M000035799

Interreligious Heroes

Interreligious Reflections

Series Editor: Alon Goshen-Gottstein,
director, Elijah Interfaith Institute

With the rise of interfaith relations comes the challenge of providing theory and deeper understanding for these relations and the trials that religions face together in an increasingly globalized world. Interreligious Reflections addresses these challenges by offering collaborative volumes that reflect cycles of work undertaken in dialogue between scholars of different religions. The series is dedicated to the academic and theological work of The Elijah Interfaith Institute, a multinational organization dedicated to fostering peace between the world's diverse faith communities through interfaith dialogue, education, research, and dissemination. In carrying out Elijah's principles, these volumes extend beyond the Abrahamic paradigm to include the dharmic traditions. As such, they promise to be a source of continuing inspiration and interest for religious leaders, academics, and community-oriented study groups that seek to deepen their interfaith engagement. All volumes in this series are edited by Elijah's director, Dr. Alon Goshen-Gottstein.

Other Titles in the Series

*The Religious Other: Hostility, Hospitality,
and the Hope of Human Flourishing*

*The Crisis of the Holy: Challenges and Transformations
in World Religions*

*Friendship across Religions: Theological Perspectives
on Interreligious Friendship*

*Memory and Hope: Forgiveness, Healing,
and Interfaith Relations*

*The Future of Religious Leadership:
World Religions in Conversation*

*Sharing Wisdom: Benefits and Boundaries
of Interreligious Learning*

Also by Alon Goshen-Gottstein

Coronaspection: World Religious Leaders Reflect on COVID-19

Interreligious Heroes

Role Models and Spiritual Exemplars for Interfaith Practice

Essays Offered in Friendship to
Rabbi David Rosen at Seventy

EDITED BY
Alon Goshen-Gottstein

WIPF *&* STOCK · Eugene, Oregon

INTERRELIGIOUS HEROES
Role Models and Spiritual Exemplars for Interfaith Practice

Interreligious Reflections Series

Copyright © 2021 Wipf and Stock Publishers. All rights reserved. Except for brief quotations in critical publications or reviews, no part of this book may be reproduced in any manner without prior written permission from the publisher. Write: Permissions, Wipf and Stock Publishers, 199 W. 8th Ave., Suite 3, Eugene, OR 97401.

Wipf & Stock
An Imprint of Wipf and Stock Publishers
199 W. 8th Ave., Suite 3
Eugene, OR 97401

www.wipfandstock.com

PAPERBACK ISBN: 978-1-6667-0960-5
HARDCOVER ISBN: 978-1-6667-2189-8
EBOOK ISBN: 978-1-6667-2190-4

09/29/21

Quotations from the *New Revised Standard Version Bible*, copyright © 1989 National Council of Churches of Christ in the United States of America, all rights reserved worldwide, are used by permission.

Contents

Transforming the Catholic Church

Revisiting Theological Foundations

The Spiritual Quest

Increasing Understanding

Engaged and Peace Activism

Fathers and Children

Conclusion: Appreciating Interreligious Heroes | 397

Endnotes | 407

About the Contributors | 433

Introduction

Dr. Alon Goshen-Gottstein

The coming into being of this book illustrates one of the salient theses it presents: it's all about relationship, all about friendship. This is as true of relations between members of different faiths as it is between members of our own faith. Had it not been for a friendship of over a quarter of a century, this collection of essays would not have been born. And had it not been for the simple and concrete fact of being together, sharing a very particular space—David Rosen's study—after a long year marked by COVID-19 limitations, the reader would not be reading these lines. It took a moment of being together, a thought, an inspiration, an action of the will, and the subsequent galvanizing of will, thought, and word of over forty friends for this collection to come into being.

I had gone to David's home in order to have him sign some papers related to the Elijah Interfaith Institute, with which he has been associated for twenty-five years. As members of its administrative board, as well as of the Elijah Board of World Religious Leaders, but above all, as close collaborators and kindred interfaith spirits, there is much we share. As we chatted about global and family matters, it dawned on me that David would soon be celebrating his seventieth birthday. Among academics, it is customary for friends to come together and to honor a friend in the form of a *Festschrift*. The subject matter and the specifics of what is being offered are often secondary to the very act of convening to honor a scholar who had attained a noteworthy age. David deserves honor and recognition from colleagues, I reasoned. Yet, not being an academic, no one will think of putting together a collection in his honor. In any event, he should be honored in a way that is particular to him. The Talmud relates a discussion between Moses and Pinchas, in the framework of commenting on Num 25.[1] In the context of an imagined dialogue between the two relating to zealotry, the Talmud employs what has become a frequently used phrase: the messenger is the one to act. In other words, if you have received the message, the idea, the inspiration, be the one to carry it out. So, for a few days following our meeting, I mulled over in my mind what might be a fitting tribute to David, one that I could meaningfully undertake, drawing on my own history as convener of interfaith projects and on the interfaith networks of leaders and scholars that David and I share, jointly and independently.

A day or two later, my wife Therese and I, lounging on our sofa after a Shabbat Eve meal, continued reflecting on what might be a fitting topic for a book that would honor David, but more meaningfully advance inter-faith understanding and serve as an educational and reflective asset. I had just had an exchange with Rabbi Or Rose a few days earlier about a related project, so the idea of focusing on a broad range of interreligious exemplars emerged as a subject worthy of the cause.

Here was the concept. We would turn to close friends and associates of David (his one thousand closest friends, as the joke goes) and invite them to offer brief essays focusing on whom they consider to be their interreligious heroes. The assumption, largely borne out by the outcome, was that David's wide range of contacts would likely come up with a fairly comprehensive list of individuals who have left their mark in the field of interreligious relations, who have a lesson to teach, and who can provide continuing inspiration for the broader interfaith movement or for those who are active in it, especially religious leaders. Only friends of David were invited to contribute, and they were asked to write not about David himself but about any figure of broader interest. In this way, we would avoid the book being so narrowly focused on David and his interests as to be of interest only to a small circle of friends. Moreover, as the individuals to whom we turned were leaders of religious organizations, communities, and thought, the goal was to create a collection of essays that has broad appeal and interest, irrespective of the person being honored. Contributors were asked to focus on an interfaith personality whom they considered a hero and to leave reference to David only to a concluding paragraph or two. In fact, referring to David was left as optional.

The entire process was to be completed in a matter of several weeks, given the imminent birthday anniversary. This, of course, placed some pressure on authors. What is remarkable, a sign of the depth and extent of relations that David enjoys with individuals around the world, is how many people said yes and met the very specific guidelines of this publication. With the help of David's wife Sharon and Avril Promislow, assistant direc-tor for international interreligious affairs at the American Jewish Com-mittee and David's righthand person, a list of prospects was soon drawn up. The list numbered close to one hundred individuals. I had imagined we would come away with about twenty contributors, given the tight time frame, the high-ranking level of many of the prospective contributors, and the very specific mandate. That the present volume contains over twice that number may suggest the appeal of the topic, but more than anything it speaks to David's friendships and the depth of loyalty that his friends feel towards him. If we add to this figure the individuals who offered to write but for a variety of reasons could not complete the task, as well as those who offered to write on subjects other than the volume's specific focus, we emerge with a positive response rate of sixty percent, which is nothing short of staggering. Even before a single word was written, the project already pointed to one important message: the importance of friendship across religions and the power, benefit, and message that emerge from relations built up consistently over the span of decades.

We do well to introduce the project with the letter of invitation that was sent out to potential participants.

> The choice of topic stems from the recognition that all those who are working in the field have been and are inspired by figures who preceded them and who serve as inspirations and role models. What we would like is to learn:
>
> a. Who is a figure who inspires your interfaith work?
>
> b. How does this figure inspire you, and what lessons, applications, and concrete expressions has this inspiration taken in your life?
>
> The writing should be personal but grounded in the objective reference to the figure.

While the title was given as *Interreligious Heroes*, nothing regarding heroes and a definition for them was suggested. The request was for contributions towards the construction of a gallery of figures whose primary characteristics are inspiration and impact on the authors.

As a consequence, many of the authors wrote about "my interfaith hero." Many of the authors spoke of individuals they knew, who had direct influence upon them. As the group of authors are activists and leaders engaged in interfaith, this would naturally yield a significant picture of interfaith actors going back one generation and more.

It was interesting to note the breakdown of interfaith heroes. Church hierarchs tended to write about other hierarchs; children wrote of their parents; women tended to write of other women. Most heroes were chosen from one's own religion, a fact easily explained in view of the premium placed upon inspiration. There are, as this volume indicates, some notable exceptions. Some individuals found their inspiration in figures of other religions. Significantly, the figures profiled in other religions are inadvertently teachers and scholars, rather than religious leaders in any organizational sense. Scholars provide a neutral bridge that allows inspiration to be shared beyond one's own religion.[2]

With the focus on inspiration and personal friendship as motivations for contributing to this volume, there was little room for a rigorous or systematic approach to the subject. This meant two things.

1. There was not a list of individuals who had to figure in this collection. We did not start with a list and then seek out the best equipped authors to describe figures on this list. The process was, rather, the reverse. Individuals offered whomever seemed to them to befit the designation interfaith hero, and the sum total of the effort, remarkably, has been a fairly comprehensive catalogue of outstanding individuals. I did, nevertheless, review the list as it took shape and invited contributions from among David's friends where I felt a major figure had not been addressed. So, with a certain amount of editorial compensation for the pressures and limitations of a short timeline for production of the book, I hope we were ultimately able to produce a fairly comprehensive volume. If, however, a reader finds that his or her chosen hero is not present, I ask that this not be taken as reflection on the significance of that particular individual. It is purely an outcome of a process characterized by great freedom and spontaneity. I am certain that the list could have been doubled, had the scope of the project allowed.

2. There was also no attempt to define an interfaith hero.[3] The procedure here is the opposite of that undertaken in another project, where careful consideration and definition of a category, that of religious genius, preceded its application.[4] The assumption, and I believe it has proven itself, is that there is something intuitive in the appeal to a hero and that authors would naturally respond to the category. The final part of this book is an attempt to draw together various insights that have emerged from the book. One could consider such a synthetic review as a kind of thick description of what makes an interreligious hero. However, the goal was never to construct the category per se. Its uses, and eventually its usefulness, emerged from the process.

This is not to say that the category went completely unchallenged. Two individuals commented on the difficulty in using it. Mary Boys, in private communication, expressed concerns related to the category's usefulness from a feminist perspective. Swami Atmapriyananda, from a theological perspective, queried its applicability to figures whom he considered Christlike, namely avataras and great prophets. Notwithstanding these queries, all authors, including the two just named, found a way of working with the category. It does bear stating that several attempts to identify an alternative category failed to deliver one that was problem-free, universally recognizable in an intuitive way and able to do the same work. The ultimate justification for continuing appeal to interreligious heroes is in the fact that it works. That fact is established by the collection of essays presented here.

Some words are in order regarding the editorial process. My job as editor consisted largely of the attempt to get all authors to do more or less the same thing and to describe their chosen hero in line with some key questions. I am grateful to the authors who had the patience for working with me on bringing out the best of their chosen interreligious hero, sometimes in as much as four different drafts.

Attaining consistency across the essays, given the broad scope of authors—religiously, geographically, culturally and institutionally—required making some decisions. One of these concerns was the titles given to essays. Most authors titled their essay by the name of their chosen hero. Only about a quarter of the authors chose a title that offered greater specificity, sometimes a particular angle that the author considered relevant to the chosen hero. In an attempt to maintain uniformity across the volume, all essays are titled by reference to the name and title of the chosen hero only. In those cases where the original title offers a window upon the person, the author's original title is listed in an opening note.

One expression of diversity in the essays relates to style. I left it up to authors whether to take a more informal approach or to apply a more academic approach, while gently pointing them to an emphasis on the former. Styles vary across the essays, so some are more academic, others a little more personal. Relatedly, some authors wrote with no footnotes; others offered substantive documentation for their claims. In an attempt to accommodate this difference, all notes have been moved to the end of the individual essay, thereby making the reading of the essays themselves consistent throughout the book, a free-flowing text that does not visibly feature a second stratum of information in the form of footnotes. Similarly, some authors chose to provide materials for additional reading. I have kept this variety, rather than forcing a uniform standard on the many contributors.

One of the challenges of putting this project together has been to decide upon the sequence in which contributions will appear. I considered several options. The most banal was alphabetic, listing either authors or heroes alphabetically. Only slightly less banal was the possibility of presenting heroes in accordance with their religious traditions, grouping all Jews together, etc. I finally opted for a thematic breakdown of the volume. In an attempt to tease out the various possible dimensions of interreligious heroism, I broke down the presentations into smaller groups, each of which has its own particularity. Let me dwell briefly on each of these groups.

The first group, titled "Spiritual Inspiration and Precedent," features figures of old, great teachers and models who continue to inspire and impact the lives of believers today. The volume opens with a juxtaposition of Saint Francis and Pope Francis, suggesting the historical span of the book and the basic dynamics of how interreligious heroes can inspire others, generating in turn other heroes. Several other figures of old taken from the context of the spiritual life of India are then featured, as well as a notable Muslim exemplar. The ability to draw on classical precedent is a potential of all religions and is especially relevant as believers seek precedents and examples for their present-day engagement across religions.

The next batch of essays is grouped under the title "Academic and Philosophical Foundations." These too engage foundations and precedents. However, the figures discussed are not great spiritual exemplars but rather scholars and thinkers who contributed to the formation of the present-day interreligious environment. These figures laid the groundwork, philosophically or historically, allowing us to take for granted much of what we do today. They are some of the founding parents, so to speak, of the engagement and interaction across religions that is characteristic of the interfaith movement.

A special group of essays is titled "Transforming the Catholic Church." In terms of contributors to the volume, it stems from the fact that David's most important and perhaps broadest network of friends and associates is within the Catholic Church. Cardinals and bishops make up 20 percent of the contributors to the present essay. Most of these are Catholic, and of these, the great majority refer to processes within the Catholic Church and the exemplars for engagement across religions that it has produced. Grouping these contributions is not only a function of the composition of authors for the present volume. As David is fond of saying, the Catholic Church is the group responsible for the single greatest transformation in teachings in relation to other religions that humanity has ever seen. The momentous processes relating to the promulgation of *Nostra aetate* and its various later expressions—pedagogic, institutional, and personal—occupy a place of honor in the gallery of figures represented in this book.

Advancing interfaith relations involves understanding the other. But it also involves a reexamination of one's own view of other religions. This is one of the great hallmarks of *Nostra aetate* and is a precondition for making meaningful advances in interfaith relations, regardless of how one conceives of their purpose. The next group of essays is accordingly devoted to individuals who have rethought the theoretical foundations of their religion's views of other religions. It is therefore called "Revisiting Theological Foundations."

The following sub-categories in the gallery of interreligious heroes are broken down in accordance with the particularity of interest and approach that characterize the different figures. One group of heroes is characterized by its specific spiritual interests. Under the rubric "The Spiritual Quest" are listed individuals for whom interfaith engagement has served, above all, a spiritual purpose and formed part of their personal spiritual quests. The examples of deepening the spiritual life by engaging other religions then provide paths and precedents for others, in particular for schools and disciples associated with these figures.

A complementary purpose for engaging across religions is described as "Increasing Understanding." This cluster of essays focuses on individuals who have made a contribution to and whose efforts were geared towards increasing understanding across religions. It may be that increasing understanding is not a goal in and of itself. This goal may be construed as subservient to some of the other purposes and goals, reflected in the sub-groupings of this project. Nevertheless, enhancing understanding is a distinct approach and purpose of interfaith engagement. It involves religious leaders, especially scholars who have been devoted to the history of particular relationships, as well as theologians in quest of a better understanding of their religion and that of the other.

Perhaps the most common cause for present-day interreligious engagement is not so much the view of the other but the ways in which engaging the other serves the needs of society. The most frequent needs in today's interfaith scene are advancing peace or taking care of what David, following Pope Francis, refers to as our common home. It is therefore no surprise that the most populated sub-group in the present volume is the one that describes individuals whose efforts can be described as "Engaged and Peace Activism." Note the *and* in this title. Engaged activism is a broader category that relates to various forms of engaging other religions in pursuit of a common public agenda, described as activist. Within this group, peace is perhaps the most important and common concern, often serving as the primary motivator for interfaith relations on the ground.

The final group is not so much a description of types of interfaith activity as it is a reality of the present project. As it turns out, interfaith activity is a cross-generational reality. Several contributors chose their fathers as interreligious heroes. This is suggestive of the depth of engagement of the figures described, figures that had the power to communicate to the next generation. It also points to the important challenges of interfaith work—continuity, communication to the next generation, and, in particular, engagement of youth. As we learn from Rabbi Shlomo Dov Rosen, David's nephew, David himself is already a second-generation interfaith practitioner. The sub-category is therefore valuable for an appreciation of the person who is being honored in this volume.

Let it be recognized that the breakdown into different types of inter-religious involvement is far from scientific or strict. It is adapted to the essays and seeks to identify trends within them. It does not grow out of a cold analysis of the forms of interfaith practice. As it turns out, it does a pretty decent job of analysis, but this is an ex post facto achievement, not the outcome of a more careful analysis. More importantly, the decision to include an individual in one category rather than another is far from exact or foolproof. Many of the individuals could be appreciated through more than one category. Classification ends up functioning as a means of interpreting and appreciating these individuals and deciding what matters most or what should be featured most clearly in their work. That decision is ultimately my own, and others may take issue with it. Thus, to classify the Dalai Lama as seeking to increase understanding among religions, rather than as someone who practices interreligious dialogue with the goal of ad-vancing peace, is already offering a particular reading of the Dalai Lama. The same is true for the decision to describe Gandhi's or Chiara Lubich's relation to other religions under the rubric of "The Spiritual Quest," which pronounces a view on how and why these major figures engaged in interre-ligious relations. The grouping can be defended, and I believe it says some-thing important about the individuals who have been variously grouped. Nevertheless, we must recognize the partial nature of such groupings. An interreligious hero should, ideally, operate in more than one area and draw on more than one dimension of religion. I am not sure that any of the figures presented cover all the bases. That would probably be asking too much. Individuals have their particularities, and their contribution to rela-tions across religions reflects some specific focus and special gifts, while relating in some way to other areas. Even if these particularities have not been at the center of attention of the chosen hero, they may still be relevant to the hero, either as preconditions or as consequences of his or her work. Thus, to appreciate an interreligious hero is to identify his or her strong traits and unique contribution, to recognize the area within the broader field of interfaith relations to which the individual has contributed, and to explore the possible links and impact that this particularity has to other domains within the broader interfaith field.

All of which brings us to the interreligious hero being celebrated—Rab-bi David Rosen. I have intentionally left the presentation of David, master-fully crafted by his wife and lifelong partner Sharon, to the end, rather than featuring his work at the beginning of the volume, as would be typical of a classical *Festschrift*. It seems to me that we can best appreciate David when his particular profile is seen against the historical and conceptual backdrop of which he forms the most recent chapter. Getting to David at the end of the volume, then, is a way of affirming the history of a movement, of situating a present-day hero in relation to that history, and of appreciating his achievements only after we have a fuller grasp of the field and its potential expressions and combinations. I believe this affords us the best perspective to appreciate and celebrate David Rosen, and my own words in the final chapter of this volume seek to bring this understanding to light.

The final chapter in this book is my own. In it, I try to draw conclusions and to identify broad trends that emerge from the project as a whole. Having studied forty-three cases, David included, what can we say are the traits and characteristics of an interreligious hero? As I suggest, these are the depth dimensions that make an interreligious hero. They cut across the different areas in which interfaith work takes place and are therefore not dependent on one particular kind of activity or approach.[5] Recognizing these allows us to point more readily to who is an interfaith hero. Consequently, they also allow us to shape future interfaith heroes. If some categories, such as saints or religious geniuses, assume something inimitable,[6] the present category of interreligious heroes assumes that such heroes can be formed, through education, encounter, friendship, and certain experiences. If the logic of the present book is intergenerational, moving from historical roots, to founding parents of the field, to immediate precedents and biological fathers, this logic also points to the future. Interreligious relations are based on hope, and hope points to the future. Recognizing what it is that makes interreligious heroes and how their virtues are carried into different domains is a key to transmitting such heroism to future generations.

I would like to conclude this introduction with words of gratitude. No project is carried out as a solo project. This is particularly true of a project that required the engagement of dozens and dozens of individuals, many high-ranking, all with their particular personalities, needs, and styles of working. Thank you to all of the contributors to this project, in their diversity and richness. Thank you for the contribution and thank you for working with this editor and his *own* particular personality and style.

Sharon Rosen and Avril Promislow deserve special thanks for advice and support all along the way.

As with so many other projects over more than a decade, I depend heavily on Peta Pellach Jones, director of educational activities at the Elijah Interfaith Institute. Her good reason, common sense, broader perspective, understanding of key issues, literary and linguistic skills, and editorial abilities are assets that I never take for granted and for which I remain grateful.

Elisabet Meltvik, Elijah's secretary, has been and is always available, with good cheer and dedication, to realize a slew of practical tasks that are required to achieving the end goal. This is also true of this project, whose smooth flow was facilitated by her skills and dedication.

Paul Mendes-Flohr provided much needed bibliographical help, with his characteristic wisdom and humility. Thank you.

Wipf and Stock has become home to many projects. It is hard to communicate the sense of trust and collaboration that have developed with James Stock and K. C. Hanson, both of whom played a crucial role in the realization of this project, as well as of the series *Interreligious Reflections*, within which it appears. A dedicated team, which includes Rebecca Abbot, Calvin Jaffarian and Matt Wimer, has made this project a pleasing reality. Working with Shannon Carter on the book's design was fun, pleasure and inspiration. May their labor find favor in the eyes of the book's future readers. To all of them, heartfelt gratitude.

Spiritual Inspiration and Precedent

St. Francis and Pope Francis[7]

PETER CARDINAL TURKSON

St. Francis of Assisi

THERE WAS ONCE A man in love with God, shaped by prayer, animated by love for the poorest, concerned for creation, a man among men, a brother among brothers, open to friendship, passionate about dialogue and respect for others, an apostle of peace between men, peoples, and religions. This man was Saint Francis of Assisi. He lived at the turn of the twelfth and thirteenth centuries (1181/82–1226), but, throughout the centuries and up to the present day, his ideal has continued to inspire millions of men and women who cherish fraternity, love, and dialogue without borders, well beyond the great families of the Franciscan Order that he founded, an order formed by men who made the radical choice of poverty and devotion to the service of God and men. Their founding father is rightly considered a precursor and an apostle of interreligious dialogue.[8]

A Jesuit Pope Called Francis

On March 13, 2013, after his election to the See of Peter, the faithful who had been waiting for the announcement of this *gaudium magnum* in St. Peter's Square, held their breath when the new Pope, successor to Pope Emeritus Benedict XVI, was presented to the jubilant crowd by Cardinal Jean-Louis Tauran, the Protodeacon, who from the central balcony of St. Peter's Basilica announced that Cardinal Bergoglio, having just been elected by the conclave, had taken the name of Francis. After the acclamations of the faithful, there was a moment of wonderment. He is the first Jesuit Pope in history and, at the same time, the first to bear the name Francis. But which Francis is it, and why did he give himself this name? A few months after his election and during a meeting with media representatives, the Holy Father explained the name he had given himself: "Some people wanted to know why the Bishop of Rome wished to be called *Francis*. Some thought of Francis Xavier, Francis De Sales, and also Francis of Assisi. I will tell you the story. During the election, I was seated next to the Archbishop Emeritus of São Paolo and Prefect Emeritus of the Congregation for the Clergy, Cardinal Claudio Hummes: a good friend, a good friend! When things were looking dangerous for me, he encouraged me. And when the votes reached two thirds, there was the usual applause (by the Cardinals in conclave), because a Pope had been elected. And he gave me a hug and a kiss and said: 'Don't forget the poor!' And those words stuck with me: the poor, the poor. Then, right away, thinking of the poor, I thought of *Francis of Assisi*. Then I thought of all the wars, as the votes were still being counted, till the end. Francis is also the man of peace. That is how the name came into my heart: Francis of Assisi. For me, he is the man of poverty, the man of peace, the man who loves and protects creation .... He is the man who gives us this spirit of peace, the poor man .... How I would like a Church which is poor and for the poor!"[9] Consequently, the goals that Pope Francis will set for his pontificate are closely linked to this trilogy: poverty, peace, care for creation.

Poor in the Service of Universal Fraternity, a Culture of Love, and Encounter

Returning to St. Francis of Assisi, but this time to the Basilica of Spoliation in Assisi: when Francis went nude, shedding his clothes (his *spoliation*), he did not say no and goodbye to the world; rather, he found himself saying hello. He was free—free to go, free to do, free to be. With no master but Christ, and no possession but his soul, he was free. In his poverty, he found the means to pursue and to live his relationship with all, starting with his religious family and extending it to sultans. Thus it is said that in his religious family, Francis was not a leader; he was rather a brother, and all his followers and companions were a band of brothers. For Francis, the only relationship available for us in which to live is the relationship of brotherhood. When this relationship is with everything that exists, as God's creation, then Francis lived in a universal brotherhood with everything that exists.

Additionally, Francis believed in the universal ability and duty of all creatures to praise God, wherefore he saw creation as sharing with him the vocation to praise God. From this universal vocation, Francis deduced again a sense of the universal brotherhood[10] of everything that exists. From a universal function of the praise of God, Francis concluded a universal sense of sharing a common nature, of belonging together, all being brothers. Thus, Franciscans profess, individually and collectively, to respond with unbound joy to all creation.[11] They call themselves minor, because they humble themselves before each other, not imposing themselves on anyone, but cherishing the points of view of the other, as listeners, in order to facilitate dialogue and conversation.

So, Francis's choice of poverty did not only mean personal destitution. His poverty was the seedbed of a culture of love, compassion, and encounter: a missionary openness to everyone and to everything that existed in God's creation, including a sultan.

A Life of Fraternity without Borders: A Dialogue of Life and Dialogue of Faith

It is significant that Pope Francis, who took the *Poverello* of Assisi as his patron and model, recalls, at the beginning of his encyclical letter *Fratelli tutti: On Fraternity and Social Friendship*, the saint's visit to the sultan, Malik-el-Kamil, in Egypt. This visit of the saint, according to Pope Francis, "shows his openness of heart, which knew no bounds and transcended differences of origin, nationality, color or religion."[12] Pope Francis observes further, "Saint Francis went to meet the Sultan with the same attitude that he instilled in his disciples: if they found themselves 'among the Saracens and other non-believers' . . . not to 'engage in arguments or disputes, but to be subject to every human creature for God's sake.'"[13]

Following in the footsteps of the saint of Assisi, Pope Francis has been a veritable apostle of dialogue without borders, as his apostolic journeys to the four corners of the world have shown. Among the most significant are those to Israel and Palestine, Egypt, the United Arab Emirates and Iraq, Japan, Myanmar, and Bangladesh—all predominantly non-Christian countries—Cuba, the United States of America, the Central African Republic, Nairobi, and Uganda, where he met with representatives of other faiths. As the Holy Father himself explains it, his relationship with Jews began when he was archbishop of Buenos Aires. "Our relationship is very close to my heart. Back in Buenos Aires, I used to go to the synagogues and meet with the communities gathered there. I would follow the Jewish festivals and commemorations and give thanks to the Lord, who gives us life and who accompanies us throughout history . . . . In interreligious dialogue it is fundamental that we encounter each other as brothers and sisters before our Creator and that we praise him; and that we respect and appreciate each other and try to cooperate. And in the Jewish-Christian dialogue, there is a unique and particular bond, by virtue of the Jewish roots of Christianity:

Jews and Christians must therefore consider themselves brothers, united in the same God and by a rich common spiritual patrimony,[14] on which to build and to continue building the future."[15]

Pope Francis: *Laudato sì* and *Fratelli tutti*, Integral Ecology and Universal Fraternity

In Pope Francis, the Saint of Assisi has come alive again, not only in his love for the poor, for peace, for the care of creation, and for encountering people of other faiths. Rather, in his two encyclical letters, inspired by the Saint of Assisi (*Laudato sì: On the Care for our Common Home* [2015] and *Fratelli tutti: On Fraternity and Social Friendship* [2020]), Pope Francis applies the Christian faith and the collective wisdom of other faiths, as well as the principles of Catholic social teaching, to the *res novae* (new developments of our day): the ecological and climate crisis, migration and refugees, inequalities, poverty, joblessness, the economy, disabilities and vulnerabilities, etc., to affirm that the creation and humanity affected by these *res novae* are not themselves problems or issues. Creation and the human family are inseparably and interdependently bound together as God's gifts for our care, as brothers and sisters, members of a fraternity without borders, members of a universal and a cosmic fraternity. This is how he does it:

Laudato sì, Pope Francis's landmark encyclical letter on care for our common home, is woven around the central theme of communion (the equivalent of the French notion of *fraternité*), our communion with the rest of the cosmos, with the biotic world and all creatures, with our fellow brothers and sisters, and ultimately with God the Creator.

In what follows I shall explore in the underlying relational metaphysics of *Laudato sì* the truth that everything is interrelated and interconnected, as everything exists in communion. I will also dwell on the implications of our vocation to live in communion, namely, the need to treat the rest of creation and our fellow brothers and sisters with respect. All this has significant consequences for our vocation to live in communion, for interfaith dialogue.

The underlying metaphysical foundation for the integral ecology of Pope Francis in *Laudato sì* is the truth and conviction of the interrelatedness of the whole of reality and the interdependence of all created entities. "We are all connected" is the mantra repeated throughout the document. We are connected to the rest of the human family, to the created world, and to those who will come after us in future generations. Communion or fraternity is a sort of ontological glue that holds together the encyclical's main premises and arguments.

Already in the introduction to the encyclical, while enumerating the main themes of the text, Pope Francis speaks of "the conviction that everything in the world is connected."[16] The pope notes that the reality of the interconnectedness of all things is a revealed truth found in the very first chapters of the book of Genesis. While referring to the biblical episodes, the pope remarks: "These ancient stories, full of symbolism, bear witness to a conviction which we today share, that everything is interconnected, and that genuine care for our own lives and our relationships with nature is inseparable from fraternity, justice and faithfulness to others."[17]

The truth of the interdependence of all reality is the core of Christian belief and doctrine as affirmed by the *Catechism of the Catholic Church,* which the Pope quotes in the encyclical.

As the catechism teaches: "God wills the interdependence of creatures. The sun and the moon, the cedar and the little flower, the eagle and the sparrow: the spectacle of their countless diversities and inequalities tells us that no creature is self-sufficient. Creatures exist only in dependence on each other, to complete each other, in the service of each other."[18]

As the pope reminds us, "we are not disconnected from the rest of creatures but joined in a splendid universal communion. As believers, we do not look at the world from without but from within, conscious of the bonds with which the Father has linked us to all beings."[19] It is precisely our profound communion with the wider earth community which makes us feel our brokenness and alienation from each other, "the desertification of the soil almost as a physical ailment, and the extinction of a species as a painful disfigurement."[20]

Pope Francis sees human life as a pilgrimage in communion along with the rest of God's creatures, bonded together by God's love. He writes: "Everything is related, and we human beings are united as brothers and sisters on a wonderful pilgrimage, woven together by the love God has for each of his creatures and which also unites us in fond affection with brother sun, sister moon, brother river and mother earth."[21]

Our ontological communion with the rest of creation requires that we treat every creature with respect. "Because all creatures are connected, each must be cherished with love and respect, for all of us as living creatures are dependent on one another."[22] The truth of the universal communion of the entire creation is the basis of a common fraternity "that excludes nothing and no one." We cannot be at peace among ourselves if we are not at peace with creation. With deep psychological insight, the pope writes: "We have only one heart, and the same wretchedness which leads us to mistreat an animal will not be long in showing itself in our relationships with other people."[23]

Our universal and cosmic fraternity has implications for our social life, too. According to Pope Francis, we cannot live in communion with the natural world when we do not live in communion among ourselves. He writes:

> A sense of deep communion with the rest of nature cannot be real if our hearts lack tenderness, compassion and concern for our fellow human beings. It is clearly inconsistent to combat trafficking in endangered species while remaining completely indifferent to human trafficking, unconcerned about the poor, or undertaking to destroy another human being deemed unwanted. This compromises the very meaning of our struggle for the sake of the environment.[24]

Our universal communion with the rest of the human family and with the whole of creation has concrete consequences. One of this is the "common destination" of all Earth's goods which "are meant to benefit everyone."[25] Pope Francis reminds us that Pope John Paul II wrote in 1991, "God gave the earth to the whole human race for the sustenance of all its members, *without excluding or favouring anyone.*"[26] The unequal distribution and consumption of our planet's life-essential resources, and the tragic fact that nearly one in seven of our fellow humans goes to bed hungry every night, remind us that we have failed to live in true communion with our fellow brothers and sisters. Thus, quoting a passage from the statement of the Catholic Bishops' Conference of New Zealand, Pope Francis writes:

> The natural environment is a collective good, the patrimony of all humanity and the responsibility of everyone. If we make something our own, it is only to administer it for the good of all. If we do not, we burden our consciences with the weight of having denied the existence of others. That is why the New Zealand bishops asked what the commandment "Thou shalt not kill" means when "twenty percent of the world's population consumes resources at a rate that robs the poor nations and future generations of what they need to survive."[27]

Another consequence of our universal communion, the result of our interconnectedness and our interdependence, is the fact that none of the elements and features of our interdependence is an independent variable. Every violation of our solidary communion and of our civic friendship is bound to upset relations among us and in our society. Recognizing this, it is of the utmost importance that we avail ourselves of all tools and instruments to consolidate our fraternity and social friendship. Religion and dialogue between the adherents of different faiths have a significant role to play in this. As Pope Francis observes, "The different religions, based on their respect for each human person as a creature called to be a child of God, contribute significantly to building fraternity and defending justice in society. Dialogue between the followers of different religions does not take place simply for the sake of diplomacy, consideration or tolerance. In the words of the Bishops of India, 'the goal of dialogue is to establish friendship, peace and harmony, and to share spiritual and moral values and experiences in a spirit of truth and love.'"[28]

Appreciating Rabbi David Rosen

It has been a great pleasure to pay tribute to Rabbi David Rosen with these reflections inspired by two important figures of the Catholic faith, namely St. Francis of Assisi and Pope Francis, who bears his name. Three subject areas and themes dominate my own knowledge, friendship, and working relationship with Rabbi David Rosen. These are peace issues, ecology (the environment), and interfaith dialogue. As a member of the World Conference of Religions for Peace, and in context of the celebrations of the World Day of Peace in Assisi and in the different places in which Sant'Egidio continued to celebrate the event, it was always a delight to meet Rabbi Rosen. The emergence into prominence these decades of ecological issues and concern for the well-being of God's creation have made Rabbi Rosen a comrade in arms. Engaging in any way with Rabbi Rosen in these areas of his passion and, indeed, in any other area of the Vatican, entails one's bringing to bear on the conversation the different expressions of the popes and the Roman Curia on the matter, especially the writings of the current Pope Francis: *Evangelii Gaudium,* which sets the trajectory of his pontificate; and his two encyclical letters, *Laudato sì* and *Fratelli tutti.* In this tribute to Rabbi Rosen, I have attempted to sketch briefly how Rabbi Rosen's special passion for interfaith dialogue finds resonance and strong underpinnings in the ministry of Pope Francis and the Saint of Assisi in whose shadow and footsteps he treads, and how especially the last two encyclical etters of Pope Francis *Laudato sì* and *Fratelli tutti,* put together the teachings of universal fraternity and integral ecology to freshly present humanity's vocation to live in dialogue and communion for harmony and for peace.

Chaitanya Mahaprabhu[29]

Acharya Shrivatsa Goswami

Swami Vivekanand once said:

Among the great acharyas of *bhakti*, Sri Chaitanya Dev[30] has been the supermost. Being God himself, he has followed the path of the *acharyas* (religious teacher). Huge devotional waves originating from him have flooded not just Bengal but the entire masses. His path of love accepted no limits. He has not discriminated amongst honest-dishonest, pious-sinner, Hindu-Muslim, pure-impure, fallen-harlot, this nation-that nation, this country-that country, this sect-that sect and the like. He was merciful to everyone. Despite its weaknesses. his community has become the place of shelter for poor, weak, outcasts, fallen, inferior, sinner, distressed and persons having no place in the society. What a magnanimous proposition it is. Till now no other Hindu *acharayas* have performed in such a way, due to their narrow sectarian communal outlook. His *Sikshastakam*[31] (Eight Teachings) are applicable for one and all.[32]

Chaitanya Mahaprabhu (1486–1533)[33] was born into a family of pious scholars in Navadvipa, a center of learning in eastern India. Graduating in philosophy and logic, he soon had his own seminary. He was an arrogant scholar, enjoying scholastic debates and much feared by his opponents. After the untimely death of his wife, he married again. But soon his life took a different path. His encounter with Isvara Puri, a respected spiritual leader, dramatically turned the arrogant scholar into a seeker suffering from the pangs of separation from the Divine. He saw misery in the ritual-shackled Hindu society. With an intimate group of friends and admirers, Chaitanya launched a liberation movement based upon the chanting and singing of divine names. As it caught the imagination of masses, so it did the attention of the non-Hindu rulers of Bengal at the beginning of the sixteenth century. The persecution of Chaitanya and his fledgling movement was harsh—especially the ban on the public display of religious practice, with its violation resulting in severe physical punishment and, many times, in death.

This was the moment when Chaitanya became my interfaith hero. He was challenged by the opposing power. History is full of such instances and also records rebellion towards others, in most cases violent rebellion. Chaitanya chose to rebel, but differently. Violent response as a solution has endless chain reactions and thus brings continual destruction. Chaitanya rebelled not because of religious discrimination or persecution. For him, it was a denial of the fundamental human right, i.e., freedom of his faith-practice. Bereft of political and economic power, Chaitanya adopted the path of peaceful disobedience. The greatest power a human being has is to say no to injustice of any kind. He then succeeded in persuading the ruling Islamic authority to restore the freedom of religious expression, especially in public.[34]

His contributions are many, but the one I most value, from the point of view of interfaith relations, is the reestablishment of Vrindavan, the theater of Krishna's love dance. One of the holiest centers of Hindu faith, Vrindavan, was a gift from a Muslim Mughal emperor to the Hindu Goswamis. This is a unique and unparalleled case of interfaith relations, where a holy center of a faith (Hindu) was literally created and gifted by another faith (Islam).[35]

This was made possible through the interfaith sensitivity of Chaitanya. In 1515, Chaitanya made a long pilgrimage from the eastern shore of India to the northern heartland, in order to visit Lord Krishna's holy land, Vrindavan,[36] which had an overwhelming presence in religious, literary, and artistic traditions, though it lacked a physical, geographical corollary. This sacred area of Braj, with lost Vrindavan as its heart, in the early sixteenth century, was the marching route of the invading armies between Agra and Delhi. Chaitanya, during his nine-month-long stay in Braj, almost lost his life twice due to the hostilities. He faced the challenge firsthand.

Chaitanya responded to this volatile situation not violently, but with a well-thought-out plan of peaceful dialogue with the other. To that end, he created a team known as the Six Goswamis. Its three most prominent members came from a Muslim background, holding high positions in Hussain Shah's court. After Chaitanya's appointment, which involved no ritual conversion back into the Hindu way, they were most identified with their Hindu names as Sanatana Goswami, Rupa Goswami, and their nephew Jiva Goswami.[37] The fourth belonged to a lower caste. The other two members held powerful priestly positions.

These Goswamis, as per Chaitanya's guidance and plan, engaged with the imperial Mughal court. This was a Hindu and Muslim dialogue, but, more importantly, a sincere dialogue of religious with political powers. The Goswamis engaged with the imperial Mughal court, with the mediation of Hindu Rajput kings and nobles, who held high positions in the Mughal court. It is interesting to note that these dialogue participants all held positions of strength and were seekers of power, either religious or political. On the religious dimension of this interaction, the Hindu Goswamis and the Muslim ruler Akbar were well grounded in their own faiths. At the same time, the Goswamis were sure of their religious power, in parallel to the court's political power. Thus, both these powers engaged in dialogue, leading to a successful outcome.

The result was Emperor Akbar establishing Vrindavan as a separate revenue entity and gifting the recreated town, along with generous monetary grants, to the Goswamis. The Goswamis, in their turn, blessed the Mughal emperor. They recognized his greatness not just for these land and monetary grants but for something greater. A 1590 inscription reads: "When His Highness Akbar ruled over all the world with ease, the virtuous people found total happiness in practicing their own faith openly. The faithful Vaisnavas always joyfully blessed him."[38]

This dialogue reclaimed the lost Vrindavan for the Hindus. Moreover, it was like a pebble thrown in the pond, which triggers further ripples. It helped to create an overall peaceful environment, leading to overall development. Historians have named the sixteenth century as India's golden era, from economic to artistic, intellectual to spiritual creativity. Music, literature, art, architecture, philosophy, trade, and industry reached new heights. Basically, it was an era of mutual cooperation and harmony, not just between different ethnic and religious communities, but also when religion and politics could work together for the good of humanity.

Chaitanya and his followers led this dialogical dance. They were privileged to be part of a long-standing dialogical culture, which from its earliest times has believed in the fact that "truth is one; the wise describe it variously" and "let noble thoughts come to us from all directions." This openness in interacting with plurality did not happen in the abstraction of a philosophical world. It has a history of encounters in the real politics in India. From the earliest known and unknown pages of history, India has received visitors and invaders of many shades of political and cultural variety. India has responded diabolically as well as dialogically. The preferred way was harmony and embrace through dialogue. Quite often, the political and religious forces talked and worked with each other. The result was the growth of the popular understanding that "the truth comes out through various viewpoints." Chaitanya was part of that tradition and not shy of religion and politics working together for human welfare. However, he was also conscious of the fact that a solid base of ideology and thought process is required for dialogue to be successful. Chaitanya provided that basis.

The theater of this dialogical dance in its religious mode had two stages on which to perform. One was for intrafaith Hindu dialogue. Through intrafaith dialogue, Chaitanya engaged creatively with his own tradition to reform and revive its social and religious systems. For that, he developed a philosophical tool. As we know, Hindus agree upon the nature of ultimate religious realization as unique and essentially non-dual. Yet, they disagree on the ways of attaining this goal. Thus, Hinduism becomes a celebration of a variety of experiences, which move between pairs of known opposites: I and you, man and woman, subject and object, day and night, pleasure and pain, noumenal and phenomenal, and so on. Hindu metaphysical and logical theories have a rich history of this dialectic.

On the metaphysical realm, this polemics of binary opposites has, on the one hand, an objective absolute as pure being, from the standpoint of knowledge (*jnana*); on the other hand, it has a subjective absolute as pure will, from the standpoint of *karma*. In both these cases, there is a loss of the subjective or the objective, respectively. There is also no possibility for the confusion of the two. However, Chaitanya would go for a confusion.

Accordingly, he preferred the emotive path of *bhakti* (love and service), where the absolute is pure feeling, and where the absolute manifests as relational and dipolar, neither of the two *relata* being discarded. On the paths of cognitive knowledge (*jnana*) and will (*karma*), reality emerges as essentially non-relational. Reality for Chaitanya should instead conform to experience, and relation is a fact of experience. Relation needs two terms to relate. In love, separation is suffering. There is always an attempt to overcome that separation in suffering through union, where the sense of mutual exclusiveness of I and you, subject and object, is transcended. As a modern philosopher concludes: "It is the nature of feeling that it is a unity which militates against any aloofness or emphasis of one side against the other . . . . It might be seen that feeling is more primitive and basic than the other two [i.e., knowing and willing]; it is 'thicker.'"[39]

Chaitanya prefers the thicker path of feeling. Intellectually, this needed to be supported by a well-defined logical system. Hindu or Vedantic logic thrives upon a long history of oscillating dialectically between the binaries of difference (*bheda*) and non-difference (*abheda*). Again, Chaitanya did not choose one way of thinking as opposed to other. To resolve the dilemma of the logic of binary opposites, he formulated a logical system of "inconceivable difference and non-difference" (*acintya bhedabhedavada*). It is understood as the relation between the sun and its rays, the ocean and its waves. Essential non-difference and functional difference defines this logical system. Difference and non-difference are relative terms, hence the reality can be fully comprehensible only in the logical category of difference in non-difference, which is inconceivable from the viewpoint of binary opposites.

His dialogical stances and the path of love and *bhakti*, with the absolute as its goal, were based in a unique dialectic of inclusive transcendence, where the pairs of opposites are neither rejected nor preferred, one over the other. It is *bhakti* or feeling that includes and transcends knowledge and *karma*. His dialogical metaphysics requires a pair of others, who are related as two living beings. His system of logic is essential for a successful dialogue where different identities are respected, always keeping room for another possibility or identity to take shape. Chaitanya celebrates dialogue through the aesthetic model of Rasalila, or the dance of love, where the pair of male and female dance together for the highest aesthetic experience. Here, different pairs like male and female, humanity and divinity, subject and object, religion and politics, economy and aesthetics, Hindu and Muslim, and so on can complement each other for a "thicker" experience. This dialogical metaphysics and logic provided a firm ground for Chaitanya to engage with the other, both within the Hindu tradition and outside.

Any fruitful interfaith dialogue is based upon respect for the other. For Chaitanya, the other is valuable. He engaged with Buddhism, Islam, and other traditions and integrated various persons and elements from these others. The main category of the metaphysical system *advaya*[40] (non-dual absolute) seems to be derived from the Buddhist system. The main spiritual practice or ritual for Chaitanya is Nama-Sankirtana (chanting of the divine name), and that has a Buddhist background and flavor. The artistic ritual of *sanjhi*, the sand paintings in the Chaitanyaite temples, is a close cousin of Buddhist mandala paintings and Kalachakra ritual. The Islamic tradition trained his three most trusted and respected Goswamis, the Mughal emperor created and gifted Vrindavan to Hindus, and, even today, the Muslim community fully participates in the religious life of Vrindavan. They build ashrams and temples, decorate deities with dresses and ornaments, craft ritual vessels and thrones for Hindu gods and goddesses. The trade of sacred cows is an enterprise of the Muslim community in Vrindavan.

For successfully directing this dialogical dance, Chaitanya drew upon the *Bhagavata Purana* as his primary source. One of the most sacred texts for the Hindus, the *Bhagavata* responds to the fundamental question about the variety of paths taken by a religious seeker and which is best among them. As we have indicated above, the journeys to the non-dual goal are various, and they depend upon the psychological and spiritual makeup of a seeker. Hindus put them under three categories of the cognitive (knowledge, *jnana*), the conative (will, *karma*) and the emotive (feeling, love, *bhakti*). The *Bhagavata Purana*[41] is a serious dialogue between these three paths. To be a true text of dialogue, it also has to be a text in which an alliance is forged between speaker and listener, humanity and divinity, humanity and nature, and so on. Since dialogue and alliance are its focus, the *Bhagavata* turns out to be the text of dance, of dialogue plus alliance. The five chapters[42] on the *rasalila*[43] are the essential five vital breaths of this text.

Here *bhakti* includes and transcends *jnana* and *karma* and thus becomes mother to both. Chaitanya's dialogical understanding comes from the absolute dictum of the *Bhagavata* itself: "One can have full faith in *Bhagavata,* only if one resolves to never disrespect and denounce others' holy book."[44] This perspective went a long way in shaping the interfaith history of India.

This dialogical dance requires a relationship, and that has to be grounded in love. What is that love? For Chaitanya, love is evident only when we act for the good of other. "Love for the satisfaction of oneself is merely a self-centered desire. Whereas desire for the satisfaction of other is love."[45] "A true seeker does not consider his own pleasure or pain. The sole occupation of his/her mind is to make the other happy."[46] Love and service are not bound by religious and social distinctions of caste, creed, gender, etc. *Bhakti* or service out of love is not just a lofty philosophic idea supported by an inclusive metaphysical and logical system. For Chaitanya, the discipline of *bhakti* is the means or way to reach the highest spiritual goal, which is *bhakti* itself—love and service (*premabhakti*). This cannot be taught through mere words; it has to be lived. "For this reason I myself take on the role of a servant, preach and practice *bhakti.* If I do not do it myself, the values (*dharma*) cannot be taught," says Chaitanya.[47] His life is his teaching.[48] His own words succinctly tell us about the guiding principles of his life—a dialogical dance:[49]

> More humble than a blade of grass,
> As forbearing as a tree,
> Having no conceit,
> Always respecting others,
> One should always sing the Hari.

> O Jagadisa (The Lord of Universe),
> I do not desire wealth, or offspring, or a beautiful women,
> nor poetic genius,
> But that from birth to birth selfless service be in me towards you.

Sri Chaitanya Mahaprabhu lived in the fifteenth and sixteenth centuries in India. But he is alive. He is alive in a thriving Hindu Vaisnava community of millions, not just in India but throughout the world.[50] Sri Chaitanya and his tradition is my existential ground. My family[51] has served at Sri Radharamana Temple almost since the time of Chaitanya. I grew up experiencing the environments guided by the Chaitanyite tradition. Even before Mahatma Gandhi's famous movement of permitting entry into temples for low-caste Hindus, our elders were initiating them in their religious life. Along with them, the temple doors were open for non-Hindus as well, despite having a very rigid ritual regimen.[52] The temple supported and continues to support artistic activities of *sanjhi* and *phul-bungala* (houses of flowers for the deities), exemplifying intertextuality with Buddhist rituals and Islamic architecture respectively.

This open, existential education was supported with my early education at a school run by J. Krishnamurti in Varanasi. Higher studies at Banaras Hindu University gave me an opportunity of widening my horizons. Christians and Buddhists were my close friends who attended my marriage in Vrindavan. Then, I was invited by Harvard University as a visiting scholar. I shared my own religious and philosophical tradition with an international interfaith community of scholars, while I benefited from the opportunity of studying Christian history and theology. In that period, I spent time visiting centers of new faith movements in the 1970s United States.[53]

My father, who was a respected Chaitanyaite figure, entrusted the task of construction of our present ashram to a Muslim mason, Mohammad Taslim. We are grateful for his great services. In the early 1980s, I was active in the interfaith group of the World Council of Churches, traveling widely. Then, for a couple of decades, I participated in the governing council of the World Council of Religions for Peace, now Religions for Peace. The icing on the cake is my participation in the activities of the Elijah Interfaith Institute. It provided the inspiration for rigorous questioning and deeper understanding, along with the commitment to translate into action the ideas we deliberate in the interfaith dialogues. It is the gift of this institute that it has created a large family of sincere and committed men and women. Here, I had the occasion to think, interact, and share with Rabbi David Rosen. Certainly, he shines like the Star of David in the interfaith sky. Like Chaitanya, I find him to be a good listener, eager to learn, yet firmly and uncompromisingly grounded in his own tradition. His deep roots in the Judaic tradition give him the freedom to fly high in the interfaith sky. He vindicates Chaitanya, who said that the prerequisite for dialogue is strength. And that strength flows from faith in oneself and compassion for others. My heroes Chaitanya and David share that.

Guru Nanak Dev Ji

Bhai Sahib Bhai Mohinder Singh Ahluwalia

In the classic nineteenth-century text *On Heroes, Hero Worship, and the Heroic in History*, the British historian and philosopher Thomas Carlyle set out his vision of heroes. For Carlyle, "Universal history, . . . the history of what man has accomplished in this world, is at bottom the History of the Great Men who have worked here."[54] These great men—and Carlyle recognized only men—appeared "always as lightning out of Heaven."[55] In every age, he wrote, "we shall find the Great Man to have been the indispensable saviour of his epoch;—the lightning, without which the fuel never would have burnt."[56]

What is useful about Carlyle, although he was writing in a very different context, is the insight about having an "indispensable saviour" who acts as the lightning, the kindling that awakens the divine spark embodied deep within each of us. An interfaith hero who more than fulfils this criterion—who has the capacity to exalt other men and women so that they in turn can become heroes and godlike themselves—worthy of hero worship, is Guru Nanak Dev Ji.

Guru Nanak Dev Ji as an Interfaith Hero

Guru Nanak Dev Ji was born in 1469 into a Hindu family during the Renaissance, a period of seismic changes in Europe. An equally monumental change on the subcontinent loomed with Guru Nanak Dev Ji's birth. At his birth, when the midwife noticed that he came smiling into the world rather than crying, she immediately knew that he shared divine attributes. He was a divinely blessed child who came to change the world. From the very beginning, he challenged orthodoxy and sought a much deeper understanding of the religious traditions, rituals, and sacred texts that were prevalent in India. His education included Sanskrit, Arabic, and Persian studies, which he mastered in a very short time. For example, at the age of eleven, he challenged the Brahmin priest who was to bestow him with the sacred thread of the Hindus by questioning its use. When the priest was unable to provide a satisfactory answer, he refused to wear the thread only for the sake of ritual. Instead, he implored the priest to focus on inner purification:

> Out of the cotton of compassion, spin the thread of content-ment, tie the knot of continence, and the twist of virtue; make such a sacred thread; O Pundit, for your inner self.[57]

The message of Guru Nanak Dev Ji after emerging from the river Bein, three days after he had been in communion with God, was the open-ing of the Japji Sahib—the Mool Mantar that described the oneness of God and his attributes. He emphasized that God existed and was synonymous with truth before time, was present throughout the ages, is present now, and will be forever present in the future. He declared that: "There is no Hindu, there is no Muslim."

This declaration established the foundation of Guru Nanak Dev Ji's universal message for humanity. This was an interfaith message that he first expounded in Sultanpur Lodhi, where he engaged in a weeklong dia-logue with both Hindus and Muslims. As a consequence, he came to be widely accepted as both a guru and *pir* (Sufi saint) by Hindus and Muslims respectively. For Guru Nanak Dev Ji, his mission became to enlighten a humanity entrapped in falsehoods and to meet with those who were im-bued with the love of God.

Interfaith Journeys

"There is a famine of truth; Falsehood prevails, and the blackness of the Dark Age of Kal Jug has turned people into phantoms."[58]

Being acutely aware of this famine of truth that was prevalent at the time, Guru Nanak Dev Ji undertook four interfaith journeys to different parts of the world, accompanied by a Muslim musician, Bhai Mardana, and sometimes a Hindu, Bhai Bala, to take his particular message to the world. He covered incredible distances, walking approximately 20,000 miles, al-most exclusively on foot, through all kinds of terrain. Throughout these journeys, neither knowing where he would spend the night nor where he would eat, Guru Nanak Dev Ji demonstrated his unwavering love, commit-ment and trust in God. The first twelve-year journey was made eastwards across India, visiting cities sacred to the Hindus, such as Hardwar, Ayodya, and Varanasi. This was followed by a five-year journey southward to Sri Lanka, returning to the Punjab via Gujarat and Rajasthan. A further two years were spent going northwards into the Himalayas as far as Tibet, and a final four-year journey was made westwards into the Middle East, visiting the sacred Islamic cities of Mecca, Medina, and Baghdad, returning through Iran, Iraq, and Afghanistan.

During Guru Nanak Dev Ji's journey northwards, he had extensive dialogues with the Siddhs, some of the greatest sages and ascetics who had renounced the world and resided in the caves of the Himalayas. The dialogue recounted in the Guru Granth Sahib Ji is known as the Siddh Gosht. The Siddhs sought spiritual enlightenment and peace through renouncing the world. They were intrigued by the visit of Guru Nanak Dev Ji, who was far younger than they. They addressed him as "dear child" and posed many deep philosophical questions. Reflecting on one of the most significant exchanges with the Siddhs, Bhai Gurdas Ji writes that Guru Nanak was asked: "How are things going down below in the world?"[59]

Guru Nanak replied that the world was drowning in sins and injustices, burning in falsehoods, and pleading for rescue and asked the Siddhs about their responsibilities. Furthermore, he asked what hope there was when the spiritually adept had taken refuge in the mountains, in ignorant bliss of the world's plight. What hope would the world have to be redeemed from its suffering?

In his travels to Mecca, when faced with the question of which civilization was greater, the Hindu or the Muslim, Guru Nanak Dev Ji simply responded that neither was greater because their followers are caught "in meaningless rituals." He was prepared through sheer love to uplift the people whom he met, to ensure that they were not caught in mere ritual but rather that they had a deep understanding of their own faith. For example, in his dialogue with some Muslims he encountered, he defined a true Muslim:

> It is difficult to be called a Muslim; one must be so, to get himself called a Muslim. First, he ought to accept the Deen (Religion as presented by Prophet Muhammad) as sweet (good), and then with this scraper, let him scrub his ego clean and let his pride of possession be scraped away. To become the true follower of the Islamic faith, let him break the illusion of his life and death. And heartily submit to the Will of Rab (God), worship the Creator and efface self-conceit. Says Nanak, if he is merciful to all creatures, then he is truly acclaimed as a Muslim.[60]

Guru Nanak Dev Ji's four journeys, lasting twenty-three years, led him to meet with people from different areas and regions of the world. He visited "holy places of major religions, particularly Hinduism, Islam, Jainism, and Buddhism, to share his divine message."[61] Guru Nanak Dev

Ji taught those he encountered to respect their own faith and to remain true to it but also to respect and even protect other faiths. He was against proselytization and forced conversions.

In an encounter in Mecca, Guru Nanak Dev Ji was resting with his feet pointing towards the holy Kaaba. When the Qazi, Jeevan, came to him, he abused him for disrespect. Bhai Gurdas Ji captures the incident in his writings:

> Now he sat in a mosque where the pilgrims (haajis) had gathered. When Baba (Nanak) slept in the night spreading his legs towards the alcove of mosque at Kaaba. The Qazi named Jeevan kicked him and asked who this infidel was enacting blasphemy. Why this sinner is sleeping with his legs spread towards God, or Khuda.[62]

At this point we learn, when Jeevan hastily grabbed hold of Guru Nanak Dev Ji's legs to move them, miraculously the whole of Mecca seemed to be revolving. When Jeevan questioned Guru Nanak Dev Ji about the incident, indicating that it was not right to point your feet towards the Kaaba, he retorted, "Then please point my feet in the direction where Allah does not abide. That act was a lesson that made the Muslims gathered there realize the omnipresence of God."

These long arduous journeys signify his deep concern for the suffering of humanity and his wish to share God's message. Buoyed by his interfaith dialogue at Sultanpur Lodhi, Guru Nanak Dev Ji was adamant that members of all faiths should discover God's message within their own faiths, but, even more, he was driven to expose the superstitions, falsehoods, and rituals that had come to dominate their faiths.

The overarching message was one of love and peace, as well as the truth and the oneness of God. He asked both Hindus and Muslims to be true to the essence of their religions. He stressed the need to live in the world, inspired by a sense of loving duty towards not just the Creator but the whole of creation. His teachings were expressed in lyrical verse, urging us to live up to those qualities latent within us that make us all in the image of God—such as love, compassion, forgiveness, truth, and selflessness. Through dialogue, he explained universal principles for all of humanity.

The Spirit of Guru Nanak Dev Ji
and the Unique, Lasting Legacies of the Gurus

Guru Nanak Dev Ji's teachings were new, revolutionary, coherent, systematic, and extremely articulate. The foundation of Guru Nanak Dev Ji's teaching was *Ik Oankar*—one universal Creator God.[63] This established a hierarchy that recognized above all else that there was one God. He preached the oneness of God and the universality of humanity, stressing that humans need to visualize and accept the existence of a divine universal Sovereign, God. Guru Nanak Dev Ji explicitly and lovingly places all the world's religious faiths under the same Sovereign by addressing all of humanity as children of the same God:

> There is only one breath; all are made of the same clay; the light within all is the same. The One Light pervades all the many and various beings.[64]

Guru Nanak Dev Ji prohibited marginalization, exclusion, and radicalization. He promoted truthful living, along with love and equality for all. He promoted respect of other faiths and considered support and help for another faith noble.

> He is in the temple as he is in the mosque, he is in the Hindu worship as he is in the Muslim prayer; all humans are one, though they appear different. The Hindus and the Muslims are all one; each have the habits of different environments, but all have the same eyes, the same body. Thus, the Abhekh of the Hindus and the Allah of the Muslims are one, the Qur'an and the Purânas praise the same Lord. They are all of one form, the One Lord made them all.[65]

Guru Nanak Dev Ji's teachings and writings are enshrined in the Guru Granth Sahib Ji. The former Indian prime minister Dr. Manmohan Singh wrote that the teachings

> of the *Guru Granth Sahib* seek to harmonize the world as we know it. These teachings synthesize the essential wisdom of all the religions and earlier mystic saints and the ancient traditional cultural and civilizational ethos of the Indian people. In doing so, it sets out a powerful and appealing message of gender equality, concern for women and concern for our natural environment. It defines a moral compass for humanity to follow, but without adopting an imperative approach. Most of all, it sets out an agenda for social equity that is most relevant for our society today.[66]

The Guru Granth Sahib Ji is the sacred text that Sikh gurus passed down from Guru Nanak Dev Ji to Guru Arjun Dev Ji, who compiled the writings to install in the Harmandir Sahib Amritsar, popularly known as the Golden Temple. Guru Gobind Singh Ji added the teachings of Guru Tegh Bahadur Ji and completed the scripture, having infused his own spirit into the Guru Granth Sahib Ji and the *Khalsa* (the pure ones), which he had created in 1699. He proclaimed and enthroned the Guru Granth Sahib Ji in Nanded, Maharashtra, as the eternal Guru of the Sikhs from 1708.

> They shared the One Light and the same way; the Sovereign Guru has changed body.[67]

Jaswant Singh Neki succinctly captures what the eternal Guru encapsulates. He writes that it is

> not a historical document, nor an album of mythology, nor a treatise about ritual, nor even a corpus of canonical statutes. It is a collection of lyrical songs ensconced in which is the guidance about how to live a God-oriented life. It does not include the works of the Sikh Gurus alone, but also those of many other holy men from both the Aryan and the Semitic fold. It addresses the entire mankind. No one is alien, none a stranger in its persuasion.[68]

Guru Granth Sahib Ji, understood as the embodiment of the living spirit of all ten Sikh gurus, is a perfect example of interfaith harmony, comprising the verses of Sikh gurus as well as Hindu and Muslim saints.

The Guru Granth Sahib Ji was composed predominantly by six Sikh Gurus and contains the poetic teachings of thirteen Hindu *Sant* and two Sufi Saints. The Sacred Sikh Scripture can thus be considered as a unique interfaith sacred scripture. Guru Nanak Dev Ji explains that what is recorded in the Guru Granth Sahib Ji is eternal wisdom, which is revealed by the Guru who is attuned and one with God. This truth applies to all the contributors to the eternal Guru, regardless of their religious affiliation.

An Interfaith Journey:
To Be Religious Is to Be Interreligious

In 1999, while in Amritsar, following divine intervention, I decided to formally engage with what can broadly be described as the interfaith movement or what has now become my interfaith family. I have always been committed to the values, principles, and ethics of respect and love of all humanity and the need for all of us to live in harmony. These underlying values are most clearly a manifestation of my faith and understanding of Guru Nanak Dev Ji's teachings as expounded in the Guru Granth Sahib Ji. They are also part of my own lived experience, albeit that the inspiration comes from Guru Nanak Dev Ji, who implored us to engage in dialogue:

> As long as we are in this world, O Nanak, we must listen to others, as well as express ourselves to others.[69]

Guru Nanak Dev Ji has taught me to respect all religions, inspiring me to venture into dialogue with other faiths, to cooperate and collaborate with believers of other faiths to formulate and enact joint projects with them.[70] This has entailed working and participating in interfaith events, seminars, conferences, and projects aimed at better understanding amongst the world's faith traditions. It is vital that humans gain consciousness of their divine interconnectedness and interdependence. Spiritual realization improves our relationships, our solidarity, and leads to the realization that our fate and future are dependent upon one another. This naturally fosters mutual respect, collaboration, and cooperation.

From the very moment that I committed myself to be immersed in interfaith work and dialogue, I realized that to successfully engage in interfaith, one had to have a profound knowledge of and commitment to one's own faith tradition. However, involvement in interfaith work went beyond simply being grounded and well versed in my own faith. I realized that, as a Sikh, one of my fundamental convictions was that to be religious is to be interreligious. My conviction was founded on several key historical and scriptural underpinnings. The influence of Guru Nanak Dev Ji and the centrality of the eternal guru, Guru Granth Sahib Ji, have continued to guide me. Above all else, it was Guru Nanak Dev Ji's humility that is both unique and phenomenal, his practical approach emphasizing daily practice, as opposed to philosophizing and theorizing about it. He is my absolute divine role model. His explanation of faith is rather explicit and simple to understand. His divine teachings and message inspire, motivate, and are in perfect harmony with the Sikh notion of always living in ascending optimism.

I am reminded also of the importance of interfaith acts that were crucial to the formation of a Sikh identity. The foundation stone of the Sikh's most sacred shrine, Sri Harimandir Sahib, also known as the Golden Temple, was laid by a Muslim saint, Mian Mir, at the behest of the fifth guru, Guru Arjan Dev Ji. It is at the Sri Harimandir Sahib that I had the honor and privilege of undertaking the restoration and gold gilding after 165 years.

Similarly, the ninth guru, Guru Tegh Bahadur Ji, made the supreme sacrifice, giving his life to protect the freedom of religious belief and practice of a faith other than his own, the Hindu Dharam or faith. He said: "We should not just better and elevate ourselves, but we should support and help all those who come to be associated with us."[71] Guru Gobind Singh implored us to recognize the whole human race as one family, when he proclaimed:

> Recognize all mankind as one
>
> The same Lord is the creator and nourisher of all
>
> Recognize no distinction among them
>
> The temple and mosque are the same
>
> So are the Hindu worship and Muslim prayer. People are all one.[72]

Finally, I am always conscious that every Sikh congregation ends with a prayer invoking blessings for all humankind, "Sarbhat da Bhalla."

Simply put, my convictions rest upon the knowledge that the Sikh *Dharam* holds a profound spirit of universality at its core. *Dharam* for Guru Nanak Dev Ji is the divine law that humans must follow. He makes me respect all faiths; he places all of them under one universal divine Sovereign and one universal sovereign God Almighty. He refers to God as our divine loving Mother, Father, Protector, and Guide. Guru Nanak Dev Ji makes me understand one's responsibilities and rights, recognizing that God is ever merciful and forgiving and that we all share the sparks of the same divine light or *noor,* and, as such, we are all worthy of respect.

The message of my interfaith hero Guru Nanak Dev Ji and the Sikh gurus is a universal message. The ethical relationship is one that hinges on the responsibility one has to the other. The other here has a double meaning, signifying all the species that inhabit the planet, as well as the infinite Other, who is always omnipresent yet difficult, indeed impossible, to comprehend, being attainable only once the self is transcended.

Guru Nanak Dev Ji knows me, inspires, and motivates me, more than anyone else. He consoles, supports, and guides me to success and happiness under the most difficult situations and circumstances. All this makes me appreciate that he is much more than an interfaith hero; he is the intermediary between me and God. However, Gurbani also convinces me to be conscious that "Gur Parmesar eko Jan"—consider guru and God the same.[73]

The sharing of my interfaith hero Guru Nanak Dev Ji and his profound influence over me, as well as my own engagement with the interfaith family, reminds me how much affection and love I have for Rabbi David Rosen and his dear wife Sharon. David Rosen is one of my closest friends and an interfaith brother. As I reflect on David's commitment and passion for interreligious relations and practice, the Papal Knighthood (KSG) that we have both been bestowed, his ethics and values, his vegetarian diet and his deep love for the Creator and his creation, I am sure that he is, at his core, an outstanding Sikh. He encapsulates the true spirit of Guru Nanak Dev Ji and is a contemporary interfaith hero who has been exalted by the sacred divine spirit that he has lovingly embraced to be the outstanding rabbi that he is today.

Śrī Rāmakṛṣṇa[74]

SWAMI ATMAPRIYANANDA

Introducing Śrī Rāmakṛṣṇa in the Words of Romain Rolland

MY INTENTION IS TO provide a glimpse into the life and teachings of Śrī Rāmakṛṣṇa, one of the outstanding mystic-saints of the modern era, about whom Romain Rolland, the famous French savant, litterateur, and 1915 Nobel Laureate, wrote, "his inner life embraced the whole multiplicity of men and Gods." Ramakrishna, although born in the orthodox Hindu tradition, was catapulted by a hunger of the soul to various other traditions to which he had access in his time. Realizing in the inner depths of his own being the oneness of the ultimate truth in all the religious traditions, he pronounced in his own inimitable style: "'The Ultimate Reality is Infinite and the paths leading to It are also infinite."[75] Romain Rolland, in his famous work *The Life of Ramakrishna*, first published in 1929, nearly four decades after the passing away of Ramakrishna, introduces this nineteenth-century saint and mystic in the following telling words:

> Allowing for differences of country and of time, Ramakrishna is the younger brother of our Christ . . . I am bringing to Europe, as yet unaware of it, the fruit of a new autumn, a new message of the Soul, the symphony of India, bearing the name of Ramakrishna. It can be shown (and we shall not fail to point out) that this symphony, like those of our classical masters, is built up of a hundred different musical elements emanating from the past. But the sovereign personality concentrating in himself the diversity of these elements and fashioning them into a royal harmony, is always the one who gives his name to the work, though it contains within itself the labour of generations. And with his victorious sign he marks a new era.
>
> The man whose image I here evoke was the consummation of two thousand years of the spiritual life of three hundred

million people. Although he has been dead forty years, his soul animates modern India. He was no hero of action like Gandhi, no genius in art or thought like Goethe or Tagore. He was a little village Brahmin of Bengal, whose outer life was set in a limited frame without striking incident, outside the political and social activities of his time. But his inner life embraced the whole multiplicity of men and Gods . . .

Very few go back to the source. The little peasant of Bengal by listening to the message of his heart found his way to the inner Sea. And there he was wedded to it, thus bearing out the words of the Upanishads:

"I am more ancient than the radiant Gods. I am the firstborn of the Being. I am the artery of Immortality."

It is my desire to bring the sound of the beating of that artery to the ears of fever-stricken Europe, which has murdered sleep. I wish to wet its lips with the blood of Immortality.[76]

Birth and Childhood

Śrī Rāmakṛṣṇa was born on February 18, 1836, in Kāmarpukur, a remote village of Bengal in the district of Hooghly, about sixty miles northwest of Calcutta (now Kolkata). His family name was Gadādhar Caṭṭopādhyāy. He was from an orthodox family of Brāhmaṇas, the priest-class devoted to prayer and worship, cultivation of spiritual knowledge and ministry. His father, Kṣudirām Caṭṭopādhyāy (1775–1843), was highly revered in the village for his impeccable integrity of character. His mother, Candramaṇi Devī (1791–1876), was a pious lady, loving and deeply caring. She inculcated her values in her children. The life of an orthodox Brāhmaṇa in India is devoted to asceticism and self-denial, cultivation of higher knowledge and worship. Śrī Rāmakṛṣṇa's parents epitomized this very ideal. When he was just five, Gadadhar experienced his first trance, called *samādhi* in the Hindu religious tradition. He felt such intense God-absorption that he remained for hours in a state of total oblivion of the external world. In fact, this experience of *samādhi* in God-absorption became his second nature, due to its repeated occurrence. Throughout his life, *samādhi* became as natural to him as breathing. When he grew to become Śrī Rāmakṛṣṇa, he came to be regarded and worshipped as a Paramahaṁsa, a name by which saints of highest spiritual attainments and those belonging to the highest order of monks (called Saṁnyāsins in Hindu tradition) are called in the Hindu parlance.

Contemporary Backdrop

In 1835, Lord Macaulay announced a proclamation of a New Education Policy for India, whose stated objective was to bring about a complete change in the mindset of Indians. His intention was that they would consider their traditional Hindu spiritual culture primitive, obscurantist, superstitious, and unscientific and that they would eventually forget it. By this time, Hinduism had itself lost much of its glory, having fallen into the narrow trap of casteism. The original sublime concept of caste based on aptitudes and temperaments had degenerated into caste by birth, resulting in inhumane discriminatory practices. Notwithstanding the claim of oneness and sameness at the theoretical philosophical level, there was the practice of inequality, inequity, and discrimination at the ground level in society. Narrow sectarianism had thus reduced the grand Hindu religion to a bundle of lifeless ritualistic practices that became the institutionalized monopoly of the upper caste. The powerful onslaught of materialism and the challenges of Western science were also powerful forces with which to reckon. Any attempt at turning this oncoming tide was met with the stoutest opposition, howls, and protests from the orthodox, as it challenged their monopoly.

The following angry outburst later by Svāmī Vivekānanda, the chief apostle of Śrī Rāmakṛṣṇa, who attempted such a task of reformation of Hinduism against a narrow orthodoxy, gives an indication of how tough was the opposition: "Do you mean to say that I am born to live and die as one of those caste-ridden, superstitious, merciless, hypocritical, atheistic cowards that you find only among educated Hindus?" In such a scenario, there was an urgent need for a mighty spiritual force for the restoration of the spirit of true religion that was the eternal legacy and wisdom of the human civilization. The pure and pristine spirit of the teachings of religion—not only of the Hindu religion but of all the religious traditions of the world, as embodied in the Avatāras, prophets, saints, and sages of all religions—needed to be resuscitated and revivified.[77] Against such a backdrop, it is perhaps not just a fortuitous coincidence that in the very next year of Macaulay's proclamation, in 1896, Gadādhar was born. His life and teachings exemplify the universal ideals of purity, holiness, truth, and godliness. They helped reassert the true spirit of religion in the broadest and widest setting of interreligious understanding and harmony. The story of Śrī Rāmakṛṣṇa has therefore been called a phenomenon by Christopher Isherwood,[78] his twentieth-century American biographer.

Spiritual Practices (*sādhanā*) and Attainments (*siddhi*)

The transformation of the unsophisticated youth Gadādhar into Rāmakṛṣṇa Paramahaṁsa is a great saga. He passed through an intense period of spiritual practices called *sādhanā*, which lasted for nearly sixteen years. Being endowed with a highly scientific temperament, Gadādhar would not accept anything unless it was actually realized and directly experienced. The spiritual scientist in him was constantly investigating and examining, exploring and penetrating into the mysteries of God, the ultimate reality, and the true nature of consciousness. He manifested a colossal spiritual capacity to take the kingdom of heaven by violence, as it were, as described by Śrī Aurobindo, another mystic-saint of the modern era who came after Śrī Rāmakṛṣṇa.[79] Thus, Śrī Rāmakṛṣṇa, the worshipper of the Divine Mother Kālī at the Dakṣiṇeśvar temple, restlessly questioned whether the Divine Mother was actually living in the image or if it were mere imagination. He spent his time performing *sādhanā*—intensely praying, meditating, crying and yearning for direct and immediate realization of the Divine Mother. He was oblivious of the surroundings and indifferent to social norms to such an extent that people considered him mad. Indeed, what a divine madness it was! When the intensity of his yearning and longing was in white heat, he saw luminous waves of divine light engulfing him in a divine rapture, overwhelming him and throwing him into a state of *samādhi,* as he himself described later.[80] That was in 1856, when Śrī Rāmakṛṣṇa was just twenty years old. From then on, his spiritual voyage became more intensive, even as it was extensive. He was buffeted by the divine ecstatic waves in the course of his journey in the unchartered sea of the supreme reality, swimming in this ocean and exploring the truths of various religions, through each of which he attained the same supreme truth. His is a remarkable story in this modern age of skepticism and unbelief, serving as a beacon of light to all sincere spiritual seekers. Śrī Rāmakṛṣṇa's divine exploration into the mystery of God was not born, as is commonly understood, out of his desire or intent to prove or vindicate the veracity of all the religious traditions as valid paths leading to the ultimate truth. Rather, it was his intense and spontaneous desire to taste the divine sweetness of God, to attempt, however infinitesimally, to experience his inexhaustibility and infinity in various ways in unceasing childlike wonderment. This led him to move from one religious tradition to another in a mad, relentless pursuit. He has been likened to a glutton in the spiritual field[81] with an insatiable passion for tasting God in innumerable ways. He began to practice, one by one, the various traditions within the Hindu fold—the worship of various personal forms of God, leading ultimately to the highest impersonal reality without qualities and attributes, under the competent guidance of a number of gurus (spiritual teachers). From such a vast treasure house of rich personal spiritual experience that became the natural state of his being originated his liberal doctrine of "infinite paths to infinite Reality, all equally valid and true."[82]

Practice of Other Religions—Infinite Paths to the Infinite Reality

Śrī Rāmakṛṣṇa realized that the infinite reality is comprehensible and realizable in countless ways and through infinite paths. He became possessed of deep longing to realize God through other religions, following meticulously their own traditions and modes of worship. This is one unique characteristic that distinguishes Śrī Rāmakṛṣṇa from ordinary spiritual aspirants and perhaps even other saints: whereas they practice disciplines of one tradition and achieve their goal through them, Śrī Rāmakṛṣṇa practiced with insatiable gusto the disciplines of different cults and religions, the entire vast-ranging gamut of the various cults of Hindu religion, as well as some other major religions of the world. He began his spiritual journey as a humble image worshipper in the Kālī temple at Dakṣiṇeśvar; passed on to the tantra mode of worship of Śaktī or Power, attaining *siddhi* (acme of attainment) through a rich variety of traditionally known sixty-four tantric methods of *sādhanā* under the guidance of his woman-guru Bhairavī Brāhmaṇī; thence to the various bhāvas (spiritual attitudes or moods) known to Hinduism, namely, thinking of oneself as the mother and God as the Divine Child (called Vātsalya Bhāva), oneself as the humble eternal servant and God as the Divine Master (Dāsya Bhāva), oneself as the bride and God as the Divine Bridegroom (Madhura Bhāva); finally culminating in the realization of the ultimate truth as the impersonal absolute, formless, nameless, attributeless (Advaita Vedānta) under the guidance of Totā Purī. Even this did not satisfy his divine hunger. Like a glutton in the spiritual realm, Śrī Rāmakṛṣṇa began to explore other religions. He meticulously went through the practices of Christianity and then Islam, attaining the acme of realization in each of them. He is thus unparalleled in the spiritual and religious history of humanity as having undertaken the practice of the various religions as an *insider*—becoming a Christian, a Muslim, and so on and realizing God through each of them, thus establishing that each of these religions was a valid and true path to attain the supreme reality. Thus he enunciated one of the most liberal religious doctrines of the modern age: 'The Ultimate Reality is Infinite and the paths leading to It are also infinite.'[83] Svāmī Vivekānanda, his chief disciple and foremost exponent of his teachings, commenting on how Rāmakṛṣṇa seamlessly moved across various forms of *sādhanā*, said that Śrī Rāmakṛṣṇa could be considered as an extraordinary searchlight that reveals the whole scope of Hindu religion and that he had, in fifty years, lived the five thousand years of national life.[84]

Śrī Rāmakṛṣṇa's significant legacy is the Rāmakṛṣṇa Order of monks working through the twin organizations Rāmakṛṣṇa Maṭh and Rāmakṛṣṇa Mission for *ātmano mokṣārthaṃ jagaddhitāya ca* (Sanskrit), that is, "for the liberation of oneself and for the good of the world," established by Svāmī Vivekānanda in 1897 at the command that he received from Śrī Rāmakṛṣṇa before the latter passed away.[85] These twin organizations have been working in the East and the West since their inception for the all-round welfare of the whole world—physical, mental, intellectual, moral, aesthetic, and spiritual—irrespective of caste, creed, religion, and nationality, preaching the gospel of universal harmony and peace. On a personal note, I have been so deeply influenced and overwhelmed by the life and personality of Śrī Rāmakṛṣṇa, the intensity and extent of his teachings that find expression as living traditions and practices through the Ramakrishna Order in daily life in the midst of the complexity of the modern world, consumed as it is by the unmistakable sway of science and technology, that I chose, at a very young age, to dedicate my entire life to the deal of *ātmano mokṣārthaṃ jagaddhitāya ca*, "for the liberation of oneself and for the good of the world" as delineated above. I consider myself blessed to be a part of the holy order of Śrī Rāmakṛṣṇa devoted to the above ideal, and my learning experience is growing richer and deeper with every passing day.

Philosophy of Harmony— Essential Teachings of Śrī Rāmakṛṣṇa

The teachings of Śrī Rāmakṛṣṇa, based as they are on his profound spiritual realizations were summarized by his chief disciple, Svāmī Vivekānanda. Freely rendered, these teachings are:

1. Religion is realization, direct and immediate, of the ultimate reality or truth, which is personal-impersonal. This realization is the essence of true spirituality. To acquire this first and become a dynamo of spirituality is the greatest service we can do to humanity.

2. The ideal of harmony is preeminent and paramount—harmony of all religious paths as equally valid paths to the ultimate reality. This leads naturally to universal acceptance, not mere toleration.

3. Various religions of the world are but manifestations of one eternal religion of God. Truth may be One and many at the same time, that we may have different visions of the same Truth from different standpoints. Therefore the watchwords are help and not fight, integration and not destruction, harmony and peace and not dissension.

4. The Many and the One are the same Reality, perceived by the same mind at different times and in different attitudes.

5. Every soul is divine. However, this divinity is not recognized. The Goal is to manifest this Divinity within by controlling Nature, external and internal and attain Freedom by any path: this is the whole of religion; doctrines or dogmas, rituals or temples, books or forms are but secondary details.

Is Śrī Rāmakṛṣṇa an Interreligious Hero?

Having chosen to present Śrī Rāmakṛṣṇa in a volume dedicated to interreligious heroes, one would expect the final section of this paper to be an affirmation of his status as such, rather than a question to be pondered. There are several reasons why the title of this section concludes with a question mark. At the same time, including him in this collection of essays constitutes a decision to legitimate a view that considers him through the lens of interreligious hero.

The first challenge in applying the category stems from the fact that certain exceptional beings, be they prophets in other traditions or divine incarnations or avatars, as these are known in India, defy categorization. That is particularly true for their followers. From this perspective, an interreligious hero would be a fitting designation for a human achievement. What if the person under discussion is considered divine, as are India's great teachers? Does the category not belittle his status?

A second challenge stems from the fact that Śrī Rāmakṛṣṇa did not engage in interfaith relations in the sense that we do today. He did not represent one particular faith in its encounter with another. The path described above is one that affirms all faiths, while transcending them, in entering the one common divine reality. Interfaith encounter was not a social reality of his day.

Notwithstanding these challenges, there are good grounds for viewing Śrī Rāmakṛṣṇa in the present context because of his testimony, because of what he makes possible for those who seek to engage other religions, and because, indeed, from him flows a lengthy chain of activity and engagement of his disciples and followers in interfaith activities.

Considering interfaith engagement as commonly practiced, one recognizes that a landmark event in the history of interfaith relations was the first World Parliament of Religions, which took place in Chicago in 1893. This was the moment when Svāmī Vivekānanda made his first major appearance on the global stage, presenting Hinduism in the framework of other religions and launching a movement that has continued ever since, the movement of sharing the wisdom and spirituality of India with the West or, more correctly, with all humanity. Śrī Rāmakṛṣṇa's chief disciple and primary interpreter is an interfaith hero by any definition. Yet, the vision he brings to the interfaith table engagement is that of his master. The same is true for the numerous swamis of the Ramakrishna Order, who for over one hundred years have been engaging other faiths in a variety of local and international contexts. All of them not only follow Svāmī Vivekānanda's example; they draw their inspiration and grounding from Śrī Rāmakṛṣṇa.

Śrī Rāmakṛṣṇa's unmistakable contribution lies in the field known nowadays as theology of religions.[86] The scope and meaning of interfaith engagement are a function of implicit and explicit views of other religions. The experience lived by Śrī Rāmakṛṣṇa and his articulation of its philosophical and theological meaning are therefore foundational to the approach of his followers to interreligious relations. It is the key to their openness and to their interest in engaging other religions.

More significantly, Śrī Rāmakṛṣṇa suggests a special approach to relations across religions, one that is often overlooked and one that is sorely lacking in the broader interfaith arena. His is not the activist's quest for peacemaking or social reform. His is the quest for God, and God alone. Crossing over to other religions is part of a spiritual quest, a yearning for tasting God in his infinite expanse and wealth. Śrī Rāmakṛṣṇa therefore not only provides the philosophical and theoretical foundations for interfaith engagement; he holds out a vision of what the highest form of interfaith engagement looks like. It is an encounter of the spiritual gluttons, who seek to enrich each other in the process of tasting and experiencing divine reality.

Few, if any, are able to follow the exact same path the master followed. In fundamental ways, he is, like all great masters, inimitable. However, there is an important teaching for others in his path. Grounded in his Hindu framework, Śrī Rāmakṛṣṇa was able to enter the spiritual reality of other religions and to find God in the highest dimensions. The quest for finding God need not compromise religious identity. Nor should it be applied casually to a supermarket mentality of picking random experiences off the proverbial shelf. There is, however, a serious, disciplined approach that may be termed a tasting approach to interreligious engagement. This is the approach of the spiritual seekers, the serious practitioners, whose quest and thirst for tasting God leads them to discover divine reality in the religious experience of the other, as part of the discovery of God's very infinity. I believe in this regard, Śrī Rāmakṛṣṇa is a unique teacher in the modern times. As a role model for this approach, he may be considered an interfaith hero. The heroic practice of his own path to God points to a way of practicing relations across religions that is not only particular but serves as an important reminder and corrective to much that takes place in the present-day encounter of religions.

'Abd Al-Qâdir Al-Jazâ'irî

Imam Yahya Pallavicini

The Life of the Emir: "Emir among the Saints and the Saint among Princes"

A LITTLE MORE THAN two centuries after the birth of Emir 'Abd al-Qâdir, it is surprising to see how much prejudice against him is still present, if not even enlarged and worsened. Westerners have been able to first fear, then fight, criticize, censor, and finally love the emir's personality. Few have been able to go beyond the complexity of his history to recognize the depth of his vision and intention of spiritual knowledge and obedience. A similar myopia pertains to the Arabs of the Algerian tribes, the Turkish officials of the declining Ottoman caliphate, and the mass of Syrian Muslims who lived in Damascus.

Yet, at the same time, a good minority of Jews, Christians, Muslims, Westerners, and Easterners knew how to follow him and to grasp from this warrior and humble hero, from this contemplative emir, the exceptional mastery of a harmony of opposites. In the dynamics of the history of this world, interior and exterior, war and peace, homeland and exile, poverty and wealth, slander and glory have represented only forms and aspects of a symbolic alternation of serving and obeying a just cause. In this alternation of trials, one can discern the true identity of a humble hero of Allâh, the way of an order of Islamic esotericism towards sacred knowledge in contemplation and action.

Every day, Emir 'Abd al-Qâdir, under the tent in the desert, during a fight or a peace negotiation, in the quarters of Oran, Toulouse, Istanbul, Damascus, Makka, by ship, in exile, in various residences as a guest or a prisoner, gathered his disciples and a few friends in meditation on revelation. The deepening of the subtleties of the divine language; the penetration of the profound meaning of Allâh's signs in space, time, and movement; and the search for attunement with the teaching of the masters of the various inner orders of Islam were of support to the emir and his companions to intuit the correspondences useful to win the outer combat of the moment.

The Education of a Young Sûfî in the Management of Life and Knowledge of the World

Emir 'Abd al-Qâdir al-Jazâ'irî was educated by his father Muhyî al-dîn according to the rules of the order of the patron saint Shaykh 'Abd al-Qâdir al-Jîlânî. The order of the Qâdiriyya, in fact, had developed and radiated in the eleventh century from Persia to the Middle East, where Muhyî al-dîn's father, Shaykh Mustafâ, had received initiation into this contemplative way. The doctrine of the Qâdiriyya, based on the way of practicing obedience, humility, and charity, united the Sûfî with Christian monks and priests, for whom the Qur'an reserves a condition of particular respect.

The doctrine of the Qâdiriyya brotherhood preached a simple and universal message that attracted the vocation of Muslims but also the curiosity of Jews and Christians. It was a duty for the Muslims of the order to pray and work for the good of all humanity, not only for the members of their own community and spiritual family. The founder had taught them to respect the figure of Jesus, characterized by the gift of divine goodness and the power of love that distinguished him from other prophets.

In order to realize the sacred science of spiritual knowledge, the father and master Muhyî al-dîn had taught his son and disciple 'Abd al-Qâdir the rules of the way to the Beloved:

> If you are asked what is the Way, say: it is Knowledge, purity of heart and body, patience and having excellent offspring.
> If you are asked what are the rules and discipline of the Way, say: To not utter evil words, to repeat continuously the names of God, to have contempt for the goods of this world, to fear God.
> If you are asked by what signs one recognizes people of the Way, say: By their good works, discretion in speech, gentleness, compassion, and absence of sinful behavior.[87]

His father's teachings on the contemplative path were accompanied in the education of the young 'Abd al-Qâdir by those of Ahmad ibn Tahâr, the judge of Arzew, a village near the port of Oran only two days' ride on horseback from Guetna, their city of residence.

The chronicles of the French colonizers described the Algerian society of the time as characterized by two levels of aristocracy: the nobles of religion (the *marabouts*) and the nobles of the sword (the *douads*). The latter were hunters of enemies, while the *marabouts* practiced the discipline of hunting to train in the four qualities of life: intelligence, patience, determination, and courage. It was precisely courage that was considered a fundamental virtue, alongside intellectual honesty, a sense of justice, and self-control.

His father and teacher Muhyî al-dîn demanded that his son 'Abd al-Qâdir learn the recitation of Allâh's revelation in the Holy Qur'an with deep attention and transparency: "You must learn to read the Qur'an following the mimicry of the divine breath that Allâh has inspired in man!" The Qur'an is the perfect word of Allâh, his father recommended, but it must be recited to perfection in order to grasp the spiritual influence that governs chaos: "Man is surrounded by the alternation of states and the randomness of decisions. Without the support of ritual, the world becomes unstable and disorderly."[88]

"Remember," continued the father and teacher Muhyî al-dîn, "tests are sent by God to strengthen you. Rather than turn away from Him or dare to judge Him, you must realize that He who is the First Cause of all things, also allows his creatures to become muddled in the secondary causes. He chose to give his lieutenants on earth a free will."[89]

As the father guided his son on his pilgrimage to the holy city of Mecca, he taught him about the nature of the various spiritual brotherhoods, their histories, and their patron saints, and likewise explained to him the various religious communities:

> "Abraham was a Muslim."
> "But how could he be a Muslim even before Islam?" asked his young son 'Abd al-Qâdir.
> "Because he submitted to the will of God. A Muslim is one who submits to God," replied Father Muhyî al-dîn.
> "Are Jews and Christians also Muslims?"
> "Of course, when they seek sincerely to do God's will. 'Thy will be done, on earth as it is in heaven' is a part of a prayer the Prophet Jesus gave to the Christians."[90]

Going up the Nile after the pilgrimage and going beyond the city of Cairo, Muhyî al-dîn and 'Abd al-Qâdir followed the footsteps of the prophet Moses to Mount Sinai, where they found hospitality at the monastery of St. Catherine. For hours, they dialogued with the monks about the unity of Allâh, the mystery of the Trinity, and the differences of his ways.

Abd al-Qâdir learned that Jesus was direct revelation for Christians, just as the Qur'an was for Muslims. Upon arriving in Damascus, the father arranged for his son to study with the master of another contemplative order, the Tarîqa Naqshabandiyya of the enlightened Shaykh Khâlid. In this same city, the long pilgrimage of father and son, of master Muhyî al-dîn and disciple 'Abd al-Qâdir, ended with a visit to the tomb of the holy founder of the Qâdiriyya order, Shaykh 'Abd al-Qâdir al-Jîlânî, who died in this city in 1166.

After this visit and pilgrimage, the father Muhyî al-dîn authorized his son 'Abd al-Qâdir to take the baton of command and speak in the name of their spiritual way.

A few years later, back in Algeria, this spiritual succession between master and disciple would find an outward consequence even more visible than that relating to the inner order. In fact, in 1832, the authorities of the various Muslim tribes in Algeria asked Muhyî al-dîn to become their sultan, the central pole that united the seven families of the region in defense against the armed colonization of the French. His first formal act was to abdicate in favor of his son 'Abd al-Qâdir, who would become the young emir, the commander of the believers, respected by the Arab elders, the heads of the Jewish families in Mascara, and the Christian communities in the region. At the age of twenty-five, 'Abd al-Qâdir synthesized a number of characteristics: devout son, pious sage, preacher, fighter, diplomat, administrator, judge, but, above all, spiritual authority. The banner of this Muslim ascetic and monk was colored by the virtue of obedience and service to Allâh.

The Jihâd of Humble Hero

The Emir 'Abd al-Qâdir had the intuition to make sure he was supported in his public function by a court of advisors, among which there were also some Jewish brokers and traders: Mordecai Amar, Michael Bushnach, and Judas Ben Duran. His ecumenical sensitivity found a natural correspondence with the management of power and unity of the people in their defense against the invasion of the French colonizers.

The capital city of Algiers in 1830 was a mosaic of fifty different ethnic neighborhoods, with thirty-three towers rising between furnaces, pottery factories, leather dyers, fishnet weavers, police offices, and credit institutions. There were 159 mosques, four synagogues for over five thousand Jews, and a church for Christian residents. Religion, more than any other dimension, brought together the complex social fabric of ethnic groups, tribes, and traders.

By 1835, after only four years of French civilization, the shoreline had been transformed into a plaza, where retail stores displayed unfashionable European items. Mosques had been transformed into churches, and urban planning had been adapted to accommodate streets with incomprehensible names: rue Annibal, rue du Chat, rue Sidney Smith, rue du Lotophages, rue Sophonisba, rue Belisaire. New hotels and grand cafés were the meeting places.

Beyond this veil of calm and ostentation, a war was being fought between opposing extremisms: those who wanted to drive out the infidels and those who wanted to conquer the savages. Emir 'Abd al-Qâdir had managed to maintain unity among his people and good diplomatic relations with French generals and governors. Above all, he had managed to guarantee himself dignity and autonomy of management, even though he had to suffer the criticism of those who reproached him for "having made peace with the Christians and for having betrayed jihad."

During these intense and difficult years of fighting and diplomatic negotiations, 'Abd al-Qâdir lost contact with his wife Khedira and his son Muhammad. After accepting his responsibility as emir, he had even offered his wife the dissolution of the marriage bond, which took place in times when neither of them could remotely imagine the destiny of warrior and monk that he would have to live. But his wife always remained faithful and supportive in the mission by declining the offer of dissolution of marriage.

French General Robert Bugeaud, in his report to Count Louis-Mathieu Molé, describes his meeting with 'Abd al-Qâdir as that with a monk:

> His clothes were no different than the most common Arab and resembles portraits one sees of Jesus Christ. His eyes are dark, his forehead prominent, and he has a large mouth with crooked white teeth. His entire physiognomy is that of a monk. Except at first greeting, he keeps his eyes lowered. His clothes are dirty and worn. It is clear he affects a rigorous simplicity.[91]

The Emir's Exile

Having established a kingdom in Algeria in the 30s of the nineteenth century, the emir was eventually forced to surrender to the French, leading to his exile in France, contrary to promises the French had made at the time of his surrender. The emir lived in forced exile in France from 1847 to 1852. Even the inhabitants of Pau and Amboise were curious to catch a glimpse of "the famous emir who dressed like a Trappist monk in his essential white cloak." These were particularly difficult years for Emir 'Abd al-Qâdir and his retinue of family members and disciples in exile in France, where the government of Emperor Napoleon III was unable to fulfill its promised safe-conduct to the Middle East, for fear that he might again organize an Arab resistance to French rule.

In this sojourn away from his homeland, the emir remembered the prophet Abraham, the father of monotheism who "is not a Jew, not a Christian, but a pure worshipper, integrally converted to Allâh." He wrote that he had a vision of Abraham, "the intimate friend, the beloved of Allâh," in his company.[92] Among Abraham's children, he was the one who most resembled him, who had realized a special loyalty to his heritage. This blessing of Abraham consisted of a mission to fulfill: to be a witness to the one Allâh, the Merciful, the Patient, the Beloved for all mankind. This had also been the message of Shaykh 'Abd al-Qâdir al-Jîlânî, the saint of Baghdad and founder of the Sûfî order of the Qâdiriyya, of which he was the representative by permission of his father, Shaykh Muhyî al-dîn.

In this perspective, the exiled 'Abd al-Qâdir wished to be of help to France, which he saw growing as an international power in the Islamic world, to better understand Islam and rediscover its spiritual needs. By France, the emir meant the entire Western world, which he saw as enriched in the management of material goods but fragile in its understanding of the reality of the spirit, where eternal knowledge resides.

One day, he said to Baron and General Estève Boissonet, his guardian during his detention in Amboise:

> Your savants have an impressive spirit of practical application. But where is the spirit of metaphysical speculation which will allow them to go beyond the narrow confines of material reality to attain a knowledge which serves the needs of man's soul?[93]

Emir 'Abd al-Qadir thus provoked his Western and Christian interlocutors to rediscover the memory of an intellectual light and a universal perspective of sensitivity for the sacred that would be prioritized over the thirst for an assertion of absolute power in this low world.

Damascus: The Final Goal of the Sûfî and the Spiritual Encounter with Ibn 'Arabî

When Emir 'Abd al-Qâdir finally arrived in Damascus in 1855 to spend the last part of his life in this city, he managed to surprise the Turkish dignitaries who had come to welcome him and to escort him into the city. His first request was not to meet the governor or to visit the mosque of the Umayyads but to visit the tomb of Master Ibn 'Arabî, the greatest of the masters of Sufism, and to be allowed to occupy his own residence in the Armara quarter.

Ibn ʿArabî had died in Damascus in 1240, stricken by the madness of a corrupt imam. His tomb was later honored by the Ottoman sultan Selim I the Weighed. One of his love poems is famous:

My heart is capable of wearing all forms,

Is pasture for gazelles and a monastery for monks,

A temple for idols and the Kaaba for the pilgrim.

It is the tablets of the Torah and it is the book of the Qurʾan.

I profess the religion of love, wherever the destination of its caravans may be.

Love is my law and my faith.[94]

By virtue of the principle of divine omnipresence, Ibn ʿArabî draws the conclusion that there is no space devoid of sacredness and holiness. He is with you wherever you are. "Perfection," writes the supreme of teachers, "does not come from withdrawal but from living together in society. The elect do not flee their condition; on the contrary, it is their condition that flees from them." "Spiritual retreat," he taught, is "like a hospital for the heartsick, useful for temporary treatment. But perfection is realized in life in common. . . . The lesser combat against the outward enemy is not a distraction from the greater combat against the inward enemy. The lives of the elect are united between the affairs of this world and those for eternity." Emir ʿAbd al-Qâdir shared the same perspective, but few Western diplomats recognized it.

During his exile in France, ʿAbd al-Qâdir had had the opportunity to reflect and write:

Our God and the God of the communities different from ours are in reality all one God . . . He reveals Himself to Muslims as beyond all form, to Christians in the person of Jesus Christ and monks. He reveals Himself even to pagans who worship objects. For no worshipper of something finite worships the thing for itself. What he worships through this object is the epiphany of Allâh.[95]

Emir ʿAbd al-Qadir knew the work of Ibn ʿArabi through his writings and dedicated time in his meetings with his brethren to deepen, develop, and comment on the understanding of these teachings. Once in Damascus, he requested to live in Ibn ʿArabi's house in order to experience his link as a follower of his master and to see himself according to this spiritual link. The Andalusian master Ibn ʿArabi writes in his work that every creature is the custodian also of an inner city and that this must be well managed to transmit order to the outer world: "As man is created central to the universe as God's deputy on earth and is the microcosm of the macrocosm, so the soul is central to the human being and is the deputy of the Lord within us."[96]

"I Didn't Move the Events, the Events Moved Me"

The final chapter in the emir's life was spent in Damascus. His stay in Damascus coincided with the decline of the Ottoman caliphate and growing civil unrest between Muslim citizens and Western Christian residents. In 1860, riots between Druze and Christians broke out in Lebanon and spilled over to Damascus. 'Abd al-Qâdir sheltered Christians. The act of saving their lives made international news headlines and brought broad international recognition to the emir.

> "Christians, come with me! I am 'Abd al-Qâdir, son of Muhyî al-dîn, the Algerian. Trust me, I will protect you." For many hours, the emir's Algerian companions escorted the hesitant Christians to 'Abd al-Qâdir's fortress and residence. His house's two floors and courtyard sheltered thousands of victims desperate for the sudden and irrational wave of persecution and retaliation against Christians by Syrian Muslims.[97]

The echo of this feat crossed the ocean and was reported in the *New York Times* newspaper:

> Twenty years ago, the Arab emir was an enemy of Christendom, hunted through the ranges of his native hills . . . . Today, the Christian world unites to honor the dethroned Prince of Islam, the most unselfish of knightly warriors, risking limb and life to rescue his ancient foes, his conquerors and the conquerors of his race and religion, from the outrage and from death. For 'Abd al-Qâdir this is indeed a chapter of glory, and of the truest glory. It is no light thing to record that the most uncompromising soldier of Muhammadan independence became the most intrepid guardian of Christian lives and Christian honor in the days of political downfall and in the decline of his people.[98]

Allâh is Greater. Witnessing the Truth of Islam

But why did Emir 'Abd al-Qâdir behave as he did? Some wondered in amazement why the emeritus leader of the Algerian resistance had not used this opportunity to take revenge for the suffering that France had caused his people and his land. Others thought he had become more French than Arab. The very words of Emir ʿAbd al-Qâdir help us to recognize the character of his personality and the motive of his action: "I was doing my duty in saving the lives of innocents, it was my sacred duty. I was only an instrument; the praise belongs to Allâh who guided me."[99]

Later, in a letter sent to Bishop Louis-Antoine Pavy, the emir wrote:

> That which we did for the Christians, we did to be faithful to Islamic law and out of respect for human rights. All creatures are part of God's family and those most loved by God are those who do the most good for his family. All the religions of the book rest on two principles—to praise God and to have compassion for his creatures . . . the law of Mohammed places the greatest importance on compassion and mercy, and on all that which preserves social cohesion and protects us from division. But those who belong to the religion of Mohammed have corrupted it, which is why they are now like lost sheep. Thank you for your prayes and good will toward me.[100]

In another account for why he acted as he did, directed to a fellow Muslim freedom fighter, the emir wrote:

> Vice is condemned in all the religions, for to be led by vice is to swallow a poison that contaminates your body . . . . When we think about how rare are the real champions of truth, and when one sees ignorant people who imagine that Islamism is about severity, hardness, excess and barbarism,—it is time to repeat these words: patience is godliness, trust in God.[101]

Islam was the only compass for Emir ʿAbd al-Qâdir—not a sectarian interpretation of Islam, but a universal Islam, the Islam of the primordial nature present in all things visible and invisible that are subject to the order of Allâh. The emir's faith reposed in a great Allâh, greater than all human frailty and greater than any religion of this world, including Islam: "Every believer worships Him and knows Him in some ways and ignores Him in other ways." We are therefore all in error when we equate the oneness of Allâh with the diversity of creatures or the specificity of our modes of worship.

In this last teaching of self-criticism of Emir ʿAbd al-Qadir on the decadence of Muslims in the authentic interpretation of Islamic identity in the Arab world, we find an important reminder for the orientation also of interreligious relations in contemporary society. The forgetfulness of metaphysics and of the universal dimension in religion risks replacing confessional belonging with an assertion of nationalistic power, as in the case of the French, the Turks, or the Syrians, identifying religious and cultural differences as an enemy to be fought or conquered.

The Teacher of Patience

In a previous quote, the emir states, "Patience is godliness," a lesson that goes back to the catechism he received. One of the heroic aspects of Emir 'Abd al-Qadir is his patience in trying to develop a dialogue on the values and virtues of life. This dialogue was carried out in line with the education he received as a believer and as an intellectual, based on the common roots of every civilization and the particulars of his religious community. His heroic patience manifests itself in the different chapters of his life. It was required during his exile in France, in the boring salons where the Western middle class could enjoy his company in the same way they enjoyed their Persian carpets. It was previously required in Algeria, as well as later in Damascus, as he faced narrow-minded Muslims, who prefered to react with violence to injustice, rather than trying to practice justice against injustice as Emir 'Abd al-Qadir did.

The Emir as an Interreligious Hero

The interreligious wisdom of Emir 'Abd al-Qadir teaches us to react in different ways to injustice, ignorance, or barbarism. Diplomatic mediation and intellectual testimony ought be the natural articulation of a witness and representative of a religious wisdom, while the sacred principle of defending the life of a people, whether Algerian Muslim or Western Christian, can never be the object of ideological compromises or vulgar cultural corruptions. One always searches, interprets, and defends the truth without ever absolutizing one's own belonging in an exclusive way but cultivating a dialogue for knowledge and the common good.

I wish to offer this meditation on a hero of interreligious dialogue to a close friend who is like a brother to me, who lives with his wife Sharon in the blessed city of Jerusalem: Rabbi David Rosen. His love for the intelligence of justice, truth, and peace is accompanied by the eloquence of the testimony of the Torah in its universal teachings and in the interpretation that Rabbi Rosen generously offers among the communities, peoples, and regions of the world.

Together with the inspiration of love and the gift of the word, Rabbi Rosen integrates and offers a practical orientation of guidelines for the tangible impact of Jewish doctrine in the specific fields of intellectual, social, and political challenges, updating the reading of ethics, not as formal moralism but as a method of religious application and coherence.

Academic and Philosophical
Foundations

Claude Montefiore

Dr. Edward Kessler

Introduction

Claude Goldsmid Montefiore (or CGM, as he was sometimes called) devoted his life to academia, philanthropy, and the formation of Liberal Judaism in Britain. However, it is his pioneering contribution to the study of Judaism, Christianity, and Jewish-Christian relations and, to a lesser extent, to dialogue between Jews and Christians that secures his place as an interfaith hero.

CGM was born into Anglo-Jewish aristocracy. His youth witnessed the height of the British Empire, when Gladstone and Disraeli took turns at being prime minister. Born in 1858, the year in which Lionel de Rothschild became the first Jew to take his seat in the House of Commons, his father was a nephew of Sir Moses Montefiore and his mother was daughter of Isaac Goldsmid, one of the founders of the non-sectarian University College, London, and of the West London Reform Synagogue.

Montefiore's early years indicate how he was able to obtain an understanding of both Judaism and Christianity. At Oxford University, he was trained by liberal Christians such as Benjamin Jowett (Anglican theologian, scholar, and master of Balliol College) and was able to quote the classical poets and dramatists freely. Jowett was to be a lasting influence. He encouraged Montefiore to devote himself to Judaism and wrote, "I cannot advise you for or against the ministry, but I would certainly advise you to lead an ideal life, by which I mean a life not passed in the ordinary pleasures and pursuits of mankind; but in something higher, the study of your own people and their literature, and the means of elevating them. No life will make you as happy as that."[102]

After CGM secured a first class degree, he traveled to the Hochschule in Berlin, with the intention of becoming a rabbi. There he was assigned to and was deeply impressed by a young tutor called Solomon Schechter, already an outstanding biblical and rabbinic scholar. Schechter formed a contrast to his student—a native of Romania, from a Chassidic family, who received a traditional yeshivah education in Lemberg (Lwow) in Galicia. Montefiore helped bring Schechter to Britain, where he taught at Cambridge University and was involved in the discovery of the Cairo Geniza. By the time Schechter had emigrated to the US to become president of the fledgling Jewish Theological Seminary, Montefiore had become a scholar of rabbinic as well as biblical Hebrew. He made clear his debt to Schechter in private correspondence, as well as in public lectures and writings.[103]

Montefiore's output was prolific, and his works cover many aspects of Jewish life, including biblical studies, rabbinics, Hellenistic and Modern Judaism. He also examined significant aspects of Christian teaching, including the New Testament and theology. His writings, both published and unpublished, could have been produced only by someone steeped in the Jewish tradition, with a profound knowledge of Christianity.[104]

His familiarity with Christianity was based not only on academic research and publications but also on personal encounters and engaging in dialogue with leading Christian figures. For example, he befriended the Catholic theologian Friedrich von Hügel, and together they founded the London Society for the Study of Religion in 1904. The society provided a fertile ground for early modern Christian-Jewish dialogue, as it brought together thoughtful men (there were no female members at that time) who remained faithful to their own traditions, while having more in common with one another than with most members of their own denominations.[105]

Montefiore also co-founded the *Jewish Quarterly Review* in 1889 with Israel Abrahams (the *JQR* remains the oldest English-language journal of Jewish studies) and was the first Jewish scholar to deliver the Hibbert Lectures in 1892. These attracted enormous attention, because Montefiore courageously accepted many of the results of modern critical scholarship, paid tribute to the teachings of Jesus, and vigorously defended Judaism from Christian criticism.

In the Jewish community, the benefit of Montefiore's robust response to Christian criticism overshadowed the sentiment of alarm that his opposition to the Mosaic authorship of the Pentateuch, as well as commendation of the Gospels, might have aroused. He argued that the essence of the Bible is most truly shown at its best and not at its worst; its true tendency is found not in Esther but in Jonah. According to Montefiore, the Bible was divine "because of its religious excellence, because of its righteousness and truth, because of its effects for righteousness and truth."[106] In other words, the Bible's value did not depend upon its divinity, its divinity depended upon its value and excellence.

Christianity

Throughout his life, Montefiore reflected on the role of Christianity and, in particular, the significance of Jesus and the New Testament. He called on Jews to abandon the traditionally negative attitude towards Christianity and criticized Jewish scholars who tended to denigrate gospel teaching through a lack of impartiality. He emphasized the importance of balance and sought to achieve it, when reflecting on Christianity.

Previously, it was the norm for Jews to look for defects in Christian works or for parallels in rabbinic writings. "What was true could not be new, and what was new could not be true" summarized many Jewish approaches towards Christianity, demonstrated by the writings of Abraham Geiger and Gerald Friedlander. Montefiore took a more balanced approach. As far as Christians were concerned, he did not have to assume that Jesus was always right; with Jews, he did not feel obligated to always defend the rabbis. As a result, Christian scholars attacked him for being too Jewish and Jewish scholars for being too Christian.

The appropriate moment had arrived, Montefiore proposed, for a Jewish reappraisal of Christianity and a Christian reappraisal of Judaism. It was time for the two to stop judging each other by their defects. Since Montefiore had an understanding of Judaism and Christianity, he believed he was well placed to undertake this task.

Indeed, like a small number of Jewish scholars interested in Christianity before the subject came into vogue, he suggested, with Victorian optimism, that Judaism was on the threshold of a new age that would mark a turning point in Jewish attitudes towards Christianity. Tragically, his optimism was misplaced. Decades would pass, and six million Jews would perish, before such a turning point would be reached, illustrated by the Jewish statements *Dabru Emet* (2000) and *To Do the Will of Our Father in Heaven* (2015).[107]

In many ways, CGM was ahead of the times, illustrated by a desire to introduce the New Testament to Jews, which, he argued, was part of Jewish literature and in which were no Christian elements but which was an entirely Jewish book. He was in favor of Jews studying the whole work, including its anti-Jewish polemic. This, he suggested, should be understood in its historical context, since the early church suffered persecution from many quarters, including the synagogue. Consequently, New Testament authors showed little neutrality when writing about Jews.

Montefiore admired enormously the figure of Jesus, whose teaching was "a revival of prophetic Judaism" and in some respects pointed forward to Liberal Judaism.[108] Jesus emphasized inward goodness at the expense of outward forms, adopting a prophetic attitude towards the Torah. Jesus,

CGM argued, should be viewed as a great and wise teacher, but in no sense God. Referring to Maimonides, he explained that the significance of Jesus lay in the fact that "he started the movement which broke down the old barriers and brought about the translation of Judaism into the Gentile world— the translation of Judaism with many modifications, curtailments, additions both for the better and worse, good and evil."[109]

Just over seventy-five years before *Dabru Emet* was published, Montefiore's writings on Christianity reached their climax in a call for implementing a reassessment of relations with Christianity, both theological and historical. In *The Old Testament and After* (1923), he argued there was a need to look at Christian ideas; were there Jewish equivalents? By too wholesale a rejection of all Christian concepts, Montefiore felt that Judaism may have discarded what was true as well as what was false, resulting in a narrowing of its own outlook. A study of Christianity could lead to the rediscovery of Jewish truths and so to a greater understanding of Judaism.

As well as attacking Jewish ignorance of Christianity, Montefiore responded vigorously to Christian misconceptions of Judaism. His demolition of the anti-Jewish stereotype that the violent and jealous God of the Old Testament could be contrasted with the loving and merciful God of the New is worth quoting in full. In the following passage, Montefiore comments on Matt 25:41 ("Then shall he also say unto them on the left hand, Depart from me, ye accursed, into the everlasting fire"):

> Such passages as Matt 25:41 should make theologians excessively careful of drawing beloved contrasts between the Old Testament and the New. We find even a liberal theologian Dr. Fosdick saying: "From Sinai to Calvary—was ever a record of progressive revelation more plain or more convincing? The development begins with Jehovah disclosed in a thunderstorm on a desert mountain, and it ends with Christ saying: 'God is Spirit: and they that worship Him must worship Him in spirit and truth'; it begins with a war-god leading his partisans to victory, and it ends with men saying, 'God is love; and he that abideth in love abideth in God, and God abideth in him'; it begins with a provincial deity loving his tribe and hating its enemies, and it ends with the God of the whole earth worshipped 'by a great multitude, which no man could number, out of every nation, and of all the tribes and peoples and tongues'; it begins with a God who commands the slaying of the Amalekites, 'both man and woman, infant and suckling,' and it ends with a Father whose will it is that not 'one of these little ones should perish'; it begins with God's people standing afar off from his lightenings and praying that he might not speak to them lest they die and it ends with men going into their inner chambers, and, having

shut the door, praying to their father who is in secret" (*Christianity and Progress*, 1922, p. 209). Very good. No doubt such a series can be arranged. Let me now arrange a similar series. "From the Old Testament to the New Testament—was there ever a record of retrogression more plain or more convincing? It begins with, 'Have I any pleasure at all in the death of him that dieth?'; it ends with 'Begone from me, ye doers of wickedness.' It begins with, 'The Lord is slow to anger and plenteous in mercy'; it ends with, 'Fear Him who is able to destroy both body and soul in Gehenna.' It begins with, 'I will dwell with him that is of a contrite spirit to revive him'; it ends with, 'Narrow is the way which leads to life, and few there be who find it.' It begins with, 'I will not contend for ever; I will not always be wrath;' it ends with, 'Depart, ye cursed, into the everlasting fire.' It begins with, 'Should I not have pity on Nineveh, that great city?'; it ends with, 'It will be more endurable for Sodom on the day of Judgement than for that town.' It begins with,' The Lord is good to all who call upon Him'; it ends with, 'Whoever speaks against the Holy Spirit, there is no forgiveness whether in this world or the next.' It begins with, 'The Lord will wipe away tears from off all faces; he will destroy death forever'; it ends with, 'They will throw them into the furnace of fire; there is the weeping and the gnashing of teeth.'" And the one series would be as misleading as the other.[110]

Rabbinic Judaism

Naturally, the study of the New Testament led Montefiore to investigate parallel developments in Judaism, but Christian criticism, especially from German Protestant scholars, also stimulated Montefiore's interest. Many showed a disdain for "late Judaism," while German scholarship and anti-rabbinism went hand in hand with anti-Semitism. It was therefore not surprising that Montefiore should write that "my German masters . . . led me to defend the Rabbis."

Scholars such as Wilhelm Bousset argued that rabbinic Judaism viewed God as remote, while Christianity emphasised God's nearness. As a result, it was argued, by the time of Jesus, Judaism had become barren. Jesus filled this void, bringing the transcendent and unique God to become the indwelling and immanent God.[111] CGM, following in the footsteps of Schechter, was acutely aware of the need to respond to contemporary Christian anti-Jewish polemic.

In his response to Christian contemporaries, he made clear that by the end of the biblical period God had not become remote and "purified away." Indeed, the rabbis had expanded the concept of Torah, which Montefiore compared to the role of Jesus. The "Law supplied the motive force, the passion, the love, which the death of Christ and the risen Christ supplied to Paul."[112]

His approach paralleled that of Franz Rosenzweig, who wrote that "we are Christian in everything. We live in a Christian state, attend Christian schools, read Christian books, in short our whole 'culture' rests entirely on Christian foundations."[113] Montefiore was similarly influenced, and his language is in many ways Christian, particularly when his writings are directed towards a Christian audience.

Reaching a Christian readership was one reason he collaborated with Orthodox Jewish scholar Herbert Loewe, producing A Rabbinic Anthology (1938), in which they offered separate introductions and regularly disagreed with each other's interpretations. The book remains not only an excellent example of an Orthodox and Liberal Jew working together but a fine introduction into rabbinic literature for Jews and Christians alike.

Montefiore accepted that rabbinic Judaism was legalistic and that rabbinic legalism was greater than the legalism of the Bible. He accepted that there existed dangers to legalism but was critical of the dangers of legalism, not of legalism itself. He argued that, for the most part, these dangers were avoided. This was because the rabbis successfully developed a number of biblical teachings that offset such dangers and made the service of God into a passion. Rabbinics scholar Louis Jacobs commended Montefiore for teaching Christians that the Torah did not become a burden but a joy. He also criticized CGM's attitude towards the rabbis as condescending.[114]

In Rabbinic Literature and Gospel Teaching (1930), Montefiore explained why Christian theologians were unable to appreciate the rabbis' love of the Torah. "To them [the rabbis] the Law was a delight and no burden and in practice and life all this talk of 'endless' injunctions and minutiae is largely a figment of Christian theologians. They only knew and know the Law from outside. How it really affected and affects life they knew and know not."[115]

Although Montefiore was willing to express criticism of the rabbinic writings, criticism was tempered by comparison with the development of a Christian tradition. For example, he criticized rabbinic writings on circumcision, which drew out some biblical crudities, stating that "reflected or justified imperfections are worse than naïve and spontaneous ones." He went on, however, to compare this to the concept of hell in the Gospels, which was "bad enough," but what was said about hell "by St Augustine is far worse."[116]

The conflict between Jesus and the rabbis was tragic but inevitable. Both sides were right, but CGM's sympathies appear to lie with Jesus. Although the rabbis were logically right, the teachings and actions of Jesus were on a higher order. For the rabbis, the ceremonial and moral were equal. For Jesus, the moral came first. Montefiore compared the position of the Torah to that of Jesus: both supplied the motive for love and passion; both became mediators between God and the people and the means of bringing God close to the people. In effect, the Torah was the means of maintaining Israel's closeness with God. Partly as a result of his position of interpreter of Jews and Judaism to Christians, he often explained rabbinic concepts in quasi-Christian terminology.

Conclusion

Montefiore was influenced by both Jewish and Christian thought, which led him to perform an important role in Jewish-Christian relations and in the Jewish study of Christianity. Israel Zangwill once described Montefiore as a "queer mixture, half-Jew, half-Christian,"[117] and it is this queer mixture that allowed the controversial Jewish scholar to gain the respect, if not the approval, of both Jews and Christians.

His positive attitude towards Christianity will not shock us as it did his contemporaries, but a careful reader will notice his courage in tackling anti-Jewish stereotypes during a period of intense Christian criticism. His optimism may have been misplaced in pre-Holocaust Europe; but we would do well to rediscover Montefiore, particularly his writings on the relationship between Jews and Christians, both in New Testament times and in the present day.

Montefiore was an Anglo-Jewish leader and scholar. What makes him an interfaith hero and relevant to a volume in honor of David Rosen is that he was also a pioneer in the study of Judaism, Christianity, and Jewish–Christian relations. The rise of virulent anti-Semitism in Europe in the first half of the twentieth century prevented the inauguration of a new era in Jewish-Christian relations; but CGM's contribution, both in terms of his life and work, contributed towards a more positive relationship, which developed in the second half of the century. David has built on the legacy of many interfaith heroes, among whom CGM should be counted.

Claude Goldsmid Montefiore possessed some of the same characteristics as David: both were passionate about and became representatives for Jews and Judaism; both were concerned with fostering good relations with and a proper understanding of Christianity; and, last but not least, both were Englishmen.

Martin Buber[118]

WALTER CARDINAL KASPER

MARTIN BUBER (1878–1955) WAS and is for me one of the most important, most interesting, most profound, and, at the same time, most challenging interlocutors in the Jewish-Christian dialogue. He is so, even though Buber cannot be aligned with any of the official directions of Judaism and is therefore controversial within Judaism.[119] Nevertheless, no Christian theologian in the Jewish-Christian dialogue can avoid Buber as one of the most important Jewish philosophers and theologians of the twentieth century.[120] After the horrific crime of the Shoah, with the Second Vatican Council declaration *Nostra aetate* (1965), dialogue has hopefully finally replaced the centuries-old anti-Judaism of the Christian churches. The very use of the word dialogue, which has become common, points to the overriding influence of the philosophy of dialogue of Martin Buber and Franz Rosenzweig.

Between the two World Wars, the world in which Buber wrote was not the global world we experience today. Nevertheless, Buber's dialogical philosophy can help us in our current situation, where interfaith dialogue is fundamental for peace in the global world. Buber's dialogical philosophy was adapted by philosophers like Jürgen Habermas and others. He also had a deep impact on many Jewish thinkers or thinkers with a certain Jewish background, who did not fit in neatly into Jewish categories but became very important in European philosophy after the Second World War and after the catastrophe of the Shoah. Thanks to Buber, there is a paradoxical revival of a certain kind of Judaism beyond Judaism in philosophy as well in theology, especially in biblical exegesis.

Martin Buber first became known through a collection of Hasidic stories and their exploration, through which he made Eastern Jewish spirituality accessible to Western Jews as well as Christians.[121] Then his impressive translation and interpretation of the Hebrew Bible, which the Jews call the Tanakh and the Christians the Old Testament, became renowned.[122] Through both, Martin Buber made the soul of Judaism—its mystical tradition, its messianic trait, its worldly piety, and its inner-worldly ethos—newly accessible to broad Christian circles.

Martin Buber found broad resonance above all in his unsurpassed translation of the Bible, through the power of the language with which he translates the biblical prophets. With great skill, he accomplished what at first sight seemed a foolhardy attempt to let the original expressiveness and force of the Hebrew language shine through convincingly in the modern German linguistic form, which is so different from it, and thus confront the reader directly with the biblical word. Buber's language creates immediate encounter. Thus, it was Buber's hermeneutic masterstroke to make God's claim, as expressed in the Bible, into a present reality in a modern Western language—at least, in the literary language of the first half of the twentieth century.[123]

Buber lived and wrote in the time before *Nostra aetate*, when there was no dialogue between Jews and Christians. Nevertheless, in the philosophy of dialogue of I and Thou (1923),[124] which was developed by Buber together with Franz Rosenzweig and others and which continues to have an effect today, especially through Emmanuel Lévinas, Buber laid the foundations for interreligious dialogue that goes beyond the Jewish-Christian dialogue and that today more than ever is fundamental for peace in the world. Just as the I can be realized only in the other and in the acceptance of the You, so it is necessary to understand the other religion in its otherness and to respect it in its otherness. Only in this way is it possible to be enriched by each other in respectful dialogue, without giving up one's own identity. Only in this way can there be a peaceful coexistence of religions beyond an exclusive fundamentalism that excludes the other and an egalitarian relativism that unifies the other.

With this, Martin Buber laid the foundation for correctly understood tolerance and for peace between religions. Tolerance does not mean indifference. The indifferent take neither the other religion nor their own religion and its unconditional claim seriously. Tolerance also does not mean syncretism, like one who chooses elements of the other religion according to his taste and mixes them with his own religion in order to build a unified religion that pleases him. Those who think that all religions are basically the same and ultimately interchangeable have not recognized the seriousness and the unconditional claim of religion and have thus missed the topic of interreligious dialogue from the outset. They have also missed the opportunity to understand their own religion better and more deeply in confrontation with the other religion.

With this conception, Martin Buber has become an uncomfortable and, precisely because of the discomfort, a helpful and further-leading interlocutor for the Jewish-Christian dialogue in the correctly understood sense. Hardly anyone has conducted the Jewish-Christian dialogue more thoroughly, passionately, profoundly, and, at the same time, mercilessly as he. Buber has emphasized the fascination of Jewish identity and at the same time its diversity from Christian identity, thus clearly marking the border to Christian self-understanding.

Martin Buber says of himself that from his youth he felt Jesus to be his great Jewish brother.[125] Thus, in contrast to Talmudic Judaism, Buber brought Jesus home to Judaism. In this, many other Jewish thinkers followed him in the twentieth century.[126] Christian theologians, conversely, against Harnack's liberal theology, rediscovered Jesus as a Jew and brought him to the fore. Jesus was born of a Jewish woman, Mary of Nazareth, and circumcised on the eighth day; thus, Jesus is the bond that connects Christians to Abraham and to Judaism. That is why, until the liturgical reform of 1970, the Catholic Church celebrated the circumcision of Jesus on the eighth day after Christmas, the feast of Jesus's birth, as a liturgically observed feast.[127] The rediscovery of the Jewish roots of Christianity made the Council declaration *Nostra aetate* possible and fundamentally changed the Christian interpretation of the New Testament in the second half of the twentieth century.[128]

The bringing home of Jesus to Judaism, as well as the rediscovery of Jesus as a Jew, means from both sides the rediscovery of the common basis which connects Jews and Christians. Christians who understand themselves rightly can therefore never be anti-Judaists and anti-Semites, because of their own faith.

But immediately in the sentence following the quoted sentence, Buber clearly distinguished himself from the Christian understanding of Jesus as the Christ, the Messiah, the Redeemer, the Son of God. Shalom Ben-Chorin put this dialectical definition of the relationship in the well-known, often repeated formula: "The faith in Jesus unites us, the faith in Jesus Christ separates us."[129]

According to Buber, Judaism and Christianity are characterized by two different ways of faith. On the one hand, he recognized the Abraham-oriented faith as *emuna*, as holistic, unconditional personal trust in God, a faith that always makes new departures and experiences God as the unavailable. Unlike some post-Auschwitz theologians, Buber held fast to this faith, even in the face of the Shoah. On the other hand, Buber understood the Christian way of faith as *pistis*, not as faith *in* but as faith *that*, i.e., recognizing as faith the truth that Jesus is the Messiah, the Redeemer, the Son of God. Buber saw this understanding of faith in Paul, who came from Tarsus in Asia Minor, grounded in the Hellenistic Jewish diaspora. According to Buber, it signifies an "exit from history"; *pistis* neglects the historical and earthly context of faith and transcends this world to another reality.

Christian theology cannot accept this comparison. It is true that Judaism focuses more on the doing and the realization of faith, whereas Christianity emphasizes the confession of faith. But also for the Christian, it is true that he cannot confess the truth only with his mouth—that he must rather do the truth in order to come to light (John 3:21). Abraham is our common father in faith, and it is true of Jesus Christ, as Paul says, that he redeemed us in hope (Rom 8:24). The Christian faith is therefore not a pure what and that faith, but also a faith of trust; it is not an escape into the hereafter, but in the following of Jesus in doing the will of God on the way through history. The Ten Words (Ten Commandments) (Ex 20:1, 17; Deut 5:6–22) are common to us in order to contribute to the healing of the world (Hebrew: *tikkun olam*) in faithful action.

Conversely, Judaism also knows the confession *Shema Israel*: "Hear, Israel. The LORD our God, the LORD is unique" (Deut 6:4–9). Especially today, Jews and Christians will have to say this confession together. We will have to hold it up together today in a time of the eclipse of God, as analyzed forcefully by Buber. The hypothesis of God's existence has become superfluous for many, and many proclaim the death of God in the wake of Friedrich Nietzsche.[130] The word God is, as Buber elsewhere puts it, "the most loaded of all human words. None has been so sullied and tattered." "We must respect those who frown upon it because they rebel against the injustice and mischief that so readily invoke God's empowerment; but we must not abandon it." "We cannot wash the word 'God' clean, but we can raise it from the ground, stained and tattered as it is, and raise it above an hour of great sorrow."[131]

As much as one will differentiate within Martin Buber's depiction of the "Two Types of Faiths," one must be grateful that Buber has ensured with his comparison that we do not make things too easy for ourselves in the Jewish-Christian dialogue, despite all the common ground. The burdens from the dramatic and tragic history between Jews and Christians cannot be so easily removed. Moreover, there are differences that run deep. The Jewish faith has its grounding in the people of Israel and in the bond to the land of Israel (*Eretz Israel*). Buber left no doubt about this, even in his more cultural Zionism, which aimed at a balance with the Arabs.

The Christian church, on the other hand, is a church of Jews and gentiles; it is Christian freedom, and thus the identity of Christianity, to be freed from Mosaic law. Precisely because of this, Christianity was able to universalize the central message of Israel, the faith in the one God, as well as the commandments of the second table of the Decalogue, and to carry them out into the world. The connection back to Israel reminds us, of course, of the historical roots from which Jesus comes, and it saves the Christian faith from being lifted up into world-less and history-less gnosis. Conversely, Christian universalization reminds Israel of the promise made to Abraham, "Through you all the peoples of the earth shall receive blessing" (Gen 12:3), and of Israel's mission to be light for the Gentiles (Isa 42:6; 49:6).[132]

It is precisely when Jews and Christians take each other seriously in their otherness that they understand each other better. They depend on each other for their own sake. This mutual bond has persisted in a paradoxical way even in the darkest times of the relationship between Jews and Christians. Already in the second century, early Christianity made the decision against Marcion to hold on to the Hebrew Bible as the normative basic text. What would European culture be without the Bible as the book of books? What would the liturgy be without the Jewish elements and their influence on European culture? The Bible, like the liturgy, brought essentials of the Jewish heritage to Europe and reminded Europe of its eccentric identity. Today, after the Nazi madness, Europe must be aware that, without its roots in Israel, it would not be Europe as we know it. Like many other Jewish thinkers, scientists, and artists, Martin Buber made a significant contribution to European culture and philosophy, just as he, in turn, was rooted in the European educational tradition and philosophy.[133]

This path that Buber trod must be continued. It has an eschatological dimension. We will not be able to complete it within history. Unfortunately, Martin Buber understood eschatology as "history happening here and now" and pushed aside the apocalyptic dimension of early Judaism.[134] Thus he did not consider the eschatological future dimension of the Jewish-Christian relationship. It is found in chapters 9 to 11 of Paul's letter to the Romans, to which Buber unfortunately does not refer, but which have become fundamental in the conversation between Jews and Christians today.

In these chapters, Paul says that Christians are planted in the rootstock of Israel and that this root carries them. He goes on to say that Christians will find their eschatological fulfillment only together with Israel (Rom 11:13–32). It is hardly possible to express more clearly Jews' and Christians' mutual historical reference to one another. The eschatological character of their path excludes—as Bernard of Clairvaux already knew during the First Crusade—missionizing or eradicating the Jews.[135] "For irrevocable are the grace and calling which God has granted" (Rom 11:27). This is the title of the statement issued by the Vatican commission responsible for Jewish-Christian dialogue on the occasion of fifty years of *Nostra aetate*. Different and yet together, shoulder to shoulder, Jews and Christians are to go their way through history before God until the end of time.

In David Rosen, I met a Jewish interlocutor for whom the mutual recognition of the otherness of Jews and Christians was a prerequisite for a successful respectful dialogue and for a fruitful ten-year collaboration. The friendly cooperation has proven its worth in some difficult phases of the dialogue. We have acknowledged our differences in faith, but on the basis of a great common ground, we have tried together to do what Jews and Christians can already do together for the healing of a deeply wounded world. It is with gratitude that I dedicate these lines to David Rosen and offer my heartfelt congratulations. Shalom!

Bishops Nathan Söderblom
and Krister Stendahl

Bishop Lennart Koskinen

Krister Stendahl, following in the footsteps of Nathan Söderblom, was an internationally renowned Swedish theologian. He was born in 1921 in Sweden and passed away after his retirement, in 2008 in Boston, Massachusetts, in the United States.

Stendahl served as professor of New Testament studies and as dean at Harvard Divinity School. He also was the second director of the Center for Religious Pluralism at the Shalom Hartman Institute in Jerusalem.

Stendahl was appointed bishop in the diocese of Stockholm, Church of Sweden, in 1984.

MY FIRST MEETING WITH Krister Stendahl took place at the major ecumenical meeting organized by the World Council of Churches in Uppsala in 1968. I was a student of theology and philosophy in Uppsala and volunteered to co-host the meeting.

The Uppsala Cathedral was and is the biggest church in Sweden and the seat of the Swedish archbishop. Stendahl was already a famous theologian and was the one who had invited Dr. Martin Luther King Jr. to the meeting as one of the keynote speakers. Sadly, Dr. King had been murdered only a few months earlier, but Stendahl had learned some of what he had intended to say and also knew the lines of his famous "I had a dream" speech.

So Stendahl made his own version of this dream. This was very typical of him, rarely quoting anything word for word.

He stood behind the newly installed Tree of Reconciliation, a beautiful globe with two sets of crosses where candles could be lit, and presented his vision. Standing there beside the globe, he made a very powerful image. His dream incorporated different Christian interpretations of the gulf between the rich and poor and differences between nations. He has been quoted many times, but I will never forget the five candles he lit, one by one.

His first candle represented Athens and the common value of all humans and our democratic roots. He spoke about the Pnyx, established there in 507 B.C. so that any free man could climb it and speak freely. St. Paul, making his famous speech at the Areopagus (Acts 17:16–34) probably stood just there when he spoke about the unknown God: "The God that made the world and all things therein, seeing that he is Lord of heaven and earth, dwelleth not in temples made by hands. He has made of one blood all nations of men for to dwell on all the face of the world."

Much later, when Stendahl was bishop of Stockholm and I was serving as his assistant, he told me that those exact words of St. Paul, whom he had studied so much, opened for him a new understanding of the importance of interreligious dialogue, not only ecumenism between Christian churches.

The second candle represented Jerusalem, the holy city for the three Abrahamic religions. Its historic importance is self-evident, he said, but more important is its spiritual significance. It is a real historic place but also a living dream. "Next year in Jerusalem" was the living hope for Jews during more than two thousand years, and the city also served as a role model for pilgrimages to the spiritual center of the world for both Christians and Muslims. It continues to be a meeting place and inspirational site for both believers and seekers from many different religions and cultures.

Stendahl's third candle represented Rome, the symbol of Justitia, law and order, organization and perseverance, but also a remembrance of the darkness and the ever-present violence in ourselves which always has to be fought. Without the heritage from Rome, which has inspired a whole world, it is hard to imagine how our present world would look, for good and ill.

Those three sites are all well known. Stendahl gave them a partly new interpretation. But then he continued with two more.

His fourth candle represented the old Mesopotamian city Babylon, meaning "the gate of God." This gate opened up for him a deeper interest in many more Eastern traditions which too often are forgotten in the West. His interest started, he told us, when he studied the Babylonian exile of the Jewish people, mentioned in the Bible. The Jews worshipped one God only but were surrounded by polytheists. So they had to prove that their God was the strongest, as when Elijah met with the prophets of Baal in Mount Carmel (1Kgs 18).

In Babylon, they met with another old monotheistic religion, which claimed that there is only one creator of heaven and earth, whom they called Ahura Mazda. Rather than leaving their own religion and religious traditions, the Jews seem to have been strengthened in the Mosaic belief in one God during the period in Babylon. All the texts written after the exile also carry proof of that.

So Stendahl explained his choice of Babylon as the gate to the insight that there is only one universal God, whatever name he is given. For him, this belief had meant a growing respect for different religions and interpretations. Behind them all, of course, he said, there is only one God. This did not mean that all religions are equal, and he opposed such a relativistic view. But Babylon had for him been another gate to his interest in interreligious dialogue, with its base in the Jewish-Christian tradition. This his fourth candle really opened our eyes to also seek for holiness outside our own tradition and theology.

Stendahl's fifth candle represented Alexandria and the hunger for new knowledge. He lit the candle with utmost care, because, as he said, we must avoid any new devastating fires. The library of Alexandria was for hundreds of years the largest in the world, with up to a million books and scrolls. A part of it was destroyed by a big fire in 47 BC, when Caesar invaded the city, and the remains were finally eliminated at the end of the third century. But Alexandria was not famous for its library only; it was a center for knowledge, research, and inspiration, that gathered scholars from the whole known world.

The candle was a reminder of how important it is to honor such hubs of knowledge and the possibility of letting different cultures and traditions really meet and find ways forward together. Most universities today are national and predominantly reserved for students of their own countries, even if some exchange, of course, takes place. More Alexandrias are needed.

Those of us who were there will never forget this lesson, which also gave such a vivid picture of the person itself.

Fifteen years later, we met again, when he was elected bishop of Stockholm. Immediately I realized that his ambitions to be a bridge-builder had not vanished. Already at his inauguration in the Cathedral of Stockholm, he had invited not only representatives of different Christian churches but also the Jewish rabbi, whom he asked to read the Old Testament text in Hebrew—something that never had happened before. Also invited were senior representatives of other religions like Islam, Tibetan Buddhism, Sikhism, and Taoism, who were present and seated in the front rows of the old distinguished church. This was discussed and often criticized in the media for weeks, but Stendahl gave interviews and explained his intentions so well that public opinion, at least partly, changed in his favor.

But his bridge-builder ambitions did not stop there. He opened up his diocese and the hundreds of churches there for spiritual discussions and meetings with scientists, seekers, and non-believers, as well as local politicians and business leaders. Suddenly, the church began to occupy a place in the midst of society. No bishop before him had been so frequently invited to debates on television and radio.

Together we also started an Institute for Working Life, arranging seminars and discussions about ethics and the human well-being of employees, also something quite new for the traditionally conservative church.

Unfortunately, he reached retirement age much too soon, and many of his initiatives could not survive without him. But for us who had the great privilege to work with him and came to know him more closely, he will never be forgotten. His five candles and their challenge from the Uppsala Cathedral are still burning deep in my heart and have inspired me my whole life, as I know that he as a scholar, theologian, and person has influenced many, many others in the rest of the world.

An important Swedish role model for Stendahl was Nathan Söderblom (1866–1931). They never met in person, but during his growth and studies at Uppsala University, Söderblom was nothing less than a legend. His spirit was ever present in the narrow space between the Institution of Theology and the archbishop's residence in Uppsala. Söderblom really linked the two together and showed how scientific work can be combined with deep faith and the practical work of a pastor.

After his basic studies in theology and languages, he was ordained as a priest. He combined his practical priesthood as a pastor in a big hospital with continued academic studies. He has said that this was his best education in combining the practical with the theoretical, something he would continue to do all his life. In 1894, he moved to Paris and was appointed rector of the Swedish congregation there. As such, he was also linked to the Swedish embassy and learned the basics of diplomacy. He was very popular among the many Swedes in Paris, the city which was a playground for many Scandinavian artists and writers. There he also was introduced to Alfred Nobel, who at the time had aspirations to be an author. Nobel later explained how much these meetings meant to him, and the first seeds for the idea of a peace prize were sown here. Söderblom himself was awarded the Nobel Peace Prize in 1930. But true to his ideal to combine practical work with theoretical studies, he also managed to finish an extraordinary doctoral thesis at the Sorbonne in 1901.

Already the next year, he was appointed professor of history and philosophy of religions at Uppsala University and returned home. Once there, he combined his research with the practical task of serving as a priest in a nearby parish. His working capacity must have been immense. His academic output resulted in an invitation to combine his chair in Uppsala with another professorship in Leipzig in 1908.

Traveling between the two cities was very time consuming in that era, but he spent the time on the train writing articles, books, and letters and preparing new lessons for his students. He said that these long times on the train were the most peaceful and productive oases in his normally so busy life. His authorship was famous, and he was elected to a chair in the Swedish Academy in 1921. He was also appointed by the king to the Royal Swedish Academy of Science.

In 1914, Söderblom was elected archbishop of the Church of Sweden and could move into the big residence opposite the theology faculty. Until he moved in, the imposing building mainly had been the private home for archbishops, but now the doors were often opened for groups of students, representatives of both church and society, and scholars from the whole world. His wife Anna was an excellent and very popular hostess at these meetings, and he often reflected that, without her, his life would have been impossible.

Even if Sweden did not take an active part in the First World War and was formally neutral, it came to be a safe hiding place for many refugees of different religions and traditions. Meeting the asylum seekers woke up Söderblom's deep interest in ecumenism and interreligious dialogue. His most famous achievement came in 1925, when he arranged the first World Conference of Life and Work in Stockholm. It was an attempt not only to let church leaders from different traditions meet, but also to host a meeting of reconciliation between countries who had been fighting each other for so long. The Nobel Peace Prize he was awarded in 1930 was based on the results of that meeting.

Söderblom died in 1931 and is buried with his wife Anna beside the high altar in the Cathedral of Uppsala. When Stendahl came to the meeting of the World Council of Churches in 1968, the first thing he did was to pay a visit and light another candle at their grave.

Personal Reflections

We all need role models. These two persons have both been very important to me during the whole of my professional life, whether as a scholar, priest, or bishop.

Söderblom and Stendahl both shared the belief that there is and can only be one God, Creator of all humankind and all things. That paved the way for the concept of a common, holy, and unlimited human value, whoever you are and whatever faith you have. This has also been the foundation of my own thinking and practical aspirations.

Stendahl taught me how important it is to always ask the question beyond the question and the hidden assertion beyond a certain statement. This requires knowledge, and a lifelong quest for more knowledge has been for me a part of his heritage. Both of my heroes lived according to that principle. Curiosity and hard work is required, not least when it comes to the importance of understanding the other. A key role for both Söderblom and Stendahl was not only learning languages but understanding the historic and cultural setting of them. Söderblom lectured in Swedish, French, and German, spoke English fluently, and had studied Greek and biblical Hebrew. For Stendahl, English was his second language and he was also fluent in German. As a scholar, he had studied Greek and Hebrew thoroughly, of course, but also Aramaic and Latin, to go beyond the translations of texts he studied.

Both of them inspired me to study not only the biblical languages and Latin but also Sanskrit, as a help to understand some of the holy Vedic texts that are so important within both Hinduism and Buddhism. That gave me, when I was only a student, inspiration and a key for interreligious dialogue, not merely superficial discussions.

A basic rule for dialogue that both of my heroes revered was always to seek a positive interpretation of the other's views and faith, instead of letting your own prejudices and lack of understanding frame the meeting.

A third area where I have found inspiration—and, in the case of Stendahl, practical support—is in my efforts, whenever possible, to combine theory and practice. "There is nothing as practical as a good theory" is one of the lines of Stendahl that has followed me. In the footsteps of them both, I have all my adult life strived for combining practical work with research and seeking for more knowledge.

Much has happened within the interreligious movement since first Söderblom and then Stendahl died (in 2008.)

When it comes to Söderblom, dialogue was a key concept, but in the early twentieth century and in the shadow of the First World War, religious dialogue was in practice limited to the broad Christian families. His ambitions were realized as the field was opened up for broader dialogue between all religions. As a professor in the history of religions, he was of course well aware of similarities and differences and could see both possibilities and the need for a deeper dialogue. But he was in this, as in many other areas, born ahead of his time.

For me personally, I have also met with new heroes in the field of interreligious dialogue, education, and friendship. In 2004, I first participated in Seville in a meeting of world religious leaders arranged by the Elijah Institute. The topic was "From Hostility to Hospitality," and I was deeply impressed by Rabbi Alon Goshen-Gottstein and his both practical and scientific work, exactly as my early heroes had taught me. There, I also met with Rabbi David Rosen for the first time. He at once seemed to be an incarnation of the ideas and ideals I had learned from both Stendahl and Söderblom.

From that day, I have had the privilege to be a member of the big Elijah family and have continued to be nourished by the wisdom, warmth, and breadth of perspective that are characteristic of Rabbi Rosen.

Abraham Joshua Heschel[136]

Archbishop Pierbattista Pizzaballa

Passionate about God and Man

In this article, I intend to elaborate on some points where the person of Abraham Joshua Heschel has been a source of great inspiration for me. The fruits of his legacy continue to mature in this century even more than in the past: an authoritative rabbi, theologian, and philosopher with great originality, he was a hero of interreligious dialogue, having had, among other things, an active part in the preparatory work of the Second Vatican Council. His works have been read by entire generations of Christians, as well as Jews.

Born in Warsaw in 1907, Heschel was educated in the study of the Torah, Talmud, and Qabbalah in his family, which boasted great Hassidim.[137] After his university studies in Berlin (Semitic philology, history, and philosophy), where he graduated in 1933 with a thesis on prophecy, he ws chosen by Martin Buber as Buber's successor in teaching at two Jewish institutions in Frankfurt. Deported to Poland in 1938 by the Gestapo, a few weeks before the German invasion—"a lit firebrand pulled out of the fire"[138]—he emigrated to London and then to the United States (1940), where he briefly taught at Hebrew Union College in Cincinnati and then, until he died in 1972, at the Jewish Theological Seminary of America in New York.

The first thing that strikes me about this rabbi is the profound unity that he demonstrates in himself and that he tries to achieve for others: a complete man, in the biblical sense of undivided. Not only did he teach Jewish ethics and mysticism, but he also lived them, which is rare in our time characterized by the worrying separation between faith and life. This firmness in the perception of one's own identity, of one's place in the world, we consider as the secret of Heschel's capacity for dialogue. It relies on faith, understood, first and foremost, as a profound personal relationship with God even before participation in a religious tradition. The rabbi's influence was significant not only in the fields of academia and religion but also in politics and society, as shown by the fight against racial segregation—his famous march alongside Martin Luther King, the defense of Jews in the USSR, and opposition to the US war in Vietnam.

A prophetic man and, like a good Hassid, passionate about God, Heschel was also a fan of man. For the rabbi, the category that best fits the God of biblical revelation is pathos,[139] a conception far removed from the Aristotelian one of God, of an unmoved and impassive mover.[140] The relationship between God and his people is, for Heschel, existential: God, in his concern and his pathos, is in search of man. All-forbearing, he is disposed to spend himself entirely for man. That is directly reflected in anthropology, where the apathy of the stoic sage is contrasted with the sympathy of the prophet, since in the Bible, "the source of evil lies not in passion, in the heart that beats strongly, but rather in the hardness of the heart."[141] Divine passion is thus expressed in the election of the people, which, in turn, involves a partnership in that divine pathos: "There is a price to be paid by the Jew. He has to be exalted in order to be normal. In order to be a man, he has to be more than a man. To be a people, the Jews have to be more than a people."[142] Man must become an incarnate Torah: "The Torah has no glory if man remains apart. The goal is for man to be an incarnation of the Torah."[143] Heschel's reflections on the divine pathos greatly influenced Christian theologians, both Catholic and Protestant (e.g., Jürgen Moltmann and Karl Barth).

Paving the Way

Rabbi Alon Goshen-Gottstein calls Heschel "the first theorist of Judaism regarding interreligious relations" and a "trail blazer."[144] His influence, along with that of Jules Isaac (1877–1963), was decisive for the genesis and content of section 4 of the *Nostra aetate* declaration. Heschel had a deep friendship with Cardinal Bea, contact with Cardinal Willebrands, and a memorable meeting with St. Paul VI on September 14, 1964. The latter, during his audience (Jan. 31, 1973), shortly after the rabbi's death, encouraged the publication and dissemination in Italy of his works. He quoted him, stating: "Even before it is man in search of God, it was God who came looking for us." The fact that a pontiff quoted a rabbi was, at that time, extraordinary. St. John Paul II also cited Heschel on several occasions, in various hearings, and even in the apostolic letter *Dies Domini*.

Through his work and contacts, Heschel did not fail to protest the accusation of deicide and the forced conversions of Jews that caused so much pain to the Jewish people up to the immense Shoah tragedy. He strove to help Christians grasp the intrinsic value of Judaism, overcome ancient prejudices, and reject contempt for the Jewish people. Heschel, however, who within Judaism was accused of excessive orthodoxy by liberals and excessive liberalism by the orthodox, hoped that the Church would not abandon its tradition and identity.

Through his thought, Heschel sought to respond to the crisis of the Judaism of his time and the tragic failure of Western thought. Rightly referred to as a poet theologian,[145] capable of uniting the Bible and rabbinical tradition, Eastern European Hasidism and Western philosophy, he attempted to heal the rift between philosophy and faith, de-Hellenizing the exegesis of biblical revelation[146] and the concept of God and proposing a philosophy that arises from the Bible.

The categories in which biblical man conceived of God, man, and the world are so different from the presuppositions of metaphysics upon which most Western philosophy is based that the particular insights that are meaningful within the biblical mind seem to be meaningless to the Greek mind. It would be an achievement of the first magnitude to reconstruct the peculiar nature of biblical thinking and to spell out its divergence from all other types of thinking.[147]

Heschel therefore deplored—and rightly so—the "de-Judaization" of Christianity in history. Along his line, today it would be very desirable to take that step back that Paul Ricoeur accused Martin Heidegger of never having been able to take: to recognize the "radically Jewish" dimension of Christianity, without denying the Greek dimension, which, moreover, has critically influenced Judaism since before the Christian era.[148]

Building Bridges So as Not to Remain Islands

Heschel was confident that "no religion is an island," as he wrote in the eponymous, masterful article, and that humiliating the person amounts to humiliating God—indeed a *hillul ha-Shem*, a desecration of God himself. In this way, he intended to make his contribution to *tiqqun olam*, to the reparation of the world, and to help Christians to embark on a path of *teshuvah*, of return to the Jewish people and consequently to God.[149] Heschel "developed an inclusive thought in which Christianity and Judaism are inseparable parts."[150] The rabbi came to declare: "A Christian ought to realize that a world without Israel will be a world without the God of Israel. A Jew, on the other hand, ought to acknowledge the eminent role and part of Christianity in God's design for the redemption of all men."[151]

As Rabbi Goshen-Gottstein points out, Heschel, as a wise rabbi and true philosopher, taught us to ask ourselves questions; he taught us how important questions are and what are the right questions.[152] Also, as a Hassid and a mystic, he instructed us to "turn and return the Torah" (m. Avot 5:22) and, even more so, to scrutinize reality just as the Torah is scrutinized (*darash*). Among the many questions left to us, we consider the following particularly pertinent.

There is another worldwide ecumenical movement with extensive influence: nihilism. We must choose between interfaith and internihilism. Cynicism is not parochial. Should religions insist upon the illusion of complete isolation? Should we refuse to be on speaking terms with one another and hope for each other's failure? Or should we pray for each other's health and help one another in preserving our respective legacies, in preserving a common legacy?[153]

However—mind you—Heschel never preached an interfaith at the expense of faith. In other words, his call for dialogue never fell into relativism, syncretism, or vague pluralism. On the contrary, he asserted decisively: "The first and most important prerequisite for 'inter-faith' is faith."[154]

As for me, I would like to make Heschel's appeal my own. To remain isolated in our little world would be to put ourselves in the hands of the prevailing nihilism, as I expressed in my first homily as patriarch.

The continuous encounter with others, with those different from ourselves within our home, the church, should render us more capable of listening to others outside our home. The diverse character of the church in Jerusalem calls us to be a church that is increasingly extroverted, welcoming, open to others.

We are a numerically small church. That is a part of our identity, and there is no need for drama. Such a condition reminds us that we do not exist for ourselves but must enter into relationships with all whom we meet, and it encourages us to be proactive, especially with the people and faiths that are found in our land: Christians, Muslims, Jews, and Druze.

The Road Opened by Heschel and Traveled by Rabbi Rosen

Heschel, as an envoy of the American Jewish Committee (AJC), was received at an audience by Pope John XXIII and, during the Second Vatican Council, was often summoned by Cardinal Bea for consultations. On behalf of the AJC, the rabbi prepared several memos essential for the drafting of *Nostra aetate*. In a speech to the AJC, Pope Francis said:

Your organization has had close contact with the successors of
Peter since the beginning of the official dialogue between the
Catholic Church and Judaism. At the Second Vatican Council,
when a new direction in our relations took place, among the
Jewish observers was the distinguished Rabbi Abraham J. Hes-
chel of the American Jewish Committee. Your commitment to
Jewish-Catholic dialogue goes back to the declaration *Nostra
aetate*, a milestone in our journey of fraternal rediscovery.[155]

On the path opened by Heschel, this dialogue took great strides under
the leadership of Rabbi David Rosen. As Director of International Interreligious Affairs for the AJC itself, as president of the International Jewish
Committee for Interreligious Consultations (IJCIC), and as a member of
the Permanent Bilateral Commission of the State of Israel and the Holy See,
Rabbi Rosen has worked until today in the field of interreligious relations
and especially in Jewish-Catholic relations—so much so that he became the
first Israeli and the first Orthodox rabbi to be awarded the Pontifical Knight's
Honor of the Order of St. Gregory. With outstanding balance and at the same
time with admirable courage, he has made an extraordinary contribution to
the long journey of Jewish-Catholic reconciliation, which today has achieved
previously impossible goals. Among these should be counted a beautiful and
recent statement addressed to the church by the Jewish side, promoted by
Rosen.[156] As Rosen says, the political and social process of reconciliation in
the Holy Land necessarily passes through our faith:

May I, therefore, conclude with the hope that your prayers will
be with this initiative as well as for the various interfaith activities on different levels that take place in the Middle East. All
these levels have their significance and importance; that which
takes place purely at the level of officialdom and establishments
is not good enough if it is not supported by grass-roots work.
But it sends a critical message: it serves as testimony; it presents
the vision in which religion is not seen as just part of the problem but seen to be part of the solution—may it become such.[157]

Peace is a path to be achieved with a strong faith and at the same time
openness to the other, as modeled by Heschel and Rosen. In my opinion, I
can only rejoice at living in an age when a patriarch of Jerusalem and a rabbi
of international stature, such as Rosen, of the Chief Rabbinate of Israel, can
be friends and brothers.

Transforming the Catholic Church

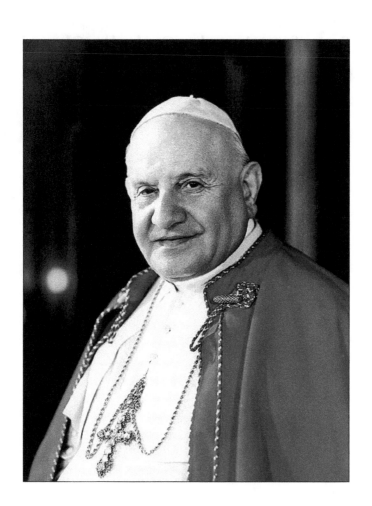

Pope John XXIII

Dr. Therese Martine Andrevon Gottstein

On April 27, 2014, John Paul II and John XXIII were proclaimed saints during a liturgical celebration in Rome, presided over by Pope Francis. The million pilgrims who poured into Rome from all over the world were there for John Paul II. But John Paul II would not have been John Paul II without John XXIII. The name he had chosen, following the premature death of his predecessor John Paul I, demonstrated an affiliation with John XXIII and Paul VI, the two key players of the Second Vatican Council. John XXIII, who had always wanted to remain in the background, was undoubtedly pleased with the honors paid to his younger brother and took his place in the background with simplicity. I had the privilege, with my husband, to be part of the Jewish delegation invited to the ceremony. David Rosen was also present. We had eaten the Shabbat meal together, and we met again the next day on the square in front of St. Peter's Basilica. I was not totally in tune with the majority, for while my admiration for John Paul II was in line with that of the crowd, my affection was for Good Pope John, whom I had discovered while writing my thesis on the conciliar text *Nostra aetate*, and for the developments of Catholic theology with regard to the Jews. It is to this pope, who was referred to with a note of disdain as a transitional pope at the time of his election in 1958, but who was mourned by the whole world on the day of his death in 1962, that I want to dedicate these few lines and explain why I consider him a hero in interreligious dialogue and how he remains a source of inspiration.

Preamble: My Definition of a Hero of Interreligious Dialogue

First of all, it is necessary to define a little better what I see behind the concept of hero of interreligious dialogue. In my opinion, we must distinguish between two categories. There are men and women who are part of the existing current of dialogue but who make an important step forward. John Paul II can be classified in this category; Catholic interreligious dialogue was not inaugurated by him, but he gave it an unprecedented boost. The other category of heroes is those who lived before the advent of interreligious dialogue and a new theology of religions. They were rooted in their own doctrine, with its limitations and closure to other religions, but they opened up gaps that allowed for the advent of the era of dialogue. John XXIII belongs to this category.

Historical Context

Angelo Roncalli was born into a very poor family of thirteen children in 1881 in northern Italy. The Catholic Church was then a body that was becoming increasingly centralized around the person of the pope. In 1870, the unity of Italy had been achieved at the expense of the papacy. The popes of this period, from Pius IX to Pius XI, considered themselves prisoners in the Vatican until 1929, refusing to leave the Vatican in order to not support the new republic. It was also the time of the unbridled development of industrialization, accompanied by workers' misery, social movements, and the spread of communism in Europe. As for Christianity in this period, we witness the beginnings of the historical-critical study of the Bible. The advent of this modernity was felt as a threat to the faith; the Catholic Church, under the pen of Pope Pius X in 1907, condemned what it called modernism.[158] All of this contributed to making the Church a bastion of resistance and to cultivating a hostile relationship with the secular world. From a theological point of view, the Catholic Church considered itself to be the depositary of the truth, while other Christian confessions qualified as heretics or schismatics, the inhabitants of mission lands as savages, and other religions as pagans. "Outside the Church there is no salvation," the adage dating back to the time of Bishop Cyprian, was interpreted literally, which raised the burning question of the salvation of souls to be saved from hell and the urgency of the mission to baptize them. If the Church was already shaking with the need to adapt to the world, the tendency to condemn the errors and wanderings of the secular world dominated their thinking. Catholics multiplied pilgrimages to support the Holy Father or the construction of basilicas in reparation of the offenses made to God. It is in this context that Angelo Roncalli grew up, studied and taught this theology, and exercised his ministry as a priest, bishop, and diplomat of the Holy See.

The Man of Dialogue and Concord

Nothing in his background prepared the peasant boy, who at the age of eleven had never been to a city, to open paths of dialogue and become a citizen of the world, embracing with his goodness all men, including those defined as enemies of the Church. Angelo Roncalli had an affable, cheerful, voluble, and resolutely optimistic temperament. He loved to meet people. From the point of view of his spirituality, he sought unceasingly to cultivate humility, simplicity, and gentleness. He had an immense trust in God. At the age of nineteen, he wrote,

> If all men are a reflection of God, how can I not love them all, how can I despise them, how can I not have respect for them? This thought must prevent me from offending my brothers in any way; I must remember that all are the image of God, and that perhaps their souls are more beautiful and dearer to the Lord than mine.[159]

These reflections seem to have guided him during his life as a pastor and diplomat. They are the foundations of a theology of religions. But Roncalli was not a theorist of dialogue. It was through his actions and his attitudes that he opened up paths of dialogue, of which we will give some significant examples. Let us specify beforehand that, although he met with Jews and Muslims, it was above all in non-Catholic Christians that Roncalli invested himself, which cannot be called interreligious dialogue. But at a time when ecumenical dialogue did not exist, there was not much difference in the discourse when speaking of so-called schismatic or heretical Christians and other non-Christian religions—except when it came to the Jews, who were the object of a very singular teaching. The former were seriously in error since they have left the true path, while the latter were in error through ignorance. Thus, to take the step of entering into dialogue with the Orthodox or Protestants was almost the same as entering into dialogue with Jews or Muslims: one must cross a line of demarcation. This is what John XXIII did.

In 1925, Archbishop Roncalli was sent to Bulgaria as a visitor, then as an apostolic delegate, even though the pope had not had a representative in that country for seven centuries. He stayed there for ten years. Immersed in a new cultural world, predominantly Orthodox, he arrived in a situation of extreme conflict between the Vatican and the Orthodox Church, coupled with tension between Latin and Eastern Rite Catholics. Roncalli had a method that he would not abandon during his life and would often repeat: to leave aside what divides and to concentrate instead on the search for what unites in love and prayer. He established contacts with the Orthodox, which was not always appreciated by Rome; exercised charity without distinction of religion during the earthquake of 1928; and mediated the marriage of the Orthodox tsar Boris III with the Italian Catholic princess Jeanne de Savoie. On December 31, 1934, he said goodbye to this country where he had lived in poverty:

> If someone from Bulgaria passes by my house—whether at night or during a difficult period in his life—he will always find a candle burning in my window. Let him knock on the door. No one will ask him if he is Catholic or Orthodox—the fact that he is a Bulgarian brother will suffice.[160]

At the beginning of the Second World War, Bishop Roncalli was sent as apostolic delegate for Turkey and Greece, where Orthodox hostility towards Rome was no less great than in Sofia. He lived in Istanbul, in a predominantly Muslim environment, and had to be in contact with the new Republic of Turkey, with other religious communities, and with the Orthodox. The Catholics, who were in a very small minority after the upheavals at the end of the Ottoman Empire, were very withdrawn, which was not to the liking of Bishop Roncalli, who wrote to them,

> We are here a modest minority who live on the surface of a vast world with which we have only superficial relations. We like to distinguish ourselves from those who do not profess our faith: Orthodox brothers, Protestants, Israelites, Muslims, believers and non-believers of other religions . . . . It seems logical that each one should look after himself, his family and national tradition, keeping tightly within the limited circle of his own coterie . . . My dear brothers and sons, I must tell you that, in the light of the Gospel and of Catholic principle, this is a false logic.[161]

Roncalli was animated by an extraordinary love for Istanbul and for the Turkish people, whose language he learned. He was the architect of the first thaw with the Ecumenical Patriarchate, which manifested itself in 1939 with the presence of Orthodox representatives at the funeral ceremony of Pius XI. Then he went to the historical district of Fanar, seat of the Patriarchate of Constantinople, where he was received with all honors by Patriarch Benjamin. This was the first time this had happened in centuries.

His dealings with the Jews were of a different nature, since they were guided by the urgency of saving lives. From 1940, since Turkey was neutral, Bishop Roncalli used his influence, his ability to create links, and his old relations, such as with Tsar Boris III, to save the maximum number of Jews from death.[162] The Shoah made such a strong impression on him that as soon as he became pope, during the Good Friday ceremony in 1959, John XXIII interrupted the ceremony so that he could repeat the oration for the Jews, deleting the traditional mention of *perfidis*. In October 1960 he greeted a group of American Jews with the words, "I am Joseph, your brother" (Joseph was his baptismal name). He was thus evoking the reunion between the Jewish people and the Church to which he aspired. But it was his meeting with the French Jew Jules Isaac that was decisive in giving concrete expression to his desire for a response from the Church to Auschwitz. This renowned historian, who had been deposed by the Vichy regime, had lost his wife and daughter in the Shoah and was co-founder of the Jewish-Christian Friendship. He was received in audience by John XXIII on June 13, 1960, and presented him with an argument for reforming Christian teaching on the Jews. The meeting lasted twenty minutes. Jules Isaac was won over by the successor of Peter, whom he described as "a round fellow, rather fat, with a face of strong and rustic features—a big nose—very smiling, willingly laughing, with a clear look, a little malicious but where there is an obvious goodness which inspires confidence." For his part, John XXIII never ceased to show understanding and sympathy for his visitor, and when Jules Isaac, before retiring, asked if he could take away some hope, the pontiff replied: "You are entitled to more than hope."[163] This was the beginning of the long journey of the conciliar text *Nostra aetate*, which in its chapter 4 put an end to the teaching of contempt for the Jews and their collective condemnation for the death of Christ.

John XXIII was seventy-seven years old when elected pope. A man of the field, rich in varied experience, including twenty years of life in the East as a minority, he was attentive to history and the signs of the times. He believed that the Church should declare peace to the world and enter into dialogue with it. He announced the convocation of an ecumenical council a few months after his accession to the chair of Peter, giving the floor to bishops from all over the world and inviting representatives of other confessions to participate partially in the work of the Second Vatican Council. John XXIII wanted Christians to enter into a movement, whose name in Italian has been preserved as *aggiornamento* (update, modernization, adaptation, renewal): this will have an impact in many areas, among others, in the relationship to other religions. Of this Council, of which he would only see the first session, he would say "it is not the Gospel that has changed, it is we who understand it better."

One should not think that John XXIII was a progressive as we say today. If his way of doing things, his love of contacts and travel, did not always please the Roman Curia, nobody questioned his orthodoxy in matters of doctrine. He is considered a conservative. So there is a paradox in him. On the one hand, he wrote: "To me and to all priests, to all Catholics, falls the very serious duty of cooperating in the conversion of the unfaithful world, in the return of heretics and schismatics to the unity of the Church, in the proclamation of Christ, even to the Jews who killed him."[164] On the other hand, he engaged in an authentic friendly dialogue with these heretics and schismatics. He was totally opposed to the settlement of the Jews in Palestine, for the traditional reasons that the Jews had been driven out by the will of God. But he worked hard to obtain the passage of entire trains of persecuted Jews to Palestine. He was fundamentally anti-communist, but he had real exchanges with Nikita Khrushchev, who wrote to him on several occasions. Obviously, his theological thought evolved—for example, at the end of his life we no longer hear him speak of schismatics but of separated brothers—but the basic line remains the same. How could exclusivism and openness be combined in him? This is what we are going to decipher in order to understand how and why this man whose vision of other religions was that of his time, inspires myself, who lives in the era of interreligious dialogue.

Inspiration

As mentioned above, Angelo Roncalli had character traits that favored his ability to enter into dialogue with the other. But we must add other parameters.

Roncalli confessed to having a real "intellectual greed." He wrote in his diary on January 8, 1902, "I feel a rage to want to know everything, to know all the authors of value, to be aware of the whole scientific movement in its multiple directions." He read and studied but also traveled. His proverbial friendliness was not superficial; it was accompanied by his curiosity to know those he met.

The Second Vatican Council introduced into its vocabulary the notion of a "hierarchy of truths" in the ecumenical process. It seems to me that this concept can be applied to John XXIII, because he knew how to make a distinction between the fundamental truths on which one does not compromise and the more circumstantial aspects of tradition—to put it briefly, between Tradition and tradition. Removing the ecclesiastical habit, forbidden in Turkey, did not pose him the slightest problem. To modify a protocol to honor the chief rabbi of France or an Orthodox dignitary seemed natural to him. All this indicates a free spirit but also a deep vision of his conception of obedience. His motto illustrates this well: "Obedience and Love." Roncalli always wanted to obey—the pope, the teaching of the Church—but his deepest obedience was to Christ and the gospel, that is, to charity. It is charity that made him take bold steps and open up gaps. His secretary, Monsignor Loris Capovilla, wrote of him: "The secret of Roncalli's success lies in a traditional but also dynamic matrix, in the apparent paradox between severe conservatism and evangelical openness."[165]

John XXIII was a profoundly free person. This freedom came from his native poverty, which he saw as a blessing and which was the source of his humility. The feeling of being poor never left him, even when he attained honors. This resulted in an indifference to mockery, accusations, and what people thought of him. He acted according to what he thought was God's will and spoke the truth as he understood it, but without trying to impose it. His awareness of his existential poverty went hand in hand with his trust in God. He had no illusions about his power, which is in the hands of God alone. He was therefore an ardent missionary, but without seeking results at all costs, and was always respectful of people.

John XXIII's life was marked by conflicts that made him obsessed with peace. The concept of just war or balance of power had no meaning for him. True concord among men of faith, among men of good will, was his deepest concern, to which he dedicated his last encyclical, *Pacem in terris*, signed a month before his death from stomach cancer. He positively believed that it is by talking to each other and knowing each other that men could resolve their conflicts. The dialogue that he practiced with simplicity and patience all his life was not a method. It was a true spirituality.

Conclusion

When asked why the Council was convened, John XXIII would have opened his office window wide and replied, "To let fresh air into the Church." Others have heard him say, "I want to open the window of the Church so that we can see what is happening outside and the world can see what is happening inside." Whether these anecdotes are entirely accurate or not, they seem to me to sum up what Pope John XXIII leaves us as a teaching for interreligious dialogue. Opening a window not only brings air from outside and renews the room but also allows one to see beyond the walls of one's home. This is basically what Roncalli did during his long pastoral and diplomatic career. Without leaving his doctrinal house, he opened the window to admire what is good and beautiful in the world and renewed the air for Christians.

Cardinal Augustin Bea[166]

Pietro Cardinal Parolin

MY PERSONAL CHOICE FOR interreligious hero would be Cardinal Augustin Bea, who played a decisive role in the Catholic Church's promotion of systematic dialogue with other Christian churches and with the world's religions. We should note from the outset, however, that Bea was initially concerned with dialogue with Judaism alone, since Pope John XXIII had asked him first to reconsider theologically the Church's relationship with Judaism. In order better to appreciate the cardinal's life and work, let us begin with some biographical details.

Cardinal Bea as a Gift from God to Humanity: Biographical Notes

Augustin Bea was born in Germany on May 28, 1881, in Riedböhringen, a small village in the Black Forest close to the Swiss border. His intellectual abilities became apparent at an early age. Consequently, the local priest gave him private lessons, including lessons in Latin, and encouraged his further education. His desire to become a priest grew, and he wanted to join the Society of Jesus, the Jesuits. At the time, however, due to the *Kulturkampf,* the Jesuits were forbidden from engaging in any activities in Germany, so he began his theological studies at the University of Freiburg. After just three semesters, and against the advice of his parents, he determined to join the Society of Jesus. In 1904, he was sent to Valkenburg in the Netherlands for his preliminary studies. Even before the final stage of his religious formation, the young Jesuit was sent to Innsbruck to study philology and later to Berlin for Oriental studies, but he remained in both places only a brief time. While still in formation and shortly thereafter, he was assigned administrative duties, ranging from acting as a house superior to becoming the first provincial of the Upper German Jesuit Province, established in

1921. Bea's talents were quickly recognized by several of his superiors. He was known to be reliable, thorough, and capable in a number of areas. In 1923, he participated, the youngest Provincial present, in a General Congregation of the Jesuits in Rome, where he was assigned the following year by his Roman superiors. In the decades that followed, he developed a rich and multifaceted ministry. In 1929, the Jesuit General decided to send him for six months as a visitor to Japan in order to chart the course for the future of the Society there. From 1930 to 1949, he served as rector of the Pontifical Biblical Institute in Rome, where he lectured in the field of Old and New Testament exegesis and published numerous studies. From 1945 to 1958, he was confessor to Pope Pius XII and consultor to several Vatican offices. Father Augustine Bea was therefore no stranger to the Vatican when Pope John XXIII made him a cardinal on December 16, 1959. The following June, he was asked by the pope to head the Secretariat for the Promotion of Christian Unity, which was charged with preparing three important documents for the forthcoming Second Vatican Council. On September 18, 1960, the pope commissioned him to draft a so-called *Tractatus de Iudaeis* for the Council, which eventually led to the conciliar declaration *Nostra aetate*. The drafting, history, and promulgation of this Council document resembles a detective novel: removed from the Council's agenda at one point, it raised a number of diplomatic concerns, and its contents were debated.

Cardinal Bea as the Father of the Conciliar Declaration *Nostra aetate*

Cardinal Bea lived during a fascinating and turbulent time for the Catholic Church, which was experiencing a period of renewal through the meeting and subsequent implementation of the Second Vatican Council (1962–1965). He had been chosen by Pope John XXIII to play a leading role in this process by introducing the drafts of conciliar documents on ecumenical relations with other Christian churches and communities (*Unitatis redintegratio*), religious freedom (*Dignitatis humanae*) and the Church's new theological relationship to Judaism. These three issues had not been treated authoritatively by any previous council, and so new ground had to be covered very carefully and with great tact and sensitivity, especially since significant resistance within the Church was to be expected. Traditional teaching had to be preserved but also reviewed in the contemporary historical context, in order to be open to the needs of the times and further development on the basis of the gospel. It was important to respect the teachings of the Catholic faith but also to communicate them in a fresh and contemporary way.

Cardinal Bea's work of presenting a *Tractatus de Iudaeis* to the Council immediately met with all kinds of difficulties that had to be gradually overcome. The reasons Pope John XXIII wanted the Council to deal with the theological question of the relationship of Judaism to Christianity—moving beyond the older theology of substitution—were clearly set forth by his private secretary Monsignor Loris Capovilla. Jules Isaac, a French scholar of Jewish descent, had claimed that, prior to the Council, the Church was marked by a teaching of contempt towards Judaism, holding that God's promises to the people of Israel had passed to the Church following the Jewish denial of the messianic status and divine sonship of Jesus. The Church thus became the new people of God, in place of the chosen people of Israel. This theory of supersession or substitution, based on the teaching of some of the early Church Fathers, had shaped Catholic theology throughout the Middle Ages and the modern era; it left no room for the Jews as God's first chosen people, retaining an uninterrupted covenant relationship with him.

On June 13, 1960, John XXIII met privately with Jules Isaac, who proposed that the forthcoming Council should reflect on the relationship of the Catholic Church to Judaism and that a theology of substitution should be definitively abandoned. The pope was open to the idea and enlisted Cardinal Bea, who had dealt with the issue in his scholarly writings. He was convinced that the Church needed to rethink its relationship to Judaism from a deeper theological standpoint. Cardinal Bea's contribution to the Church was ultimately the conciliar declaration *Nostra aetate*, whose fourth section moved beyond the theology of substitution to posit a clearly positive relationship to Judaism. The declaration, originally planned as a *Tractatus de Iudaeis*, had an eventful history. Due to political and diplomatic concerns, a document dealing solely with the Jews did not seem opportune, as Catholics living in predominantly Muslim countries feared repercussions due to the political conflict in Palestine. The Church's relationship with Muslims and, in a broader sense, with all world religions also needed to be taken into account. As a result, what was originally to be a statement on Judaism turned into a new definition of the Church's relationship to all religions, with her relationship to Judaism as a starting point and catalyst. *Nostra aetate*, which had initially been planned as an appendix to a conciliar document on ecumenism, and then to one on the Church, was thus issued as a document in its own right. At times, it was feared that a document on the new relationship of the Church to Judaism would never see the light of day, either because it was removed from the Council's agenda or because voting was postponed due to time constraints.

It was the great and lasting merit of Cardinal Bea—persistently and with the support of two popes, John XXIII and Paul VI—to move the

Council to accept this historic document in the face of opposition and resistance, both external and internal. He was a man with a task, a mission, and, thanks to his unique personality and the power of the Holy Spirit, he was able to accomplish it. *Nostra aetate*, in its section 4, was to inspire other churches and ecclesial communities, especially in Protestant circles, to advance on the path of reconciliation with Judaism.

Cardinal Bea's Personality and Commitment to the Council

Cardinal Bea exemplified several attitudes essential to interreligious dialogue. Despite the difficulties he encountered, he never thought of abandoning or betraying his mission. In the early days of the Council, it was not entirely clear to him what a mammoth task he had been asked to undertake. He later admitted: "If I had been able to foresee all the difficulties we would have encountered, I do not know whether I would have had the courage to undertake this task."[167] Yet he never grew discouraged in those decisive years, for he trusted completely in the help of God.

Stability and Flexibility

What certainly helped Cardinal Bea was his personal character, shaped by a combination of steadfastness and flexibility. These two qualities were present from his youth and consolidated by his Jesuit training. In his parents' home, he had learned the importance of fidelity to certain convictions and values, while in his religious life, he was constantly confronted by new challenges that could not be met without mental flexibility. His Catholicism was firmly rooted in traditional theological and moral doctrine, yet, thanks to his profound and solid knowledge of the Holy Scriptures in their original languages, he was sensitive to dogmatic developments down the centuries. Through his work on the Old Testament and Hebrew, he became familiar with the world of Jewish thought and its ancient traditions. At the behest of Pope Pius XII, he had also served as the head of a working group that translated the Psalms from Hebrew into Latin.

This flexibility also shaped how he dealt with the people and situations he encountered throughout his life. Again and again, he found himself entrusted with new and unexpected tasks, whose range and complexity he could not have imagined beforehand. To meet these challenges imposed by his superiors, he had to venture into new territory, without knowing where he would eventually be led. He showed great trust in God and a willingness to surrender himself completely to the Lord's will. This gave him the strength to approach things calmly, serenely, and patiently.

Humility and Determination

Cardinal Bea was not one of those people who need to be in the spotlight. Although blessed by God with rich intellectual abilities, he did not yield to pride, since he knew that these were God's gift. His modesty and common sense were valued in the religious community to which he brought his gifts and shared them alongside those of others. His leadership skills were honed in his years as Provincial of the Jesuits' Upper German Province, but especially during the period between 1930 and 1949, when he served as rector of the Pontifical Biblical Institute. The head of a religious community is expected first and foremost to show respect for his brethren, accepting them as they are, accompanying them spiritually, but also confronting them with humility and modesty. In a community of Jesuits, there is no place for a superior who exercises his power with a heavy hand and seeks to dominate his confrères. In carrying out his ministry of governance, Cardinal Bea thus gained certain social skills that were to prove useful to him at the time of the Council in his dealings with bishops.

He also showed determination in decision-making, another important characteristic of a superior, who must be able to accept advice and then judge, together with his confrères and co-workers, the next steps to take. Ultimately, of course, a superior bears sole responsibility for his decisions. To carry out his work well, he must be a man of determination and not prey to hesitation, doubts, or procrastination.

Patient Tenacity and Courageous Progress

What particularly distinguished Cardinal Bea, however, was his remarkable patience, combined with his courage to keep moving forward in spite of difficulties. In those three critical years of the Council, he could easily have given up because of the opposition he faced in drafting *Nostra aetate*. Yet he persevered tenaciously, committed to the mission he had received. If, after a discernment of spirits, he was convinced that the desired objective was in accordance with God's will, nothing could stop him. He was completely committed to the mandate given to him by Pope John XXIII.

Patience is a quality learned in the course of a lifetime, as we learn that all things have their proper time and can mature only gradually. Impatience proves destructive, since it would violently and prematurely seek to reshape reality. Tenacity, on the other hand, is marked by the confidence that, in the end, things will work themselves out with God's help. This is the only real explanation of Cardinal Bea's perseverance at the Council: he was absolutely convinced of the necessity of his mission.

My Personal Experience with Cardinal Bea

If someone feels called to be a priest and over time realizes that this is God's will, then there is always a corresponding sense of mission. At the beginning of my own priestly life, I had no idea of what God had in store for me; only gradually did it become clearer to me. I first encountered the figure of Augustin Bea as a young seminarian in Vicenza, where I completed my philosophical and theological formation (1974 to 1980).

I never met Cardinal Bea personally, but in those days, immediately after the Second Vatican Council, we studied its documents, which were to guide the Church in new directions. Naturally, I also read the conciliar Declaration *Nostra aetate* with great interest, to see how the new relationship with Judaism would be presented. Early on, then, I was impressed by Bea, the great learning and enthusiasm he brought to the task assigned to him and his refusal to be discouraged in the face of difficulties. Bea undertook something new, exploring uncharted territory and challenging traditional approaches, undeterred by opposition. My impression was that of a personable, serene, quiet, and cheerful man, but also one who was fearless. Thanks to him, Jewish-Catholic dialogue advanced following the promulgation of *Nostra aetate*. It now remains for us to continue with confidence on the path traced out for us.

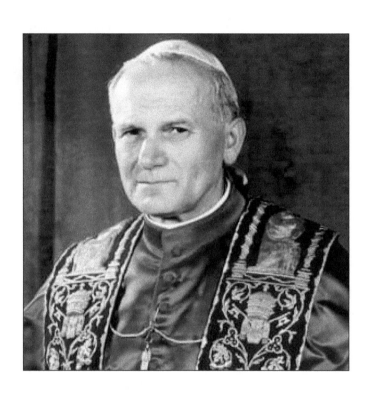

Pope John Paul II[168]

Kurt Cardinal Koch

The person I have selected as my interreligious hero is Pope Saint John Paul II, particularly because I was privileged to meet him on several occasions, and he consecrated me bishop on January 6, 1996, in St Peter's Basilica in Rome. He granted me an audience in the Vatican several times as bishop of Basel, together with the Swiss Bishops' Conference or on my own. Then in early June 2004, as the local bishop, I had the honor of welcoming him to Bern for a meeting of the young Catholics of Switzerland; that was his second-to-last trip abroad, a year before his death.

Those on the Jewish side regarded John Paul II as the great ice-breaker in Jewish-Catholic dialogue, because he was one of the first to display unforgettable gestures of friendship towards the Jews. Pope Saint John XXIII and Paul VI had already taken crucial steps to come closer to Judaism, but the commitment of the Roman Curia in this respect was above all realized under John Paul II. The preconditions for this unique interreligious activity are, however, related to his biography, at which we should first take a look.

Karol Wojtiła's Background as a Precondition for Jewish-Catholic Dialogue

Karol Wojtiła was greatly concerned to improve relations with Judaism, if only for reasons related to his own life story. He grew up in the Polish town of Wadowice, in which over a quarter of the population was Jewish. From the start, it was natural for him to associate with Jewish fellow citizens and share their daily lives. From childhood on, he had Jewish classmates with whom he spent his free time and formed close bonds of friendship. In this way, he gained intensive knowledge of the Jewish way of life. A nice anecdote has it that, as a teenager, he took a shine to a Jewish girl. What is quite certain, however, is that he remained a lifelong friend of Jerzy Kluger, a Jew who grew

111

up with him in Poland, later lived in Rome, and met regularly with him after Wojtiła became pope. For Wojtiła, it was distressing to see many of his Jewish friends disappear and be killed in the Shoah. He had firsthand experience of the horror of national socialism, of which Jews were the main victims. Subsequently, under communist rule in Poland, few people saw a need to deal with the sufferings of the Jews during World War II in any way. A veil was cast over the past, so that the decimated Jewish community was hardly able to leave any impression on the outside world.

Marked by the way both the Nazis and the communists had dealt with his Jewish fellow citizens in Poland, it was of very personal concern for John Paul II as pope to form and strengthen new bonds of friendship with Judaism. The influence of John Paul II in the Jewish-Catholic dialogue has a lot to do with his strong personality; he was a master of grand public gestures, in order to make his concern visible. To this day, the Jewish dialogue partners regard him with high esteem, and their admiration for him and his great work of reconciliation remains unbroken.

Activities of John Paul II to Achieve Reconciliation with Judaism

On June 7, 1979, in the very first year of his pontificate, he visited the Auschwitz-Birkenau concentration camp, where he dedicated a special commemoration to the victims of the Shoah at the memorial stone inscribed in Hebrew. This stone, John Paul II said, "awakens the memory of the People whose sons and daughters were intended for total extermination. This People draws its origin from Abraham, our father in faith (cf. Rom 4:12), as was expressed by Paul of Tarsus. The very people that received from God the commandment 'Thou shalt not kill,' itself experienced in a special measure what is meant by killing. It is not permissible for anyone to pass by this inscription with indifference."[169]

Yet his visit to the Rome synagogue on April 13, 1986, was even more spectacular. The symbolic picture of the embrace between Chief Rabbi Elio Toaff and Pope John Paul II in front of the *Tempio Maggiore* was seen the world over. For the first time in history, a Roman Catholic pope had visited a synagogue to publicly display his interest in and esteem for Judaism. Another very significant step for Jews took place at the end of December 1993, when the Holy See accorded the State of Israel full diplomatic recognition. An exchange of ambassadors took place in June 1994.

Finally, the request for forgiveness of March 12, 2000, must be seen against the background of the document of the Pontifical Commission for

Religious Relations with the Jews "We Remember: A Reflection on the *Shoah*," published in 1998.[170] In a public liturgy, the pope prayed for forgiveness of guilt towards the people of Israel: "We are deeply saddened by the behaviour of those who in the course of history have caused these children of yours to suffer, and asking your forgiveness we wish to commit ourselves to genuine brotherhood with the people of the Covenant."[171] It was a paper with this prayer—only slightly amended—that John Paul II then wedged between the ashlars of the Wailing Wall on his visit to Israel on March 26, 2000. His visit to the State of Israel can certainly be seen as historic and as a unique inspiration to Jewish-Catholic dialogue. He visited the Holocaust Memorial Yad Vashem, commemorated and prayed for the victims of the Shoah, met survivors of this inexpressible tragedy, took part in an interreligious meeting involving Muslims, and made the first contacts with the Jerusalem Chief Rabbinate. John Paul II received Israel's two chief rabbis in the Vatican several years later, on January 16, 2004, by what time an institutionalized dialogue had already developed between the Holy See's Commission for Religious Relations with the Jews and the Chief Rabbinate of Israel.

In fact, John Paul II frequently met with notable Jewish figures and groups in the Vatican, and on his numerous pastoral journeys, it was always a must for him to meet with a local Jewish delegation in places with a big Jewish congregation. Hence, when we consider the great commitment of this pope to Jewish-Catholic dialogue, it is clear that, during his long pontificate, he set the course for the future of this dialogue. The achievements of his pontificate are a benchmark below which we can never fall—especially as *Nostra aetate* (section 4) set unequivocal standards that remain valid.

Basic Attitudes of John Paul II in the Dialogue with the Jews

These activities of a pope to achieve reconciliation with Judaism are unique. Before John Paul II, they would all have been impossible. It is therefore his personal merit not only to have made the Jewish-Catholic dialogue fruitful with these encounters and gestures but also to have given it a completely new direction. The two subsequent popes Benedict XVI and Francis took the same steps to deepen the relations with the Jews, albeit with their own style and personal imprint.

So what can we learn from John Paul II for the current Jewish-Catholic dialogue in general? Much has to do with his charismatic personality, which no one should even attempt to imitate. Yet certain basic qualities stand out as indispensable for a propitious interreligious dialogue. There is first the openness and esteem with which this pope encountered representatives of other religions, coupled with a fundamental interest in the other and an authentic respect for the initially unknown religious traditions. With great empathy, he received them as people who, like him, owed their lives to the Creator of all things and were God's beloved creatures. He had absolutely no fear of new encounters and, time and again, was courageous enough to venture into unforeseeable situations. With a strong trust in God, he believed that the steps he had taken would lead to a more intensive friendship with the leaders of other religions. That was the basis for interfaith dialogue: successively building up trust and friendship, so that people could together tread paths beneficial to the whole of humanity. If we just think of the interreligious encounters that John Paul II founded in Assisi for peace and harmony in the world and organized on October 27, 1986, and January 24, 2002, the pope's attitude becomes visible: regarding world peace, religions were no longer to be part of the problem but part of the solution. He rightly recognized that peace in the given societal and political conditions is only possible when all world religions stand and act together.

The Political Significance of John Paul II

The second edition of the encounters for peace in Assisi in January 2002 took place in the context of the "war on terrorism" that US President George W. Bush declared in reaction to the attack on the Twin Towers in New York on September 11, 2001. John Paul II rightly feared a gradual escalation of acts of war, since countering force with force only generates more force. Shortly before the Iraq War that the US instigated in March 2003, he tried with all the diplomatic means available to the Holy See to avoid this military strike. He received several foreign ministers and politicians and pleaded with them not to start a new war. As his predecessor Pius XII said, with war, all is lost, and with peace, all is won.

John Paul II was doubtless a political pope who endeavored to achieve justice, peace, and freedom for humankind. Based on his own life experience, he knew about the material and spiritual devastation caused by war and what happens when people are deprived of freedom in ideological systems. We need only to remember his public influence on the fall of the Berlin Wall in 1989, when the communist regimes were nearing their end. As a Pole, it was extremely important to him to perform this service for his homeland; after all, it was from Poland that the freedom movements radiated out, ultimately spreading to the whole of Eastern Europe and liberating these countries from the communist yoke.

Consequently, we can learn from John Paul II that the prophetic view of the respective political situation is just as important as deep roots in your own religious tradition. He was a pious man, who included everything in his prayers but took resolute steps towards reconciliation, in order to safeguard or promote peace in the world. For him, an important means of securing peace was interreligious dialogue and prayer. Religion and politics are kept apart in largely secular societies, but ultimately every religion that seriously advocates for human beings has a political character, and all policy-making respectful of human dignity must consider the religious character of humanity. While there is a tendency in Christianity to carefully separate politics and religion, Judaism generally involves a complete view of all aspects of human life.

The Theological Significance of John Paul II in Jewish-Catholic Dialogue

As head of state of the Holy See, John Paul II was per se a politician; but as head of the Catholic Church, it was up to him to lead his flock in every sense. He was the guardian of the magisterium, the office of Catholic teaching, and, as such, he undertook key steps towards a theological reassessment of Judaism. The Church's doctrinal texts before the declaration *Nostra aetate* (section 4) of the Second Vatican Council (1962–1965) never spoke of Judaism in theological terms or used the substitution view as a premise, according to which the elect people of Israel were disinherited to such an extent that God's good promises had been transferred to the church. Not until *Nostra aetate* did a genuinely biblical and theological way of thinking develop that gave more value and appreciation to the Judaism not only of the past but also of the present. The roots of Christianity in Judaism are clearly underlined, and any form of anti-Semitism is rejected.

From this basis, John Paul II derived further theological conclusions. Already on November 17, 1980, speaking in Mainz to the Central Council of Jews in Germany, he said that the Jews continue to live in the covenant with God: "The encounter between the people of God of the Old Covenant, which has never been abrogated by God, and that of the New Covenant is also an internal dialogue in our church, similar to that between the first and second part of the Bible."[172] If now the old covenant is still valid for the Jews, then they have never fallen out of God's salvific intentions. How and in what way they will now be saved, however, is an interesting and also delicate theological question in view of the Christian confession that only Jesus Christ can be the mediator of universal salvation. This was not taken up until 2015 by the document of the Commission for Religious Relations with the Jews entitled "'The Gifts and the Calling of God Are Irrevocable' (Rom 11:29)."[173] Hence John Paul II gave new theological impetus to the Jewish-Catholic dialogue and touched upon issues that can be deepened still further.

His address in the Rome synagogue on April 13, 1986, is marked by a pointed theological statement. There he said: "The Jewish religion is not 'extrinsic' to us, but in a certain way is 'intrinsic' to our own religion. With Judaism, therefore, we have a relationship that we do not have with any other religion. You are our dearly beloved brothers, and in a certain way, it could be said that you are our elder brothers."[174] He saw Judaism and Christianity as linked not only in a historical sense but also as current religious traditions. Furthermore, he underlined the unique relation between these two religions, which is not comparable with their relations with any other religions. His calling Jews the "elder brothers" of Christians was much quoted after this historic address, and the term can still be heard today. Through his relationships with Jewish friends as well, John Paul II demonstrated the meaning of this term in an authentic way. He was a man of friendship and communication, so that it was particularly hard for him towards the end of his life to have to contend with difficulties in speaking.

We can learn a lot from John Paul II for the Jewish-Catholic dialogue. At the personal level and the practical and theological levels, he had a number of qualities that made him an interreligious hero in the truest sense of the word. Yet we must not forget from where he got these qualities and how they were enhanced: John Paul II was a man of God, deeply rooted in prayer, ultimately a saint. The Eternal placed him in this world to fulfil a specific mission. He was aware of that, and from there he drew his power, strength, and energy for interreligious dialogue, above all with Judaism.

Cardinal Francis Arinze

JOHN CARDINAL ONAIYEKAN

Introduction

I AM GLAD TO have this opportunity to celebrate a great African contemporary father of the Catholic Church, my mentor and highly respected senior ecclesiastical colleague, His Eminence, Francis Cardinal Arinze. When I was asked to choose an interfaith hero as the subject of my contribution, it did not take me long to settle on this great man of God and of the Church, an African figure that has made us Africans in general and Nigerians in particular proud through his great achievements in the Church and in the world. At over eighty-eight years of age, he is gracefully in retirement in his Vatican apartment overlooking St. Peter's Square, as an emeritus—one who has served with great merit—as archbishop of Onitsha, president of the Pontifical Council for Interreligious Dialogue, and prefect of the Congregation for Divine Worship and the Discipline of the Sacraments. He continues to be relevant in Church affairs at the highest level, as the fourth-ranked among the merely eleven cardinal bishops who top the list of the over two hundred members of the College of Cardinals. He is by all standards a hero, and I am happy to tell the story of my association with him.

His Early Life

There are many reports about the early life of Cardinal Arinze. I will highlight here only the aspects that relate to his later life as an interfaith hero. He was born on November 1, 1932, into a family of ardent and sincere adherents of the Ibo traditional religion. Very early in life, he became attracted to the Catholic faith through his contacts with missionaries, both Irish and indigenous Ibo pioneer priests, especially the now famous Blessed Father Iwene Tansi, for whom he was an altar boy. He was nine years old when he was baptized. This means that before then, he grew up in his ancestral

119

religion. As a young convert to the Catholic faith, he retained a great respect for the religion of his parents. They, in turn, embraced the Christian faith much later in his life. He grew up as an ardent Catholic, with sincere respect for his ancestral religion. In those times before Vatican II, such an openmindedness to non-Christian religions was not common, especially among missionaries and new converts.

He was drawn to the Catholic priesthood at a very young age and entered the seminary at the age of fifteen. This was not before he had managed to wear down the understandable reluctance of his father to give consent. It is significant that he considered such consent important. It is perhaps even more significant that his non-Christian father granted his consent, recognizing that his son's desire to serve God was good and deserved his support. We see here an interfaith family at work.

Priestly Formation

In pursuit of the priesthood, he did his secondary education in the junior seminary of All Hallows in Onitsha and his course of philosophy in the major seminary of Bigard Memorial in Enugu. Thereafter, his archbishop sent him to Rome in 1955 for his theological studies at the prestigious Collegio Urbano de Propaganda Fide. He finished his priestly formation with excellence and was ordained in Rome in November 1958. He continued higher ecclesiastical studies in the same Collegio Urbano and concluded them with a doctorate summa cum laude in dogmatic theology. It is worth noting that his doctorate thesis was on "Sacrifice in Ibo Traditional Religion," a work that was later published in 1970 by the Ibadan University Press as a seminal work of research in its field. We can see here his abiding interest in the religion of his ancestors. The thrust of the publication was to show the great continuity between the religious values of Christianity and our African religions, a theme that he would later develop in his many efforts to find common ground in his numerous encounters with people of different faiths.

He returned from Rome with a reputation as a young priest with extraordinary talent. We can see this in the positions of great responsibility to which he was assigned, especially as professor in the Bigard Seminary and soon as the Catholic education secretary for the then eastern region of Nigeria. This last job came with very heavy responsibility, given the important place of Catholic schools in those days before the ill-advised governmental takeover of schools. It is no surprise therefore that after only seven years of priestly apostolate, he was appointed in 1965 as co-adjutor archbishop of Onitsha at the age of thirty-two, the youngest bishop in the

Catholic world for many years. He succeeded Archbishop Heery two years later as the substantive archbishop of Onitsha.

The Nigerian Archbishop and the Second Vatican Council

The young archbishop started his archepiscopal career in grand style. Soon after his ordination, he packed his suitcase and headed for Rome, to take part in the last session of the Second Vatican Council. He is today one of the very few surviving Council Fathers in the Catholic Church, an honor that neither Pope Emeritus Benedict nor the incumbent Pope Francis can claim. That he was the youngest bishop there did not deter him from making valuable contributions to the work of the Council. The bishops who represented Nigeria at that Council were mostly foreign missionaries. Arinze was a welcome addition to the small number of Nigerian bishops. It is my belief that among all of them, both white and black, none was as conversant with the workings of the Council and its language as their youngest brother. He is on record as one of the very few African bishops who made a personal intervention on the floor of the Council, with his text in correct Latin, as was the practice at that Council.

As a Council Father, Arinze had the honor of putting his signature to all the Council documents passed in that last 1965 session. We can imagine that he would have had special interest in documents like the following: *Christus Dominus*, on the ministry of bishops; *Nostra aetate*, on the relations of the Catholic Church with other religions, which, like *Christus Dominus*, was passed on October 28, 1965; *Dignitatis humanae*, on religious freedom; and *Ad gentes*, on the Church's missionary activity, which, like *Dignitatis humanae*, was passed on December 7, 1965.

It is not surprising that he handled the Vatican II documents with an authority that comes from being personally involved in their formulation and approval.

Arinze, Archbishop of Biafra

He was a young thirty-five-year-old archbishop when the Nigerian Civil War of Biafra secession broke out in 1967, on territory that at the beginning comprised his entire metropolitan province. There were only three ecclesiastical provinces in Nigeria at that time, the other two being Kaduna in the north and Lagos in the southwest. The war put a heavy burden of pastoral and social responsibility on him and his brother bishops of the province. It was a story of great heroism and pastoral zeal, guiding the Church and the people of God through conditions in which mere survival was a severe challenge. The heroic efforts of the Church and her agents, under the leadership of Archbishop Arinze, to alleviate the misery that the war inflicted on the people has remained fresh in the grateful hearts of all those who went through that tragedy. The tremendous growth of the Catholic Church in Ibo land during and after the civil war is not unconnected to this impressive record of works of charity.

To put together the pieces of the lives of the people after the devastation of the war required a lot of hard work, patient effort, and wise management of people and scarce resources. The war was over, but the Church still had to deal with the ubiquitous presence of soldiers from all parts of Nigeria, many of whom were Muslims. The archbishop managed to work out a peaceful *modus vivendi* with everyone, largely due to his infectious cheerfulness and friendly disposition. He thus showed his ability to reach out to people across ethnic and religious lines to maintain peace and work for the common good.

Arinze in the Catholic Bishop's Conference of Nigeria (CBCN)

With the end of the Civil War in January 1970, the Nigerian hierarchy did not waste time to come together, thus giving a much-needed example of reconciliation and reunification in a new Nigeria. Archbishop Arinze played an important role in facilitating this not always easy process. The scars left by the war needed some time to fully heal. The period also coincided with the drastic Nigerianization of the Nigerian hierarchy, as largely young and relatively inexperienced Nigerians were appointed to replace non-Nigerian bishops, who retired, one after the other, home to Europe and America. Thus Arinze soon found himself with episcopal colleagues of his own age bracket.

It was this rather young episcopacy of the 1970s and 1980s that pulled the Nigerian Church through a most delicate period of our national history. This was a time that we started to see and feel the impact of a creeping political Islam. This phenomenon became accentuated with the end of military rule and the return to civil government under political parties in October 1979. This period witnessed the gradual coming together of the badly divided Christian denominations in Nigeria, which led eventually to the establishment of the Christian Association of Nigeria (CAN), with its major goal of forging a common approach to dealing with Islam. Arinze was in the frontline of this effort. It is significant that, by 1979, the bishops of Nigeria elected him as their president, a position he held with great commitment and competence until he was called to Rome by Pope John Paul II in 1984. I should note that it was under his presidency that I myself became a bishop in January 1983 and had a glimpse of his effective leadership before he was taken away from us.

Cardinal Arinze in the Vatican

Pope John Paul II called Archbishop Arinze to Rome to head the Pontifical Council for Interreligious Dialogue. He took up his office in 1984 with the title of pro-president of the council, since only cardinals were substantive heads of Roman dicasteries (departments of the Roman Curia) at that time. As was expected, in the next consistory in 1984, he was created a cardinal, to the great joy of the Nigerian nation. He set to work immediately with his usual determination and hard work.

He started his duties with a reasonable familiarity with Islam in his native Nigeria. What has rarely been appreciated was that he brought an important dimension into Christian-Muslim relations from his Nigerian experience. In Nigeria, Islam is neither a majority nor a minority religion. Christians and Muslims have roughly equal numerical strength. It is therefore a special place for both religions to work for equality and mutual respect. He brought this idea strongly into the work of the council that he headed.

Although Islam is his largest concern, his office covers all religions except Judaism, which has a separate office within the Council for Promoting Christian Unity. He reached out to Muslims all over the world and got to know them very well. He also expanded to the other world religions, especially the so-called great religions of the East: Hinduism, Buddhism, and Shintoism. He covered thousands of kilometers traveling around the world to meet these religious communities.

An area in which Arinze made a major impact in his council was in the recognition of the African traditional religions as communities that deserved to be respected like other religions. His council sent out a very important document on this matter.

One of his first and most important tasks upon taking office was to organize the first Assisi Meeting in 1986, to which over 150 religious leaders from at least fifteen faiths were invited to pray with the pope for peace. Among them was a Voodoo priest from the Republic of Benin, much to the delight of many Africans. This was obviously an event for which the pope himself called and over which he presided. That tradition has continued annually, even after both Pope John Paul II and Cardinal Arinze left their positions. We must acknowledge the great contribution of the Sant'Egidio Community in taking care of the logistics for this meeting annually. While most people speak well of this initiative, there are a few who criticize it as going too far, putting all religions on the same level. Neither the pope nor the cardinal takes this criticism seriously. I remember once Cardinal Arinze replied to them in his humorous style: "We went to Assisi together to pray. We did not go to Assisi to pray together." I am not sure this answers their query, but the distinction is valid.

In all that he did as president of the council, Cardinal Arinze was very much a Pope John Paul II man. The pope trusted him and relied on him to organize his own many encounters with leaders of other faiths, whether in their various countries or on their many visits to the Vatican.

On October 1, 2002, Pope John Paul II transferred and promoted Cardinal Arinze to head the Congregation for Divine Worship and the Discipline of the Sacraments, an exalted position that he held firmly with deep commitment and loyalty to the pope until 2008, when he retired for reasons of age. In that office that deals very much with the inner life of the Church, Cardinal Arinze did not forget his experience and the lessons he learned in his many years of service at the Council for Interreligious Dialogue.

Arinze and My Interfaith Experience

I started my episcopal service in 1983 as auxiliary bishop of Ilorin. Two years later, in 1985, I was appointed the substantive bishop of Ilorin. The city is famous as a bulwark of Islam in Yorubaland. The bishop of Ilorin cannot but be involved in interfaith efforts with his overwhelmingly Muslim neighbours. I encountered a lot of deep-seated distrust and quarrels over many unimportant issues between the two communities. I had previously engaged in theoretical dialogue with Muslim scholars at the academic level; I therefore decided to try out dialogue on the practical level. I found out that with some effort of good will, a lot could be achieved to improve relations.

It was at this time that I received a call from Cardinal Arinze from Rome, suggesting I get involved with an organization that was then called the World Conference of Religions for Peace (WCRP). I attended their General Assembly, officially opened in the Synod Hall in the Vatican, with Pope John Paul II in attendance and Cardinal Arinze organizing behind the scenes. Since then, I have been very much involved with this interfaith organization, now with the simpler name Religions for Peace (RfP). Through the RfP, I have learned much about interfaith dialogue and shared the same with many people in my country Nigeria. I have also met many very important and great men and women of faith, including our hero Rabbi David Rosen, with whom I have gained precious friendship and shared experiences.

Conclusion

I know that Cardinal Arinze has encountered Rabbi Rosen over the years. They have a lot in common, in terms of a sharp intellect, a deep faith, and warm human relations. I am glad to bring up the figure of Cardinal Arinze in this publication in honor of Rabbi Rosen.

It is on record that on October 24, 1999, Cardinal Arinze received the gold medallion from the International Council of Christians and Jews for his "outstanding achievements in inter-faith relations." I don't know if Rabbi Rosen had a hand in this honor. But I am convinced that the Rabbi himself, who already has a papal honor, deserves such a gold medallion for his own "outstanding achievements in inter-faith relations." May God continue to bless them both.

Cardinal Joseph Bernardin[175]

PROF. JOHN PAWLIKOWSKI

CARDINAL JOSEPH BERNARDIN BEGAN his ministerial service in the Catholic Church in Charleston, South Carolina, in the US. He eventually became the general secretary of the United States Conference of Catholic Bishops. As general secretary, he gave his support to the development of ecumenical and interreligious activities in light of Vatican II. In 1972, he was appointed the archbishop of Cincinnati, Ohio. It was here that he began to show promising leadership in the implementation of Vatican II's new perspectives on ecumenical and interreligious relations, primarily in dialogue with the Jewish community. The archdiocese rapidly became known as a leader within the American church with regard to ecumenical relations and Catholic-Jewish dialogue. Cardinal Bernardin served the Cincinnati Archdiocese until 1982. In 1982, he was appointed archbishop of Chicago, one of the largest dioceses in the United States. It was during his time in Chicago that he quickly acquired a reputation for the promotion and implementation of the major ecumenical and interreligious documents generated by the Second Vatican Council. His local reputation in this regard quickly spread to national recognition in this area within the American church as a whole and was recognized at the Vatican. When Cardinal Edward Idris Cassidy, in his capacity as president of the Pontifical Office for Promoting Christian Unity and its special Commission for Religious Relations with the Jews, visited Chicago for an address at the Catholic Theological Union, he proclaimed Chicago to be a model diocese for the implementation of ecumenical relations with other Christian churches, as well for the promotion of constructive Catholic-Jewish relations.

Soon after his arrival in Chicago, Cardinal Bernardin turned his attention to the implementation of the vision of Vatican II's *Nostra aetate* throughout the archdiocese. He opened and sustained a rich dialogue, both publicly and privately, within the Jewish lay and rabbinic leadership in the metropolitan region. He supported programs on ecumenical and interreligious relations within the large Catholic school system in the archdiocese. When the State of Illinois passed a mandate on Holocaust education, Bernardin made Holocaust education a priority in Catholic schools as well.

Soon after Cardinal Bernardin's arrival in Chicago, I began working with him, specifically with regard to his strong interest in Catholic-Jewish relations in light of Vatican II. He gladly responded to numerous invitations to speak at synagogues and to Jewish organizations in the Chicago area. Eventually, the invitation list expanded, as he was asked to address national and interreligious meetings in this area.

Working with the cardinal on his addresses for these various meetings gave me a good window on his basic approach to dialogue. Cardinal Bernardin was quite comfortable delivering a well-crafted theological presentation. In fact, he was rather meticulous in his preparation for such an address. I recall one occasion, when he was asked to present a formal response to a paper by the late Rabbi Byron Sherwin of the Spertus Institute in Chicago. I was on the road at the time. The cardinal made a valiant effort to reach me, so that he could discuss how to react to Rabbi Sherwin's contention in his pre-presentation text that Jesus should not be regarded as a false Messiah by Jews but rather as a failed Messiah. The cardinal was unsure as to how to react to this assertion by Dr. Sherwin. This was only one small example of a constant trait in his interreligious outreach. He felt an obligation to fully understand this provocative statement by Rabbi Sherwin prior to responding to the argument in a public setting. Here, Cardinal Bernardin was honoring the Vatican injunction in the 1974 statement celebrating the tenth anniversary of the Vatican Council's declaration on the Jews, that Catholics should come to understand Jews as they define themselves. This effort to reach me for clarification on Rabbi Sherman's perspective impressed on me an image of the cardinal as a person who felt that accurate understanding of the other was central to any realistic and authentic approach to interreligious dialogue.

In my years of working with Cardinal Bernardin on Catholic-Jewish issues, I came to recognize another essential component of successful dialogue and outreach to another faith community. That was the centrality of deep personal relationships. On the ecumenical front, he developed a very close working and personal relationship with two of his counterparts in Christian religious leadership in the metropolitan area. The presiding bishops at the time in the Episcopal and Lutheran communities became close personal friends, as well as consistent collaborators in religious outreach to the Chicago area society. This mindset led the cardinal to eventually co-found the first ever official leadership organization in Chicago for societal outreach. The Council of Religious Leaders of Metropolitan Chicago championed by the cardinal was instrumental in adding a religious voice to many of the critical issues facing the Chicago region.

Cardinal Bernardin's vision for the metropolitan leadership group went beyond the limits of inter-Christian collaboration. He reached out to a prominent rabbinic leader, Rabbi Herman Schaalman. Their collaboration eventually evolved into a deep spiritual friendship. They became true soulmates over the years. This is a further illustration of the high regard Cardinal Bernardin placed on human friendship and spiritual sharing as core elements in interreligious dialogue.

These personal characteristics of Cardinal Bernardin were clearly visible during an interreligious trip he led to Israel and Palestine. This journey took on a high profile in the Chicago media and became a time of significant spiritual experience for those of us who accompanied the cardinal in visits with religious and political leaders in the region. The joint visit to the Holy Sepulchre where the Cardinal presided at a special Eucharistic liturgy, the celebration of a Shabbat meal together, the walk of the entire delegation down the Via Dolorosa in Jerusalem became moments of profound spiritual sharing that built lasting bonds among the Catholic and Jewish participants. They also became teaching moments back in Chicago, as the major television stations provided extensive coverage of the trip during their nightly newscasts.

Through his ministry of public witness and effective collaboration throughout his tenure in Chicago, Bernardin created a model of how a particular diocese could implement the new interreligious vision generated at Vatican II. It was the basis for the previously mentioned remark by Cardinal Cassidy of the Vatican that Chicago had truly become a model for the concrete implementation of the Church's new thinking about its relations with Jews and Judaism. Another recognition of the high regard in which Cardinal Bernardin was held in Chicago came at the time of his death and funeral. During the time he was lying in state at Holy Name Cathedral, the Jewish leadership of the city cooperated with the Archdiocese of Chicago in an unprecedented ritual celebration of the cardinal's life and accomplishments. This high honor was recognized by both ordinary Jews and Catholics. The attendance at the celebration was so large that the fire marshal ordered the doors of the cathedral to be locked to prevent overcapacity. Many of the people who had accompanied the cardinal on the memorable journey to Israel/Palestine joined in the final tribute to this great interreligious leader.

During his time as a religious leader in metropolitan Chicago, Cardinal Bernardin spoke to many of the important theological and social issues of the day. A collection of his many addresses was published by the Chicago- based Liturgy Training Publications under the title *A Blessing to*

Each Other: Cardinal Joseph Bernardin and Jewish-Catholic Dialogue.[176] The volume was presented to the cardinal's sister during the ritual event at the time of his funeral.

Cardinal Bernardin maintained a full schedule of speaking engagements while continuing his ministry to the Archdiocese of Chicago. The collection of his writings published upon his death, cited above, provides eloquent testimony to his public influence. Addresses on the Catholic-Jewish relationship (with implications for the encounter with other faith communities) demonstrate his significant contributions to public theology. In the area of Catholic-Jewish relations, the cardinal spoke to the continuing disease of anti-Semitism, to the implications of the Holocaust for the Church and human society, and the theological ramifications for Christian self-understanding that have arisen from the profound turnabout in the understanding of the Church's relationship with Judaism and the Jewish people. Without quoting him directly, Cardinal Bernardin, particularly in a 1988 address delivered at the University of St. Thomas in St. Paul, Minnesota, echoed the statement made by Canadian theologian Gregory Baum (an official expert at Vatican II and involved with the very early stages of section 4 of *Nostra aetate*). Baum had stated at a meeting of the Catholic Theological Society of America that section 4 of this declaration represented the most profound change in the ordinary magisterium of the Church to emerge from the Council.

Regarding the Holocaust, the cardinal spoke of its implications at Emmanuel Congregation in Chicago, where his close friend Rabbi Schaalman ministered for many years, and very poignantly at the national memorial to the Holocaust in Israel while on the interreligious delegation's visit. His remarks on the latter occasion were made inside the special building honoring the more than one million children who perished at the hands of the Nazis. Those in presence there, myself included, could see how visibly moved he was by this memorial.

Cardinal Bernardin also brought contemporary issues into the dialogue with Jews in such areas as religion and power at the 1990 National Workshop on Christian-Jewish Relations in Chicago and on the topic of creational responsibility at the 1992 meeting of the official dialogue of the Vatican and international Jewish leadership in Baltimore. Bernardin was prophetic in raising the issue of the necessary care for creation in that speech well before it became a widespread issue. This brings him into a significant link with Rabbi David Rosen, who has become a passionate advocate for the urgent need to address climate change on the part of religious communities.

The centerpiece of Cardinal Bernardin's many addresses came at the Hebrew University in Jerusalem, while with the Catholic-Jewish visiting delegation of Chicago. His focal point in that memorable 1995 speech was anti-Semitism. Once again, he was on target in terms of the concrete realities still confronting the Catholic-Jewish dialogue. His speech is commemorated yearly since then in the Archdiocese of Chicago with a public lecture, extending his contribution to the present day.

As we recall Cardinal Bernardin's record as an interreligious giant, we see how closely it dovetails with the life and work of Rabbi Rosen, celebrated in this volume. Certainly on issues such as creational responsibility and the continuing challenge of anti-Semitism, the two leaders' wavelengths coincided. While somewhat more reserved in terms of personality than Rabbi Rosen, both have exhibited a shared passionate concern for human dignity and human responsibility for planetary survival. It has been a personal privilege to have worked with them over the years.

Revisiting Theological Foundations

Rabbi Irving Yitz Greenberg[177]

Shmuly Yanklowitz

HAVING BEEN RAISED IN an interfaith home, I arrived in the rabbinate with deep sensitivities toward religious pluralism. I felt alone, though. I didn't see models of teachers who shared my robust Jewish fervor yet also my religious pluralism. It seemed, at times, that one must either be a religious fundamentalist or leave passionate religious discipline altogether—that is, until I stumbled upon the writings (and later the very close mentorship) of Rav Yitz.

Undoubtedly, Rabbi Dr. Irving "Yitz" Greenberg is one of the most significant voices in our time. His years of service in the rabbinate as organizational leader, author, lecturer, and longtime activist for a multitude of spiritual causes have been responsible for spreading Jewish values across the spectrum of other religious traditions and cultures. Rav Yitz is this generation's consummate bridge builder: He constructs bridges within the Jewish community, as well as between different faiths and over the vast gulf that separates tradition and modernity. While committed to Orthodoxy, Rav Yitz has made great contributions across all of Jewish life, always remaining rooted within a forward-looking *halakhic* observance. He is that rare pedagogue who has demonstrated the relevance of a modern Judaism while assembling and nurturing the vibrant Jewish institutional landscape that we know today.

Rav Yitz's preeminence in Torah thought is but a minor aspect of his larger role in shaping contemporary Jewish attitudes towards the entire world. From the time he was ordained at Beth Joseph (Novaredok) Rabbinical Seminary and earned a PhD in American history at Harvard University in the 1950s, to his tenure as a professional in stimulating the Jewish community, Rav Yitz has been a tireless proponent of a more engaged Judaism.

I appreciate his contributions both to social justice and to interfaith dialogue: his advancement of Jewish ethics on a global level; his expansion of modern conceptions of *tzelem Elokim*, theology, and *tikkun olam* values; and the clarity and accessibility he has brought to epistemic pluralism. In some cases, the two values of social justice and pluralism come together:

> The only way to wholeness is to heal the world and to work to take the poison out of absolutism without eroding all values and truth in the process. Post-Shoah [Post-Holocaust], the yearning for perfecting finitude, properly harnessed, can fuel the drive for *tikkun olam* (mending the world), politically and economically as well as religiously and philosophically.[178]

Rav Yitz has never been merely an armchair philosopher. He has lived a life committed to serving and advocating for public service. For him, there is no worthy task without personal involvement and heavy lifting. Moreover, Rav Yitz has a unified vision of the Jewish people. We Jews have a unique ethical, religious, and moral obligation to serve our communities, and thus we must be active participants in building a more just society:

> Personal service must be brought to the fore as a central value of Jewish traditionand culture. Every synagogue, school, and organization must teach this norm. Even unaffiliated Jews recognize education and family as synonymous with Jewish values: so should personal service become known as the indispensable expression of Jewishness . . . .
>
> A Jew is commanded not just to do individual acts of *chesed* (kindness) to others but to set aside regular time for volunteering and giving personal service. What is the minimum number of hours a week, a month, or a year that one must dedicate to nurturing the equality and uniqueness of other human beings? We must create a Jewish culture in which the final measurement of "was this life worthwhile" will be: Did one set aside regular times for nurturing other human beings?[179]

We must not be confused. This is not watered down Judaism nor is it "Judaism lite." It is, rather, an expansive conception of Jewish action in the world. This approach demands rejecting mindless relativism, instead encouraging respectful and empowered pluralism. One teaching from Rabbi Greenberg has always stayed with me. It goes like this:

Pluralism means more than accepting or even affirming the other. It entails recognizing the blessings in the other's existence, because it balances one's own position and brings all of us closer to the ultimate goal. Even when we are right in our own position, the other who contradicts our position may be our corrective or our check against going to excess.[180]

There is humility found in this pluralism, an acknowledgement that we cannot see the full picture ourselves. We need others to complete the vision, even those who are different from us in temperament and persuasion and with whom we disagree. Only when we open our hearts to all valid views of the world can we learn from all. Rav Yitz continues:

> The essential difference between pluralism and relativism is that pluralism is based on the principle that there still is an absolute truth. . . . Pluralism is an absolutism that has come to recognize its limitations.[181]

In his understanding of Judaism, pluralism is the ideal, while narrow particularism must be eschewed as a remnant from earlier, more precarious times. Rodger Kamenetz's book *The Jew in the Lotus* contains perhaps the most succinct summation concerning Rav Yitz's concern for expanding the vocabulary of Jewish social action: "There was no question in [Rabbi Greenberg's] mind that Judaism takes place in real history and that Jews had to learn from other cultures . . . . [He] was particularly concerned that Orthodox Jewish culture had withdrawn into itself, shunning contact with the challenge of pluralism."[182]

The concept that human beings are created *b'tzelem Elokim* (in the image of God) is the foundation of Rav Yitz's theology. He explains that this principle implies that humans are endowed by God with three intrinsic and ineradicable qualities: infinite value, equality, and uniqueness. His proof text for this is the Mishnah found in Sanhedrin 37a. For Rav Yitz, this is not an abstract truth relegated to a certain human experience but a living truth that must permeate our existence. He writes:

> The principles of human infinite value, equality, and uniqueness not only regulate the realm of society and collective behavior. They are equally the ethical principles that are meant to govern all human relationships.[183]

We are able to actualize our human potential filled with dignity only because God has engaged in *tzimtzum* (giving space to humans to exercise free will). Our covenant with God and our partnership with the Divine make a difference, because every person has a different, unique role to play in repairing the world. *Tzelem Elokim* theology tells us not only about the essence of humanity but also about God, which we can discern from studying the Holocaust and its ramifications:

> After the Shoah (Holocaust), the value of *Tzelem Elokim*—of nurturing the infinite value, equality, and uniqueness of every person—is crucial. Such confirmation is the only credible statement about God one can really make. This is the true glorification of God in an age when God is profoundly hidden, in a time

where there has been a serious assault on the credibility of faith because of the great destruction of human life.[184]

Rav Yitz's teachings were for our times—for the twentieth and now the twenty-first centuries. He grounded his teachings in a world where God's presence may be less obvious. In the world today, God is hidden. We do not witness divine providence (*hashgachah*) the way some used to. We can only look back at God's action in history. "God now acts primarily, at least on the visible level, through human activity—as is appropriate in a partnership whose human participant is growing up."[185] Although God does not act for us, we feel God's closeness:

> *Hashgachah* means that God is with us; God is interested in and concerned about every detail of our lives. There is not a moment in life that is cut off from God. But *hashgachah* is not to be interpreted as meaning that God is doing the fighting and, therefore, is guaranteeing the outcome for us.[186]

In this situation, he taught that our human responsibility is greater than ever, as God continues to retract from participation in this world. We no longer look toward the heavens to find divine intervention, rather to the divine image for human solidarity in fulfilling our covenantal mission.

Commitment to channeling the Divine into the mundane arenas of the world extends from the interpersonal realm to politics as well. That *tzelem Elokim* theology translates into political advocacy is a uniquely Greenbergian innovation:

> The definition of the state of *tikkun olam*—the arrival of the messianic kingdom—is when the actual legal, political, social institutions in the world will be structured so that each human being will be sustained and treated as if he or she is an image of God. The world must become rich enough to spend an unlimited amount of money to save one life. The world must be reorganized so that there cannot be systematized degradation or discrimination against people; there must be no inferiority imposed by law or by practice.[187]

Part of what, theologically, enables us to truly encounter another with the full dignity of that one's faith commitments is holding some skepticism in our own. That is to say that we must not check our religious fervor at the door, but we must check our fundamentalism at the door.

Only in the modern world, observed Rabbi Greenberg, have Jews been able to participate fully in shaping their own attitudes towards others and in interfaith dialogue. No longer subservient to the Church, as in medieval times, or living in a state of fear of their neighbours, Jews today choose both to be Jews and how they relate to other religions. Rav Yitz famously and most controversially writes about the voluntary covenant:

> As long as the covenant was involuntary, it could be imposed from above in a unitary way . . . . In the new era, the voluntary covenant is the theological base of a genuine pluralism . . . . [This] is a recognition that all Jews have chosen to make the fundamental Jewish statement at great personal risk and cost.[188]

We can experience, with more humility than ever perhaps, just how wide the gap is between God's word and our knowing minds. In building interfaith bridges, we not only tie our fate more connectedly to other groups, but we also liberate ourselves in our self-determination. For centuries, Jews defined themselves as those who clung to the covenant in the face of the error or sin of so many who turned to Christianity. Rabbi Greenberg observes:

> In defining Judaism by negating Christianity, Jews paradoxically were being controlled by the very religion to which they were so antagonistic.[189]

This is not only about liberation but about humility.

> Of course, one cannot write a truly theocentric perspective; in the end, we are human and not G-D. We are locked up in our mortal bodies, embedded in our socio-economic-cultural contexts, which filter our received evidence and shape our interpretative schema.[190]

The opportunity to engage in interfaith bridge building is increasingly present, because of

> what I would call the universalization of culture. This means the extraordinary capacity of modern culture to communicate, i.e., the extraordinary openness of the cultural medium in which we live. It has thrown us together and by exposure and involvement has made us part of each other's consciousness.[191]

We have redefined self. In modernity, the self was autonomous, individual, and separate. In postmodernity, the self is connected, fluid, and mixed with less distinct boundaries. Rav Yitz demands the best of us. We cannot just preach *tikkun olam*, but, rather, we must put our hands in mud. Furthermore, as religious people, this is the dream that we must work toward each day:

Tikkun olam, then, is the process whereby humans transform the world or improve it to the point where it truly sustains each image of God in appropriate dignity. Part of the process involves upgrading the economy. If the world is poor, it cannot support people at the needed level of dignity. Similarly, to reach the messianic stage, humans have to overcome war because wars take lives; armies kill and waste images of God. If the society, by law, opposes equality, then there will be no equality. If people are equal, then every vote should count just as much as every other. This is what democracy is all about.[192]

Today, more than ever, we need to learn from his teachings and modeling on interfaith dialogue and partnership. It seems that more than ever human affairs are undergoing a breakdown in community, respect, and civil discourse. Many prefer a retreat into solitude rather than engaging with others who are different from them. The process of othering based upon gender, sexual orientation, race, nationality, and religion is now rampant. In Orthodoxy, tribalism—and a political slide to the far right in America and in Israel—creates more distance from our neighbors.

Rabbi Greenberg warns us that othering is the dehumanizing of people created in the divine image. Many try to fuel nightmare narratives by insisting that the others are coming for us and that they are taking over. This was done toward Jews fleeing the Holocaust and is done today toward Muslim refugees fleeing from Syria, toward people of color, toward immigrants in America, and toward the Arab minority in Israel. How can we collectively ensure that all adult citizens come to value plurality, complexity, and difference? Rav Yitz offers a way with his emphasis on education.

We owe sincere gratitude to Rav Yitz for helping the Jewish people deal with the complexities of the twenty-first century. He has woven together a theology of pluralism with an ethics of *tzelem Elokim*, an epistemology of skepticism, and a passionate religious worldview. His contribution is not unidimensional; it is interwoven. He truly believes in fostering a discourse that is morally fervent yet also leaves room for the other. This is true on the interpersonal level, the familial level, tribal-communal level, and the global interfaith scene. He models the best practices on all fronts. I am forever grateful for him and his mentorship.

It is a great honor to reflect on the legacy of my dear teacher Rabbi Dr. Yitz Greenberg. What makes it even more delightful is to write this essay in honor of another teacher, Rabbi Dr. David Rosen. Rabbi Rosen has, for me and so many others, been a great model of scholarship and *Menschlichkeit* (humanity). I have watched his global leadership closely and continue to be in awe of how far-reaching his impact is and how deep is the content he provides. He is the top ambassador for the Jewish people around the world, representing Jewish values and the Jewish people. Rabbi Rosen does not need to write the books that Rav Yitz needed to write to make the early case for why this work matters. He can simply live it and take its importance for granted. His coupling of interreligious dialogue, along with paying attention to pressing social justice issues (climate change, warfare, intolerance, animal abuse, human rights, etc.), is a model for an integrated model of service and realizing a deep Jewish vocation. And may I add on a final personal note: it has always meant a lot to me that Rav Yitz is a vegetarian and Rav David a vegan. This demonstrates their spiritual sensitivity toward suffering and how their mercy, like God's, extends toward all life.

Abdurrahman Wahid

KH. Yahya Cholil Staquf

Abdurrahman Wahid and Interreligious Relations

IN A 2007 *WALL Street Journal* article titled "The Last King of Java," Pulitzer Prize-winning American journalist Bret Stephens described Abdurrahman Wahid as "the single most influential religious leader in the Muslim world" and "easily the most important ally the West has in the ideological struggle against Islamic radicalism."[193]

Popularly known as Gus Dur, Abdurrahman Wahid (1940–2009) was and remains one of the most influential religious and political figures in modern Indonesian history. In 1926, his paternal and maternal grandfathers established Nahdlatul Ulama (NU)—the world's largest Muslim organization—in direct response to the Wahhabi conquest of Mecca and Medina.

Gus Dur mastered a wide array of classical Islamic disciplines at a young age, studying with many of Indonesia's preeminent Muslim scholars. He went on to attend Cairo's Al-Azhar University and the University of Baghdad in the 1960s. What Wahid experienced in Iraq, and how it affected his subsequent life, was described in an article the Jewish Telegraphic Agency (JTA) published in 2008:

> In its telling, the story of a notorious lynching of Jews is not unusual. The storyteller, however, is: Abdurrahman Wahid, the former Indonesian president, and a leading Muslim scholar, visiting the U.S. to preach his message of Muslim tolerance, revealed the root of his understanding of the risks and perils of Jewish existence.[194]

Wahid was a twenty-nine-year-old student at Baghdad University in 1966, earning his keep as a secretary at a textile importer, when he befriended the firm's elderly accountant, an Iraqi Jew he remembers only by his family name, Ramin. "I learned from him about the Kabbalah, the Talmud, everything about Judaism," Wahid recalled of the four-year friendship that included long lunches, quiet walks, and talks at the city's legendary Hanging Gardens.

In 1968, the Iraqi government effectively had come under the control of Saddam Hussein, whose title at that time was deputy to the president, Ahmad Hassan al-Bakr.

At Saddam's behest, Iraqi courts had convicted fourteen Iraqis—nine of them Jews—on trumped-up charges of spying for Israel, and they were hanged that day in Baghdad's Tahrir Square, just steps away from where the textile firm had offices.

Ramin came to his friend Wahid and wept, wondering what would become of Iraq's ancient Jewish community. "I said, 'This is not only your fate, it is my fate,'" said Wahid, now frail and in a wheelchair. Wahid said he decided then that "the Islamic people should learn" about the Jews and their faith.

Ramin's worst fears were realized: the community that dated to the Babylonian exile heard Saddam's message loud and clear, and by the early 1970s it had dwindled to barely a hundred Jews. By 2007, there were fewer than ten, according to media accounts.

His voice quavering with emotion as he spoke forty years after these tragic events, President Wahid told an audience of over 900, including many of Hollywood's elite, that he had never forgotten his promise to Ramin. The occasion was a Simon Wiesenthal Center tribute dinner at the Beverly Wilshire Hotel in Southern California, held in President Wahid's honor.

Abdurrahman Wahid "made good on his pledge" to his Jewish friend, the JTA article continued. "The apex of this effort, conducted jointly with the LibForAll Foundation, a group that promotes moderate Islam, and the Simon Wiesenthal Center, was the Holocaust conference last year in Bali, Indonesia." During the conference, President Wahid issued a firm repudiation—which was broadcast and reported worldwide—of Mahmoud Ahmadinejad's Holocaust denial. Gus Dur also wrote an op-ed that the *Wall Street Journal* published on the day of the conference. Co-authored by former chief rabbi of Israel and child Holocaust survivor Israel Meir Lau, the op-ed called upon the world's religious leaders to "not only refute the claims of terrorists and their ideological enablers, but also defend the rights of others to worship differently," and "face up frankly to the evils of Holocaust denial."[195]

While serving as general chairman of the Nahdlatul Ulama Executive Board from 1984 to 1999, Gus Dur strove to renew (i.e., reform) Islamic discourse and thereby ensure that Islamic teachings and practice embody what he and Nahdlatul Ulama regard as the primary message of Islam, namely, *rahmah* (universal love and compassion). In the words of his *New York*

Times obituary, Wahid was "the single most important figure not merely in Indonesia's transition from Suharto's centralized autocracy to a decentralized democracy but in ensuring that the new democracy was committed to religious and ethnic pluralism."[196]

In 1992—at a national gathering of religious scholars held in Lampung, under the leadership of HE Kyai Haji Abdurrahman Wahid—the NU explicitly acknowledged that the changing context of reality necessitates the creation of new interpretations of Islamic law and orthodox Islamic teaching. At this same congress, the NU issued a formal decree stating that if the Muslim community cannot find individuals who meet the exacting criteria of a *mujtahid* (one qualified to exercise independent reasoning to create Islamic law), then *ulama* (scholars of Islam) must assume the burden of responsibility and perform collective *ijtihad* (the use of independent reasoning to formulate Islamic law), which is called *al-istinbath al-jama'iy*. *Ulama* have endowed the Indonesian nation state (NKRI) with profound theological legitimacy by advancing a number of strong religious arguments in its favor. The theological rationale that Indonesian *ulama* employed to legitimize NKRI was the product of new *ijtihad*, which cannot be found within the authoritative texts of *fiqh* from the canon of classical Islamic thought. Moreover, this new *ijtihad* succeeded at securing the support of an overwhelming majority of Indonesian Muslims, while simultaneously helping to shape their religious views and mentality.

During his brief term as Indonesia's fourth president (1999 to 2001), Wahid restored civilian control of the military, eliminated the army's role in politics after thirty-two years of dictatorship, implemented regional autonomy and the establishment of Indonesia's anti-corruption agency, restored civil and political liberties to Indonesia's ethnic Chinese population, and preserved the political foundation of Indonesia as a multireligious and pluralistic nation-state in the face of serious challenges posed by Muslim extremists and their opportunistic political allies.

Gus Dur's friendship with Jewish leaders continued after he was no longer in office. In 2003, he visited Israel and signed a public declaration, along with the Sephardic chief rabbi of Israel, Eliyahu Bakshi-Doron, titled *Combating Terrorism*. In their joint declaration, President Wahid and Rabbi Bakshi-Doron stated that God is "merciful and compassionate and calls upon us to be compassionate and merciful accordingly. Causing suffering in the name of God is opposed to the will of God. We affirm the highest religious value to be the sanctity of human life."[197]

President Wahid's idealism also found expression in his commitment to engage in interreligious dialogue across all traditions, not only the Abrahamic faiths. Serving as the Elijah Institute's Muslim convener, President Wahid invited other prominent Muslim figures to join the Elijah Board of World Religious Leaders, thereby launching this important international interreligious body, with which the author of the present essay is also affiliated.

Gus Dur defended religious minorities throughout his life and, in moments of crisis, took decisive, timely action to deter violence and uphold the Republic of Indonesia's unique brand of inclusive, multireligious, and multiethnic nationalism. Writing in the *Boston Globe*, Jeff Jacoby observed:

> There is no doubting Wahid's commitment to interfaith harmony. He tells Indonesian Muslims that they can learn from Christianity and Christian life, and has dispatched armed members of Nadhlatul Ulama to protect Christian churches from Islamist violence. Not long ago, one of Wahid's Muslim adherents was killed when he discovered a bomb in a church and used his body to shield the Christian worshipers from its blast. That stunning act of selflessness is a powerful reminder that Muslims no less than non-Muslims have a great deal riding on the defeat of the Islamofascists, and that we will not win the war against radical Islam without Muslim allies like Wahid.[198]

President Wahid's wisdom continues to shape Indonesian society more than a decade after his death, and many of his sayings have become virtual proverbs. Nearly every Indonesian is familiar with Gus Dur's pithy statement "*Tuhan tak perlu dibela*" (God needs no defense). The same is true of a phrase—"*Gitu saja kok repot*" (That's just how it is: no problem)—which he often used to calm or prevent public disturbances, by encouraging the acceptance of cultural and religious differences as an expression of divine will. For as Gus Dur often said, "The greater a person's knowledge of religion, the greater his tolerance. The primary message of religion is one of peace, while extremists behave as if the opposite were true. We need a loving and compassionate Islam, not an Islam full of anger."

As President Wahid explained in his introduction to the massively influential book *Ilusi Negara Islam* (*The Illusion of an Islamic State*):

> People who are convinced that they know more than anyone else about Islam, and yet are full of hatred towards any of God's creatures who do not travel the same path with them; and those who claim themselves to be in possession of the absolute truth, and for that reason entitled to act as God's vice regents on earth (caliphs) and to dictate how everyone else must live—clearly, their words and behavior will not lead us into the presence of God. Their dream of an Islamic state is merely an illusion, for the true Islamic state is not to be found

in the structure of any government, but rather, in hearts which are open to God and all His creatures.[199]

Continuing Gus Dur's Legacy

I had the privilege to serve as Gus Dur's presidential spokesman. My uncle, Kyai Haji Mustofa Bisri, was Gus Dur's best friend. My great-grandfather, Kyai Haji Cholil Harun, established Nahdlatul Ulama with Gus Dur's grandparents. For fifteen years, I lived at Pondok Pesantren al-Munawwir Krapyak, an Islamic boarding school in Yogyakarta, Indonesia, and studied with Gus Dur's own spiritual master, the revered Islamic scholar and chairman of the NU Supreme Council, Kyai Haji Ali Maksum (1915–1989).

Afterwards, I moved to Jakarta and, at Gus Dur's direction, helped coordinate the establishment of what soon became Indonesia's largest Islamic political party, PKB, which was founded in 1998 by senior NU leaders, including Wahid and Mustofa Bisri. At Gus Dur's behest, I also served as one of the first members of Indonesia's newly established Commission for General Elections (*Komisi Pemilihan Umum*, or KPU). Much to my regret at the time, Gus Dur—the chairman of PKB, which served as the political vehicle for his ascent to the presidency—forbade me from assuming any kind of political office. Although I could not then fathom his reasoning, in retrospect I consider this to have been an enormous blessing.

Knowing and working with Gus Dur completely changed my life. It would be fair to say that I was a typical conservative Muslim before I met Gus Dur and took his teachings to heart. The manner in which he taught and thereby shaped his disciples involved far more than rigorous intellectual exchange. Rather, I experienced a direct spiritual connection with Gus Dur, through which he deliberately and systematically transformed me.

Through this process, I developed a far more comprehensive understanding of my own previous masters, including Kyai Ali Maksum, my father, my uncle Mustofa Bisri, and others. Thanks to Gus Dur, I learned to see, not just cognitively but also spiritually, that they had risen to the same exalted station (*maqam*) as Gus Dur. They were all friends of God, or saints (*awliya'*). Their primary motive, in every action, was to serve the truth and foster the well-being of humanity, by recognizing and submitting to God's will.

In 2004, my father, Kyai Haji Cholil Bisri, passed away, and I returned to the small town of Rembang in north-central Java to run our family *pesantren*, or Islamic boarding school. In December of 2009, Gus Dur himself, to use a phrase he once laughingly employed, "vanished from the face of the earth," but not before setting in motion a grand strategy to realize

Indonesia's potential as an engine of spiritual progress for all humanity. In 2010, I joined two of Gus Dur's close friends—Mustofa Bisri and C. Holland Taylor—in this effort, which subsequently gave rise to the Humanitarian Islam movement and the Center for Shared Civilizational Values.

Inspired by Gus Dur and alarmed by the threat that a resurgent Islamist current poses to the unity of Indonesia and its people—and to the future of humanity as a whole—the spiritual leadership of NU has launched a long-term, systematic, and institutional campaign to reform what we have not hesitated to describe as "obsolete and problematic tenets of Islamic orthodoxy." These tenets—including the religious obligation to establish a caliphate, wage war against infidels, and consign religious minorities to a subordinate status—are still taught by most orthodox Sunni and Shi'ite institutions worldwide as authoritative and correct. Needless to say, these tenets readily lend themselves to political weaponization by enjoining religious hatred, supremacy, and violence.[200]

Acting under the authority of Kyai Haji Achmad Mustofa Bisri ("Gus Mus")—then chairman of the Nahdlatul Ulama Supreme Council—in 2014, we launched the *Islam Nusantara* (East Indies Islam) movement to counter the threat posed by Islamist extremism in Indonesia. The term *Islam Nusantara* describes indigenous forms of Islam, practiced by the vast majority of Indonesians, which are deeply rooted within South and Southeast Asia's ancient traditions of spirituality, religious pluralism, and tolerance. This campaign, publicly endorsed by President Jokowi, helped to re-enliven Indonesians' appreciation of their distinct civilizational heritage and rally Muslims across Indonesia's vast archipelago against Islamism at a time when the Islamic State, or ISIS, was wreaking havoc across the Middle East.

In recent years, Humanitarian Islam leaders have drafted a series of historic declarations that were adopted by Nahdlatul Ulama and/or Gerakan Pemuda Ansor, the NU's five-million-member young adults movement. NU leaders have also developed—and begun to operationalize—a global strategy to reconcile Islamic teachings with the reality of contemporary civilization, whose context and conditions differ significantly from those in which classical Islamic law emerged.

As a result of these pioneering efforts, a large body of Sunni Muslim authorities are now engaged in a wide-ranging, concerted, and explicit project of theological reform for the first time since the late Middle Ages.

This reform process has attracted the attention and support of major institutions across the globe, which have endorsed the Indonesia-based Humanitarian Islam movement and its efforts to preserve and strengthen a rules-based international order founded upon universal ethics and humanitarian values.

In February of 2019, at a national conference of Nahdlatul Ulama Religious Scholars, over 20,000 NU theologians and their disciples gathered to abolish the legal category of infidel (*kafir*) within the modern nation-state, while simultaneously affirming the theological legitimacy of the nation-state and of laws formulated through modern political processes. Classical *fiqh* prescriptions regarding the treatment of infidels have long been weaponized by Sunni ultra-conservatives to prohibit religious freedom, encourage social vigilantism, and legitimize terrorist acts committed against those perceived to be non-Muslim.

In October of 2020, the Hudson Institute's Center on Islam, Democracy, and the Future of the Muslim World published an in-depth analysis of these efforts, concluding that "Nahdlatul Ulama has emerged as a formidable challenger to powerful state actors in the battle for the soul of Islam . . . . This struggle has and will affect the prospects for the emergence of a truly more tolerant and pluralistic interpretation of one of the three Abrahamic religions."[201]

The Nahdlatul Ulama Supreme Council has closely studied ISIS ideology and behavior. This careful examination of Islamic State propaganda led us to conclude that ISIS systematically draws upon established and authoritative tenets within classical Islamic law (*fiqh*) to justify even its most horrific actions. As a result, it is easy for groups such as ISIS and al-Qaeda to convince many young Muslims that they are implementing the true teachings of religion.

These observations led many of us to a simple and straightforward conclusion: there can be no lasting peace between religions without the recontextualization (i.e., reform) of obsolete and problematic tenets of religious orthodoxy. Saint Pope John XXIII reached an analogous conclusion as a result of the Holocaust, whose horrors spurred the assembled bishops of the Catholic Church to adopt *Nostra aetate* in 1965.

Gus Dur and David Rosen

In 2002, Gus Dur visited the United States and addressed the American Jewish Committee's annual Global Forum. Upon his return to Indonesia, he wrote that a Jewish friend he met at the forum had shared an idea of great significance: efforts to achieve a just and lasting peace between Israelis and Palestinians cannot succeed without incorporating an additional element, namely, religion. The name of this Jewish friend was David Rosen.

Gus Dur told Indonesians that he agreed with his friend and proceeded to elaborate on his idea by stating that religions not only embody the noblest aspirations of humanity, but are also characterized by problematic historical and contemporary dynamics. Unless we address these dynamics, religion will often exacerbate rather than prevent conflict.

In 2018, I too addressed the American Jewish Committee's annual forum. For the first time in AJC's 112-year history, its Global Forum was held in Jerusalem. When I spoke at the opening session, it was in the form of an on-stage discussion with Rabbi Rosen. I told the audience that I was following in the footsteps of President Wahid.

Prior to my visit to Jerusalem, many Indonesians warned of the severe criticism to which I would be subjected by Muslim extremists and their political allies. When deciding whether or not to accept AJC's invitation, I thought of Gus Dur and something he often said, both publicly and privately: "*Selalu jujur dan terbuka; tak perlu takut*" (We should always be honest and open; there's no need to be afraid).

I try to live my life by this principle, which Gus Dur instilled in me. At the conclusion of my discussion with Rabbi Rosen, at the AJC Global Forum in Jerusalem, I said:

> Religion is often used as a weapon. We people of religion have to ask ourselves: is this the proper function of our religion? Or is there a way that religions can function so as to offer a solution to all these conflicts? The way I see it, the way Nahdlatul Ulama sees it, is that all sides need to change.

For as the Qur'an states: "Verily, God will not change the condition of a people until they change what is in their hearts" (Qur'an 13:11).

What is left to us is simply the choice—the very fundamental choice—that can provide us with an opportunity for a solution. It is to choose what, in Islamic terms, we call *rahmah* (universal love and compassion). If we choose *rahmah*, we can begin to talk about justice, because compassion is not about demanding justice for ourselves but about willingness to provide it to others. If people do not have *rahmah*, or compassion for others, they will never be willing to provide justice to others. So if I may use this opportunity to issue a call to the world, it would be this: let us choose *rahmah*. Let us choose compassion.

Fethullah Gülen[202]

Ibrahim Anli

FETHULLAH GÜLEN, AN IMAM and preacher by training, pioneered the first interfaith dialogue initiative of modern Turkey in 1994. The success of this early initiative inspired many individuals in his audience to initiate similar platforms in many countries. The very idea of a Muslim scholar of deep devotion and his predominantly observant Muslim audience engaging with peoples of other traditions had a lasting peace-generating impact in numerous settings across the globe. These efforts prevented aggressive interpretations of Islam from monopolizing the religious discourse within Muslim communities. They also helped to prevent possible intercommunal tensions in a post-9/11 world. Gülen's dialogue is based on a genuine conviction rooted in the Qur'an and the Sunna and is by no means a mere convention. His overall contribution to the global interreligous endeavor can be summarized as a fruitful encounter between Islam's millennia-old Sufi-scholar tradition and the contemporary age.

Foundations

Fethullah Gülen is an imam, preacher, civic leader, and author. Born in 1942 in Turkey's conservative eastern Erzurum province, he spent his formative years within a profoundly observant Muslim family and a social environment where traditional Islamic instruction merged with Sufi teachings. His sermons, written work, and social innovation efforts throughout the last half century culminated in a transnational faith-inspired movement known as Hizmet ("service" in Turkish) that is actively involved in education, interreligious dialogue, and humanitarian relief.

Gülen's story as a preacher begins in the early 1970s in Turkey's coastal city of Izmir, where a totally different urban secular culture shaped the worldview of his audience. By the early 80s, he was already a nationwide figure credited for his moving sermons that attracted an unusually young audience to the mosque. In the meantime, Gülen succeeded in mobilizing a network of educators and business owners to start education initiatives in the form of mentoring centers and dormitories, making university education accessible to underprivileged students from Turkey's conservative periphery. By the beginning of the 90s, this core group had managed to build a nationwide educational network that included some of Turkey's most competitive private schools.

Gülen's education model is a wholistic one that advocates dialogue of faith and reason. "In its true meaning," Gülen argues, "religion does not oppose or limit science or scientific work"[203]—hence these schools' emphasis on character building on the one hand and a science-focused curriculum on the other. Gülen further notes:

> The word of God, which is a ladder of light taking man to God, is manifested in historical form in the Qur'an and the Old and New Testaments. Nature and, on the micro plane, man are manifestations of the will and might of God. Thus, there can be no real conflict between religion and science which examines nature and man.[204]

With the end of the Cold War, this education model became transnational, as Gülen encouraged Hizmet participants to open schools in the post-Soviet countries of the Balkans and Central Asia. The effort was welcomed by the host countries, giving international visibility to a version of Islam that positively engages with modernity, stays away from politics, and emphasizes personal spirituality, while being open to dialogue with others. Thanks to their non-confessional curricula, equal admissions policy, supportive scholarships, and impressive success record, these schools attracted a diverse array of students from all ethnic and religious backgrounds wherever they operated. The schools also contributed to the transition into a free market economy, as their Turkish sponsors expanded their business ventures into these host countries. Most importantly, there is a large consensus that this climate of diversity built by a faith-inspired group had an impact that went beyond quality education. At a critical juncture in history, Hizmet schools contributed greatly to preserving intergroup harmony during the complexities of early post-Soviet years and prevented radical groups from taking root by exploiting political uncertainties. Such impact is by no means a surprise given Gülen's uncompromising stance against blending religion with politics:

> Such a book [the Qur'an] should not be reduced to the level of political discourse, nor should it be considered a book about

political theories or forms of state. To consider Qur'an as an instrument of political discourse is a great disrespect for the Holy Book and is an obstacle that prevents people from benefiting from this deep source of divine grace.[205]

Dialogic Sufism

It was in this atmosphere of the early 1990s that Fethullah Gülen began communicating with leaders of non-Muslim communities in Turkey. The early informal conversations paved the way for large public gatherings. The landmark event was an iftar (the meal after sunset that ends the daily fast during Ramadan) in 1994 hosted by the Journalists and Writers Foundation (JWF), where Gülen was the honorary chairman. These public gatherings were unquestionably bold steps, given the prevailing suspicious attitudes towards non-Muslims and to whomever amicably interacted with them. It was not too long before hardliner religious and nationalist segments started attacking Gülen with provocative headlines and a smear campaign that questioned his loyalty to his country and his faith. JWF's Istanbul headquarters was bombed in April 2000, shortly after the large Abrahamic convention that the foundation held in Harran. Nevertheless, Gülen stayed the course of dialogue, and the JWF continued its work as the first nongovernmental interfaith platform in the history of modern Turkey.

Gülen's concept of Sufism merits particular attention. The contemporary practice of Sufism and its institutionalization in terms of *tariqas* (Sufi brotherhood/sisterhood orders) is a form that was developed after Islam's fifth century. Prior to that, Sufism did exist as a mystical school but had not branched into different *tariqas*. It is this earlier Sufi tradition that Gülen follows and revives. He was never initiated into any specific Sufi order and therefore neither taught nor led any Sufi ritual. Gülen rather devoted decades to reviving the early Sufi tradition of Islam's first five centuries, an effort that culminated in his magnum opus *Key Concepts in the Practice of Sufism*. The name of some chapters will give an idea of his focus: Self-Reflexivity, Heart, Piety, Humility, Modesty, and Love. While the history of Islam records occasional disagreements between mystic and legalistic schools, Gulen assumes a reconciliatory tone:

> In fact, Sufism and jurisprudence are like the two schools of a university that seeks to teach its students the two dimensions of the Shari'a so that they can practice it in their daily lives. One school cannot survive without the other, for while one teaches

how to pray, be ritually pure, fast, give charity, and how to regu-
late all aspects of daily life, the other concentrates on what these
and other actions really mean, how to make worship an inseparable part of one's existence, and how to elevate each individual
to the rank of a universal, perfect being (al-insan al-kamil) a true
human being. That is why neither discipline can be neglected.[206]

Every interfaith pioneer brings his or her own unique voice into this
noble endeavor. One such landmark contribution stands out in Gülen's
record: guiding millions of Muslims to liberate themselves from the mis-
conception of dialogue being a foreign practice to Islam. Gülen's dialogue
is because of Islam, not despite it. His interfaith work is the unsurpris-
ing result of a foundational understanding of devotion and openness not
being mutually exclusive. Over the decades, Gülen has successfully communicated the idea that one can well be anchored in his or her faith and
can warmly welcome those from other confessions. Gülen frequently cites
the numerous Qur'anic verses that command peaceful engagement with
non-Muslims and the Prophet's efforts to put them into practice. Among
those are the Medina Charter as a pluralistic constitution and the Farewell
Sermon as a bill of rights. In a clearly Sufi tone, Gülen reminds us that such
attitude is an essential part of personal piety:

> Love is the foundation of the world. God created it as such. Ev-
> erything in the world is a magnificient art. To demean a piece of
> art is the same as demeaning the Artist. Everything deserves to
> be exalted, respected and loved due to their relationship to their
> Creator, God. We base our relation with the created order on the
> principle of loving them because of their Creator.[207]

It is a figure like him, whose Islamic credentials combine solid Sufi
foundations with an equally strong training in textual sources, who could
achieve such an impact on masses. In fact, just like the thirteenth-century
master Rumi, Gülen's scholarly profile is a peaceful blend of mysticism and
orthodoxy. While his Sufi training grants him a vision of Islam with love at
its center, his scholarly authority enables him to lead large audiences into
such a vision. This is well summarized in his frequent emphasis on being
humans first, then Muslims, Christians, Hindus, Jews, or others second.
Like all tenets of his "dialogic Sufism,"[208] Gülen bases this approach on the
Qur'an and the Sunna:

> O humanity! Indeed, We created you from a male and a female,
> and made you into peoples and tribes so that you may get to
> know one another. Surely the most noble of you in the sight

of Allah is the most righteous among you. Allah is truly All-Knowing, All-Aware (Qur'an, 49:13)

(The Prophet) one day stood up as a Jewish funeral was passing by. One of the Companions at his side said, "O Messenger of God, that's a Jew." Without any change in attitude or alteration of the lines on his face the Prince of Prophets gave the answer: "But he's a human being!"[209]

Vision and Legacy

Generating a vision is one task, and communicating it is another. A key component of Gülen's success is his skill in communicating his perspective through a relevant discourse that combines confidence in one's faith with personal humility. Through this balanced discourse, Gülen was able to convince his audience that Islamic tradition can negotiate with modernity, without having to resort to the distortions of either a superiority or an inferiority complex. This conviction is vital, as a sense of equality between sides is a precondition for successful dialogue. Gülen notes:

> Differing opinions, differing attitudes should not be a barrier to dialogue. These differences should be communicated with utmost comfort by neither neglecting the respect to the position of the other nor assuming a sense of exceptionalism. No one should consider the self superior to others nor give any such impression and all must be unassuming.[210]

On a no less important front, Gülen powerfully argued in *Key Concepts in the Practice of Sufism* that Sufi concepts are universal enough to be put to practice in all areas of contemporary life. Gülen's genius was to prove that Muslims are not marginalized cultural orphans of this age, and they have all the abilities at their disposal for a fruitful engagement with it. Thus he fulfilled the role of a transformative leader by highlighting the viability of dialogue and by empowering his audience with the notion that they possess all the agency to perform it.

It helps at this point to have a closer look into Gülen's discourse in order to highlight some insights and ideas that function as its building blocks. Gülen, in a distinguishably Sufi way, is a pathbreaker. His story is one of bridge building between faith and reason, mysticism and text, East and West, as well as secular and pious. His central insight that informs this characteristic is a reconciliatory worldview as opposed to a binary one. When asked about whether a certain region is *dar al Islam* (abode of Islam) or *dar al Harb* (abode of War), he refused to adopt the medieval dichotomous conception and rather responded by calling the entire world as *dar al Hizmet* (abode of Service). This inclusive worldview does not need clashing with a constitutive other to establish itself but rather embraces diversity as divine will. Therefore a social climate where diversity prevails is the best environment for this vision to blossom. This is summarized in yet another Gülen concept, "living, so that others may live," because "life is meaningful if we are living to let others live, otherwise it means we are living in vain."[211] Gülen also highlights the need to build "islands of peace." It helps to note that this metaphor is one of humility rather than compartmentalization, as Gülen's vision of peace embraces society as a whole:

> We should direct our efforts toward helping people build a so-ciety of peace, on both a national and global scale. This society will be purified of all contemptible feelings and directed toward lofty ideals. Its individuals will rest in the serenity of their con-science. Peace begins in the individual, resonates in the family, and from there pervades all parts of society.

Guiding principles of substantive dialogue are emphatic acceptance, transparency, equality, humility, and a genuine desire to learn. The op-erational creed while putting these ideals into action, in Gülen's lexicon, is known as *musbet hareket* (positive action). This is evident in his discourse, where he characteristically focuses his energy on communicating what he is for rather than what he is against.

Gülen's dialogical approach has made significant achievements in the realm of interreligous engagement. First and foremost, it has made the idea of dialogue a central notion across a global network of like-minded non-profits, making it a grassroots practice that transcends scholarly and clerical circles. This not only means greater impact at the societal level, but also means the culture of dialogue sustains itself through individual activism. At a more concrete level, one of the most important achievements in Gülen's record is the wave of interfaith efforts mobilized by the Hizmet networks in the aftermath of 9/11. At a historical moment of deep suspicion towards Muslims, coupled with a profound interest in learning more about them, Gülen-inspired institutions in Western Europe and North America such as the Dialogue Society (UK), Dialogue Platform (Belgium), Stiftung Dialog (Germany), Rumi Forum (US), and Intercultural Dialogue Institute (IDI) initiated grassroots campaigns for local interfaith outreach. Through a variety of engagements such as informal conversations, scriptural studies, interfaith iftar and prayer gatherings, academic conferences, and study trips to Muslim majority destinations, these efforts played a vital role in softening the rhetoric, addressing misunderstandings, and building rapport between Muslims in the West and their neighbors.

Rabbi Rosen: Eyes on the Horizon

It is this profound commitment to dialogue and its elaborate framing by Gülen that has shaped the last two decades of my life. At a foundational level, his principle of avoiding merging religion with politics is my North Star in dialogue. An ensuing Gülen imprint in my mind and soul is the idea of dialogue being an Islamic concept firmly connected to the Qur'an and the exemplary life of its Messenger (*pbuh*). A third key inspiration is a solid belief in the inherent value of dialogue, a merit that can be neither measured with conventional cost-benefit calculations nor appreciated with a short-sighted outlook. Rather, it is a relationship-building marathon that deserves years, if not generations, of meticulous investment, no matter what the circumstances dictate. This vision eventually inspired me to choose Israel as an academic destination after graduate school. Shortly after my first semester at the Hebrew University, I received a call from the late Cemal Usak of JWF, another interreligous hero, and was kindly invited to join a breakfast with Rabbi Rosen and his wife Sharon. The connection we established then on the shiny blue Bosphorus has remained as strong and lively since that day.

Few have been gifted with *Silm*—a deeply settled peace—in their souls, and only such souls are perfectly sheltered and able to shelter others from the daily ups and downs of life. In an age when a plethora of distractions are competing to derail and discourage dialogue, leaders like Imam Gülen and Rabbi Rosen stand out with their sights constantly on the horizon. Throughout my fifteen years of acquaintance with him, I have observed Rabbi Rosen always persevering on this line of thought and action: his faith in the indisputable necessity to build mutual positive regard among adherents of faiths and his trust in the Creator that this vision can be realized. It is with such firm commitment and conviction that he has been able to carry out his demanding task during testing times. Moreover, a principled dialogue between the realms of faith and politics, as opposed to compartmentalization, is essential, and Rabbi Rosen pioneers his exemplary version of *muspet hareket* (positive action) in that dimension. He is a pathbreaker and bridge-builder in a variety of ways, including his principled interaction with decision makers. His way of engaging with leaders is full of lessons for all those who are committed to dialogue, who may easily lose sight of the goal in the temptation to protest. Last but not least, interreligous dialogue is by no means a set of external protocols or conventions. It is not an easy realm to navigate without a profound belief in the God-given value of every human being and appreciation of the image of God within. It is no wonder that Sufis who considered a human's heart to be of equal value with the holy Qa'ba were the interreligious heroes through ages. Rabbi Rosen shines with that trait. Even a brief interaction with him will suffice to manifest his profound appreciation of each and every individual and his embracing attitude towards every soul.

Dialogue is a worthy endeavor in which to invest our time and energy, simply because it is dialogue. Valuing the process over outcomes is an invaluable skill for those engaged in interreligious work, as we might be tempted to harbor short-term expectations as far as outcomes are concerned. Dialogue is a long journey. It is leaders like Imam Gülen and Rabbi Rosen who, with their actions, keep reminding us that the process has inherent value in itself.

Sheikh Abdullah Bin Bayyah[212]

Mufti Mustafa Ceric

A Man of Soft Heart in a Cruel World

IT IS NOT TALKING but walking interfaith dialogue that matters. I know that from my personal experience in the reality of war and peace. I lived under the siege of the city of Sarajevo, which lasted 1425 days. It was not easy in the face of the cruelty of genocide to have a soft heart, an open mind, and a willingness to listen to the call for interfaith dialogue. You need a faithful brother of faith and an honest friend of humanity to help you overcome a desire for vengeance. I was lucky to have had both—a brother who softened my heart and a friend who opened my mind.

HRH Prince Ghazi bin Muhammad bin Talal of Jordan softened my heart by his initiative of "A Common Word between Us and You" in 2007.[213] This initiative was launched on October 13, 2007, as an open letter signed by 138 Muslim scholars and intellectuals addressed to church leaders and Christian communities throughout the world, starting with Pope Benedict XVI. The essence of this letter, as affirmed in verses of the Qur'an and the Bible, was that Muslims and Christians share values of the utmost importance, namely love of God and love of neighbor. Building on this common ground, the letter called for peace and love between Christians and Muslims throughout the world.

Dr. William Fray Vendley, the secretary general of the World Conference of Religions for Peace (WCRP), precisely at the time of my inner struggle between considering an offer for interfaith dialogue and feeling wrath and need for revenge against the Serbian Orthodox Church, opened my mind to see the future of my country, Bosnia, in the Interreligious Council of Bosnia rather than in the law of retaliation, "an eye for an eye." It was then that I fully grasped the significance of the Qur'anic saying "But whoever forgives it, that would become expiation for him" (Qur'an, 5:45). This idea was the first most important step toward an opening of a process of truth, justice, peace, and reconciliation in my country.

With a soft heart and open mind, I met Sheikh Al-Allamah Abdullah bin Maḥfūẓ bin Bayyah at a peace summit conference that was convened in the Turkish city of Mardin (*mardin* means "the abode of peace") at the Artuklu University campus on March 27–28, 2010, under the auspices of the Global Center for Renewal and Guidance (GCRG) based in London. The reason for this conference was the reevaluation of the Ibn Taymiyya's classification of his Mardin fatwa, which went beyond the classification that was common among past Muslim jurists: dividing territories into an abode of Islam (in which the primary state is peace), an abode of *Kufr* (unbelief) (in which the primary state is war), and an abode of *'Ahd* (covenant) (in which the primary state is truce), among other divisions that they had stipulated. Now, the Mardin conference under the leadership of Sheikh bin Bayyah concluded that Muslims today are bound by international treaties through which security and peace have been achieved for all humanity and in which they enjoy safety and security, with respect to their property, integrity, and homelands.

Indeed, here I found in the thought and in the figure of Sheikh Abdullah bin Bayyah what I was looking for in the context of a universal as well as particular interfaith dialogue that was founded on a genuine Muslim belief and tradition. Since then, Sheikh bin Bayyah has become my guide in interfaith dialogue but also in intrafaith dialogue with some of my fellow Muslims who are opposed to interfaith dialogue. In the company of Sheikh bin Bayyah on many occasions, I have found in him a soft heart in a cruel world, exemplifying courage, not weakness. He highlighted the well-known verse of the Qur'an: "O men, God has created you from male and female and made you nations and tribes so that you may know one another. But, indeed the most noble of you is the most morally correct among you. God knows and is well informed about everything" (Qur'an, 49:13).

In the light of this Qur'anic teaching, Sheikh bin Bayyah initiated, in partnership with the Moroccan Ministry of Endowments and Islamic Affairs, a constructive dialogue with religious communities living among majority Muslim societies. Thus, the *Marrakesh Declaration on the Rights of Religious Minorities in Predominantly Muslim Majority Communities* of January 2016 was launched in Morocco amid much fanfare.[214] It was declared as a response to the persecution of religious minorities by ISIS in Iraq and Syria. Key among the declaration's proposals offered as a solution was the development of constitutional laws based on the objectives of the Charter of Medina in countries with Muslim majorities. It was also argued in this declaration that "the United Nations Charter and related documents, such as the *Universal Declaration of Human Rights* (*UDHR*), are in harmony with the Charter of Medina."

Furthermore, another step that Sheikh Abdullah bin Bayyah took was to revive the historic example of the faith plurality of the Charter of Medina (622) that Muhammad, the Messenger of God, made between the different religious and social groups of the city of Medina with an aim of establishing and maintaining a stable and factionally mutual coexistence within a majority Muslim society. The Charter is considered an important historic document of Abrahamic dialectical spiritualism. It is a unique testimony of the spirit of the peaceful faith of Islam, as well as of an early peaceful Muslim community. It was initiated as a result of the crisis of relationship between the early Muslim and Jewish communities in Medina. It is considered to be an exemplary advanced document for the kind of social contract that was forged by Jean Jack Rousseau, John Locke, and Thomas Hobbes as a guiding sociopolitical idea in Europe.

Then, on top of that, came the New Alliance of Virtue, which seeks to bring together religious leaders of good will for the benefit of humanity. This alliance is reminiscent of the Islamic tradition that when Muhammad was about twenty years old, a grave injustice involving one of the Quraysh leaders happened in Mecca. At this, al-Zubayr Ibn 'Abd al-Muttalib stood up and cried: "This must stop!" He gathered noble elders of Mecca, and they made an alliance: "We will be allied [lit., one hand] with the wronged against the wrongdoer until he receives his fair share, and as long as the sea lasts and as long as mounts Thabīr and Hirā' stay firm. And we will give each other mutual sustenance." The Quraysh called this covenant *Ḥilf al-fuḍūl*, the Alliance of Virtue, which was an inspiration for Sheikh bin Bayyah to initiate a New Alliance of Virtue to be as an example across religions to enable their members to live side by side in peace and happiness. It does not seek to bridge theological differences but rather to cooperate on the basis of a theology of God-given human dignity, seeking virtue and the benefit of all.

My testimony to the virtue of Sheikh bin Bayyah being an inspiration for me in interfaith dialogue both locally and globally is based on my personal experience of war and peace in Bosnia. During the war and postwar time in Bosnia, it was hard to find a peace initiative from a credible and sustainable Muslim group or institution to help me engage in dialogue and trust-building with others. Sheikh bin Bayyah closely followed what was going on in Bosnia (1993–1995) with Bosnian Muslims and helped me to cope with my dilemma as to how to engage in a process of reconciliation through interreligious dialogue. This was very helpful to me, as peace initiatives were coming mainly from the Christian and Jewish groups or institutions that by this very fact had an advantage in presenting their case in the context of war and peace. So, when later a major Muslim peace initiative of a global scope was introduced by Sheikh bin Bayyah in 2014 in Abu Dhabi, I was delighted to be invited to join it.

It is the lesson I have learned from Sheikh bin Bayyah that no one has a monopoly on Islam, but everyone has the duty of *farḍ-i' ain* (personal responsibility) and *farḍ-i kifāyah* (collective responsibility) to behave in such a way that does not corrupt the moral teachings of Islam and does not compromise the right image of Islam and Muslims in the world for the sake of personal gain. The work of Sheikh bin Bayyah is due to his sense of *farḍ-i ' ain* (personal responsibility) and *farḍ-i kifāyah* (collective responsibility) for improving a damaged picture of Islam and Muslims in the world because of some radical and extreme so-called Islamic groups who have claimed to act on behalf of Islam. Those who do not understand this message are out of touch with reality and thus cannot claim to be the right guide for the Muslims, especially in the West. Those among the Muslims, wherever they are, who still support the catastrophic violence that has happened recently in some major Muslim countries ought to be advised that suicide is not in the nature of Islam. True Islam has never been a religion of destruction. Indeed, Islam has always been a religion of construction, inclusive culture, and civilization.

Based on that notion of Islam, Sheikh bin Bayyah is a man of faith in a time of faithless people, a man of morality in a time of promiscuity, a man of tranquility in a time of turmoil, a man of knowledge in a time of ignorance, a man of sound mind in a time of foolishness, a man of trust in a time of betrayal, a man of guidance in a time of misguidance, a man of dialogue in a time of conflict, a man of hope in a time of despair, a man of humanity in a time of brutality, a man of civilization in a time of barbarism, a man of peace in a time of war—a man who is an example for both Muslims and non-Muslims to be followed in the genuine work of interfaith dialogue for the common future of humanity.

This is Sheikh Abdullah bin Maḥfūẓ bin Bayyah, who was born in Tambadeha, eastern Mauritania, in 1935. He was brought up in a house of knowledge and piety, where he acquired the knowledge of his father, the prolific judge, the famous scholar Sheikh Maḥfūẓ (1879–1973), who was the president of the first conference of Mauritanian scholars, which was held in Nouakchott shortly after the country's independence. Sheikh bin Bayyah took his understanding of Arabic studies from the scholar Muhammad Salem ibn al-Shin and of the Qur'an from the scholar Sheikh Bayyah ibn al-Salik. With the dawn of independence, Sheikh bin Bayyah was sent to Tunisia as part of the first group of trained judges there. He was ranked first in the cohort.

As a man of knowledge, tranquility, and trust, Sheikh bin Bayyah was transferred to several judicial positions in the Islamic Republic of Mauritania, including his appointment as head of the Sharia department in the Ministry of Justice, then vice president of the Court of Appeal, then vice president of the Supreme Court, then head of the Islamic Sharia department in this court. After that, he was appointed high commissioner for Religious Affairs at the Presidency of the Islamic Republic of Mauritania, where he proposed the establishment of a Ministry for Islamic Affairs. He was the first minister of this ministry.

As a man of reason, guidance, and dialogue, Sheikh bin Bayyah held the following positions as well. In 1971, he was appointed minister of Basic Education and Religious Affairs; in 1973, he was appointed minister of Justice and Legislation and Keeper of Rings; in 1975, he was appointed minister of Human Resources and Religious Affairs with the rank of deputy prime minister; in 1976, he was appointed minister of National Guidance and Party Organizations (this ministry included the Ministries of Information, Culture, Youth, Sports, Post and Telegraph, and Islamic Affairs); in 1987, he became permanent secretary of the ruling Mauritanian People's Party and was a member of its political office and its permanent committee from 1970 to 1978. In 1978, Sheikh bin Bayyah was tasked with declaring the application of Islamic law in Mauritania and was focused on completing the Arabization of administration in the institutions of the Mauritanian state.

With his belief, thought, and work as a man of trust, renewal, and reform, Sheikh bin Bayyah initiated the establishment of important Islamic institutions, where he was assigned to lead and manage them for the benefit of the local and global community as well. He is now chairman of the Emirates Council for Sharia Fatwa; president of the Forum for Promoting Peace in Muslim Societies; president of Al-Muwatta Foundation for the Graduation of Scholars; head of the Global Center for Renewal and Rationalization in London; president of the Ghaza Institute for Arab and Islamic Sciences—Eastern Mauritania; co-chair of Religions for Peace, Banu York; and chairman of the Supreme Academic Council of Mohammad Bin Zayed University.

Although he is of a different tradition—the Jewish tradition—Rabbi David Rosen is my hero in interfaith dialogue as well. He has similar attributes to Sheikh bin Bayyah as a man of peace in a time of war and a man of interfaith dialogue in a time of faith xenophobia—anti-Semitism and Islamophobia. Indeed, Rabbi Rosen is a beacon of faith in God and trust in humanity. Honoring him on this occasion by introducing a champion of interfaith dialogue and global humanism like Sheikh bin Bayyah is an honor in itself. Indeed, it is my personal honor to be their brother and friend as well.

I am sure that if we had more people of faith like Sheikh Abdullah bin Bayyah and Rabbi David Rosen, our world would be in a much better condition. We should keep in our prayers that God Almighty would give them a long life so that we can benefit from their courage and wisdom, so that we, too, may have the courage to change what we can change for better, the wisdom to perceive what we cannot change, and the knowledge of the difference between the two—courage and wisdom. Amen!

The Spiritual Quest

Mahatma Gandhi

Prof. Anantanand Rambachan

Raghupati Raghava Raja Rama

Lord Rama, chief of the Raghu family
(raghupati raghava rajaram)

the uplifter of the fallen
(patita pavana sitaram)

Your names are Ishwara and Allah
(ishwara allah tero naam)

Bless us with wisdom to understand
(saba ko sanmati de bhagavan)

All are equal
(uncha nicha eka samana)

Bless us with wisdom to understand
(saba ko sanmati de bhagavan)

As an expression of my gratitude for the friendship of Rabbi David Rosen and for his contributions to building interreligious relationships, I wish to share a theological reflection on one of Gandhiji's favorite Hindi religious songs (*bhajan*) that is sung by Hindus in every part of our world. It is one of the earliest songs of my memory. My grandfather, a Hindu priest, regularly sang this song when he led worship services. It is a song that has gone deep into our hearts and awakens special religious sentiments whenever we hear its lyrics. That song is "Raghupati Raghava Raja Rama." Its composition was inspired by Mahatma Gandhi and it became one of his favorite hymns for worship. Through my exegesis of this song, I hope to highlight some of Gandhi's special contributions to interreligious thinking and his inspiration for me. I want to begin therefore with thoughts about Gandhiji.

Mahatma Gandhi was a devotee of God as Rama. Although open to the many names and forms for God in the Hindu tradition, Rama had special significance for him. As a child, Gandhi had a tremendous fear of ghosts and spirits. His babysitter, an elderly woman named Rambha, suggested that he adopt the practice of repeating the name of Rama. Gandhi had deep faith in his babysitter and took her advice seriously. This childhood religious practice of repeating the name of God, that we know as *japa*, was his earliest religious observance and remained with him throughout his life. Gandhi was introduced to the actual narrative of the life of Rama a little later in his life. During his father's final illness, his family gathered each evening at his bedside to listen to the reading and exposition of the life story of Rama as written by the sixteenth-century poet Tulasidasa, himself a great devotee of God as Rama. Gandhi described himself as being enraptured by his first exposure to the singing of Tulasidasa's composition. This experience of listening to the text while his father lay on his deathbed laid the foundation of his devotion to the Ramayana which he came to regard as the greatest book in all devotional literature.

Among the many names for God in the Hindu tradition, it was the name Rama that moved Gandhi the most. He found the word God too abstract and impersonal. Gandhi described his love for the name Rama by referring to the famous incident of Rama's devotee and servant, Hanuman, tearing open his chest and revealing that his heart was occupied by Rama and his spouse, Sita. In the words of Gandhi:

> Hanuman tore open his heart and showed that there was nothing there but Ramanama [the name of Rama]. I have none of the power of Hanuman to tear open my heart, but if any of you feel inclined to do it, I assure you, you will find nothing there but love for Rama whom I see face to face in the starving millions of India.[215]

This is a revealing quotation for the fact that when Gandhi's chest was literally opened by an assassin's bullets, his final words, "Hey Rama [O Rama]," came directly from his heart. No other words were spoken before life left his body.

When Gandhi sought a description for the India of his dreams, it does not surprise us that he turned to the Ramayana of Tulasidasa and referred to this utopian kingdom as Rama Rajya (the kingdom of Rama). It was a kingdom in which no one suffered or died prematurely, where people were educated and healthy, where love prevailed and violence was eradicated.

Rama was Gandhi's favorite form of God, referred to in the Hindu tradition as one's *ishtadeva*. From among the many names and forms of

God available in the Hindu tradition, each Hindu has the opportunity to choose a favorite one as the object of worship. With such a deep love for God as Rama, it does not surprise us that Gandhi's favorite religious song then was one dedicated to Rama.

Many attribute this famous song to the Hindustani musician Vishnu Paluskar, a contemporary and follower of Gandhi who died in 1931. Paluskar sang this song in Gandhi's presence, and it clearly captivated him. It was regularly sung during Gandhi's daily evening worship (*satsangh*), and it was the song that millions sang as they accompanied his body on its final journey to cremation at Raj Ghat in New Delhi. The song became extremely popular in 1930 when it was sung by Gandhi and his followers along the 241-mile route from his community (*ashram*) in Sabarmati, Gujarat, to Dandi on the coast of India. This march of protest, which has come to be known as the Salt March, was an act of organized protest against British rule in India. It was an act of defiance against the British control over the manufacture of salt. Gandhi's lifting of a handful of salty mud from the ocean was a signal that inspired mass civil disobedience across India.

Why did the lyrics of the song "Raghupati Raghava Raja Rama" appeal so strongly to Gandhi? The most obvious answer is that it is addressed to and praises his favorite form of God, Rama; this, however, cannot be an adequate explanation. Let us therefore look at the structure and lyrics of this song more carefully and unpack its significance for interreligious relationships.

The traditional version of the song consists of a chorus and two verses. The chorus (*raghupati raghava raja rama / patita pavana sita rama*), with which it begins and which is repeated after each verse, contains a number of familiar names of Rama: *raghupati* (lord of the Raghus), *raghava* (belonging to the Raghu family), and *raja rama* (Lord Rama). The most important name of Rama, however, in the chorus, is *patita pavan* (the support or lifter of those who have fallen), and this name was particularly significant to Gandhi for several reasons.

First, the entire nation was in a fallen state of poverty and powerlessness as a consequence of British exploitation and control. The nation was also in a fallen state because of internal oppressive practices such as untouchability. One of the important roles of religion and faith in God, for Gandhi, was the empowering of people to lift themselves and each other from this fallen condition. For Gandhi, the struggle for social justice is inseparable from the practice of nonviolence. Second, since God existed in all beings, the only way to find God, for Gandhi, was to see God in all beings and to identify oneself with all. The way to identify oneself with others is through love. This love requires active and dedicated service of others.

This was, for Gandhi, the meaning of liberation (*moksha*), and he saw his political action as inseparable from his quest for spiritual liberation. *Patita pavana* (the supporter of the fallen) was one of his favorite names for God, but it was also a human ideal. God is *patita pavana* to us, but we must become *patita pavana* to each other.

The communities (*ashrams*) founded by Gandhi in South Africa and India always included people of other faiths—Jews, Muslims, and Christians. Traditionally, an *ashram* is a place for religious practice with the aim of attaining spiritual liberation. Gandhi, however, invited members of these diverse faiths into cooperative action on behalf of the poor and the oppressed. "Man's ultimate aim," wrote Gandhi, "is the realization of God, and all his activities, political, social and religious, have to be guided by the ultimate aim of the vision of God. The immediate service of all human beings becomes a necessary part of the endeavor simply because the only way to find God is to see Him in His creation and be one with it."[216] His *ashrams* were founded for service, and such service, for Gandhi, was a fundamental purpose of interreligious relations. Gandhi was one of the earliest to advocate that the overcoming of suffering is one the highest purposes of cooperation across religious differences. I believe that this has continuing relevance for us.

The movement from the chorus to the first verse is deliberate, profound, and instructive. The chorus, as already noted, is centered on Rama, and uses many of Gandhi's favorite names of Rama. From this very particular and specific naming of God, the first verse moves to referring to God by employing two names, *Ishwara* (Lord of blessings), from the larger Hindu tradition; and *Allah* (the God), from Islam. It proclaims these to also be the names of God (*ishwara allah tero naam / sabako sanmati de bhagavan* [bless us to understand that your names are Ishwara and Allah]). What is the significance of this movement? Although it is important that we have our own preferred names for God and our special ways of worshipping and understanding God, Gandhi considered it wrong to regard our preferred name to be the only correct or true one and all others to be untrue or inferior. I regard this as a fundamental interreligious insight for which Gandhi labored throughout his life and that inspires me deeply.

Ishwara is one of the names of the Divine in Hinduism that is used across different Hindu traditions, even as Allah is used across Islamic traditions. Allah is used in this song because Muslims constitute the largest religious group in India after the Hindus. "I believe," wrote Gandhi, "in the absolute oneness of God, and, therefore, of humanity."[217]

Call Him Ishwara, Allah, God, Ahura Mazda. His names are as innumerable as there are men. He is one without a second. He alone is great. There is none greater than He. He is timeless, formless, stainless. Such is my Rama. He alone is my Lord and Master.[218]

The use of Allah reminds us of a truth that is important for Gandhi. Our neighbors of other faiths, whose names for God differ from our own, are addressing and relating themselves to the same God. Our understanding of God, in other words, must not become so particularized that we overlook God's oneness and universality. For Gandhi, there is virtue in particularity, as with his preference for Rama, but not particularity at the expense of divine universality. This insight found repeated expression in his writings and speeches.

Our failure to recognize God's oneness, as articulated in this song, has had and continues to have tragic consequences. It leads to the negativization of God outside of our traditions as inferior or false. Such negativization leads, in turn, to the devaluation of other religions. The devaluation of the other religion leads in turn to condemnation of followers of those faiths who are perceived to be of lesser worth. Such condemnation creates the conditions for verbal hostility that then easily intensifies into violence. The second line of the first verse (*sabako sanmati de bhagavan* [bless us with wisdom to understand]), therefore, is a prayer for all humans (*sabako*) to awaken to the truth of God's oneness within and outside of their own particular religions. We should see this line not as a general and abstract call for goodness, but as a very specific prayer for the dawning of wisdom to recognize God's oneness across religions and the overcoming of hostility that is the consequence of seeing the other's God as alien or false. Gandhi's life was devoted to helping people of different religions awaken to this truth. This song does not allow for the existence of a Christian, Muslim, Jewish, or Hindu God. It does allow for different understandings of God but not different gods.

> All prayer, in whatever language, or from whatever religion it was, was prayer addressed to one and the same God and taught mankind that all belonged to one family and should bear love to one another.[219]

> Just as a tree had a million leaves, similarly though God was one, there were as many religions as there were men and women though they were rooted in one God.[220]

Just as the first verse of the song is meaningfully connected with the chorus, the second verse (*uncha nicha eka samana / sabko sanmati de bhagavan* [all are equal; bless us with the wisdom to understand]) is intimately connected with the first. The consequence of understanding God's oneness within and across religions is the affirmation of the equal dignity and worth of all human beings. Our failure to see God as the God of all leads often to a privileging and higher valuing of those who belong to our own religious community and to the thought that those outside of this community have lesser value in the eyes of God and may deserve ill treatment and even death. Each religion has its own special derogatory terms of abuse for those who do not belong. The purpose of the second verse in this song is to remind us that our understanding of God, and especially of God's unity, is incomplete, unless it finds expression in an ethic of human equality and dignity. This is a truth to which we must also pray to be awake. In Gandhi's words, "We are all children of one and the same God and therefore absolutely equal."

In his own time, Gandhi saw the devaluation of human beings as rooted in at least two sources. One is the devaluation and inequality that came from religious rivalry, especially between Hindus and Muslims, and the perception of each other as deserving of lesser consideration. He was also combating an internal inequality within Hinduism that expressed itself in the practice of untouchability and the demeaning of millions who were regarded as inferior on the basis of birth and work.

This truth of human equality and dignity was therefore particularly important to Gandhi as a Hindu. The Hindu tradition teaches not just the oneness of God but, just as important, the equal existence of God in all beings. The value of the human being comes from the fact of this divine origin and immanence and not from wealth, profession, religion, gender, race, or language. "I am endeavoring," said Gandhi, " to see God through the service of humanity, for I know that God is neither in heaven, nor down below, but in everyone."[221] It was this vision that led Gandhi into a life of human service. Since God existed in all, the only way to find God was to see God in all creation and to be one with it. Love was the means of this identification, and love expressed itself actively in a life of dedicated service to others. Speaking on behalf of the Muslim community in India was a courageous and bold action on the part of Gandhi and cost him his life. He teaches us by words and example that interreligious leadership is risky and requires the willingness to challenge one's own community on the basis of a commitment to divine and human unity. It is a lesson that I strive to bring to the work I do as a Hindu scholar, teacher, and practitioner.

The song "Raghupati Raghava Raja Ram" was important to Gandhi for at least four important reasons, all of which are instructive to us and all of which are important to our understanding of Gandhi's interfaith commitments and his leadership.

First, it enabled him to affirm and celebrate his Hindu religious identity through his devotion to God as Rama. Preserving the uniqueness of each religion was important to him. Our understanding of God's oneness is not to be at the expense of our own particular religious expressions. The is the reason for the Hindu emphasis on *ishtadeva*—the importance of choosing a form of God that is most meaningful to us. Gandhi's ideal was not one world religion. What he hoped for was that "people belonging to different faiths will have the same regard for other faiths that they have for their own."[222] Gandhi was always searching for commonalities among the world's religions but was not an advocate of homogenization. His ideal was one of unity in diversity. He used many metaphors to convey this truth:

> For me the different religions are beautiful flowers from the same garden, or they are branches of the same majestic tree . . . each distinct from the other, though having the same source.[223]

Second, the song affirmed the unity of God across traditions. Although devoted to God as Rama, Gandhi did not think of Rama as a tribal God of Hindus. Rama represented a precious name, form, and understanding through which the one God of the universe is worshipped and understood. There are Hindu names for God and Hindu beliefs about the nature of God as there are Muslim and Christian ones, but there does not exist a Hindu God, a Christian God, or a Muslim God, separate and different from each other. We have an obligation to learn from each other by earnest study and inquiry.

> I hold that it is the duty of every cultured man or woman to read sympathetically the scriptures of the world. If we are to respect others' religions as we would have them respect our own, a friendly study of the world's religions in a sacred duty.[224]

Third, the song affirmed the unity of humanity. The one God is the source of all life and, in the Hindu understanding, present equally in all beings. From this is derived the equal worth and dignity of all beings. Human dignity is not exclusive to the followers of particular religions. Faith and understanding of God must unify and not divide humanity. "I believe," wrote Gandhi, "in *advaita* [nonduality], I believe in the essential unity of man and, for that matter, of all that lives. Therefore, I believe that if one man gains spiritually, the whole world gains with him and, if one man falls, the whole world falls to that extent."[225]

Fourth, and finally, "Raghupati Raghava Raja Ram" affirmed, for Gandhi, the unity of life. This implies that our understanding of divine and human unity must find expression in a life of active and dedicated service to the poor and oppressed. His political work was as important to his search for God as his religious worship. Life is indivisible, and our values must be consistent in every field of activity.

> I do not conceive religion as one of the many activities of mankind. The same activity may be governed by the spirit either of religion or irreligion. There is no such thing for me therefore as leaving politics for religion. For me every, the tiniest, activity is governed by what I consider to be my religion.[226]

The celebration of particularity, the unity of God, reverence for and learning from other traditions, the unity of humanity and the unity of life are central teachings of this song that embody principles of interreligious activism dear to Gandhi. These values, I know, are also fundamental to the commitments of Rabbi Rosen as I know of and experience his participation in numerous interreligious events and contexts. This simple and profound song was a part of Gandhi's daily religious practice. May its teaching find an appropriate space and expression in our lives.

Thomas Merton

BISHOP FRANK GRISWOLD

IN RESPONDING TO THE invitation to contribute to this volume of essays about interfaith heroes who exhibit the same breadth and generosity of spirit that are reflected in the work and personal witness of Rabbi David Rosen, I was hard-pressed to settle on a particular person until a friend suggested Thomas Merton, a Cistercian monk and a prolific writer, thinker, poet. He was born in France in 1915 and died in Bangkok, Thailand, in 1968 while taking part in an interfaith gathering of Christian and Buddhist monks, drawn together to explore their different monastic traditions of contemplative practice and prayer.

In his autobiography, *The Seven Storey Mountain*, published in 1948, Merton describes his early years as a time of flux. His mother died when he was six. He then traveled from place to place with his artist father. At sixteen, he became an orphan when his father died, and he found himself under the care of a guardian. School in England and a year at Cambridge, then a move to New York and Columbia University led him to the Roman Catholic Church. Up until then, his student days in both Cambridge and New York might be described as a season of loose living, such as was common at universities in both countries. At Columbia, though fully engaged in study and enjoying the heady atmosphere of the city and university life, underneath it all Merton was experiencing an emptiness which he described as "bleeding to death." His movement toward faith was a slow process: "Books and ideas and poems and stories, pictures and music, buildings and cities, places, philosophies were to be the materials on which grace would work."[227]

His writings overflow many a bookcase, mine included, and books about him abound; there is even *The Thomas Merton Encyclopedia*. Merton's acute ability to inhabit and draw wisdom from other religious traditions made him a friend and brother to religious leaders and teachers of the three Abrahamic faiths as well as Buddhist and Hindu monks. In fact, a Hindu monk, Bramachari, whom Merton met while at Columbia, played a role in Merton's conversion when he recommended that he read the *Confessions of Augustine* and *Imitation of Christ*. Merton also drew profit from Confucianism and the Taoist sage Chuang Tzu.

Hiroshima, the Holocaust, issues of social justice, peace, civil rights, and many other issues provoked his responses and reflections rooted in his life as a monk. Though called to a life of solitude, he was in touch with a wide range of writers, thinkers, and religious leaders. While in his later years he lived apart from the community in a hermitage, he was not shy in receiving visitors from his wide circle of friends and correspondents.

One of his correspondents was Rabbi Abraham Joshua Heschel, the noted theologian and philosopher, who had been formed in the Hasidic tradition and combined a life of prayer with social action. When asked about his prayer while marching with Martin Luther King Jr. in Selma, he exclaimed, "I felt my legs were praying!" Merton and Heschel had much in common. In 1964, Heschel visited Merton out of his concern about Vatican II and what might be put forth in its declaration on the relation between Christians and Jews. Merton took up Heschel's concern, making it his own, and dispatched a letter to Cardinal Augustin Bea, the president of the Pontifical Council for Promoting Christian Unity, and a strong believer in dialogue and friendship between the two faiths, both children of Abraham.

Though I never met him, Merton has been a conversation partner of mine for many years. What has particularly drawn me to him, in addition to the breadth of his interests and capacity to dig below the surface in search of wisdom and insight, is the fact that his life was rooted in prayer. For me, the expansiveness of his vision and understanding, as well as his ability to ingest illumination from an array of spiritual traditions, have been the gift of our ongoing conversation. Therefore, in this essay, I would like to explore some of Merton's thought in relation to the inner life and its outworking in our multifaith world. Perhaps, across our traditions, there are some points of convergence that can deepen and enrich our interfaith relations and offer hope to the battered and divided global community to which we all belong.

Merton's route from Columbia to the Trappist Abbey of Our Lady of Gethsemani in Kentucky involved several stages, leading up to a Holy Week retreat at the abbey in 1941. At that point he found his true north, and, in a very real way, home. He also found something else: he found a container that could withstand his passionate, expansive spirit and protect him from what Merton's disciple, Matthew Kelty, identifies as a monk's "destroying angel." Speaking for himself, and I suspect for his monastic mentor as well, Kelty writes, "A destroying angel is near every poetic soul.

Humble though my own gifts may be, I am none the less more than conscious of a self-destructive urge that is active within me . . . . In monastic
life, submission to the abbot is central . . . and for the man called to the
monastery, that form of discipline is superb, for he needs a firm hand. Not
a hand that crushes him, but protects him from the forces that fight against
him, his own self-destroying urges."[228]

The *Order of Cistercians of the Strict Observance*, called Trappist, is—as
the name implies—strict in its life of prayer, simplicity, and labor. At the heart
of its life is the sixth-century *Rule of St. Benedict* which lays out a pattern for
daily life of a monastery and its members. The first word in the prologue to the
rule is "listen." Indeed, the whole rule is about listening not just superficially,
but with the ear of the heart, to God speaking through Scripture, "reputable
and orthodox fathers," and especially the Psalms, which constitute the nucleus
of the various hours of corporate prayer spaced throughout the day. The rule
includes as well listening to the days of the week, the seasons of the year, the
other monks, the abbot, and the community. "O that today you would listen
to God's voice," a verse from Psalm 95 chanted at the beginning Vigils, serves
as a daily reminder to the monk to listen to everything at the heart of his
prayer as a potential word from God, albeit mediated by another monk, a
book, the abbot, a visitor, the seasons of the year, or the annual sequence of
feasts and fasts that constitute the liturgy.

Merton was by inclination and monastic formation a careful and attentive listener. He was trained in the practice of *lectio divina*, a fourfold pro-
gression: *reading* and absorbing; savoring and *meditating* upon the received
word; placing the fruit of the meditation in *prayer* before God; receiving
through *contemplation* the initial word's further unfolding and fruitfulness.
It is my sense that this monastic discipline, about which he wrote, over time
became the spirit in which Merton read life (what Bernard of Clairvaux
called the Book of Experience). Life included the lives—and one might say
the personal scripture—of men and women whom he called words, inasmuch as they had been spoken into life by God and shared in God's image.
I think of Merton in relation to the words of Isaiah, "Morning by morning [God] wakens—wakens my ear to listen as those who are taught" (Isa
50:4). As a result, he heard God's voice in many places, languages, sacred
symbols, sacred texts, contemplative practices, and ways of prayer. Above
all, he heard God's voice in the lived scripture of those who wrote him and
with whom he engaged in dialogue, such as his friend, D. T. Suzuki, the
noted Zen scholar. Another friend, the Buddhist monk Thich Nhat Hanh,
describes him as "open to everything," and said Merton wanted to know
about his life: "He wanted to know more and more . . . . He was constantly
asking questions. And then he would listen."

Another friend in the Spirit was the Dalai Lama, who received Merton in 1968 during his trip to the East. In his *Asian Journal,* Merton reflects upon the meeting: "At the end I felt we had become very good friends and were somehow quite close to one another. I feel a great respect and fondness for him as a person and believe, too, that there is a real spiritual bond between us."[229] After Merton's death, the Dalai Lama offered his own reflection upon their encounter: "We looked on each other's faces and expressed things, and with each word, each minute, there was deeper understanding."[230] These examples, and there are many more, reveal the depth with which Merton read the lives of those whom he met and those whom he came to know intimately through their correspondence. Again, *lectio divina,* I believe, provided a pathway for Merton to widen and deepen his sense of God's activity and presence through an array of relationships that were illumining, expansive, and reciprocal.

For Merton, prayer "means yearning for the simple presence of God, for a personal understanding of his word, for knowledge of his will and for the capacity to hear and obey him."[231] This yearning is not self-generated but is the action of God within us, as in Psalm 27:8: "You (God) speak in my heart and say, 'Seek my face!' Your face, Lord, do I seek." Such prayer of the heart is initiated by God in our personal depths and wells up from within. It then breaks through into our consciousness as yearning toward mystery, the "Abyss of the unknown-yet-present-One," who, in the words of Augustine, "is more intimate to us than we are to ourselves."[232] This, however, is not an invitation to self-absorption, because the more we are drawn into the mystery of God, the more we see ourselves and the world around us as God sees us, including those who, by virtue of their creation, have been made like us in God's image. To be made in God's image and according to his likeness (Gen 1:26) is reflected in our capacity to love and receive love. "God is love, and those who abide in love abide in God and God in them . . . . We love because [God] first loved us" (1 John 4:16, 19). Love is the name we give to the divine energy that has been planted within us. By its very nature, it must express itself; it must go forth from itself in order to be love. Origen, an early Christian writer, in reflecting upon Genesis 1:26, makes a distinction between image and likeness. Image is given; likeness is the fruit of how we exercise the given, in this case, love. What is clear to Merton is that love that goes out to others "is a stimulus to interior life, not a danger to it, as some mistakenly believe." For Merton, others were very much part of his unfolding likeness and a stimulus to prayer and attention to God's voice—even, quite remarkably, people hurrying along the sidewalk in downtown Louisville as he stood on a street corner observing them: "I was suddenly overwhelmed with the realization that I loved all those people, that they were mine and I was theirs, that we could not be alien to one another, even though we were total strangers. It was like waking from a dream of separateness, of spurious self-isolation in a special world, the world of renunciation and supposed holiness. Not that I question the reality of my vocation or my monastic life . . ."[233]

The paradox here is that the strict regimen of silence and solitude and prayer that appears as separation from the world, in order to be drawn ever more deeply into union with God, moves in the opposite direction and returns us to the world with a compassionate heart that, in the words of Isaac of Syria, "burns with love for the whole of creation."

The Rule of St. Benedict, which is at the heart of Cistercian Strict Observance, is rooted in love of God and one another, most concretely expressed in loving one's monastic brothers, but also more widely the sorts and conditions of women and men beyond the monastery walls. Love knows no bounds; and, like the burning bush Moses encountered in the wilderness, the living flame of love is never spent. "But as we progress in this way of life," Benedict tells his brothers, "we shall run on the path of God's commandments, our hearts overflowing with the inexpressible delight of love."[234]

"To say that I am made in God's image," writes Merton, "is to say that love is the reason for my existence, for God is love. Love is my true identity. Selflessness is my true self. Love is my true character. Love is my name."[235] But later in the same chapter, he makes clear that love can be costly and difficult: "As long as we are on earth, the love that unites us will bring us suffering by our very contact with one another, because love is the resetting of a Body of broken bones. Even saints cannot live with saints on this earth without some anguish, without some pain at the differences that come between them."[236]

When we look at Merton's extensive interfaith involvements and his ability to enlarge his sense of the Holy One, who transcends the limits of our conceptions and our categories—the Holy One, who replies when Moses asks his name, "I am who I am"—we discover in Merton more than an inquiring mind. We find a heart that burns with love for the other in the integrity of their faith and the life it sustains. At the same time, as his metaphor taken from Ezekiel 37 suggests, he was not under any illusions about the pain of the resetting process. In a telling phase, "the slag of an inescapable egoism," Merton touches upon one of the most intractable impediments to overcoming or reaching beyond our boundaries, namely, the ego that abides in our various religious traditions. Here, however, the most intense struggle is sometimes an intrareligious one, as different schools of thought or practice vie with one another, claiming to be the authentic voice of that particular tradition.

For me, one of Merton's most important contributions to an interfaith consciousness is his emphasis upon the classical understanding of the Logos, the Word, God's self-expression and self-disclosure who, for Christians, assumes our humanity in the person of Jesus, the Word made flesh. This Word, according to the Gospel of John, has been "with God" since the beginning, and "all things came into being through him, and without him not one thing came into being" (John 1:1–3). Thus, the Logos is the agent of creation: "God creates things by seeing them in His own Logos."[237] I think here of God, speaking through the prophet Isaiah, who declares, "For as rain and snow fall from the heavens, and return not again, but water the earth . . . so in my word that goes forth from my mouth; it will not return to me empty, but it will accomplish that which I have purposed, and prosper in that for which I sent it" (Isa 55:10–11). That word is the Logos who "pitches his tent among us" and returns to God and, through the working of the Holy Spirit "sustains all things" in webs of relationship or, more accurately, the dynamic of communion. The Logos, therefore, transcends categories. For Christians, the Logos became incarnate in the person of Jesus. However, the Logos is active in the universe and is present in other traditions as the source of an existential unity that binds us together beyond all our divisions religious and otherwise. This, I believe, was very much Merton's perspective born from his own exploration of other traditions and personal relationships with those who embodied them. In this regard, Merton had a profound sense of that unity as he addressed his Buddhist and Christian monastic brothers at the fateful meeting in Bangkok: "And the deepest level of communication is not communication, but communion. It is wordless. It is beyond words, and it is beyond speech, and it is beyond concepts. Not that we discover a new unity. We discover an older unity. My dear brothers, we are already one. But we imagine that we are not. And what we have to recover is our original unity. What we have to be is what we are."[238]

As I reflect upon Merton's deeply rooted interfaith relationships and his capacity to look always for the underlying communion that binds those of different faiths together in virtue of the original unity of our creation and participation in the being and likeness of the One beyond all names, I sense a similar inquiring mind and generosity of spirit manifest in the person and ministry of Rabbi David Rosen, who with his family, warmly welcomed my wife and me to their home some years ago for Shabbat. We both serve as members of the Elijah Board of World Religious Leaders and have been together on a number of occasions, both in Israel and in other parts of the world, including Canterbury and a meeting of the Lambeth Conference of Bishops from the worldwide Anglican Communion. Among the many awards Rabbi Rosen has received, I am especially pleased that he received a special award from the archbishop of Canterbury in recognition of his contribution to the work of interreligious relations. To which I can only add my own gratitude and thanks and say, "Amen."

Rabbi Zalman Schachter-Shalomi[239]

Rabbi Or Rose

Introduction

Rabbi Zalman Schachter-Shalomi (1924–2014) was one of the most creative, controversial, and influential Jewish religious figures in recent decades, weaving together various strands of Eastern European Hasidism and American counterculture to create the Jewish Renewal Movement. Among the core elements of his neo-Hasidic project was an innovative approach to interreligious engagement. In his later years, he would come to describe this vision as "deep ecumenism" (a term coined by his Christian colleague and friend Matthew Fox). Beginning in the mid-1940s, Reb Zalman (a less formal title he preferred) began participating in various experiments in dialogue, study, contemplative practice, and theological reflection. This included transformative experiences with such Christian luminaries as Howard Thurman and Thomas Merton, and later with various Sufi, Hindu, and Buddhist practitioners, including His Holiness, the fourteenth Dalai Lama. By the time of his death, Reb Zalman was widely recognized as one of the great ecumenists of our time.

In this brief essay, I explore four key elements of Reb Zalman's approach to interreligious engagement, including both conceptual and practical matters. I do so as a rabbi and educator intensely involved in interfaith and cross-cultural initiatives and as a lifelong student of Reb Zalman. It is my hope that this appreciative reflection will be helpful in bringing to light his contributions to the interreligious movement and stimulate further discussion about the individuals and groups who paved the way for the sacred work we seek to do today.

"Seek God's Face Evermore": Humility and Curiosity

Reb Zalman often referred to himself self-mockingly as a "spiritual peep-ing tom." I would describe his curiosity in much more positive terms. As a person ever searching for insight into life's great mysteries, he was humble enough to recognize that no one person, community, or religion possesses ultimate truth or all of the tools to undertake this lifelong quest. In his memoir, *My Life in Jewish Renewal*, he describes a turning point in his spiri-tual development. After emigrating to the United States in 1940 from Nazi-occupied Europe, he studied in the HaBaD-Lubavitch yeshiva in Brooklyn, New York, for several years. Even before completing his ordination process, in 1946, he was dispatched by the sixth Lubavitcher Rebbe, Rabbi Yosef Yitzhak Schneersohn, to help create Jewish youth programs in New Haven, Connecticut. As Reb Zalman writes, this was part of a broader effort to re-store traditional Jewish life in the aftermath of the Shoah, an effort that was shot through with messianic fervor.[240]

Shortly after arriving in New Haven, Reb Zalman prepared for his outreach work by making a visit to the local public library in search of resources on child development. As he glanced at the books on the new ac-quisitions table, he came upon two titles that would change his life. One of these books was Robert Ballou's *The Bible of the World* (1939), a large an-thology of sacred writings drawn from humanity's major religions. As Reb Zalman stated in his memoir, "Today, hundreds of such works exist, but published on the cusp of the Holocaust . . . such ecumenism was unusual and almost visionary."[241] The other book was *Difficulties in Mental Prayer* (1944) by a Cistercian monk named Eugene Boylan from the Abbey of Mt. Joseph in Ireland. The title of this devotional manual immediately caught the young rabbi's eye: "It intrigued me, for outside Lubavitch Hasidim, no Jews I had yet encountered even mentioned the reality and nature of 'men-tal prayer.'" This discovery, he writes, "awakened my soul to the realization that other religions besides Judaism hold real wisdom and effective tools for drawing closer to God."[242]

I find this comment particularly powerful given the fact that Reb Zalman had only recently escaped the Nazis and was now passionately involved in a post-war Jewish educational project that he believed bore the seeds of cosmic redemption. Further, many of the classical sources of Ha-sidism—including the *Tanya*, the foundational text of HaBaD-Lubavitch—speak in negative terms about non-Jews and non-Jewish religions. Finally, Reb Zalman experienced the pain of anti-Semitism and Christian chauvin-ism as a child even before Hitler's rise to power. Given these facts, it is remarkable that he was open to learning from a Catholic monk and from various other religious sources at this stage of his life. Like his older colleague and fellow neo-Hasidic teacher Abraham Joshua Heschel, Reb Zalman made a deliberate choice to engage in interreligious and cross-cultural activities, rather than shield himself from such encounters. As he matured, Reb Zalman spoke passionately about the urgent need for such ecumenical undertakings and their redemptive potential.[243]

Rooted Engagement: Know Thyself and Others

While Reb Zalman spread his interreligious wings far and wide, it is important to point out that he did so with deep roots—knowledge and lived experience—in Judaism. Further, he believed that thoughtful engagement with non-Jewish interlocuters would contribute to the growth and vitality of the Jewish people. As an example of what I am calling rooted engagement, I turn to his humorous but poignant reflection on his first visit to the Abbey of Our Lady of Gethsemani in rural Kentucky to meet his beloved pen pal Thomas Merton (they began corresponding in the winter of 1960).

> It was already evening [when I arrived at the monastery] and the gate was officially closed . . . . To my dismay, the entrance bell announcing visitors was attached to a rope with a cross at its end. As a Hasidic rabbi, I really didn't want to grasp the cross, but it was necessary to pull the rope in order to ring the bell. After a moment's thought, I grabbed the rope above the cross and yanked. The bell instantly rang! Suddenly a Trappist monk emerged from the shadows, where he had obviously been standing silently all along. Striding over, he opened the gate for me and said, smiling, "An interesting solution to a problem of conscience."[244]

As this anecdote demonstrates, while Reb Zalman was excited to make this interreligious pilgrimage, standing at the front gate of Gethsemani, he bumped up against a personal religious boundary. To be sure, Reb Zalman's borders would shift dramatically over time, but, repeatedly, this ever-evolving rabbi would seek to devise creative responses to such problems of religious conscience. Even in his more radical periods, he maintained an understanding that his calling—*shelihut* in the language of HaBaD Hasidism—required him to venture forth as a Jew and return to the Jewish community with gifts from his journeys. Reb Zalman increasingly felt that Jewish life could be reinvigorated by carefully incorporating teachings and practices from other traditions. As one might expect of a Hasid, he was particularly attracted to mystical and liturgical sources from the world's religions.[245]

In using the term rooted engagement, I also wish to point out that Reb Zalman was a dedicated student of other religions. Reading through his correspondence with Thomas Merton, for example, one is struck by the fact that much of what these interreligious pioneers discussed were Jewish and Christian sacred texts and manuals on religious practice. In one touching moment in a letter Reb Zalman sent to Merton in the fall of 1963, the Hasid tells his Trappist friend to be on the lookout for a recent English translation of a Jewish mystical text called *The Tract on Ecstasy*.[246] In lending the book to Merton, he writes, "Would you please (this is one of the conditions of the loan) as you read it, mark it with pencil as to the comparisons and so forth. That will make the reading of the book, for me, a delight."[247] This dedication to learning about the other is an essential teaching for anyone interested in interreligious engagement. Not only does it demonstrate genuine interest and respect for the religious other, but it allows for more sophisticated and nuanced conversation and reflection.

Dialogues of Devotion: Cultivating Personal Relationships

According to Reb Zalman, one of his most formative religious experiences was studying with the distinguished African American pastor Reverend Howard Thurman in the mid-1950s. Following a decade of intensive training and work within the HaBaD orbit, Reb Zalman enrolled in a graduate program in the psychology of religion at Boston University, for which Thurman served as an academic advisor. Reb Zalman began this educational undertaking with real trepidation, despite several positive interactions with individual Christians leading up to this experience: "Deep down in my guts I felt anxious about entrusting my soul to a Christian . . . . I wanted to make sure Minister Thurman was trustworthy—that is, that he wouldn't try to convert me to Christianity."[248]

To Reb Zalman's credit, rather than holding tightly to this negative generalization and retreating from the scene, he met with Thurman and honestly explored his ambivalence with the acclaimed Baptist leader. In a one-on-one meeting with Thurman (resembling a traditional counseling session with a Hasidic master), the young rabbi explained that he was not sure if his "anchor chains" were "long enough" to be mentored by a non-Jewish spiritual guide.[249] Reb Zalman was deeply moved by Dean Thurman's answer to him: "With a pensive expression, he put down his coffee mug. His graceful hands went back and forth, as though mirroring my dilemma. Howard Thurman looked right at me and said, 'Don't you trust the *Ruach Ha'Kodesh* (Holy Spirit)?'"[250] Feeling that this response—a theological query consciously expressed in Hebrew—was a sign of deep respect and understanding, Reb Zalman carefully considered the question for the next few weeks and then went on to apprentice with Thurman, whom he lovingly referred to as his "Black *Rebbe*."[251]

Throughout the rest of his life, Reb Zalman sought out mentors and companions from various religious and cultural communities with whom he could engage in spiritual experimentation and deliberation. In reflecting on his friendship with Thomas Merton, for example, he described it as a "dialogue of the devout"—"I love God, you love God, so let's talk about how we're getting on with God and with our prayer."[252] In this case, Reb Zalman felt comfortable enough sharing with his Catholic pen pal the ups and downs of his religious journey. In a 1964 letter to Merton, the rabbi spoke openly about the frustration he felt about the fact that his hectic professional schedule had severely curtailed his prayer life: "It is so difficult to think about G-d, always being His errand boy, then I say to myself: 'I didn't ask for the errand. It was sent to me. Maybe He wants my errands more than my meditations.'" Reb Zalman closed the letter playfully with the following words: "So, I will pray for you and please pray for me, and we will keep in mind, won't we, that whatever curve we get pitched, we will try to bat. And after all, what is the business of the cross all about if not that."[253]

While religious leaders regularly engage in public interreligious initiatives—often in response to social and political crises—Reb Zalman invested much of his interreligious efforts in cultivating personal relationships. As he moved further from the Lubavitch community, he craved the intimacy and intensity he once shared with his peers and teachers in the more insular world of Hasidism. Often, he developed relationships with others, like him, located on the edges (or "growing edges"—borrowing from Howard Thurman's spiritual lexicon) of their communities. Reb Zalman's emphasis on the cultivation of meaningful interreligious relationships is an important reminder of the power of such connections in shaping who we are, both personally and professionally. Further, it is my experience that such relationships are invaluable when facing challenging issues involving different religious communities, as there is a level of trust already established before attempting to resolve a given matter.

The "Skillful Means":
Cultivating the Spirit

Throughout his many years of interreligious exploration, Reb Zalman always had a passionate interest in learning about the "spiritual technologies" of other seekers and devotees. What, he wanted to know, helped a Sufi sheikh feel God's loving presence in his life? Which prayers did a Catholic nun find most useful in cultivating her capacity for compassion? Reflecting on this point, Reb Zalman wrote that what drew him and Merton together was their shared interest in the *upaya* (from Sanskrit: skillful means), the practices one undertook to help facilitate personal and communal transformation. Using Jewish and Christian terminology to explain the point, Reb Zalman added that they sought to better understand what would help with *tikkun ha'midot* (repair of one's attributes) and *conversatio morum* (growth, lit., fidelity to, in the monastic life). The fundamental question was, "How do I move from my *is* to my *ought?*"[254] For Reb Zalman, this approach to interfaith engagement flowed from his understanding of Hasidism as a devotional path in which spiritual growth (*halikhah*) is intertwined with sacred practice (*halakhah*). In his interreligious explorations, Reb Zalman actively sought to learn about different ways of connecting with God, refining one's character, and building intentional community.[255] He believed that thoughtful practitioners from different religious and cultural contexts could help one another expand their consciousness and become more refined devotees and effective leaders.

In the latter stages of his life, Reb Zalman spoke of the relationships of the world's religions in "organismic" terms. Using the metaphor of the human body, he taught that each spiritual tradition should be viewed as a different organ, at once serving a distinct function while also acting interdependently within the body. In this post-triumphalist vision, one must hold the tension of particularity and universality, working to maintain the integrity of one's own community while also engaging reciprocally with other communities—sharing "vital nutrients" for the health of the heart, lungs, brain, etc., and of the organism as a whole.[256]

Conclusion

Reb Zalman was a pioneer in the North American interreligious movement. A person of great intellectual acuity and spiritual curiosity, he undertook a unique religious journey that took him from Brooklyn, New York, to Bardsdale, Kentucky, to Daramsala, India, to his final resting place in Boulder, Colorado. A self-described mystic, he believed that God's mysterious presence animated and infused all of existence and that no single person or community had full or unobscured access to the Infinite. While he remained deeply rooted in the Jewish tradition throughout his career, Reb Zalman also actively explored other religious and cultural traditions. A gifted autodidact, he learned a great deal from his studies but prized his relationships with practitioners from other communities. He was particularly drawn to fellow "renewalists," teachers and leaders working to reinvigorate their traditions and the broader world using an eclectic blend of traditional and contemporary methods. Speaking of his fondness for the Dalai Lama, for example, he stated, "We each want to preserve as much of the ethnic and traditional material that we can, but to transform it so that it can be practiced in the present."[257]

As a rabbi who spends much of his work life engaged in interfaith and cross-cultural educational and activist endeavors, I feel greatly indebted to Reb Zalman for his innovative bridge building efforts. Through his daring, eclectic, and heartfelt experiments, he paved the way for others to work creatively across communities for healing and transformation, while also attending to the particular needs of one's tradition. May Reb Zalman's memory continue to serve as a source of blessing and inspiration.

Raimon Panikkar[258]

Archbishop Felix Machado

I FIRST HEARD OF Raimon Panikkar in the course of my seminary studies in Mumbai in the 60s. Panikkar was a world-famous thinker whose contribution to dialogue among religions has been considered important, significant, and unique in approach, method, and conclusions, despite criticism. He initially impressed me with his groundbreaking book *The Unknown Christ of Hinduism*.[259] The book contributed towards a more critical Christian self-understanding at a very crucial time. It invites the reader to a contemplative insight into that Mystery that can be named only in the vocative and whose name is a super name chiseled upon a white pebble that can be properly kept only in the cave of the heart of the world. It does not claim to unveil this mystery or dictate the language that the believer in Christ is to use. The book is addressed to Christians who must encounter Hinduism in order to know Christ. The genuinely Christian attitude is to call forth that truth of Hinduism without destroying the latter's identity. To Christianity, Hinduism in turn offers the authentically Hindu gift of a new experience and interpretation—a new dimension, in fact—of the Mystery.

After my priestly ordination in the Archdiocese of Bombay, I was asked to continue my studies in New York. When I arrived in the States, the semester had already started and I could not be admitted to the university. As I was waiting for the following semester to begin, I came to know that Raimon Panikkar was scheduled to teach a course at Maryknoll School of Theology in Ossining, New York. I registered for the course in the master of arts progam, and it is there that I came in close contact with Panikkar. Our common journey gradually developed into friendship. Later, on several occasions, Raimon also came to visit me in India, spent time with my family, and visited places of interest in my village. Panikkar usually spent six months in India and six months in the US and/or Europe. In India, he taught at the Benares Hindu University; in the US, at Harvard University in Boston, before moving to the University of California at Santa Barbara.

While I worked in the Vatican as under-secretary for the Pontifical Council for Interreligious Dialogue (1993–2008), Panikkar would send me excerpts, extracts, articles, and books of his by post, motivating me to read them. Although Panikkar taught officially at the University of California at Santa Barbara and I was a student at Fordham University, New York, an arrangement was made for me to have Raimon Panikkar as my doctoral guide, together with Dr. Ewert Cousins.

Who is Raimon Panikkar? It is difficult to introduce him. He himself would often say that he was born at a crossroads: a Christian who discovered that he was Hindu and later converted to Buddhism, without ever having left Christianity. Son of an Indian father and a Catalonian mother, Raimon grew up in Barcelona in a Catalonian traditional Catholic Christian family. As an adult, Raimon decided to become a Catholic priest and so pursued that formation and became a priest. He had obtained a doctorate in science (chemistry) and later completed two other doctorates, one in philosophy and one in theology. Gifted with sharp acumen, ability, and readiness to learn, he mastered various ancient and modern languages. All this, as well as his hard work, brought Raimon Panikkar into the world of great thinkers, as expressed in dozens of books, some of which are lengthy tomes.

Panikkar's Groundbreaking and Original Thought: Intra-Religious Dialogue

Panikkar sought to bridge the gap between traditional ways of knowing (*scientia*) and those of modern science. He sought to extend discourse from an in-house discussion among Christians to a genuine dialogue between religions, a dialogical dialogue rather than a dialectical one, that is, one that involves discovery of the other as a being who speaks and acts in his or her own name, a true other. This also implies an awareness of our own individual limitations and hence a certain relativization of our personal opinions. For Panikkar, dialogue cannot be constrained by rules of the game laid down from one side or the other. No single religious or cultural tradition exhausts the millennial human experience. Panikkar categorically states that nobody has a monopoly on being human.

Panikkar's famous book *The Intra-Religious Dialogue*[260] has been groundbreaking in the field of interfaith dialogue. In it, Panikkar explains elaborately that when one studies the doctrines of the various religions, it is called inter-religious dialogue; but, more rarely, the dialogue catches hold within the very person and removes his mask of being a religious spokesperson within his own tradition. That is intra-religious dialogue, which in itself becomes a religious process. One then seeks the meaning of life in light of the experiences that have crystallized within the various traditions and which are already more or less assimilated by the actual person with whom one is dealing. This intra-religious dialogue oftentimes leaves the individual in a solitude that can be purifying or destructive. In brief, the true meeting between religions is itself religious. It takes place in the heart of the human person in search for his or her own way. It is then that the dialogue is intra-religious; as a religious act in itself, it becomes, moreover, a quest for salvific truth. One participates in such a dialogue not only by looking above, towards the transcendent reality, towards the original tradition, but also horizontally, towards the world of other humans who themselves have found paths leading to the realization of human destiny.

Intra-religious dialogue hardly makes a sound. It goes on within the depths of the person. It is open and deep dialogue with oneself that is no longer locked in the jail of egotism. It is deep, because one does not dialogue exclusively with one's own tradition or with others as others but with a self that has assimilated, in its own way, a view of reality that has drawn upon different sources. When the contact with others is superficial, it is easy to show tolerance and even sympathy towards them, but one does not ask oneself the personal question of truth. Too often, a respectful attitude hides a contemptuous indifference.

Intra-religious dialogue is an internal dialogue in which one struggles with the angel, the demon, and oneself. One asks if one can have access to the whole of religious truth, since the neighbour seems to have other convictions that are as radical as one's own. But this internal dialogue is neither a monologue nor a simple soliloquy with God. Nor is it merely a meditation on the partner's belief or on another religion. In this dialogue, one is in search of one's salvation, but accepts being taught by the other and not only by one's own clan. Intra-religious dialogue is, of its very nature, an act of assimilation—which Panikkar calls eucharistic, alluding to the central sacrament in Catholicism. It tries to assimilate the transcendent into our immanence.

Panikkar here anticipates some probable questions: "Isn't there the beginning of religious apostasy in intra-religious dialogue? Shouldn't I first try to better understand the riches of my tradition before venturing into unknown ways? Doesn't intra-religious dialogue smack of a tendency towards eclecticism and syncretism, which betrays my lack of faithfulness and my shallowness?" Panikkar's answer is that intra-religious dialogue, in its most authentic aspect, is not to be found at the purely sociological or historical level. It is, in a word, a constitutive element of one who is a nexus of relationships, a person—not an isolated individual, nor an unconscious atom, nor a number—within a democratic complex. It is our human constitution that beckons us to discover within ourselves the human universe and also all of reality. When we speak of one as a microcosm, this does not mean that one is then considered as another world in miniature, side by side with a multiplicity of small worlds; but it means that one is the miniaturization of the only world, that a person is the world on a human scale.

Intra-religious dialogue, by helping us discover the other in ourselves contributes to the personal realization and mutual fertility between the traditions of mankind that can no longer live in a state of isolation, separated from each other by walls of mutual mistrust, or in a state of war, which is more or less camouflaged by emulation and competition. Even peaceful co-existence is often but one form of political strategy in order to maintain the status quo—although preferable, undoubtedly, to war. Panikkar, professing his Christian faith, writes:

> When I shall have discovered the Atheist,[261] the Hindu and the Christian in me, when I shall consider my brother as another myself and when the "other" will not feel alienated in me . . . then we shall be closer to the Kingdom of God.[262]

Not Dialectical but Dialogical Dialogue

Among Panikkar's innovative cross-cultural studies, one cannot ignore *Myth, Faith, and Hermeneutics: Cross-Cultural Studies.*[263] The book brings together the major essays that best illustrate his method of understanding the truth of more than one religious tradition from within. Panikkar writes in his book, "If intellectual activity divorces itself from life, it becomes not only barren and alienating, but also harmful and perhaps eventually criminal."[264] Myth is the fundamental area of human experience. A living myth does not allow for interpretation, because it needs no intermediary. Myth is that which we have taken for granted, that which we do not question; and it is unquestioned because, de facto, it is not seen as questionable. The myth is transparent like light. It purifies thought, bypasses thought, so that the unthought may emerge and the intermediary disappear. Faith is understood as that dimension in humankind that corresponds to myth. Belief articulates the myth in which we believe without believing that we believe in it. Hermeneutics is the art and science of interpretation, of bringing forth significance, of conveying meaning, of restoring symbols to life and eventually of letting new symbols emerge. Hermeneutics implies going out from my own "stand" in order to "under-stand" another world view.[265]

When reflecting on culture and tradition, Panikkar values the dimension of myth. Man cannot live without myths. Much is discussed about the insufficiencies of one's own cultures and religions, and one realizes that no one has the monopoly on kindness and truth. Even though reality is much complex and nuanced, Panikkar offers five typological moments in order to uncover the emerging myth in the study of the history of encounter between the religious traditions of mankind. One must understand the five moments which have been mentioned below in a *kairological* (rather than chronological) sense, as interpenetrating and combining moments, thus giving birth to dynamism and tensions in the life of people and peoples.[266]

1. *Isolation and ignorance*: Each culture develops with the self-sufficiency of one's own group. Hardly any interest is shown outside of the unavoidable contacts with neighbours. Basically, the other does not exist.

2. *Indifference and contempt*: The other is considered, at best, nothing more than a problem of rivalry.

3. *Condemnation and conquest*: From rivalry, one tends to consider the other as someone to convert, even by honest means. The other almost becomes a threat we must do away with, a challenge to be taken up.

4. *Coexistence and communication*: Sooner or later, peoples realize that mutual tolerance and peaceful and sincere communication are the source of reciprocal and durable advantages. The other begins to intrigue us. There is a progressive takeover by the other while remaining faithful to one's own culture. Care is taken not to alienate the other while having the other integrated within.

5. *Convergence and dialogue*: True dialogue requires not only a welcoming and listening disposition but also a capacity to understand or the possibility to do so. The other starts to become another pole of ourselves. Confrontation tends towards complementarity. New ways of life appear, not without causing victims on both sides (in matters of identity and alterity).

In our times, these five moments mentioned above seem to be recognized, but we have not yet moved beyond them. Panikkar adds five other words to situate the present encounter between the religious traditions:

1. *Inevitable*: General feeling of all that peoples and world religions can no longer live in isolation and mutual indifference.

2. *Important*: Religions are the soul of every culture, and, because of this, they play an essential role in this world of ours, which is becoming more and more one.

3. *Urgent*: For better or for worse, today's world is in effervescence, and, even more, it is at a boiling point. If mankind's venerable traditions do not contribute in forging a new mentality, the latter will be formed without their immediate impact. There is no way we can avoid the urgency of the situation.

4. *Upsetting*: Meeting of religions troubles one's peace of mind, disrupts the most deeply rooted beliefs, creates confusion which can lead to internal and external breakups. It questions that which, up until then, remained undisputed, even indisputable. Oftentimes, negative criticism gains ascendancy over positive criticism, because it is almost impossible to build before having cleared the field.

5. *Purifying*: None of us is self-sufficient. Nobody can lay claim to universality when the very way of expressing it is sectarian. This coming to awareness has a purifying effect. Other systems and other beliefs, other habits and ways of life, can not only compare with our own but also purify, complement, correct, enhance, and even change what, till then, were considered definitive and hence untouchable acquisitions of mankind.

Panikkar warns about a danger of our times, namely, a hasty and short-sighted synthesis. He suggests that before coming to some sort of wholistic view, we must study doctrines, know the facts, and discover the spirit of another tradition. Panikkar uses two terms: concrete and universal. Although concrete and universal are not opposed, they do appear to be paradoxical; e.g., when one claims to be concrete, one then ceases to be universal; when one claims to be universal, one appears to be abstract, i.e., ceases to be human in a practical sense. Accordingly, Panikkar asks whether it is possible to be concrete without losing one's own identity and universal without losing one's sense of what is human. The question he asks is the following: how is one to arrive at true growth in awareness, to a personal synthesis, that spontaneously informs all of one's life and translates in a new way, expressive of that synthesis? Panikkar further questions: "How, from a given perspective, can one come to understand another viewpoint?" He answers the question by proposing that conflicts of loyalties and commitments must be resolved to allow for a real assimilation, obviously, without either indigestion or juxtaposition; this is an enormous task. The first stage to cover is to know other traditions the best way we can, to develop empathy and understanding, to be aware that to discover another religion is at the same time to deepen and purify our own, and that to learn another tradition can only enrich us.

Panikkar and Mysticism

I would like to conclude this essay on a more personal note, beginning with reference to Panikkar's deep impact on my own way of being, thinking, and acting in this world. One book in particular is relevant here: *The Vedic Experience Mantramanjari: An Anthology of the Vedas for Modern Man and Contemporary Celebration.*[267] This monumental achievement of Panikkar is important for all who desire cross-cultural studies. For me, as a Christian in India, this volume has become my close companion after the Bible. Panikkar himself declares in his forward to his *opera omnia* that "his writings are not the fruit of mere speculation but, rather, autobiographical—that is, they were first inspired by a life and praxis that have been only subsequently molded into writings." Panikkar reveals that he did not live for the sake of writing, but he wrote to live in a more conscious way so as to help his fellows with thoughts not only from his own mind but also from a superior Source, which may perhaps be called Spirit—although he does not claim that his writings are in any way inspired.[268]

Panikkar wrote a rather long preface to my own book, *Jnaneshvari: Path to Liberation,* which is about a revered and most dear Maharashtra Hindu mystic of the twelfth century who lived in my native place. Jnanadev, the Hindu mystic, is the father of a distinct theology, spirituality, and culture of the Marathi Indians. The book takes us into the realm of mysticism. Mysticism is the very heart of life itself. It encompasses active, intellectual, and emotional aspects of human life. This is why human survival has been difficult, if not impossible, without mystics. Panikkar begins his preface by writing: "This book presents a rare quality, and it could become a seminal work for a still relatively virgin field, that of Comparative Mysticism."[269] Elsewhere, he writes:

> Mysticism should not be seen as the special province of the few but rather as one essential dimension of humankind—although present in a somewhat withered form in today's technological and scientific culture, which approaches human reality through rigorously bifocal lenses (the senses and the ratiocinating reason), in spite of the protests of artists and the passive resistance of ordinary people . . . . Mysticism means integral experience of Life . . . . It is the holistic experience of reality . . . . Every person has a mystic hidden in him.[270]

I conclude with reference to the special occasion for writing this modest piece, namely, to honor a friend. I consider Rabbi David Rosen my friend, not simply because we have been meeting over the years at different venues of our international conferences in the context of promoting, strengthening, and deepening interfaith dialogue. No less importantly, in Rabbi Rosen, I see the hidden mystic of Jewish religious tradition. Its outer expression is found in his personality and work. He is down to earth, relating to everyone around him, inspiring, encouraging, and persuasively influencing all who enjoy meeting him.

Ad multosannos! दीर्घायुष्मान्भव! (Sanskrit)

Thich Nhat Hanh

Prof. Sallie B. King

Thich Nhat Hanh is a hero of interreligious friendship, a hero of peace-making, a poet, and the prolific author of over one hundred books. A Zen Buddhist monk from Vietnam, Thay (meaning teacher, the name with which his students and others address him) was one of the leaders of the Buddhist effort to end the war in Vietnam and has contributed greatly to the modernization of Buddhism. He is one of the founders of the Engaged Buddhism movement, which advocates the engagement by Buddhists in social issues on the basis of universal goodwill, principled nonviolence, and Buddhist ethical ideals. Along with the Dalai Lama, Thay has been a tremendously important teacher of Buddhism in the West. Certainly, he has been a most important teacher to me.

There are two major foundations to Thay's ability to connect deeply with people in other religions: interreligious friendships and the emphasis on religious experience over doctrine.

Interreligious Friendship

An important element in good interreligious relations, for Thay, is interreligious friendship.

Thay's closest personal interreligious relationships are with Christians and with Christianity itself. He has written two major books offering his personal view of the meeting place of Buddhism and Christianity: *Living Buddha, Living Christ* and *Going Home: Jesus and Buddha as Brothers*. A third book, *The Raft Is Not the Shore: Conversations Toward a Buddhist-Christian Awareness*, by Thich Nhat Hanh and Jesuit priest Daniel Berrigan, is a record of a series of conversations between Thay and Berrigan in 1974.[271]

Thay himself feels a close connection with Christianity. He puts it this way:

It is possible to know the Buddha and at the same time know Jesus. There are people who have roots within both the Buddhist tradition and the Christian tradition. In my hermitage, I put a lot of Buddha statues on my altar . . . . I also have a statue of Jesus as my ancestor. I have adopted Jesus Christ as one of my spiritual ancestors.

During the Vietnam War I worked very hard in order to stop the killing. When I was in Europe and in North America I met with a number of Christians who really embodied the spirit of love, of understanding, of peace, of Jesus. Thanks to these people I have touched deeply Jesus as a spiritual teacher, a spiritual ancestor.[272]

One of the most important of Thay's relationships with Christians was his relationship with Dr. Martin Luther King Jr. They met only twice, in 1966 and 1967. Thay had come to the United States to urge Americans not to continue to pursue the war in Vietnam. After their first meeting, King wrote to the Nobel Prize committee to nominate Thay for the Nobel Peace Prize. He wrote:

I do not personally know of anyone more worthy of the Nobel Peace Prize than this gentle Buddhist monk from Vietnam. I know Thich Nhat Hanh and am privileged to call him my friend. He is a holy man, for he is humble and devout. He is a scholar of immense intellectual capacity. His ideas for peace, if applied, would build a monument to ecumenism, to world brotherhood, to humanity.[273]

After their second meeting, King came out publicly against the war in Vietnam, at considerable political cost to himself.

Thay has said of meeting King:

It was only . . . through friendships with Christian men and women who truly embody the spirit of understanding and compassion of Jesus, that I have been able to touch the depths of Christianity. The moment I met Martin Luther King, Jr., I knew I was in the presence of a holy person. Not just his good work but his very being was a source of great inspiration for me. And others, less well known, have made me feel that Lord Jesus is still here with us.[274]

To commemorate their meeting, a monumental statue of Thay and King was erected on the grounds of Thay's monastery in Mississippi. Together, they are depicted as holding a document on which is written, in Thay's calligraphy, "Beloved Community" (a famous goal of Dr. King's: the just, nonviolent, and loving society for which both he and, in his own way, Thay worked).

Thay has also engaged in a long life of dialogue with Christian contemplatives. One of them, Thomas Merton, wrote: "Thich Nhat Hanh is more my brother than many who are nearer to me in race and nationality, because he and I see things in exactly the same way." When Thay's life was under threat due to his anti-war activism, Merton pleaded in an open letter: "If I mean something to you, then let me put it this way: do for Nhat Hanh whatever you would do for me if I were in his position. In many ways I wish I were."[275] Thay also spoke warmly of Merton, praising his openness. Linking his own approach to Merton's, Thay went on to say: "My Buddhism has been one without boundaries, not imprisoning myself in every narrow, locked space."[276] Indeed, it has. And he invites us all to such a spirituality, whatever its religious home.

Thay has also had a long friendship with Benedictine monk David Steindl-Rast.[277] When Brother David met Thay through Merton, he wrote:

> I recognized in him a brother in the Spirit.... He speaks of God out of his own living experience. And he speaks with enthusiasm—with the voice of the divine Spirit in his own heart.... For Christian readers, it would be a great loss to overlook this voice of insight and compassion.[278]

Religious Experience over Doctrine

How can Brother David speak of Thay, a Buddhist, as speaking of God out of his own living experience? Thay speaks to the question of God and Buddhism thus:

> The Buddha was not against God. He was only against notions of God that are mere mental constructions that do not correspond to reality, notions that prevent us from developing ourselves and touching ultimate reality.[279]

The teachings of the Buddha are indeed rigorously apophatic. Buddhism as a tradition very often (not always) follows a strict *via negativa* in speaking of ultimate reality, but this is all in the service of opening the door to experiential knowledge of ultimate reality. Names and concepts are believed in Buddhism to interfere with direct, experiential knowledge, and only the latter has the ability to touch reality and truth. Of course, one must speak; but, in Buddhism, this is often understood to be speaking only to guide, to point the student in the right direction. Actual knowledge of truth is found only in experience. It is a given in Buddhism that language cannot capture ultimate truth.

This view of religious language has been at the heart of Thay's teachings from the beginning. While still in Vietnam, he founded the Tiep Hien Order (Order of Interbeing) as a new Engaged Buddhist order within Zen Buddhism. The first precept of this order states:

> Do not be idolatrous about or bound to any doctrine, theory, or ideology, even Buddhist ones. All systems of thought are guiding means; they are not absolute truth.[280]

Acting on this understanding, Thay shifts our focus away from theology or doctrine and toward religious experience. In so doing, Thay is opening the door to that which, he believes, unites us and away from that which divides us.

How then would Thay guide us? Thay offers teachings that are designed to usher the practitioner into direct touch with reality, in its depths, in the present moment. This is a kind of universal spirituality that, in his view, can stand on its own or be paired with other religions, a spirituality based upon mindfulness practices that cultivate in the practitioner the ability to directly touch the deepest level of reality.

In Thay's experience and teaching, ultimate reality and ordinary, everyday reality coincide in the present moment. Therefore, given the right quality of awareness, ultimate reality can be experientially accessed in each moment. "We have the distinction between the ultimate dimension and the historical dimension, but in fact the two dimensions are just together."[281] This is pure Zen Buddhism. Japanese Zen Buddhist master Dogen writes:

> When a person attains realization, it is like the moon's reflection in water. The moon never becomes wet; the water is never disturbed. Although the moon is a vast and great light, it is reflected in a drop of water. The whole moon and even the whole sky are reflected in a drop of dew on a blade of grass.[282]

The moon here represents Buddhahood, supreme reality. This is a teaching of radical immanence; the holy is present in its fullness right here and now in things just as they are. With sufficient mindfulness (awareness of the present moment in the present moment) and concentration (energetic focus), we can get in touch with and directly experience that noumenal reality in the here and now, in the experience of any phenomenal reality. Thay often emphasizes accessing that experience through the gateway of sensorial experience: sight, sound, touch.

Here is an example of such a thing in Thay's teaching:

> When you come up here for chanting, when you listen to the chanting, you have to involve all your body and mind. If you do so, you are in concentration, you are in mindfulness; you come into phase with the Sangha [the practicing community] and you become one with the Sangha, like a river. You don't exist anymore as an individual; you become the river of the Sangha.[283]

The you who stands apart from other things is gone. What remains? Dogen's moon is fully present in the dewdrop; here, it is present in the chanting. In the next moment, one may hear it in the birdsong or feel it in the cool breeze on one's face. One only needs to get oneself out of the way in order to realize it. This could be true whether one were chanting in a Buddhist, Christian, other religious, or entirely nonreligious context. No one owns this kind of natural spirituality.

> In the teaching, the practice, the tradition of Buddhism, there is really no distinction between meditation and prayer, because when you are mindful, concentrated, when you have insight, you get in touch with the Buddha land, with the Buddha, with the Sangha. When you really pray, you get in touch with Jesus, with the Kingdom of God.[284]

In his Buddhist-Christian dialogue books, Thay does not hesitate to speak of religious experience using both Buddhist and Christian language. Above, he uses the terms Buddha land and Kingdom of God interchangeably to speak of ultimate reality here and now.

Living with Two Traditions

Thay does not encourage people to convert to Buddhism. He writes:

> I think rootedness means a lot for dialogue. We don't want people to get uprooted from their traditions. We want them to go back. Buddhist practice may help them to go back to their own roots. In my country we had suffered a lot because missionaries had tried to pull us out of our own traditions. They said we could only be saved by giving up our ancestral traditions, our Buddhist practices. We don't want to do the same thing to our friends.[285]

He goes on to say that he has seen many Vietnamese who want to move to the West and forget their roots, as well as many Europeans and Americans who want to become a Buddhist because they have hated everything related to their roots. Have they succeeded in leaving everything behind in order to become something completely new? The answer is no . . . . A tree without roots cannot survive. A person without roots cannot survive either.[286]

Buddhism is a universal religion, and, of course, Thay accepts converts, both lay and monastic. But he also encourages those who come to practice with him not to leave the traditions of their birth and culture but to return to their own traditions, taking with them what they have learned to help them to be better members and practitioners of their own traditions. I have seen people scoff when I have related this, but I have heard Thay say this in retreats, and I have seen this several times in print and in transcribed interviews. I personally know people who came to Thay alienated from their own traditions and who returned to those traditions with renewed interest and enthusiasm after practicing with Thay.

Here is how Thay put it on one occasion:

> The right attitude is not to encourage people to be uprooted from their tradition. The right attitude is to urge them to go back to their traditions, and the practice of Buddhist mindfulness, concentration and insight should be able to do this. I think there are enough Buddhists; we don't need to convert more people to Buddhism. Just taking care of the Buddhists we have now takes a lot of energy already. Many of them don't practice. So let us not worry about making more Buddhists.[287]

When Thay says "the practice of Buddhist mindfulness, concentration and insight should be able to do this," what he means is that all religions have an experiential dimension, a dimension of making direct contact with ultimate reality, but Buddhism (along with some others) has particularly emphasized the development of practices to intentionally cultivate practitioners in such a way as to enable them to be capable of making this direct contact. Thay offers these practices to persons of any or no religion, to enable them to touch reality in its depths, and he invites them to take such experiential knowledge as they gain from these practices back with them to their own religious traditions.

Thay is a peacemaker. To enhance the possibilities for peace, he knows it is important for the religions to be on good terms with one another. In this age when, coronavirus notwithstanding, the global movement of people and electronic communications have transformed the nature of human life, it is crucial to work out ways to live together, sharing our beautiful planet. One question that inevitably arises in interreligious circles, as people wander and mingle, is what to think about interreligious marriage. Thay has a simple solution:

> When two people from different traditions marry, the young man could make a vow to learn and practice the spiritual tradition of the young woman, and the young woman could make a vow to learn and practice that of the young man. In that case, both of them would have two roots instead of one, and this can only enrich each person. When they have a family, the children should be raised in such a way that they can appreciate the best things in both traditions. The parents should encourage their children to have two roots and to have both the Buddha and Jesus within their life. Why not?
>
> This will open up a new age where people are more tolerant, where more people can see the beauty and value of other traditions . . . . You love the apple; yes, you are authorized to love the apple, but no one prevents you from also loving the mango.[288]

I have been privileged to make the acquaintance of Rabbi David Rosen through Elijah, having served over multiple days as a small group dialogue facilitator that included him. In writing about Thay in honor of Rabbi Rosen, I have reflected on similarities and differences between the two. Both highly value interreligious friendship, but, in other respects, there are marked differences. Thay has no problem with double religious belonging and interreligious marriage, whereas for Rabbi Rosen, affirming boundaries established by religious identity is an important part of religious commitment. Of course, Thay is well known as a liberal or radical, whereas Rabbi Rosen is more traditional or conservative. It is clear that the foundations of the religious life for Thay and for Rabbi Rosen are quite different, so we do not expect them to end at the same point. Yet, I believe that they could meet each other at a midway point that I have enjoyed discovering: their mutual championing of a vegan diet, which is deeply important to them both, for reasons of compassion and ethics first and foremost but also for environmental and health reasons. Here we can reflect on the important possibility of people who are otherwise different to each other and who have different life commitments potentially being able to be strong and committed allies to each other. There are many ways to build bridges. Friendship is a great way; being allies is another.

Chiara Lubich

PROF. JOSEPH SIEVERS

TRENT WAS NOT KNOWN for its ecumenical or interfaith relations. The Council of Trent (1545–1563) is usually seen as an event that cemented divisions rather than formed mutual understanding. In that city, Chiara Lubich (1920–2008) was born and raised in a family that included unusual diversity. Her mother was a devout Catholic, her father a convinced Socialist and temporarily agnostic, and her elder brother an active member of the Communist Party and, during World War II, coordinator of a resistance group. He was incarcerated, tortured, and threatened with the death penalty by the Nazis. Despite their different worldviews, the family remained united. Chiara was especially close to her father and to her brother, although she herself was already active in leadership positions in Catholic organizations in her teenage years.

This firsthand experience of unity in diversity seems to have had a formative influence on her for the rest of her life. At age twenty-three, in one of the most critical phases of World War II in 1943, she decided to dedicate her life to God, whatever that would mean. Soon thereafter, a growing number of women joined her, with the idea that living for God meant serving him in the neediest and helping to build the unity for which Jesus had prayed (cf. John 17). Members of the movement that became known as Focolare now are engaged in many different professions as teachers, health professionals, researchers, artists, lawyers, judges, law enforcement officers, and politicians across different political parties. Instead of just helping individuals, Focolare has inspired and encouraged businesses that try to create just and sustainable jobs and working conditions and to promote relations with customers and suppliers based on the same principles. Perhaps without speaking of it, this can be seen as love in action, fighting poverty while contributing to well-being, harmony, and unity.

Already in 1947, Lubich wrote the following brief reflection concerning unity in diversity. This was long before Vatican II, and she was not thinking about interreligious dialogue. Yet, it seems very pertinent to her involvement in interfaith relations.

> Think of the sun and its rays. Take the sun as a symbol of the will of God, which is God himself. Imagine the rays symbolize God's will for each individual. Walk to the sun in the light of your own ray, diverse and distinct from everyone else's, and fulfill the marvelous design God has for you.
>
> There is an unlimited number of rays, all pouring from the same sun . . . each a single will, special for each of us.
>
> The closer the rays get to the sun, the closer they get to each other. We too, the closer we get to God, by doing his will more and more perfectly, the closer we get to each other.
>
> Until we shall all be one.[289]

Thus she realized, in a way that was not at all common at the time, that a Christian's task was not to push or convince the other to a particular path but to help him or her to find their own way. Early on, she emphasized that God's will was above all that we love God as well as our fellow human beings, as expressed in the twofold command to love based on Deuteronomy and Leviticus and combined by Jesus in the Gospels. One further step for her was the Johannine injunction "this is my commandment, that you love one another as I have loved you" (John 15:12 NRSV). For her, this meant to be willing to give one's life for the others as Jesus did, even in small daily installments.

From the late 1940s, single men along with married persons as well as families began to join Lubich and her companions. Soon this group was noticed in Church circles in Trent and beyond. The archbishop of the city realized that this was an initiative that did not fit into existing structures of Catholic lay organizations. He gave local approval to the Focolare (hearth, fireplace, hence a synonym for family in common usage), as it came to be known. Lubich remained the inspiration for the group, although for some time she was barred from having leadership roles, especially because of resistance by bishops in other parts of Italy against lay—and especially female—leadership. At the same time, bishops in other countries appreciated the new movement. The Catholic Bishops Conference warmly welcomed them in East Germany (the then Democratic Republic of Germany [DDR]) in particular, where, since 1959, some Focolare members had moved to fill medical needs but also to assist Christians in the difficult situations in this and other Soviet Bloc countries. They did not go there to fight communism but to bring love, through concrete service as doctors and nurses in hospitals and in other ways. Lubich was able to inspire, encourage, and even visit them. During one of her visits to Germany, a chance encounter with Lutherans provided the initial spark for an ecumenical dimension of Focolare, with the discovery of a mutual desire to live a scripturally oriented life. Similarly, interreligious dialogue was not part of any strategic plan but was a natural outgrowth of a spirituality based on love for everyone with the goal of building unity without barriers.

Lubich managed to remain firmly rooted in the Catholic Church. She had close relations with Pope Paul VI, for whom she also served as a go-between with the Ecumenical Patriarch Athenagoras I, and with Pope John Paul II, who decided, upon her suggestion, that her successor as president of the Focolare Movement should always be a woman. Yet she opened doors of dialogue in many different directions within the Catholic church and with members of other churches, followers of different religions, and persons without religious affiliation. Her openness was rewarded with many civil, academic, and religious awards, among them more than a dozen honorary doctorates on four continents, the UNESCO Prize for Peace Education in Paris (1996), and the Gandhi Peace Award (2000) in Coimbatore, India.

In 1977, Lubich was one of the first recipients of the prestigious Templeton Prize. In her acceptance speech she said:

> The . . . expansion of the Movement brings us face to face with persons of other faiths. With the faithful of the noble and tortured Jewish people dialogue is easy. We share with them part of Revelation. We are grateful to them for having given us a Jewish Jesus, Jewish Apostles. And Mary too was Jewish.
>
> In Muslims we admire their tenacious love for religion. They are an example to us. The mystic of the Islamic tradition, Al-Hallaj, wrote: "In His Essence (In the essence of God), Love is the essence of essences."
>
> In Asia we met Buddhists. It is good . . . to remember the words of Buddha: "Like a mother who even at risk to her own life watches and protects her only son, so with a great soul we must . . . love the whole world. . . . "
>
> The words of the Indian mystic Ramakrishna strike us: "Only love matters. Have love for everyone: nobody is any different from you. God lives in everyone and nothing exists without him."
>
> We are in contact with Hindus and also with Shintoists. The dialogue which the members of the Movement established with these brothers of other religions is not made up of words. We love them as they are, concerning ourselves about everything to do with them and therefore also about their religious life.[290]

This occasion was not only an important recognition of the achievements of Lubich and her movement, but it was also a point of departure, bringing a new awareness of the possibilities and the need for dialogue, in particular interreligious dialogue. Since that time, such dialogue is not an optional aspect of the Focolare Movement but a central feature, enshrined in its statutes and its practice. Members of different churches and of different faith communities, as well as people without religious affiliation "who, in accordance with their conscience, wish to share the Movement's goals, practicing respect and unconditional love toward every fellow human being in a spirit of brotherhood and sisterhood"[291] can be and are part of Focolare. This openness was realized in an unexpected and exemplary way in Algeria.

In 1966, a former Benedictine monastery in Tlemcen, Algeria, was offered to the Focolare. Lubich with her council decided to accept this challenging offer and sent a small group of *focolarini* there. Working as teachers and auto mechanics in a population that is almost 100% Muslim, they were able to build ties of trust and friendship with many individuals and families. Since then, this mostly Muslim Focolare community has grown and has remained united and active even during the most difficult times. Without speaking about interreligious dialogue, relations between Muslims and Christians slowly grew to unexpected depths, as people confronted together crises and tragedies, as well as everyday life, on the basis of mutual love, inspired by the Focolare spirituality.

Especially after receiving the Templeton Prize, Lubich fostered and entertained contacts and spiritual friendship with many religious leaders, such as Rev. Nikkyo Niwano (co-founder of Rissho Kosei-kai and of what is now Religions for Peace), Imam W. Deen Mohammed (leader of the then American Society of Muslims), the Venerable Ajahn Tong Sirimangalo, a leading Buddhist monk and teacher in Thailand. In these and other cases, Lubich not only kept personal contacts but was invited to speak to their followers, often in the thousands. She had similarly significant encounters with Gandhian and other Hindu leaders, with Sikhs and others. Several of her earliest companions assisted her in these contacts, especially Natalia Dallapiccola and Dr. Enzo Fondi, whom Chiara entrusted with the founding of an international Center for Interreligious Dialogue. These relations continue to be maintained and nurtured by current generations of Focolare with their various counterparts in different religious traditions in various parts of the world. Lubich engaged with Jewish leaders in Italy, the United States, and elsewhere. In Argentina and Uruguay, members and organizations of various Jewish communities have been in regular dialogue with Focolare for some time. In 1998, Chiara accepted an invitation to address them in Buenos Aires. Her presentation stressed the spiritual bonds that link Jews and Christians, first of all in their common biblical roots, but also in expressions that are different but somewhat analogous. She cited rabbinic traditions such as the Golden Rule and encouragements to seek doing God's will that are amply paralleled in the New Testament and in Christian teaching. Above all, she added, these bonds between Jews and Christians can evolve from present encounters, where differences can be used to build bridges instead of creating chasms. Chiara expressed her goals as follows:

> First of all the desire to get to know you at least a little. Secondly, to engage in a relationship with you as one does with brothers and sisters, . . . a concrete relationship nourished possibly with reciprocal gifts. Brothers and sisters who discover one another as such after a long time and love one another."[292]

Especially in interreligious contexts, she often cited the Golden Rule, present in different forms in most religious traditions and even in some formulations of secular ethics. For her, the art of loving, as she called it, was of primary importance in every human relationship and, in a special way, in interreligious relations. She understood this to mean accepting and respecting the others in their own identity, without any attempt at proselytizing but with an openness to learning from each other:

> Always fix your gaze on the one Father of many children. Then you must see all as children of the same Father. In mind and in heart we must always go beyond the bounds imposed on us by human life alone and create the habit of constantly opening ourselves to the reality of being one human family in one Father: God.[293]

An important concept to which she often referred was "making ourselves one with the other," somewhat analogous to putting ourselves in the other's shoes.

> This practice . . . demands a complete emptying of ourselves: setting aside our thoughts, our feelings, our intentions, our plans so as to understand the other. . . . Making ourselves one requires poverty in spirit so as to be rich with love.[294]

Many people, from political and religious leaders to children, experienced this loving openness and attention of hers. A posthumous appreciation was offered by Lisa Palmieri-Billig at a meeting on Chiara Lubich and World Religions. Palmieri-Billig had met Lubich on a number of occasions and has been in regular contact with Focolare members in different parts of the world:

All of us here today, Christians, Muslims, Jews, Buddhists, Hindus, Sikhs, and perhaps even some agnostics and non-believers, coming from all over the world, have been enthralled by Chiara's simple and clear, yet charismatic message. We are all here today as brothers and sisters, as partners in a common commitment to find and cultivate the good in humankind everywhere. We believe this is the most effective weapon against all violence. Evil is the opposite of love; evil is the absence of love. We are here these days, as Chiara and our traditions taught us, to engage in construction, the opposite of destruction.[295]

She further observed:

The words "tolerance" and "integration" are much in use in our contemporary multi-religious and multi-ethnic societies. But Chiara used a different vocabulary. She was far ahead of her times. She preferred to speak of love.[296]

On an earlier occasion, an imam in Italy declared: "Thanks to Chiara Lubich and her Movement I too came to believe in the human family and to refute the friend-enemy logic; indeed, I learned to look upon the others with the certainty of discovering something good and important."[297]

Imam Ronald Shaheed, from Milwaukee, Wisconsin, described the relationship between Imam W. Deen Muhammed and Lubich in the following terms:

We have tried to describe our interfaith dialogue and the best description we can come up with is that we are a family of believers and when we get together, it's a family reunion. As one who has been intimately involved in the growing relationship between Chiara Lubich and her International Focolare Movement and Imam W. Deen Mohammed and his community of Muslims, I can say with the utmost confidence that we have been blessed to have an interfaith relationship that is a model for the whole world. I believe that God and only God could have made this possible.[298]

Personally, I first met Lubich when I was barely a teenager. Over the years, I learned a lot from her about the love that is all-embracing and about the unity that enables people to address sufferings and divisions. The private exchanges I remember best were brief but significant. I wrote to her at times when I felt that an expression she used relied on questionable interpretations of the New Testament. She listened and was willing to learn and make adjustments, even if the advice came from a young graduate student like me.

When my mother fell seriously ill in Germany, while I was a member of a Focolare community in New York, Lubich called me personally, suggesting that I go home to see my mother. A worldwide family for her was not only an idea but a living reality, always to be renewed. As a matter of fact, she said during a very trying time of her life back in 1973, "If I should have to leave this world today and you were to ask me for a single word, one last word that sums up our Ideal, I would say . . . '*Be a family.*'"[299] Later, she often repeated that concept. In this family, there is a safe and welcoming space for members of all religions and even for those who do not have any religious affiliation.

David Rosen, whose interfaith travels and contacts span the world of many faiths and organizations, is included in this open family, since his first meeting with Natalia Dallapiccola and Dr. Enzo Fondi back in 1989. He has been an active and much appreciated participant in many activities of the Focolare Movement. When Chiara Lubich passed away, he wrote: "Chiara's legacy is one of the greatest spiritual blessings of our time." It is an honor to dedicate this brief essay to him.

Increasing Understanding

The Dalai Lama

Dr. Alon Goshen-Gottstein

Tenzin Gyatso, who is the fourteenth Dalai Lama, is known universally as the Dalai Lama or as His Holiness. Born in 1935 in Tibet, he has been living in exile in India since his escape from Tibet in 1959. Since that time, he has become well known internationally, earning both the Nobel Peace Prize and the Templeton Prize. He is, after the pope, the best known religious leader worldwide and is particularly recognized for his teachings of nonviolence and his work towards peace. Within this context, his approach to interreligious relations stands out in particular. It is one of the main pillars of his work internationally, for over half a century. The Dalai Lama has engaged throughout this period in multiple interfaith initiatives, both undertaken by him and undertaken by others. He is a champion of the cause of interfaith relations on all levels. And he has contributed significantly both to the public practice of interreligious relations and to the development of theory that accompanies it. He is arguably the world religious leader most deeply and consistently engaged in interreligious dialogue.

I will present the Dalai Lama as an interreligious hero by appeal to his own account of the method and centrality that interreligious relations occupy for him. I will do so through an analysis of the contents of a book that he penned, that is dedicated to the subject. The book is titled *Toward a True Kinship of Faiths: How the World's Religions Can Come Together.*[300]

In this book, the Dalai Lama records his journey into other religions and the theories he has developed as a consequence of this journey. The Dalai Lama emerges as a global religious leader, setting an example and offering a path and a theory that is meant for all of humanity's religious practitioners.

Being in exile forces the Dalai Lama into an encounter with other religions. This encounter provides the opportunity for a lifelong process of learning. Exile has allowed him to redefine his role as a religious leader and, by means of encounter with other religions, to develop a teaching that is global in reach. Early in the book, the reader is exposed to the Dalai Lama's self understanding of his task as a religious leader, summarized in three points:

1. The promotion of basic human values, especially compassion;

2. The promotion of interreligious understanding and harmony; and

3. The pursuit of a happy and satisfactory solution to the crisis of Tibet and its people.

One notes that the traditional and inherited task of the Dalai Lama is listed third, while other, more universal concerns, undertaken by him voluntarily, are listed earlier. In all of this, the Dalai Lama does not even define himself as a religious leader, responsible for the propagation of teachings of the Vajrayana school of Buddhism. The Dalai Lama identifies himself more as a religious person, thinker, practitioner, and monk than as a religious leader, even though he does not shun his official leadership role. But rather than define his role as a religious leader in traditional terms, he has redefined it to include broader teachings, aimed at all of humanity.

The first lesson that can be learned from a close reading of how the Dalai Lama describes his various encounters with other religious leaders is that the Dalai Lama does not meet ideas, institutions, or even leaders. He meets people, with whom he forms friendships, who impress and inspire him, and who provide him with the living testimonies of the power of faith in their lives, the power in light of which his recognitions and theories are formulated. Interreligious friendship is the foundation of the Dalai Lama's journey. The Dalai Lama is always appreciative of his various meetings and prepared to learn something meaningful from the representative of another religion. However, some people touch his heart, and those seem to provide the true foundation for his reflections. Not surprisingly, the people that touch him most are the practitioners whose lives and teachings offer testimony to the depth of the power of spirit in their lives. Again, not surprisingly, the figures that seem to touch him in the deepest way are those who have an openness to the spirit that extends beyond the boundaries of their own religion. Thomas Merton's is the first and formative relationship that defines what the Dalai Lama finds most significant in relations with practitioners of other religions. Rabbi Zalman Schachter stands out as the most prominent Jewish leader, in many ways a spiritual brother to the Dalai Lama: a practitioner with broad intellectual interest, keen spiritual senses, and an existential openness to other religious traditions. The Dalai Lama acknowledges that his deepest friendships have been with Christians. While he considers this to be a consequence of his early encounters with Merton, it may be that Christianity produces more men and women of faith who, like the Dalai Lama, seek to deepen their own faith experience through an engagement of other faiths.

In highlighting some religions rather than others, the Dalai Lama gives us further testimony to the foundational principle of his journey: a true encounter with other religions is made possible through personal friendships and the meeting of heart, mind, and spirit they produce. The Dalai Lama admits that he has had little opportunity to interact with Muslims. He knows of Islam from the native Tibetan Muslim community, from books, and, recently, from visits to Jordan and Malaysia. But it is clear that his engagement with Islam lacks the same basis of personal depth and engagement that characterizes his relations with other religions. His speaking out on behalf of Islam as a nonviolent religion is consequently all the more meaningful, as it is a principled assessment, not one colored by personal relationships.

The Dalai Lama encounters, reads, and interprets Christianity, Judaism, and Islam in a strikingly original way, born of his personal encounter and process, and his readings are noteworthy. When the Dalai Lama encounters Christianity, he understands the supreme act of sacrifice of Jesus on the cross, taking on himself the suffering of others, as commensurate with his own daily practice, offered for the sake of others, though obviously not on the same scale as Jesus's sacrifice. He also notes another great symbol of compassion, the image of Mary holding the baby Jesus, pointing to how motherhood provides the ground for compassion. Similarly, when he reflects on the meaning of what it is for Judaism to be a chosen people, taking his cue from the (non-Jewish) scholar of religion Huston Smith, he reads it in terms of the suffering servant of Isaiah 53, leading him to see in Judaism "an ideal community of selfless bodhisattvas working for the good of all beings." His reading of Islam is even more principled: as Islam is a religion of absolute submission to God, and as God is understood as compassionate and merciful, true Islam must be understood as "absolute submission to the ideal of universal compassion." Based on this reading, he launches a defense of Islam as a nonviolent religion, proclaiming the violence committed in the horrific crimes of 9/11 as "the deeds of a handful of mischievous Muslims" who are not representative of true Islam.

The Dalai Lama offers a reading of other traditions in which he finds what he considers to be the highest values in his own worldview: compassion. In doing so, the Dalai Lama presents for our consideration the hermeneutics of interreligious understanding. Within each tradition, there are multiple presentations or, using the language of internal discourse, "theologies." Each theology is an attempt to describe the religion, making fundamental choices concerning what is really important about a given religion and how it should be portrayed. The Dalai Lama's reflections challenge us to consider what kind of constructive theology can be undertaken through the encounter with another faith tradition. One may argue that the outsider will corrupt the understanding of the religion, but one may equally argue that it is precisely the outsider who is able to offer a fresh composite reading of the religion, in light of the categories that govern his or her own native religious understanding. The Dalai Lama has in fact launched a new theological modality of interreligious hermeneutics or even of interreligious theology.

The Dalai Lama brings to the theology of religions the principles of a positive appreciation of another religion through attempting to find what is best in it and how it best serves its practitioners. Not once does the Dalai Lama criticize another religion. Not once does he argue with it. Rather than ask whether the teachings of a religion are true, the Dalai Lama seeks to identify the benefits that the teaching and practices have in the lives of believers. A declared nontheist, the Dalai Lama appreciates time and again the value of faith in God, not in theological terms but in terms of the benefits of such faith for the believers. The depth of religious empathy as practiced by the Dalai Lama cuts across the most basic theological divides. His empathetic approach, true to the philosophical tendencies of recent decades, highlights the effects of religious beliefs on the lives of people, rather than worrying whether individual beliefs are true in and of themselves. His appreciative inquiry seeks to establish how a given faith works in the lives of believers and what benefits it brings to them.

The book constantly returns to the theme of mystical experience as possible common ground between the religions. In part, this is a consequence of the many sessions of Buddhist-Christian dialogue in which he has participated, particularly those arranged by practitioners with a contemplative focus. But the point seems to go deeper. When engaging Judaism, he actively seeks out the wisdom of the Kabbalah and Judaism's mystical experience. He turns to Rumi as the prime example of Muslim mystical experience. While the book's official thesis is that compassion is the common ground between religions, there is a second thesis that emerges from it: that the mystics of different religions share significant common ground. His interest in the questions of mysticism once again points to what is most important for him in the spiritual life and in his own self-identity, the identity of a Buddhist monk who cultivates a powerful interior life based on the resources of his tradition.

The Dalai Lama does more than describe his interreligious itinerary as moving from the level of personal encounter to engaging the theology and understanding of other religions. The sum total of his encounters and recognitions amounts to a theory, and the latter part of the book is devoted to broader theoretical considerations. Two main theses emerge. The first concerns compassion. The Dalai Lama goes beyond offering readings of specific religions or key moments and concepts within them as expressions of compassion. He develops a theory according to which the cultivation of compassion—therein included love, altruism, etc.—is the common purpose of all religions. Compassion is thus the common ground of all religions that seek to take the individual beyond the ego-centered self and to transform one in fundamental ways. Our religions seek to take us beyond ourselves and to develop a self-transcendence that would allow us to cultivate universal compassion, which extends beyond the interests of the self, culminating in the love of the enemy. His discussion of the stages of compassion and spiritual transformation as universals that apply to all religions is a major contribution to the comparative study of religion and certainly advances our understanding significantly beyond common perceptions that are limited to fundamental common moral teachings.

The second theoretical discussion is of the problem of exclusivity. How one religion views other religions comprises the discipline of theology of religions, and the Dalai Lama's discussion constitutes an important contribution to the field. At its heart is the attempt to reconcile how one may hold on to faith as something exclusive, maintaining the truth claims of the individual religion, while at the same time espousing an attitude of respect to other religions. The Dalai Lama is aware of the fact that for a journey such as his to have broader meaning, one needs to ground the various experiences, dialogues, and reflections within a theoretical framework within which to tackle the problem of religious exclusivism. He is able to apply a classical distinction of Buddhist hermeneutics to the broader situation. Conflicting teachings of the Buddha are reconciled by recognizing that the Buddha taught according to the needs of a given context and its potential for efficacy. Teaching is contextual. This, argues the Dalai Lama, is as true for Buddhism as it is for religion in general. Every religion is suited to the psychological, national, and other conditions that are specific to its adherents. Diversity in religion corresponds to the diversity of human character and the need for teaching. Multiple ways can be upheld, because ethical teachings are universal. Doctrines, metaphysics, and the view of the afterlife do indeed vary from religion to religion. In relation to these variations, the Dalai Lama counsels that adherents of every faith hold with absolute fidelity to their own unique metaphysical vision.

The Dalai Lama's threefold division of religion into ethics, doctrines, and cultural specifics provides a convenient framework for an attempt to reconcile absolute and exclusive faith with respectful acceptance of others.

He speaks not only of respect but of deep reverence towards other faiths for what they produce. In modeling an attitude of deep reverence, he has captured the essence of his own journey to other religions. Reverence is the kind of respect afforded from the depth of a spiritual sense of reality, within which another religion can be validated for the positive fruit it bears in the lives of its followers.

What makes the Dalai Lama's case so powerful and credible is that it is grounded in a personal journey at one end and leads to a broad theory of religion at the other. We can follow the experiences, the readings, the hermeneutical moves, the overall attitude, and, finally, how the theory has been born. It is this totality of vision that calls us not only to follow its conclusions but to follow the entire course set out by the Dalai Lama. He has presented a path and offered a model. There is not a single other world religious leader who has undertaken such an extensive and thorough journey within world religions, who has approached them with such openness, and who has attempted to integrate his personal experiences into a comprehensive theory of interreligious relations. There is probably no other major world religious leader with the broad reach that the Dalai Lama has, no other leader who considers interreligious activities as centrally part of his or her job description as does the Dalai Lama. And few have attempted to make the native spiritual understanding of their tradition a foundation for broader understanding and exchanges that could be relevant to all religions. (Another contemporary Buddhist teacher who may be described in this way is Thich Nhat Hanh, who is also featured in the present volume). By virtue of the path set out in this book, the Dalai Lama redefines what it is to be a truly global religious leader, perhaps in ways that are unique to him. But this uniqueness is an invitation for others to follow, making the reach and impact of the teachings of each of our religions part of the shared message that religions have to offer to their followers and to all of humanity.

The Dalai Lama is not only an interreligious hero by virtue of his encounters and philosophical reflections. He is also an educator and a world visionary, who offers a program for interreligious relations as such. His Holiness proposes four stages for the encounter between the faithful. The Dalai Lama's program for the promotion of interreligious harmony and understanding is based on the following four key elements:

1. Dialogue between scholars of religion on the academic level regarding the convergences and divergences of their respective faith traditions and—more importantly—the purpose of these different approaches;

2. Sharing of deep religious experiences between genuine practitioners;

3. High-profile meetings of the religious leaders to speak and pray from one platform; and

4. Joint pilgrimages to the world's holy places.

Viewing this program, one is struck by how a practical vision is shaped by spiritual pursuits. One notices that His Holiness does not emphasize collaboration in common global causes, which is possibly the most practiced aspect of interfaith encounter, and one in which he himself also engages. Rather, his vision is based on sharing of spiritual experience, sharing of knowledge, and a grounding in prayer and the spiritual experience that is made possible through pilgrimage. It is a program shaped by a monk who is a spiritual seeker, who recognizes spiritual reality across religious differences and who recognizes that the deepest kind of encounter with the religious other must be grounded on the very same concerns that are foundational to his own spiritual path.

I first met the Dalai Lama when he was on pilgrimage to the Holy Land in 1999, as part of a group pilgrimage of religious leaders. That meeting included components of all four aspects outlined above. The local contact and representative for the group was none other than David Rosen. As he has done consistently over a quarter of a century, with me as well as with others, he opened up the contacts and opportunities he had and shared them. So it was that he invited me to take part in a program with the Dalai Lama. One of the many gifts that I have received through him was that particular comprehensive experience but, more importantly, contact and access to the Dalai Lama himself. That initial introduction led to the Dalai Lama's membership in the Elijah Board of World Religious Leaders and to his hosting of and participating in a variety of initiatives. The most recent initiative is his involvement in the "Make Friends across Religions" initiative and the signing of the *Declaration of Friendship*. Friendship, then, emerges as the central thread that ties together the Dalai Lama's journey, his engagement with Elijah, and my own relationship with the person who was the instrument for my and Elijah's ongoing relationship with His Holiness the Dalai Lama.

Swami Dayananda Saraswati

Rabbi Daniel Sperber

Introduction

One might wonder why an octogenarian rabbi and Talmud scholar with strong moorings in Christian art history, as well as the history of Jews among Christians and Muslims, would choose, of all possible interfaith heroes, to relate to an Indian spiritual and philosophical teacher. The following essay is an account of this choice. It is a testimony to the man I will present, Swami Dayananda Saraswati, who passed away in 2015 (as distinct from his famous namesake, who lived a century earlier). But, even more importantly, it is a testimony to the power of authentic interreligious engagement. In short, looking back at decades of engagement with faith leaders of many religions, the single most transformative relationship for me has been my relationship with Swami Dayananda, and that is why I have chosen to feature him as my interfaith hero.

On Swami Dayananda

Swami Dayananda was one of India's most noted teachers of the unitive philosophical system known as Advaita Vedanta, a philosophical system that affirms the unity of God and the unity of all being. Crucial to this understanding of unity is the recognition of God as both transcendent and immanent, a fact that is germane to the discussions that follow. The swami's intelligence and wit were legendary. India's Prime Minister Modi considers himself Swami Dayananda's disciple, which tells us something of his reach. Swami Dayananda had schools and centers of spiritual retreat and learning in various locations in India, as well as in the United States. This international perspective may have contributed to his expansive vision that was not only philosophical but also practical. Swami Dayananda understood the global contemporary need for interfaith dialogue and

233

engaged in it wholeheartedly. He engaged in various Hindu-Buddhist dialogues, but for present purposes I will limit my impressions to the Hindu-Jewish dialogue in which I participated and through which I came to know Swami Dayananda.

Swami Dayananda was also a practical man. Complementing the vision of unity that he preached philosophically is a vision of unity within the vast and often confusing diversity of Hinduism. Swami Dayananda recognized that for Hinduism to meet certain contemporary challenges, it must bring together diverse schools under one organizational umbrella. To this end, he created the Hindu Dharma Acharya Sabha as a body that unites Hindu faith communities under one roof. In so doing, he sought to give Hinduism a united voice, identity, and representation.

Initiating the Dialogue with Judaism

Swami Dayananda was the driving spirit of a series of Jewish-Hindu dialogue encounters that took place over several years, beginning in 2007, in Delhi, Jerusalem, and the United States. What was it that drove Swamiji to this dialogue? The concern was neither philosophical nor spiritual, in an abstract sense. It was an attempt to deal with a pressing social-religious-political problem that Swami Dayananda considered a threat to the survival and integrity of Hinduism. Swami Dayananda, like many other contemporary Hindu leaders, was concerned about missionary work in India and about the loss of membership of the Hindu community to other religious communities, as a consequence of such missionary work. While recognizing the legitimacy of religious choices, based upon deep personal conviction, he felt that broad missionary work, especially such that introduced wrong motivation into religious identity, must be avoided. Hinduism had to be protected, and the way of doing so passed through alliances with other religions that were confronted with similar challenges. He identified, not incorrectly, Judaism as a religion that was similarly threatened—in fact or in its own self-understanding—by missionaries. The purpose of the dialogues, from his perspective, was to seek allies and to launch collaborative efforts at stemming such activities. What actually transpired at the summits of Jewish and Hindu leadership that resulted from his initiative was broader in scope and teaches us fundamental lessons about the dynamics of interfaith relations.

The Jewish-Hindu Summits

Early in 2007, a Jewish delegation went to participate in the first Hindu-Jewish Leadership Summit in New Delhi. The Jewish delegation was headed by the Ashkenazi Chief Rabbi of Israel, Rabbi Jona Metzger, and he was accompanied by Mr. Oded Weiner, director-general of the Israeli Rabbinate (and my first commanding officer in the Israeli army), and Rabbi David Rosen, the preeminent Jewish spokesman on interreligious discourse. I too was invited, probably primarily because of my acquaintance with India, having served as a rabbi in Calcutta during the mid-60s. While the Indian interests in the summit were as described above, the Jewish party entered the dialogue with different motivation. From the Jewish, and more specifically Israel viewpoint, besides whatever religious dimension the meeting had, there was primarily a desire to foster greater social, political, and economic ties with what was regarded as an upcoming superpower. This is why Israel's foreign ministry encouraged the participation of the Israel Chief Rabbinate.

Motivations for entering dialogue are one thing, and what transpires in the dialogue itself is another. As it turns out, the actual encounter between Jewish and Hindu leaders, the first ever of its kind, ended up being a primarily religious encounter, touching on issues that are fundamental to the faith of both communities. My own interventions played an important role in this emerging focus and the meeting, in turn, has reshaped my own spiritual and intellectual agenda for years to come.

In the early stages of that discussion, I voiced my own personal feelings of unease at my very participation in this summit, for, I explained, Judaism views idolatry in a very negative manner, so much so that it even forbids any Jew from entering into a place of such worship. "But I see idols on every street corner, small crypts in every shop and private house, and people regularly prostrating themselves in pujas [ceremonies of worship] before these idols, and most especially on the banks of the sacred Ganga. "How then," I asked, "do I find myself in such a place of blatant polytheistic idolatry? How can I justify to myself my participation in this conference?"

Here is where Swamiji comes in, and here is the foundation of my personal relationship with him. Swamiji, his eyes twinkling through his round spectacles, gently responded with a humorous twist on his lips, "We are not idolators. We do not worship idols. We pray to a supreme entity which one might call Brahman." And in his beautiful English style, simply and elegantly, but with great inner depth and feeling, he continued:

> We do not bother with this one-God-many-Gods business. In fact, we go one step further and say there is only God. Everything

for us is sacred. We take nothing for granted. The light of the sun, the air we breathe, the water, the stars, the solar system, mother earth, all is Ishwara, God. This is the view that underlies all the lineages within the Hindu tradition.[301]

He then continued, stating that:

The point of dialogue is to look for the common features behind one's religious philosophies and practices while gladly accepting our differences. We should learn to live in harmony. Although we might differ in some respects, we can agree to differ, and work for the common good of humanity.

He added: "Other views are not tolerated by us, but highly validated." He thus seamlessly combined theology and ethics, in this way setting the tone for the whole meeting.

For me this understanding of Hinduism was a complete eye-opener, as it was in direct opposition to everything that earlier I had thought. Cautiously, I suggested that his formulation of Hinduism was suggestive of pantheism, but he immediately disabused me of such an interpretation, suggesting, in a personal conversation, that I would do well to come and spend some time with him to learn what was truly Hinduism and, more specifically, Advaita Vedanta. This indeed I did on a number of occasions during my subsequent visits to India, sitting proverbially at his feet as an acolyte before his master.

The primary outcome of that summit—there were others that followed—was the *Declaration of Mutual Understanding and Cooperation*, which has eight clauses, the most important of which, in my opinion, was the first affirmation that the

respective traditions [of Judaism and Hinduism] teach Faith in One Supreme Being who is the Ultimate Reality, who has created this world in its blessed diversity and who has communicated Divine ways of action for humanity for different peoples in different times and places.[302]

Note the blessed diversity, etc., which was a key notion in Swamiji's teachings. Even though the concerns of proselytism were addressed in other clauses of this declaration, as well as the subsequent declaration of the second meeting of religious leaders in Jerusalem in 2008, I consider the significant breakthrough of the declaration and of the meeting itself to have been the theological engagement and clarification.

In practical terms, two scholars' groups were established, a Jewish one and a Hindu one, with myself as a chairperson of the Jewish group and,

of course, Swamiji as the obvious leader of the Hindu one. This arrangement paved the way for those subsequent meetings, which have been very
important for me personally.

The Impact of the Encounter with Swamiji

Beyond my function in these meetings and, more importantly, for me personally, the meetings of the scholars' groups cemented the relationship between
pupil and master. In all honesty, while the formal setup suggested reciprocity
between Swamiji and myself, from my personal perspective, I feel there was
little that I contributed in these meetings. For me, these were supreme learning experiences. For Swamiji already knew a good deal about Judaism, while
I saw my part as primarily involving absorbing his Eastern wisdom, in order
to try to understand it in Western terms and to reconcile apparent differences
with Jewish belief. Consequently, this turned out to be, for me, a process of
self-discovery. I realized that Judaism too had its use of images—the cheru-
bim in the holy of holies of the temple, the brazen serpent in the wilderness—
images that served to help direct one's attention beyond the material to the
transcendent deity. This led me to realize how, much in the same way, through
both iconic and aniconic Hindu images, the Hindu worshipper was seeking
some manner of union with the Supreme Entity.

Thus, one of the most important consequences of this unique confrontation—or, better stated, encounter—was the recognition that in seeking to understand and appreciate the position of the other, I was actually
gaining a new and deeper insight into and understanding of my own position. I also came to realize that the attempt to appreciate the validity of the
views of the other, which must be the cornerstone of any interreligious
discussion, was not merely a theological issue. It was also an ethical concern, one of supreme significance.

As a consequence of that first meeting in 2007, I have, for the last decade
and a half, sought to study Eastern religions, compare them with those of
the West, and reveal their strengths over the many weaknesses of the West's
one-dimensional thinking, lack of tolerance, feelings of superiority, etc. I am
now in the process of summarizing my insights and conclusions in a number
of publications that will soon appear. I see them as a tribute to the memory
of that outstanding personality, Swami Dayananda Saraswati of blessed
memory, one who transformed the lives of thousands, served as a teacher of
teachers, and left a precious legacy of respect and understanding that is so
important in our age of tension resulting from diversity.

Concluding Reflections on Dialogue

One often refers to interfaith dialogue as though it were a specific, well-defined, and monolithic activity. Reviewing my engagement and transformation, through my encounter with Swami Dayananda and his view of Hinduism, brings to light multiple dimensions of interfaith engagement. It also suggests how they open up to one another. Swamiji's initial concern was with the social and political stability of India. Israel's foreign ministry was concerned with political relations. Both motivations gave way to another kind of dialogue, theological in nature, that occurs when people of faith seek to understand one another. Swami Dayananda was a master at such engagement. But this dialogue in turn gave way to another level of dialogue and engagement, namely the personal transformative journey that opened up to me through encounter with Swami Dayananda. If I refer to him as teacher and master, this suggests the deep reverence with which I think of him. It also suggests one possible, if rare, dimension of interfaith dialogue. Dialogue can become an invitation to move from the external social concerns to the more objective theological concerns and eventually points to the internal, transformative spiritual concerns that allow for a revisiting and relearning of the meaning of self, in light of the other. Swami Dayananda was a spiritual teacher who was capable of engaging all these levels and was able to dance the dance of dialogue, leading to its higher spiritual levels. It is for this reason that I consider him my interfaith hero.

Eva Fleischner[303]

Prof. Mary Boys

My essay honors the memory of Eva M. Fleischner, who died in July 2020 on the eve of her ninety-fifth birthday. I knew her through our mutual involvement in Jewish-Christian relations, a field she came to only in her forties. Yet her earlier experiences gave her Jewish-Christian work maturity, wisdom, and intensity. Although increasing frailty had prevented her from active involvement in the interreligious realm for the past decade or more, her death has not diminished her luminosity.

In different circumstances, Fleischner might have led a conventional life, given her upper-class childhood in Vienna, Austria. Her father Konrad was a prominent lawyer and amateur musician, and her mother Gabrielle (Schoenfeld), a Francophile, was also intellectually inclined. Their spacious apartment housed a library of 7000 books. A governess tutored Eva and her younger brother Hans in French to complement their native German. Both children had music lessons and enjoyed summer camp in Switzerland. The Fleischner family was nominally Catholic, attending Mass on Christmas and Easter; her Jewish father had converted in 1936.

The Nazi Anschluss in March 1938 interrupted their comfortable life. Konrad's business contacts and resources enabled the family to send Eva to an English convent boarding school in July 1938, just two weeks after her thirteenth birthday. The following November, her parents also sent Hans to school in England and were themselves able to escape to England in early 1939. Ultimately, they attained a visa to emigrate to the United States in March 1940 through sponsorship by Konrad's brother Felix, a physician in the Boston area. Eva rejoined her parents in 1943, enrolling at Radcliffe College. After graduating magna cum laude in 1946, she worked as an editorial assistant at a publishing company, became engaged to Donald Monell, and became a US citizen in 1949. She was, it seemed, destined for a successful American life, albeit a conventional one.

A year in Paris, however, changed everything. A Fulbright scholarship enabled Eva to study medieval philosophy at the University of Paris in 1950. Yet it was not philosophy but the experience of the vibrancy of the post-war French church that deeply affected her. Her participation in the Circle S. Jean Baptiste, a student group that explored other religious traditions, served as a stimulus to develop a more authentic Christian spirituality. Her study under the tutelage of scholars such as the Jesuits Jean Daniélou and Jacques Audinet sparked a capacious understanding of Catholicism. This Paris sojourn, she later reflected, opened her to realities for which she had been searching all her life without knowing.

So, when her fiancé arrived in Paris at the completion of her studies, she told him that she had changed her mind about marriage. Something deeper was calling her. In retrospect, as she told Herbert Heavenrich for his brief biography *In Search of the Sacred*, "If I had to pick one word for what had happened to me, it would be 'God.'"

After her return from France, Fleischner moved to New York to work at another publisher and joined a group of Catholics who met weekly at the office of the *Catholic Worker*, the paper founded by Dorothy Day. Then, in 1951, she accepted an invitation to join an international women's movement, the Grail. Founded in the Netherlands in 1921 by Jesuit priest and scholar Fr. Jacques van Ginneken as a way to animate and advance women's contributions to the church and world, the movement came to the US in 1940. It was a movement that took women's voices seriously and that provided resources and communal support for their work for justice. It also gave its members a freedom not then possible in women's religious orders.

By the time Fleischner traveled in 1952 to Grailville, the US center outside Loveland, Ohio, to spend a year of intense formation, it had become a prominent center of women's leadership and church renewal foreshadowing the Second Vatican Council, especially in liturgy and in Scripture-based study and prayer. Five years later, she took an oath to live a life of devotion to God through the mission of Grail. As she told Heavenrich: "It was through the Grail that I found purpose and meaning in life . . . and with a whole new commitment which I didn't know was possible before." The Grailville years allowed her to obtain a master's degree in liturgical studies at the University of Notre Dame—and to gain renown as the head of the Grail's bakery. According to one source, she personally baked about 130 loaves a day. Some of her family and friends regarded the time devoted to the bakery a waste of her superb education, but Eva thought of it as her salvation, "bringing a wonderful balance to my life."

The deep commitment to women's leadership manifest in the Grail movement at times led to conflict with ecclesiastical authorities, as Fleischner experienced in an unforgettable encounter in 1963. The Grail had sent her to Rome for the second session of Vatican II as a reporter for its publication *Ecumenical Notes*. As an accredited journalist, Fleischner was included in an invitation to the otherwise all-male US press corps to attend Mass on October 30, 1963, in St. Peter's Basilica. As the approximately twenty-member US press corps joined the communion procession, a Swiss guard physically restrained Fleischner, preventing her from receiving communion and leaving her in "tears of rage." Some thirty years later, Eva recounted this experience at a meeting. Time had not diminished her rage.

Her discomfiting experience at the Vatican presaged a much longer encounter with Christianity's sinfulness. In the late 1960s, she began doctoral studies at Marquette University in historical theology. Seminars on early church writings and on Martin Luther revealed the animosity toward and vilification of Judaism. Shaken by her confrontation with anti-Judaism and anti-Semitism, she resolved to uncover its theological origins. It also prompted her to seek greater knowledge of Judaism, about which she knew little, despite the fact that her father was from an assimilated Jewish family. Although he had converted to Catholicism when she was eleven, she knew her paternal relatives were Jews and that her Aunt Mariana had perished in Auschwitz. Her father, too, would likely have been killed, had he not been able to get a visa to the US. In the Third Reich, a Jewish convert to Catholicism was still a Jew. And yet, somehow, while she had been affected by the Second World War, it was not until her time at Marquette that the Shoah came into her awareness.

During her Marquette years, Fleischner began an intense study of the Holocaust. Significantly, she developed friendships with Jews, thus also encountering a living Judaism. Through her mentors at Marquette, she met local rabbis, who in turn introduced her to leading Jewish scholars such as Irving (Yitz) Greenberg, Abraham Joshua Heschel, Michael Wyschogrod, and Zalman Schachter. She also seriously contemplated converting to Judaism, ultimately realizing that the church was her spiritual home.

Eva completed her degree in 1971 with a dissertation on *The View of Judaism in German Christian Theology Since 1945*, tracing the evolution of *Judenmission* among Protestants and Catholics in post-war Germany in seeking the conversion of Jews through an active, organized missionary effort. She considered *Judenmission* a "subtler version of the Final Solution," arguing that it depended on a dialectic of exclusion. In her concluding chapters, she maintained that dialogue must replace missionizing and discussed the necessity of religious pluralism. For Fleischner, the church's relation to Judaism was a test of its wider relationship to the world. Fifty years ago, this was a remarkable and prescient claim.

Appointed as professor of religion at Montclair State College (now University) in 1972, she developed a course on the Holocaust that she taught regularly for nearly twenty years, long before such a course became common. Fleischner had a major role in the planning and implementation of an international symposium on the Holocaust held in June 1974 at New York City's Episcopal Cathedral of St. John the Divine, editing its presentations in the important 1977 anthology *Auschwitz: Beginning of a New Era? Reflections on the Holocaust.* Later, she served on the honorary editorial advisory board of the international journal *Holocaust and Genocide Studies,* as well as the advisory board for the Secretariat for Catholic-Jewish Relations of the National Conference of Catholic Bishops.

In 1985, Eva did research in Jerusalem at Yad Vashem, the World Holocaust Remembrance Center, in the department of the Righteous among the Nations. She then went to France on a fellowship to interview Catholic women involved in resistance to Nazism and rescue of Jews. Three of these interviews were published in the 1997 book *Cries in the Night: Women Who Challenged the Holocaust,* which she co-authored with historian Michael Phayer.

Retiring from Montclair State in 1991, she went to the Netherlands for four years to work at the headquarters of Grail International. In 2000, she moved to Claremont, California, to live at Pilgrim Place, a continuing care retirement community. It was there that she spent the last two decades of her life.

My own relationship with Eva was primarily professional. She was an active member of the Christian Scholars Group on Jews and Judaism, which she had joined in 1972. I first met her when I entered the group in 1988. We overlapped as members of the Committee on Ethics, Religion, and the Holocaust at the US Holocaust Memorial Museum in Washington, DC, and on the Advisory Board of the National Catholic Center for Holocaust Education at Seton Hill University in Greensburg, Pennsylvania. Once she moved to California in 2000, I did not see her often. I did, however, spend a delightful afternoon and evening with her at her new home not long after her relocation to the West.

It may seem strange then that I've chosen to write about a person with whom I did not have a close friendship. Yet her name sprang to mind immediately when I received the invitation to contribute to this volume in recognition of the interreligious leadership of Rabbi David Rosen. News of her recent death had rekindled my appreciation for this learned Catholic woman of quiet yet fierce intensity who loved a church even as it enraged her. A title of a paper she gave at a conference in Oxford in 1988 expresses what Eva is for me: a "Memory of Goodness." In this Oxford lecture, she said that the extensive interviews she had done with French Catholic rescuers had proven salutary for her. They enabled her to "'touch,' as it were, good-ness within my tradition." Such encounters, she added, proved healing and counterbalanced the heavy burden of "prejudice, cowardice and betrayal within my Roman Catholic tradition."

So, yes, Eva's life speaks to some of my own anger with many Catho-lic leaders. As she knew, prejudice, cowardice, and betrayal have not dis-appeared. At nearly sixty years since *Nostra aetate*, few members of the hierarchy seem truly invested in relations with Jews and in developing non-supersessionist theologies. Rather, they seem to proffer what the late Rabbi Leon Klenicki termed "tea and sympathy." And because most Catholic clergy lack an adequate grasp of Judaism, particularly from the Second Temple period, their homilies on biblical texts tend to be shallow and misleading. Some fine documents emanate from Vatican offices, such as *The Jewish People and Their Sacred Scripture in the Christian Bible* (Pontifical Biblical Commission, 2001) and the more recent *The Gifts and Calling of God Are Ir-revocable* (Commission of the Holy See for Religious Relations with the Jews, 2015). Their impact on church leadership, however, has been minimal—and even less on parish priests. Eva's feisty spirit speaks to my tenacious (some might say stubborn) resolve to develop and communicate ways of making the riches of scholarship more accessible in the church.

I regret that I never asked Eva about her experience as a woman theologian, given the misogyny that continues to afflict Catholicism. I sus-pect she may have been more welcome in Jewish venues than in her own Catholic ones, with the exception of Catholic institutions of higher educa-tion. She, however, had lifelong friendships with the priests who had been so influential during her year in Paris. They encouraged her intellectual development and sensed the importance of forming a supportive com-munity. It was Père Daniélou who advised her to look into the Grail and Père Audinet, at the University of Chicago while Eva was in her doctoral studies in Milwaukee, who provided an empathetic conversation partner during her student years. Still, I wonder. What was her experience as the only woman on the six-member International Catholic-Jewish Historical Commission assigned to critically examine eleven volumes of Vatican archival material from 1939 to 1945? There were apparently tensions be-tween some of the members; moreover, in their report presented in Rome in November 2000, the commission raised probing questions that likely were unwelcome in certain quarters. While gender was surely not the only point of contention, I suspect it was not irrelevant.

A woman of simple elegance and sophisticated thought, Eva had a con-templative spirit. At Grail, she discovered the profundity of the Psalms, and they became for her an abiding sense of strength and faith. She found in them not only an expression of thirst for the living God but also a freedom to face one's rage and desire for vengeance. Because the Psalms allowed one to challenge and confront God, they permitted her to express in prayer the emotions she may have otherwise been tempted to repress. I, too, find in the raw expressiveness of the Psalms a way of living with my own shadow side.

While I consider Eva a companion in my recitation of the Psalms, I do not fully comprehend her decision in Paris to call off her engagement in order to pursue her search for the Divine—but then, such a mystical experience surely lies beyond the ken of others. Her choice, which shocked her family and friends, reveals her independent spirit. Breaking her engagement without having clarity about the next steps in her life manifests a certain audacity.

My own experience as a vowed member for over fifty years of a women's religious order provides insight into what she found so powerful in the Grail movement: women bonding in community to develop and use their gifts for the flourishing of the world. I think that she found Grail at just the right time in her life. Its communal support, liturgical vitality, ecumenical commitments, and ecclesial vision shaped her spirit for her later engagement with Judaism and fortified her for journeying into Holocaust studies. Similarly, my experience in a woman's community sustains my own search for God beyond the boundaries of Catholicism, providing a wellspring of companionship and joy.

Eva was quite well known as a scholar during her active years. Her dissertation, published in 1975 with the revised title of *Judaism in German Christian Theology Since 1945: Christianity and Israel Considered in Terms of Mission,* anticipates more recent work on mission and on religious pluralism. She was a pioneer in integrating study of the Shoah into the curriculum of higher education, particularly in Catholic institutions. By the force of her gracious charisma, she drew others into the wider world of interreligious dialogue. It is my hope that succeeding generations will recognize her pioneering scholarship and come to know her as a "memory of goodness."

Seton Hill University is currently launching a substantive project that will contribute significantly to knowledge of her work. The Eva Fleischner PhD Endowed Fund for Visiting Scholars and Students in Holocaust and Genocide Studies at Seton Hill has four components. The first funds an annual lecture in her honor and supports the participation of a major international scholar in the university's Holocaust Conference offered every three years. A second element aims at truth finding by supporting the school's faculty in teaching topics relevant to study of the Shoah (e.g., the rise of fascism, the role of conspiracy theories and of misinformation and propaganda). Oral history constitutes the third dimension, involving faculty and students in interviewing survivors. A fourth component involves the publication of three volumes: republication of her dissertation, with an extended critical analysis; a collection of her written work, with commentary; and a book that focuses on her key scholarly interests (e.g., women resisters and rescuers). The co-editors of the series, Carol Rittner and John Roth, plan to draw on younger scholars to offer analysis and commentary as a way of ensuring that her memory passes into next generations.

I regard Eva not so much as a hero as a sacrament, as an embodiment of divine graciousness. As my colleague John Thatamanil writes in his recent book *Circling the Elephant: A Comparative Theology of Religious Diversity*, "The practices and insights of others can even, in some cases, become sacraments for our way into the divine life." Eva Fleischner embodied the complex and mysterious process of living one's vocation.

Recently, I was at a meeting with Judith Banki, a contemporary of Eva and a major figure in the interreligious work of the American Jewish Committee and, more recently, of the Tanenbaum Foundation. Eva's name came up. Judy said of her: "She was radiant. She just sent out light."

"Those who are wise shall shine like the brightness of the sky, and those who lead many to righteousness, like the stars for ever and ever" (Dan 12:3). May the eternal light now shining upon you, Eva, continue to illumine our pathways.

Bishop Kenneth Cragg

Dr. Clare Amos

In 1956, the publication of Kenneth Cragg's first book, *Call of the Minaret*,[304] was a landmark and watershed in the story of Christian-Muslim interfaith relations, especially in the English-speaking Anglican and Protestant world. Over the following twenty years or so, the book, which is currently in its third edition, sparked the interest of many Christian young people, including myself, in seeking to understand more about the inner meaning, as well as the externals, of Islam. A friend of mine, Martin Forward, who has taught Christian-Muslim relations in both the United Kingdom and the USA, has described how he himself was "entranced and empowered"[305] by the book. It undoubtedly helped to play a part in encouraging a number of us to care enough about the importance of interfaith relations to make them part of the enduring melody of our own lives.

It was a remarkable book for its time in several ways. First, it did not simply explore Islam textually and historically but also engaged with the current lived experience of Muslims, not only in the Middle East but also in other parts of the Muslim world. Second, it encouraged its readership (largely intended to be Christian) to listen "to the call in the call [from the minaret] which the non-Muslim ought also to heed."[306] In other words, Cragg was suggesting that engagement with Islam required Christians to explore more seriously their own religious beliefs and ask how these beliefs were heard and interpreted by Muslims, particularly in view of the ambiguous centuries of conflict that had existed between Christianity and Islam. Thirdly, it introduced a feature that would become a characteristic of Cragg's later writing, which is deeply poetic in style. The title of the book, *Call of the Minaret*, was a deliberate wordplay, such as Cragg delighted in to the end of his life, drawing on his love for the beauty of the Arabic language, as well as his own gift as a wordsmith in both English and Arabic. Wordplay from the pen or lips of Kenneth Cragg was never simply a clever artifact but a deep digging down into the heart of both the Christian and

Muslim faiths, for both of whom the very word Word bears a particular holiness. His love for the play of language was reflected even in the double-entendre of the word *Call* in the book's title.

The positive reception of *Call of the Minaret* was a factor that led to the development by SCM Press of a series of books that explored Christian engagement with a number of other religious faiths. Cragg was invited to contribute the volume on Islam, entitled *Sandals at the Mosque*. The name of the series, Christian Presence, hints at a theme that would mark Cragg's contributions to interfaith engagement over the next fifty years.[307] As Max Warren, editor of the series, put it in his overall preface:

> Our first task in approaching another people, another culture, another religion, is to take off our shoes, for the place we are approaching is holy. Else we may find ourselves treading on men's dreams. More serious still, we may forget that God was here before our arrival. We have, then, to ask what is the au-thentic religious content in the experience of the Muslim, the Hindu, the Buddhist, or whoever he may be. We may, if we have asked humbly and respectfully, still reach the conclusion that our brothers have started from a false premise and reached a faulty conclusion. But we must not arrive at our judgment from outside their religious situation. We have to try to sit where they sit, to enter sympathetically into their pains and griefs and joys of their history and see how those pains and griefs and joys have determined the premises of their argument. We have, in a word, to be "present" with them.[308]

Presence would remain a key theme of Cragg's thinking for the rest of his life. It is no accident that the *Festschrift* that was presented to him by the archbishop of Canterbury in 2003 to mark his ninetieth birthday, which I myself was honored to co-edit, was titled *A Faithful Presence*, words chosen to describe Cragg's theological understanding but also the influence of his own life and ministry. Like myself, Cragg was an Anglican, and the ongoing importance of the theme of presence in Anglican interre-ligious theology, reflected, for example, in the 2008 report *Generous Love: The Truth of the Gospel and the Call to Dialogue: An Anglican Theology of Interfaith Relations* owes a considerable amount to his implicit influence. Presence for Kenneth Cragg bore, of course, the reality that for a consid-erable number of years he was physically present in various parts of the Middle East—Lebanon, Jerusalem, and Egypt—where Christian-Muslim relations have been lived experiences for centuries. It was where he first learned about their importance and, eventually, where he would make a significant contribution both to the life of the Anglican Church and to Christian-Muslim engagement in the area.

It was a remarkable personal journey. He had begun his ministry as a priest in what is known as the conservative evangelical part of the Church of England and arrived in Lebanon in 1939 as a missionary of the British Syrian Mission, an organization that was very uncomfortable with any notion of interfaith dialogue. The exigencies of the Second World War meant that he found himself undertaking a variety of tasks and roles in Beirut, including acting as chaplain to the Anglican congregation in the city, that he had not necessarily anticipated. In the course of these new responsibilities, he grew spiritually and intellectually. He became a wonderful listener and observer, allowing others to educate him, including people from other faiths, especially Muslims, and moved on from any superficial idea about mission as proselytism to an understanding of mission as primarily a deeper mutual engagement with the other. As a result of this, he helped many other people to make a similar voyage. That is one of his lasting legacies.

Although he was to move back to the UK in 1948 to undertake doctoral studies at Oxford University, he spent considerable periods in later years living and working in the Middle East: in the 1950s, pursuing a peripatetic teaching ministry from a base at St. George's Cathedral, Jerusalem, and then in the early 1970s, ministering in Egypt as the Anglican bishop in that country. He continued to make frequent visits to the region until only a few years before his death in 2012 at the age of ninety-nine. In spite of its faults and frailties, he cherished the local Anglican Church in the Middle East and its people, though ecclesiastical politics dictated that he was not as valued by all as perhaps he should have been. Yet thoughtful members of this Anglican community, such as Bishop Hassan Dehqani-Tafti, bishop in Iran at the time of the 1979 revolution, appreciated the gift that Cragg brought to the Christians of the region. "Kenneth has been one of those sent by God and used by God to help discern what it means to continue loving and hoping when all seems lost." An important aspect of the example that Kenneth Cragg offered to those who have followed him in the field of interfaith relations was of the need to be a full part of one's own religious community—however far from perfect it might be.

I had long known of Cragg's influence in the Anglican world, but it was only after I moved to Geneva in 2011 to work at the World Council of Churches (WCC) that I became more aware of his significant role in guiding the development of interfaith interest in ecumenical circles. Perhaps to the surprise of some, there has always been an ambiguity in the WCC about interfaith engagement, with fearful or even hostile voices surfacing shrilly on occasion. However, the lead of the Second Vatican Council and its document

Nostra aetate, promulgated in 1965, encouraged the WCC to begin to reflect in this area. Yet it seems it was a paper submitted by Cragg for a WCC conference held in Kandy, Sri Lanka, in 1967, that was a watershed in the story of the WCC and interfaith relations. "In Kandy Kenneth Cragg challenged in a fundamental way the Barth-Kraemer attitude to religions that had so dominated Protestant thinking during the previous decades."[309] Shortly after Cragg's death, I unearthed and republished his Kandy paper as a tribute to him.[310] One of its striking features is the way he draws on his understanding of the incarnation of Christ to suggest "the revelatory quality . . . of all experience." It was largely as a result of this Kandy conference that, a few years later, the WCC established its interreligious office.

Inevitably, however, part of my cherishing Kenneth Cragg as my own interfaith hero is due to the fact that, over a period of about forty years, my husband Alan Amos and I were privileged to know him personally as his and our paths crossed and recrossed many times. When my husband was Anglican chaplain in Beirut (1975–1982) we had a desk in our apartment that bore the initials K. C., for it had been Kenneth's working desk when he had acted as chaplain there more than thirty years earlier. During my own years living in Jerusalem, then Beirut, and later in Cambridge, Canterbury, and South London, it was a joy when Kenneth came to visit, normally to give a talk—or two—that was always deeply appreciated by those we had gathered to hear him. A particularly special memory is of leading a group from St. George's College, including Kenneth, though he was twenty years older than anyone else, on a seven-hour walk in the Judaean wilderness to reach the monastery of Mar Saba. Throughout all such experiences, one factor that shone through was Kenneth's prayerfulness and humility, which I both experienced for myself and heard about from others. I remember being told by a theological student in the Middle East how impressed his fellow students were that Kenneth, by then a bishop and a key speaker at their conference, had insisted on doing his share of the washing up after a meal. It was not a usual model for the Middle Eastern episcopate—but had certainly made its mark on that young student.

Ideally, Christian theology sees the cross of Jesus Christ as a model of divine humility. Notoriously, Christians have not always lived up to this example. But, along with the theme of incarnation, the cross was at the heart of Kenneth's theology and was genuinely a lived experience for him. He wrestled with the meaning of the cross for Christianity and for what it might mean for Islam. The orthodox Muslim position is that Jesus was never actually put to death by crucifixion. Yet one of the most haunting novels to spring out of Egypt in the middle of the twentieth century is Muhammad Kamel Hussein's *City of Wrong: A Friday in Jerusalem,* which explores the different perspectives of those who were there that day in Jerusalem when Jesus had been sentenced to death. Written in Arabic, it is telling that the English translation of it, whose language matched the beauty of the original, was made by Kenneth Cragg in 1959.

Kenneth would come back to the cross, seeking to tease out its meaning, again and again. Sometimes his endeavors could have their amusing side. My husband remembers listening to him addressing a group of American Christians at a conference in Canterbury, England. Kenneth had been exploring some of the difficult aspects of Christian history and ended with the flourish, "How can one be combative with the cross of Christ?" It was intended, of course, as a rhetorical question, to which the implied answer was "one cannot"; in the minds of people like Kenneth (and my husband and myself), to seek to be combative with the cross is a perversion of the cross's essential meaning. But Kenneth may have been speaking above the heads of at least some of his audience, as a couple of them then complained to my husband that the lecturer had not answered the question he had posed, and they wanted to have some examples of how they could be successfully combative with the cross.

Decades earlier, in 1956, Kenneth had concluded *Call of the Minaret* with the words, "We who, in our generation, listen to the call of the minaret may hear it most compellingly from the muezzin over Gethsemane. There we shall best understand wherewith we must answer—and how, and why."[311] In typical Craggian style, Gethsemane here is both physical place (part of the Mount of Olives) and metaphor (the approach of Christ's crucifixion). To speak of "the muezzin over Gethsemane" is to speak of the perplexity of the nearness and yet distance between Christianity and Islam and what the cross, the central symbol of the Christian faith, might have to offer to transfigure our alienation.

That reference to the place of Gethsemane is a reminder of part of the lived reality of both Kenneth Cragg and David Rosen, which draws them together in my mind. Both of them have deeply loved the Holy Land and the Holy City of Jerusalem. I am not sure if David Rosen and Kenneth Cragg ever met during Kenneth's lifetime. It is not impossible, though perhaps unlikely. Although I suspect their political views would have differed quite considerably, they would have shared in common a love for the land and the city, a fascination with the place and particularity of land and city in their respective Scriptures and religious traditions, and some sense of deep sadness about present realities. Kenneth's well-known exploration of the implications of the difference between the Meccan and Medinan strands of Islam for the relationship between religion and state has perhaps resonances for Christians and Jews as well as Muslims.

One thing that both Kenneth and David have known is the joy that comes from a deeply happy and loving marriage. This was true for Kenneth with Melita, as it is for David with Sharon. Both wives, over the years, have brought an essential contribution to what their husband offered.[312]

Mary Boys[313]

Prof. Philip A. Cunningham

"Who is a figure who inspires your interfaith work? How does this figure inspire you and what lessons, applications, and concrete expressions has this inspiration taken in your life?" These questions about an interfaith hero that were posed to the contributors to this volume brought to my mind a stream of recollections of people who have had a shaping influence on me, people who have modeled virtues that are edifying and inspire emulation.

Although there are many people to whom I owe much, Prof. Mary C. Boys, SNJM, stands out as a particularly important inspiration. From her books and articles and eventually from getting to know her personally, I came to recognize and appreciate several of the heroic virtues that are necessary for anyone hoping to advance interfaith understanding, solidarity, and collaboration. These include: 1) a commitment to trying to understand as much as possible another tradition's perspectives from within its own frames of reference and thus to learn from it, 2) a willingness to see things from the other's perspective and so be prepared to criticize one's own tradition, 3) the ability to bring multiple disciplines together, 4) a dedication to serving people in real-life contexts, 5) a willingness to work at forming deep friendships with the religious other, and 6) an openness to being transformed as a result of deeply engaging with the other.

Permit me to elaborate on these virtues as I discerned them in Mary Boys by shifting a bit into an autobiographical mode. I first came to know Mary indirectly through an article in the journal *Religious Education* that she published in 1981. At the time, I was serving as a parish director of religious education, while also pursuing a master of religious education degree. I was especially interested in biblical studies and focused my coursework on the New Testament. There, Prof. David Efroymson (another important influence on me) brought to the surface my latent interest in how the way Christians read the Bible shapes their attitudes towards Jews and Judaism. It was he who brought Mary's article to my attention.

In "Questions 'Which Touch on the Heart of Our Faith,'" Mary presented what she called an ideological scaffolding for teaching Christian faith without prejudice against Jews.[314] She offered a quick overview of previous educational efforts in that regard, together with specific concepts that should be incorporated into future religious education curricula. Her facility in bringing together the worlds of religious education, biblical scholarship, and Christian-Jewish relations fascinated me. So I eagerly read her book *Biblical Interpretation in Religious Education: A Study of the Kerygmatic Era*. The book included a forward by Prof. Raymond E. Brown, SS, a foremost biblical scholar whose works I was also studying. As one of her dissertation directors, he wrote that Mary "combined the best of two educations . . . [having] both the biblical and educational training" to research the topic of how the concept of salvation history shaped Christian education.[315] Little did I realize that, within ten years, Mary would be the director of my own doctoral dissertation.

I would later learn that Mary hailed from Seattle, Washington, and that her high school and college education occurred in the same decade as the Second Vatican Council. In fact, she entered the Catholic women's religious community of the Sisters of the Holy Names of Jesus and Mary in 1965, the same year as the promulgation of the declaration *Nostra aetate*, which would greatly shape her life's work.

Even though I would later frequently joke with her that my hair started turning white while under her tutelage at Boston College, the truth of the matter is that she modeled for her students the essential qualities of a Catholic interfaith hero. First is that Catholic theological scholarship should enrich people's lives and be in service to the church community. In this, I believe she passed along the pastoral sensitivity and commitments of her own mentor, Raymond Brown. I once heard him say that a teacher cannot just present students with a problem without also equipping them with the tools needed to begin to resolve it. That principle, it seems to me, informs Mary's teaching and writing as well.

Relatedly, Mary explicitly and repeatedly urges her students and colleagues to express themselves with as little technical jargon as possible or, if unavoidable, to clearly define any terms that might be unfamiliar to the generally educated person. This was especially clear when I became a fellow member of the Christian Scholars Group on Christian-Jewish Relations and participated in discussions that Mary led of chapter drafts for the book *Seeing Judaism Anew: Christianity's Sacred Obligation*.[316] As the editor of this volume, Mary constantly encouraged everyone to write in as widely accessible a manner as possible. This has become a guiding axiom for me in both popular and academic texts.

This goal takes on an even greater significance in the context of Christian-Jewish relations. Because of the close historical and theological connections between the two traditions, Jews and Christians often use the same words or phrases in their religious discourse. Naturally, this easily leads to the presupposition that, when they come together for interreligious conversation, they mean the same thing by these common terms. Actually, in some cases, the two traditions impart quite different connotations to such words as messiah, salvation, or commandment. It is all the more necessary, therefore, to define what speakers or writers mean by certain key expressions, as Mary made clear. She demonstrated that a basic desire for clarity and transparency in one's speech or writing becomes absolutely imperative in interreligious contexts.

The important expression *interreligious learning* emerged from Mary's collaboration from 1992 to 1995 with Jewish educator Prof. Sara S. Lee of Hebrew Union College in Los Angeles in an interreligious initiative called the Catholic-Jewish Colloquium.[317] This was followed from 1997 to 2000 by the Lilly Endowment-sponsored Religious Particularism and Pluralism project, in which I was privileged to participate. Both ventures brought together Jewish and Catholic educators and academicians for intensive study and learning together. The processes demonstrated the limits of learning about the other from within one's own faith community and the necessity of engaging in specific learning activities with members of the other faith. All the program participants found that such "learning in the presence of the other" powerfully transformed their attitudes toward the Jewish or Christian other and—perhaps even more crucially—renewed their self-understandings of their own religious tradition. Mary and Sara offered a masterclass in the sensitive facilitation and processing of the crucial affective aspects of Jewish and Christian rapprochement.

One participant, Rabbi Daniel Lehmann, effectively encapsulated the group's experience when, drawing upon the traditional rabbinic process of *chavruta* study, he voiced the hope that Christians and Jews could become learning partners: "A learning partner is someone with whom you study . . . biblical or other kinds of traditional texts . . . in order to have a dialogue. [You have] an interlocutor, with whom truth can emerge as you play out your different perspectives on the texts. And it's a kind of relationship which is very intimate, in which there is a sense of shared texts, and even a covenantal relationship, but in which the partners are not just trying to agree, but in fact, [are] trying to see how their different perspectives can enhance the other person's understanding."[318] That is precisely what was happening in the programs led by Mary Boys and Sara Lee.

Their pioneering modeling of interreligious learning has shaped my professional work ever since, including in my partnership with Prof. Ruth Langer at the Center for Christian-Jewish Learning at Boston College (2000–2007) and with Prof. Adam Gregerman at the Institute for Jewish-Catholic Relations of Saint Joseph's University (2013–present). It inspired the concept behind the original sculpture by Joshua Koffman, "*Synagoga and Ecclesia* in Our Time," which Saint Joseph's University commissioned to celebrate the fiftieth jubilee of *Nostra aetate* in 2015.[319] Since the inspiring and transformative experiences provided by Mary and Sara are possible only in certain parts of the world, and since the United States is particularly blessed in this regard, I have come to believe that American Christians and Jews have a special responsibility to learn from and with each other through shared study.

A corollary to Mary's commitment to interreligious learning stems from the fact that opportunities for Jews and Christians to learn deeply from each other have historically not existed until quite recently. In fact, after the Second World War, they had to learn whether such interfaith dialogues were even possible. It was a new historical moment for everyone involved. Therefore, people in congregations or in living rooms have much to teach us all about how Jews and Christians can build a new relationship. This came home to me during a series of dialogues Mary helped organize with the local office of the Anti-Defamation League during my doctoral studies. Mary's openness to learning from all levels of Jewish and Christian interaction provided an important life lesson.

As mentioned above, Mary's work is always in service to the church and to the actual lives of Jews and Christians alike. She wants her scholarship to make a difference in the real world. This is why the topics of education, preaching, and liturgy are always high priorities for her.[320] What is the effect on Christian congregations in hearing (and, in some cases, reading aloud) the Gospel passion narratives on Passion/Palm Sunday and Good Friday? Do preachers accurately depict Jesus's relationships with his Jewish contemporaries? Does Catholic education in general and seminary and theological school education in particular really enact the Vatican's exhortation that "Jews and Judaism should not occupy an occasional and marginal place in catechesis: their presence there is essential and should be organically integrated"?[321] How can the education of young Christians not only preclude any whiff of antisemitic attitudes, but also "impart an exact knowledge of the wholly unique 'bond' [*Nostra aetate*, section 4] which joins us as a Church to the Jews and to Judaism"?[322] These and related questions are always motivating Mary's research, writings, and presentations. This continuous dedication to promoting genuine understanding and friendship in the lives of actual

Jews and Christians is inspirational. Despite the inevitable resistance to the major reforms required by the new relationship between Christians and Jews, sometimes emerging from within our own Catholic community, Mary nonetheless perseveres. This too is inspiring.

As if this were not enough, Mary continuously encourages younger scholars to commit themselves to rapprochement between Jews and Christians, or indeed to all forms of intergroup reconciliation and solidarity. I have been blessed to have been Mary's doctoral student and still am blessed as her colleague and friend. She is unquestionably a champion of interfaith efforts for many, many people.

It is therefore very fitting that she is among the interfaith heroes in this volume celebrating the contributions and accomplishments of our mutual friend, Rabbi David Rosen. David has also been a tireless advocate in promoting understanding and empathy between Christians and Jews and among Jews, Christians, and Muslims. In his context in the Middle East, he fosters amity among Jewish, Christian, and Muslim Israelis, between Israelis and Palestinians, between the State of Israel and neighboring states, and in many other intergroup relationships.

May their examples be shining beacons for future generations of interfaith bridge-builders and activists!

Professor Akbar Ahmed

ARCHBISHOP ROWAN WILLIAMS

To BEGIN WITH A simple statement of observation: human encounters bring about positive change when all those involved recognize in one another two things: a set of shared experiences and challenges, and the possibility of learning how better to make sense of those experiences and challenges through what others have to offer. This presupposes that we begin from a confidence in who and what we are. The skills of recognition and the hope of making sense that we bring to a new encounter are ideally those we have learned in a context of communal wisdom, the perceptions of a tradition that we trust as a reliable lens for viewing the world. But the best thing that a tradition can do for us is to educate us in how to continue learning. This is why serious religious and philosophical dialogue does not entail leaving behind the corporate discernment and insight we have inherited in our communities or setting aside claims to truth or even comprehensiveness for our convictions. It means being confident that the insight we have absorbed in our own tradition is strong enough, "hospitable" enough, and "imaginative" enough both to recognize itself in the life and words of another and to see how the wisdom of the stranger can enhance it and take it to new depths of understanding and resilience. It means being confident enough to ask hard critical questions of one's own tradition and to make the spiritual and intellectual choices that will best serve the honesty and sustainability of that tradition.

These, I believe, are some of the ideals we are trying to flesh out in identifying models of interfaith engagement. The abstract points made here become fully intelligible only when we see how they shape particular intellectual and spiritual journeys. In choosing Akbar Ahmed as my paradigm for this exercise, the words "hospitable" and "imaginative" from the last paragraph come forcefully alive. I first encountered his work when he was an academic at Selwyn College, Cambridge (the first Muslim Fellow in this originally Anglican foundation), and was captivated by the clarity and freshness of his book on *Postmodernism and Islam* (1992). The same freshness and accessibility is no less present in his later work. One of his most recent essays is a brilliantly sympathetic reflection on the legacy of Moses Maimonides as a thinker who can help us open some necessary conversations between Jews and Muslims, conversations like those that were possible in some areas of the early medieval Mediterranean world that he has celebrated in numerous writings. He continues to direct out attention to what is still—for most Westerners—a shamefully unknown history of creative and sophisticated Islamic philosophy, consciously engaging with the classical mainstream and worthy of providing the same kind of intellectual reference points that we routinely extract from Plato's Dialogues. It would not be too much to say that he exemplifies an Islamic humanism parallel to the Christian humanism of some late medieval, Renaissance, and post-Reformation figures like Nicolas of Cusa, Erasmus, Richard Hooker, or even Pascal. He discusses with insight and learning the continuing evolution of such a discourse, up to and including figures like Muhammad Iqbal in the early twentieth century, figures in whom intellectual brilliance, artistic skill, and practical political insight were woven together.

So they have been in Akbar Ahmed's life. His early experience as a provincial administrator in Pakistan gave him a lasting understanding of the complex tribal and communal tensions in Pakistani society. His skill as a field anthropologist, demonstrated in a variety of scholarly studies, has served him well in his recent ambitious surveys of religious attitudes in Europe and North America and in his wide-ranging and eloquent polemic, *The Thistle and the Drone* (2013), which, with great erudition, demonstrates where the most dangerous blind spots have been in Western military policy in many parts of the Islamic world, especially in Pakistan and Afghanistan. He has served as high commissioner in London for his country and is familiar with the world of professional diplomacy. At a time when this was not exactly an easy option in his home country, he courageously defended the ideals of Muhammad Ali Jinnah, founder of the state of Pakistan, who worked so hard to hold together the vision of a political community gratefully rooted in Islamic identity with the hope for a truly inclusive democracy in which religious commitment did not define the rights of citizenship—an ideal as elusive and as vital as ever. Akbar Ahmed has continued to defend this heritage in books and films.

He, like Iqbal, continues to write as a poet, dramatist, and man of letters, not simply as a scholar or statesman (although he has a distinguished record in academia on both sides of the Atlantic and is far from lacking influence in public affairs). The imaginative depth he brings to his writing is evident in the turn his published work has taken in the last decade towards the ambitious and extremely important fieldwork represented in his series of Journey books—*Journey into Islam* (2007), *Journey into America* (2010), *Journey into Europe* (2018)—and the television films that accompanied them. These books result from prolonged periods of leading (and inspiring) a team of young researchers listening in to the variety of perceptions of Islamic identity across the world. Part of the purpose of effective dialogue is always to learn more fully how your own identity and language are seen or heard. Once again, it should be regarded as a mark of confidence to invite others to say what they see—members of other faiths but also, of course, members of the same faith who approach matters very differently. The fusion of hospitality with imagination is very clear in these unusual and very accessible books. They and the companion films will still be used, I'm sure, decades from now as sources of gauging the temperature of religious commitment and the understanding of this commitment in the wider society across the globe in our era. It was a personal pleasure to be involved in some of the conversations around the third of these pieces of work. An admiration based mostly on cordial correspondence and the printed page became a solid friendship, setting for me the highest of standards in engaged scholarship and irenic political vision.

Talking about the Abrahamic religions can be something of a cliché these days—and it can provoke annoyance among adherents to the dharmic faiths of South and East Asia. But Akbar Ahmed's work (not unlike the work of the man whom we are honoring in this book for his tireless and fearless involvement in dialogue and advocacy) helps us see that the Abrahamic perspective is a matter neither of collapsing deeply divergent confessions into a single phenomenon nor of canonizing a narrow focus on Western Asian religions. Judaism, Christianity, and Islam have all been through complex cultural processes that have taken them a long way from the Middle East. If there is some sort of common ground between Afghan or Indonesian Muslims, Ashkenazi Jews who still preserve Eastern European habits and traditions and Latin American Christians, it is certainly more than just a shared history in the Eastern Mediterranean seaboard. Ahmed is always alert to the very different interlocutors Islam has had in South and East Asia and—like many other contemporary Islamic scholars—resists an easy assimilation of Islamic to merely Arabic identity.

But what then is the nature of Abrahamic faith? Ahmed quotes Maimonides himself as celebrating the congruence of Jewish, Christian, and Muslim teaching in that all three faiths look to an ideal of obedience to God, fleshed out in common life, and all three take for granted a God whose action can redeem—that is, can transform from outside the conditions of human existence. This is not resignation to a God who can solve all problems without our freedom and our alignment with the divine will; it is, rather, a vision of how human hope is possible in the light of faith in a divine purpose that exceeds our imagining and is not defeated by our defeats and betrayals. Dharmic faith brings different (and indispensable) insights to the table, insights about the illusions that surround our models of individual selfhood, the slavery we inflict upon ourselves by ignorance and the mechanisms of cause and effect in a world of self-serving myths. But the Abrahamic perspective is one in which we are always invited to reflect on a narrative of repeated loss and recovery, the repeated rediscovery of a divine purpose never exhausted or deflected. The fragile world we know is always surrounded by an infinite agency that both demands our loving surrender and assures us of a freedom greater than our own and so of a future beyond our successes and failures. Dialogue—trialogue?—between our very different discourses about divine freedom and the gift of divine interruption and divine calling is possible not just because we have a shared ancestry but because that ancestry has shown all of us—or should have shown all of us—where hope is to be found.

Akbar Ahmed's chapter on Jews and Muslims in *Journey into America* maps with close attention some of the dividing lines of anxiety and misunderstanding, detailing with a difficult honesty both the paranoid fantasies indulged by some Muslims about Jewish control of society and the fixed beliefs of many Jews that Muslims are unequivocally culturally alien. It is notable that in these pages we find a nuanced and careful treatment of what Zionism does and does not mean and a reminder of the initiative originating with Ahmed's daughter, Amineh Ahmed Hoti, in 2008, A Call to Peace, Dialogue, and Understanding between Muslims and Jews, an initiative welcomed in unreserved terms by David Rosen. It has been said more than once that for all three Abrahamic traditions, there can be no peaceful common future that does not involve the rediscovery of a common past. That past is by no means a record of happy coexistence. There have been episodes like the *Convivencia* of early medieval Andalucia, but there have been far more periods of mutual incomprehension, fear, and violence as sharp and destructive as anything we see today. But the point is not to look back to some golden age. We can—as we have already noted—learn from the humanist sensibilities of so many great thinkers across the confessional territory, but we must not indulge in any sentimentality. No, the purpose of looking back is to see how, again and again, the same themes recur across the board in the leading minds of the faiths, how the mutual bitterness so often reflects a sense of uncomfortable closeness or rivalry rather than a radical alienness, how minorities of all kinds share the same experience of being demonized by the guardians of normative national or social identity (and this, of course, includes Christian minorities in the USA at different periods, from Catholics to Mennonites). The common past is not a glowing ideal but a source of learning.

Akbar Ahmed's fieldwork in this context is of exceptional significance. He and his co-workers have courageously gone into environments where their investigations have not been easy or welcome and have reported with clarity and dispassion, identifying both the seeds of hope and the persistence of deeply anti-humanist religiosities, Christian, Jewish, and Muslim. They have produced rounded and granular pictures of a society, not generalizations from a few straightforward and easily mapped localities. They are also, we should not forget, the product of an impressively diverse body of collaborators. The nature of the shared work illustrates the possibilities that the research itself seeks to chart, as well as the impact of their leading investigator on a younger generation.

Journey into America ends with a sober evaluation of the risks to civilized society when we are governed by men rather than laws—a situation apparently welcomed by some in George W. Bush's administration and manifestly adopted with still greater and more uncritical enthusiasm by many in the US and elsewhere today. Part of that drift away from an ideal of the rule of law is tied up with the nakedly racist and chauvinist spirit that feeds on Manichaean fictions about the Muslim world. But Ahmed is equally clear that only an Islamic world that has recovered its own humanism can respond and cooperate as it needs to with Western, especially American, society. "This coordination will only be possible if Americans and Muslims cultivate a genuine philosophic curiosity about themselves and each other," Ahmed writes.

Perhaps the really important word there is *themselves*. Dialogue should make us wonder about who we are—not in a panicky and rootless spirit that alienates us from our own origins but in a way that invites us to look harder at what has made us who we are, how our own tradition has learned and moved. What makes dialogue utterly impossible is a worldview which assumes that my/our beliefs have never changed or needed to change, that what we/I believe is so obvious that it never needed to be learned and was never new or surprising. From such a starting point, all surprise is unwelcome, and all learning is dangerous. Yet all our traditions in their diverse ways remind us that to encounter God is always to encounter a stranger, as well as to find our heart's desire. Augustine in his *Confessions* observes that he has become "a question to himself" as he wrestles with how to speak of God. Jewish religious thought has been overwhelmingly a history of passionate, principled, and inconclusive argument. Al Ghazali, as an already experienced teacher, found himself unable to open his mouth in front of his students and came to insist on the utter mysteriousness of God's action as expressed in every event in the world, moment by moment. Becoming strange to oneself and acknowledging the dizzying variety and intricacy of questing in God's presence is not some peculiar outlier in our discourse. So we engage with each other across the great confessional divides so as to find ourselves afresh—arriving where we started and knowing the place for the first time, to paraphrase T. S. Eliot.

Akbar Ahmed has devoted a vastly distinguished life of scholarship and action to this kind of discovery, helping his own community and other communities to see themselves anew, to be surprised and enlarged by that surprise. Among contemporary practitioners of dialogue between the historic faiths, he holds a very high position and exerts a wonderfully and diversely creative influence. I acknowledge his example with admiration and deep gratitude, hoping that the philosophic curiosity and animation in reasoning and imagining alike will persuade more and more to follow where his explorations have led.

Engaged and Peace Activism

Ecumenical Patriarch Bartholomew

METROPOLITAN EMMANUEL ADAMAKIS

ALTHOUGH THE ECUMENICAL PATRIARCHATE as an institution has a strong and venerable presence as a dynamic center of dialogue, reconciliation, and peace, Ecumenical Patriarch Bartholomew has shaped interfaith dialogue and the Patriarchate's engagement in it in powerful ways. The man who would become Ecumenical Patriarch Bartholomew was born Demetrios Arhondonis in 1940, on the small island of Imbros. This island was unique in all the Aegean in that it maintained a Greek majority population for centuries, stretching all the way back to Byzantium. It was only after World War II that Turkish settlers from the mainland changed the demographic homogeneity of the island overnight. Ecumenical Patriarch Bartholomew lived through the drastic transformation this entailed, and, as a personal experience, it has imbued his ministry and life with a deep understanding and desire to bear witness to the very real challenges but also great potential in encountering the other. Thus, the vocation for dialogue personified by His All-Holiness is fortified by both the long and storied history of the Ecumenical Patriarchate and his own deeply personal convictions rooted in childhood memories.

Patriarch Bartholomew has traveled more extensively than any other Orthodox patriarch in history, exchanging official visitations with numerous ecclesiastical and state dignitaries. In particular, because he is a citizen of Turkey and the leader of a Christian minority in a predominantly Muslim nation, Ecumenical Patriarch Bartholomew's personal experience endows him with a unique perspective on religious tolerance and interfaith dialogue. This is evident in the numerous interfaith meetings in which he has participated, in the interfaith programs and tracks that he or the Patriarchate under his guidance has launched, and in key messages that represent his religious worldview. All this makes him a leading global interfaith hero and the most prominent figure in this domain in the Orthodox world. The following essay offers a taste of key initiatives and key statements, with special attention to Jewish-Christian relations, as tribute to the honoree of the present volume, my close friend and collaborator, and trusted friend of the patriarch and the Patriarchate—Rabbi David Rosen.

Dialogue Initiatives and Vision
of Patriarch Bartholomew

The patriarch's interreligious outreach is expansive. It comes to expression in numerous state visits and associations with public bodies and global conferences. More particularly, several dialogue tracks have been launched by the Patriarchate. These include distinct dialogue tracks between Orthodoxy and Judaism; Orthodoxy, Islam, and Judaism; Christianity and Islam.[323] Dozens of symposia and conferences have been organized in these tracks, and these have taken place in a variety of international locations.

As is well known, His All-Holiness is often referred to in common parlance as the Green Patriarch, due to his decades-long concern with ecological matters. This has proven an important arena for interfaith collaboration. An extensive series of events demonstrate the conviction of Patriarch Bartholomew that environmental challenges must be resolved in dialogue and partnership with other religious faiths and scientific disciplines. This includes the establishment of the Religious and Scientific Committee (1995) and the organization of several international, interreligious, and interdisciplinary symposia, between 1997 and 2018, on such diverse topics as the Black Sea, the Amazon, a greener Attica, and more.[324]

Various keynote addresses given by the patriarch reveal his core philosophy of dialogue, a philosophy that comes to expression throughout his various initiatives.

> The credibility of religions today depends on their attitude towards the protection of human freedom and dignity, as well as on their contribution to peace. This is the presupposition not only of peaceful coexistence, but even the sheer survival of humanity. We can face these challenges only together. Nobody—not a nation, not a state, not a religion, nor science and technology—can face the current problems alone. We need one another; we need common mobilization, common efforts, common goals, common spirit. Therefore, we regard the present multifaceted crisis as an opportunity for practicing solidarity, for dialogue and cooperation, for openness and confidence. Our future is common, and the way toward this future is a common journey.[325]

This vision of joining forces for the global good is one major component of the patriarch's vision. Another dimension is found in the following seven principles, which capture his vision for how religions should function in the world. While articulated initially within a Christian-Muslim context, they aptly describe his broader interfaith engagement.

> First, our religions are not willing to disturb world peace to serve the deplorable military hysteria of political leaders.

> Second, our religions are not willing to overlook their teaching about the unity of the human race to serve recent ideologies of fragmentation.

> Third, our religions are not willing to replace the call put forward in their teachings for peace and justice in the world with the demand for war.

> Fourth, our religions are willing, through interfaith dialogue, to heal the wounds of the past in order to jointly serve the weak and suffering.

> Fifth, our religions are willing to jointly publicize the principles of mutual respect and understanding in educational curricula, so that blind fanaticism and religious intolerance may gradually be eliminated.

> Sixth, our religions are willing to cooperate through ecumenical dialogue to defend peace, social justice, and human rights among people, irrespective of religious, national, racial, social, or other differences.

> Seventh, our religions support governments and international organisations to achieve fuller awareness of these fundamental principles.[326]

A further quote will serve to profile the ecumenical patriarch's orientation towards dialogue.

> Inter-religious dialogue does not mean to deny one's own faith, but rather to change one's mind or attitude towards the other. So it can also heal and disperse prejudices and contribute to a mutual comprehension and the pacific resolution of conflicts. Biases and prejudices come from the misrepresentation of religion.[327]

This vocation for dialogue was found by Ecumenical Patriarch Bartholomew in the living reality of Orthodox Christians living alongside other religious minorities in Turkey. As stated, he has known what religious diversity means since a very early age, and it precisely this reality that has taught him to treasure the mission of promoting dialogue through intense interfaith activity. In 1994, at the International Conference on Peace and Tolerance, he declared:

> When [religions] inflict hurt, death and destruction, they steal more than life; they undermine faith itself—although faith defiantly remains the only way to break the cycle of hatred and retribution.

It is not surprising, therefore, to find the same idea expressed in the encyclical of the Holy and Great Council convened in Crete in 2016 under the ecumenical patriarch's chairmanship:

> Honest interfaith dialogue contributes to the development of mutual trust and to the promotion of peace and reconciliation. The Church strives to make "the peace from on high" more tangibly felt on earth. True peace is not achieved by force of arms, but only through love that "does not seek its own" (1 Cor 13.5). The oil of faith must be used to soothe and heal the wounds of others, not to rekindle new fires of hatred.[328]

This is clearly a direct influence of the ecumenical patriarch on the conciliar work.

Based on his experience, there cannot be a true and authentic dialogue without an encounter. In fact, this is the title of one of his books, *Encountering the Mystery*.[329] An encounter is a spiritual journey where the face of the other becomes a source of revelation. God's image calls us to experience relationships as a way to embody faith, hope, and love; to respect human dignity; and to promote peace and freedom.

The notion of encounter accounts for the manifold personal relationships that the patriarch has cultivated through the decades in the framework of interfaith activity. These include fraternal exchanges with three popes, as well as sustained friendships with religious leaders and scholars across religions.

Orthodox-Jewish Relations

The Orthodox Christian-Jewish relationship is a historic one. After the Second World War, the entire religious landscape changed. In many ways, this great conflict that caused so much devastation brought people of faith closer together. We began to realize the need for communication and dialogue. The ecumenical and interfaith movement began in earnest. This was a reality that the Ecumenical Patriarchate foresaw decades earlier when it took the first steps toward fostering such dialogue with two historic encyclicals, one in 1902, calling for stronger inter-Orthodox unity and communication,[330] as well as dialogue with other Christian faiths; then another in 1920, with a much more developed vision for what would become the modern ecumenical movement.[331] These first, vital steps were milestones on the path to earnest ecumenical and eventually interfaith encounters that would flower into relationships of understanding and love.

Ecumenical Patriarch Bartholomew's desire for communication and his insistence on the significance of in-person meetings has indeed born much fruit, including our present dialogue with the Jewish community, which started in 1977 with academic theological discussions at the Theological Faculty of Lucerne, co-sponsored by the Orthodox Center of the Ecumenical Patriarchate in Chambésy-Geneva and the International Jewish Committee for Interreligious Consultations. A follow-up meeting in 1979 took place in Bucharest, Romania—the first two meetings of a total of ten official Orthodox Christian-Jewish dialogues that have taken place, each one building on the goodwill and progress of the last.

We have indeed come a long way from where we were. We now have decades of experience behind us to help inform the decades that are to come. We need, however, to keep moving. There is a new generation of young academics who have made the relationship between Orthodox Christianity and Judaism the focus of their scholarship. More importantly, at the local level, Jewish and Greek Orthodox communities have engaged in fellowship and the sharing of each other's culture. The generations that preceded us have left us a solid foundation. It is the task of this generation of Orthodox Christians and Jews to build upon that foundation.

Aware of its continuity with the Old Israel, the Orthodox Church calls for fidelity to their common roots, as well as to the necessary opening for the deepening of dialogue, essential for the life of our communities, as well as for the protection of religious freedom. This relationship is perfectly encapsulated by a recent document blessed by the Ecumenical Patriarchate titled *For the Life of the World: Toward a Social Ethos of the Orthodox Church*: that reads: "Orthodox Christians look to the Jewish communities throughout the world not merely as to practitioners of another creed, but as to, in some sense, their spiritual elders in the history of God's saving revelations, and as to the guardians of that precious inheritance that is the first full manifestation of God's saving presence in history."[332]

Opposing Anti-Semitism

Bigotry and violence against Jews have long been a conspicu-
ous evil of the cultures of Christendom; the greatest systematic
campaign of mass murder and attempted genocide in European
history was undertaken against the Jews of Europe; and—while
some Orthodox clergy and laity demonstrated exceptional generosity and even sacrificial compassion to their Jewish brothers
and sisters, earning from them the honorific "righteous among
the nations"—other historically Orthodox nations have dark
histories of anti-Semitic violence and oppression. For all these
evils, Christians must seek God's forgiveness. In expiation for
those crimes against the Jewish people specifically committed
in Orthodox lands, the Church seeks both God's forgiveness as
well as a deeper relation of love and regard with Jewish communities and the Jewish faith.[333]

These words from *For the Life of the World* manifest clearly the ecumenical patriarch's commitment to oppose anti-Semitism. He visited with
emotion the Yad Vashem Holocaust Memorial in May 2014. On this occasion, he said:

In that place of such incomprehensible pain, our heart was
grieved and we mourned deeply at the realization of the human
potential for destruction. These emotions returned as we took
the walkway down into the children's memorial. It seemed as if
we had entered the abode of the dead. The location of the memorial under the earth vividly represents the inexplicable loss
that was the Shoah, the Holocaust. All who descend into the
inner chamber of the museum are free to walk away when they
chose, and return to the sunlight. Such was not the case for these
1.5 million children whose lives were taken from them through
hatred and unspeakable violence.

But for the ecumenical patriarch, it is not enough to remember: we also
need to condemn "every act of terrorism, anti-Semitism, and xenophobia.
We must publicly profess that a crime against believers of any faith is an
abomination in the face of God."[334]

I accompanied His All-Holiness when he visited the concentration
camps of Auschwitz more recently in 2019. He led the Walk of the Living,
the supreme tribute taking place every year since 1988 in memory of the
six million Jews exterminated by the Nazis in the Second World War. The
ecumenical patriarch addressed thousands of people from at least fifty-
seven different countries, who participated in the walk. The ecumenical

patriarch visited the sites where millions of people died, showing solidarity with the Jewish community all over the world who commemorate and honor the victims of the Holocaust. It was a particularly moving experience for all the participants this year.

I was profoundly moved by this opportunity given to me then to stand at this place where so many died under the bloody thirst of injustice and hatred. To this day, the world keeps mourning at the realization of this disaster. The emotion becomes even more real. I recall these uplifting remarks by the ecumenical patriarch:

> Through our prayers, we turn sadness and suffering into remembrance of one of the greatest tragedy in human history. For over twenty-five years, we have from the very beginning of our tenure as Ecumenical Patriarch denounced anti-Semitism, racism, xenophobia, but also religious extremism and fanaticism, rejecting the attempts by any faith, any state, institution to denigrate the very basic right of others to exist.

In closing, he said:

> It is not enough to remember the victims of the Shoah, we also need to do everything in our means so that this tragedy does not happen again. To us, dialogue is the only remedy to hatred.

The Saints behind the Hero

One often hears the point made that teaching relating to the other must be expressed not only in public interfaith gatherings or in official documents; it must penetrate to the community and shape the lives and attitudes of the faithful. One concrete expression of such a spiritual and educational approach relates to the heroes the Church presents to its followers, the saints. The choice of saints speaks volumes of the ideals and priorities of the Church. The ideals expressed above find particular articulation in the choice of some recent saints. It is under Ecumenical Patriarch Bartholomew's leadership that the Orthodox Church recognized as saints individuals who particularly witnessed Christian values by the sacrifice of their own lives during the Second World War. They were canonized by the Holy and Sacred Synod of the Ecumenical Patriarchate on May 1, 2004. As a Church, the memory of these great men and women of our faith motivates us to be worthy successors to their example. Saint Maria Skobtsova did wonders in finding a long-term hiding place for the persecuted Jews whom she had sheltered in Paris. Mother Maria was deported to the

Ravensbrück camp, where she was selected for the gas chambers on Holy Saturday and perished on March 31, 1945. Saint Dimitri Klepinin, along with Saint Maria, vehemently objected to anti-Jewish measures in France. Dimitri Klepinin was transferred to the Buchenwald camp, then to Dora, where he died in February 1944. In the midst of tragedy, love was the only hope. The destiny of these saints reminds us of the self-sacrificial love that transcends hope itself and becomes divine.[335]

In his foreword to her book *The Sacrament of the Brother*, the French Orthodox theologian Olivier Clément wrote:

> The life and death of Mother Maria was prophetic for us as Orthodox in West, as young people that wanted love and risk, but did not know where to find God. God is at the center, at the heart of things and beings, within the density of creation, in the suffering of shared creation, as Mother Mary used to say . . . . The Church is nothing other than the world walking towards deification; in the Church, the world is no longer a tomb, but a matrix.[336]

I would like to conclude this section by recalling the words of Ecumenical Patriarch Bartholomew, when he visited the Yad Vashem Holocaust Memorial in May 2014: "The future can be no better than the past, if people from all cultures, religions, and political thought do not learn well the lessons of the Shoah. Great tyranny and oppression were stopped in some small way by ordinary people, many of whom are commemorated in the Garden of the Righteous among the Nations." Among these righteous was Maria Skobtsova, who continues to speak through Ecumenical Patriarch Bartholomew's memory of her ideals and actions of self-sacrifice for the other.

In closing, allow me to quote Rabbi David Rosen's own words about Ecumenical Patriarch Bartholomew:

> Patriarch Bartholomew . . . serves as an inspiring example not only for his own flock and faith, but indeed for all religious communities and for all of society—a model and inspiration for which we give thanks to the One Creator and Guide of the universe.

Rev. Nikkyo Niwano[337]

Rev. Kosho Niwano

When I was little, while my family was sitting around the dinner table, the topic my grandfather enjoyed talking about, more than any other, was interreligious dialogue and cooperation. He had worked extremely hard to bring it about—in fact, more than I could have imagined. Even so, my grandfather always had something positive to say. He would assure us, "While there are many sufferings in the world, there are wonderful people trying to overcome them," or enthusiastically announce, "Today, I met a wonderful person," or "Something really splendid has happened." Thus, he told me about this world that I had yet to see for myself. I can still remember how my grandfather's eyes would sparkle, just like a little boy's, when he spoke of such things. Of course, I loved listening to my grandfather and seeing the world through his eyes, so I grew up thinking that the world is full of wonderful religions and remarkable people.

"What some people say is true, others say is false. And so, based on their prejudices, people argue with each other. Why is it that people on the Way of faith do not talk to each other about the same thing?" Shakyamuni Buddha said this some 2500 years ago, as recorded in Suttanipāta.

"In its essence, religion does not exclude others but instead teaches us to love others, just as we love ourselves. The oneness of self and others is fundamental to religion. Nothing is more paradoxical than religion fracturing into different sects and groups that fight with each other. Instead, religious people should study each other's teachings and practices, discuss issues of religious faith that are of mutual concern and, on that basis, work together to realize world peace." "There is no other way to save the modern world and humanity than through interreligious cooperation." These were my grandfather's firm convictions—my grandfather, Nikkyo Niwano, who founded Rissho Kosei-kai (RK).

Founder Nikkyo Niwano was born on November 15, 1906, in a remote mountain village, surrounded by austere natural beauty and subject to long, harsh winters. He used to say that when he was a boy, he was always being told, "Even the smallest insect somehow manages to feed itself, doesn't it? Since you were born a human being, you must become someone who is useful to other people and society." He grew up seeing how his fellow villagers devoted themselves to overcoming the sufferings and hardships they faced. He moved to Tokyo at the age of sixteen. Eventually, concern for his sick child led to his encounter with the Lotus Sutra. After listening to lectures about the Lotus Sutra, he realized that this profoundly vast, limitless sutra is a perfect, flawless vehicle for liberating everyone everywhere and capable of transforming the whole world into a peaceful, purified Buddha land. With joy that seemed to reach to the very heavens, he founded Rissho Kosei-kai in 1938.

Rissho means establishing (*ri*), in this world, the teachings of the true Dharma (*sho*), that is, the Lotus Sutra. *Ko* indicates the fellowship of good friends in the practice of the faith and the confluence of harmonious faith, in other words, that we are all many in body, one in mind (the Buddhist principle *ittai doshin*). *Sei* is the ideal of perfecting our character and ourselves becoming Buddhas. Reflecting on his motivation in establishing Rissho Kosei-kai, Founder Niwano said:

> There was only thing I had in mind: I want to liberate people from suffering. It's no different now. Nothing has changed, only the scope and scale of that liberation have greatly increased. But there is no change in the fundamental spirit of RK. After all, what does it really mean to be liberated? When you boil it down, I believe it is giving people the peace of mind that lets them live with hope.

After establishing RK, Founder Niwano, supported by the ideal of peace found in the Lotus Sutra's teaching that all human beings are brothers and sisters caused to live by the one great life force of the universe, proclaimed that the bodhisattva practices explained in the Lotus Sutra become our contributions to the cause of peace and devoted himself to grappling with the issue of world peace.[338]

Even when making RK's operating plan, he directed RK's leadership to "make a plan that not only develops our own organization, but also helps the development of other organizations and other people." Grounded in his firm belief that the true meaning of all religious faiths is one and the same and with the wholehearted support he received from RK's members, he taught us that by trying to always remember our sense of mission and determination to build the Land of Eternally Tranquil Light in every place in our communities and in the world,[339] the true form of peace would gradually manifest itself. Therefore, in 1951, he helped form the Federation of New Religious Organizations of Japan (Shinshuren, FNROJ), and in 1963, as a member of a peace delegation of religious leaders for banning nuclear weapons, he went to Europe to foster interreligious cooperation. He was particularly active in regard to the abolition of nuclear weapons. In 1978, at the first UN Special Session devoted to Disarmament (SSOD), Founder Niwano, representing the World Conference of Religions for Peace (RfP, at that time known as WCRP), delivered an address in which he made this appeal to political leaders of the US and USSR: "Instead of taking risks with arms, please take major risks for peace and disarmament," urging them to break out of a balance of power based on fear, generated by a seemingly endless arms race.

My grandfather's indefatigable work for interreligious dialogue and world peace began in earnest with his involvement in FNROJ and the nuclear disarmament movement that started in Japan in the 1950s. Then, through the auspices of Cardinal Marella, he was the only Buddhist invited to attend the opening ceremony of the fourth session of the Second Vatican Council in September 1965. The words spoken at the opening ceremony of Vatican II by Pope Paul VI were imbued with the spirit of the encyclical *Nostra aetate*, which recognizes salvation in other (non-Catholic) religious traditions and affirms freedom of religion. The following day, in a private audience, the pope told my grandfather, "I know what you are doing for interfaith cooperation. Please continue to promote such a wonderful movement. God will surely bless you in your holy work." My grandfather, inspired by the pope's words that confirmed his beliefs and the work he had been undertaking, made a resolution: "Were I to only think of my own religion, I could not fulfill my mission as a religious person. From now on, I will serve as a bridge between all religions. Since we share this common goal—peace for all humanity—interreligious cooperation is definitely possible."[340] Thereafter, he redoubled his efforts to bring about interreligious dialogue and cooperation in Japan and around the world.

As if in response to *Nostra aetate*, the 1960s witnessed a growing momentum among religious leaders from the United States, India, Japan, and other countries to take bold action for the sake of world peace. In the background of this burgeoning peace movement were the constant threat of nuclear war and a fervent desire to end the quagmire of the Vietnam War.

My grandfather was one of the driving forces leading to the realization of the World Conference of Religions for Peace (RfP/WCRP) in 1970. He flew to many places in Japan and other countries, calling on people to participate in RfP. However, at that time, some thirty years after its founding, RK was still a young organization. It was not easy for him, as the then president of RK, to call upon the leaders of religious organizations with centuries of history and ask them to consider participating in RfP. Many people were doubtful or suspicious of this new interreligious movement that my grandfather was promoting. In Germany, one religious leader asked him, "With what qualifications have you come to see us?" He replied, "I came here by order of the Buddha. In Buddhism, we devote ourselves to the essential life force that supports and manifests all phenomena in the universe. This is called the Eternal Buddha. Your God gives you the same order, doesn't He? You can hear the voice of God, can't you?" This religious leader showed that he empathized with my grandfather's words. Spurred on by the friendship and inspiration received from Pope Paul VI and his faith that God and the Buddha were watching over and protecting him, my grandfather continued to champion interreligious dialogue and cooperation in every place he visited and to every person he met.

Five years after *Nostra aetate*, in October 1970, more than 300 religious leaders representing thirty-nine countries around the world gathered in Kyoto, Japan, for the first assembly of RfP. At this very first assembly, these religious leaders drafted and adopted the *Kyoto Declaration*, which included this remarkable passage:

> Because of these convictions that we hold in common, we believe that a special charge has been given to all men and women of religion to be concerned with all their hearts and minds with peace and peacemaking, to be the servants of peace. As men and women of religion, we confess in humility and penitence that we have very often betrayed our religious ideals and our commitment to peace. It is not religion that has failed the cause of peace, but religious people. This betrayal of religion can and must be corrected.[341]

With one eye to the recent past—the dark shadows cast by World War II, which saw staggering casualties among civilians and combatants alike, the Holocaust, and the deployment of nuclear weapons—and another eye to present crises, including the Cold War's perpetual threat of total annihilation and the horrific conflict in Vietnam, the world's religious leaders gathered in Kyoto to forge this profound, enduring statement, which I firmly believe is the distillation of human wisdom.

Since then, assemblies of RfP have been held in different countries around the world once every five years. Each of these occasions has reinvigorated the ongoing search for ways that religion can make concrete contributions to solving various global issues that threaten peace. The last assembly of RfP that my grandfather attended was held in Riva Del Garda, Italy, in 1994, when he had reached the ripe old age of eighty-eight. At the time, he was still suffering from the cold he had caught in the early autumn, so he was not feeling well. I really did not want him to travel to Italy. My grandfather had already flown around the world more times than

I could count, giving his all for the sake of world peace. Nevertheless, my grandfather insisted that he must attend. "Yes, I will go, even if it means risking my life to do so," he said resolutely, even though he had always been running at full speed and never stopped to think about his own well-being. Thinking of him making such a long journey at that age, risking his own life, my eyes filled with tears. How could it be that my grandfather would risk his very life for world peace, while I was still holding back what I could contribute to such an important cause and thinking only of myself? My grandfather's example made me realize the role I must play, even though it might not always be easy to fulfill.

My grandfather has been my hero since I was little. Although he passed away in 1999, shortly before his ninety-third birthday, he is still my hero today. When faced with a seemingly impossible situation, I look for wisdom and inspiration in his words. For instance, when he went to Belgium to attend RfP II, a reporter asked him, "Mr. Niwano, do you think that your movement will bring peace to the world?" My grandfather replied, "No, world peace is not so easy. It's very difficult. But that is why I am making my best effort." If he could make his best effort against such tremendous odds half a century ago, so can I today.

Rabbi David Rosen, who will celebrate his seventieth birthday this year, has also overcome considerable resistance to make great strides for social justice and world peace. In the 1970s, he went to South Africa. He thought that in order for people to join forces against the apartheid policies of the South African government, action through religious faith was absolutely necessary, so he organized an interfaith council of Christians, Muslims, and Jews. He also initiated dialogue among Catholic, Anglican, Methodist, Muslim, and Jewish leaders for the sake of social justice. When Rabbi Rosen went to see a Christian minister, he asked him to focus on the things that bring them together rather than the things that tear them apart, so that they could work together in supporting the anti-apartheid movement. However, this minister replied, in a strong South African accent: "To tell the truth, rabbi, I disagree with your idea because the most important thing in my life is something that tears us apart. This is because I have accepted Jesus as my personal Savior and anyone who cannot share this faith will fall into hell. So I can meet you only in order to fulfill my Christian duty to try to save your soul."

This anecdote reminds me of when my grandfather was traveling all over the world, calling upon people who had little interest in interreligious dialogue and asking them to join RfP. Founder Niwano spoke about this as follows. "By its very nature, religion does not reject others, because its essence is a worldview of the unity of all living beings, in which you love others as you love yourself. It is unnatural for religious groups to be divided against or fighting with each other. Religious people should study each other's faith, talk about what they have in common, and, based upon our shared values, work together in order to achieve peace. This kind of interreligious cooperation requires engaging with people of other religious faiths and for us religious leaders, who may tend to be self-righteous and narrow-minded, it has the effect of purifying ourselves and heightening our own spirituality."

Similarly, Rabbi Rosen realized that in order to gain the cooperation of South Africans and deepen their understanding of him, he would have to deepen his knowledge and understanding of his own faith. Although he had worked with many different religious leaders and religious organizations that were the source of tremendous inspiration, he realized that he had never given enough thought to the meaning and importance of other religious traditions. He came to understand that not only do encounters with our fellow human beings and engaging with different religious faiths expand our awareness of God, such interaction also provides us with invaluable opportunities to change, broaden, and deepen our understanding of our own theology and find greater appreciation and respect for the other. Simply stated, he accepted and embraced the great challenge of openness.

Rabbi Rosen's association with RfP dates back to 1991, when he was asked to join an RfP conference on justice and peace in the Middle East that RK was hosting the following year. In 1992, Rabbi Rosen took the lead in organizing a conference of interreligious dialogue among Jewish, Christian, and Muslim leaders in Jerusalem. My father, Rev. Nichiko Niwano, was invited to attend as an international president of RfP. At that time, the situation in Palestine was extremely tense. In the midst of ongoing airstrikes by both Israel and Lebanon, he courageously made the trip alone. While my father was visiting Jerusalem, Rabbi Rosen hosted him at a Shabbat dinner in his home. The Rosen family extended such warm hospitality to my father that I am certain he will continue to cherish memories of that time for the rest of his life. Indeed, the seeds of friendship and trust planted then have blossomed into deep ties that continue to this day and are a real treasure for my family, one I feel blessed to have inherited.

Andrea Riccardi[342]

Bishop Ambrogio Spreafico

Speaking at the last Prayer for Peace meeting in the spirit of Assisi, organized by the Community of Sant'Egidio in Rome, on October 20, 2020, Andrea Riccardi said:

> Prayer and peace are an integral part of all religious traditions, even though they are so different. Religions do not speak only to politicians and diplomats, but they collect the small and large actions of all, the tears of the victims, the invocations of the humble, showing a "weak force" for peace.

The spirit of Assisi journeys from afar. The historic day of the Prayer for Peace convened by Pope John Paul II, on October 27, 1986, in the city of Assisi, the city of St. Francis, a man of peace and dialogue, was a moment of creative reception of the Second Vatican Council.[343] That day, 110 religious leaders from twenty-nine countries, representing thirty-eight different religious traditions, met in Assisi to pray for peace in a world marked by the tensions of the Cold War. It was the Polish pope who took the initiative, because he was strongly convinced that the spiritual strength of religions could be a source of peace. At the same time, the pope saw the risk that religion could become fuel in conflicts. In Assisi, religions prayed not together but side by side, keeping all the differences but no longer against or indifferent to others. In 2016, thirty years after that day in Assisi, Andrea Riccardi retraced what had happened since that historic October 27. He recalled that a few months after the event, Wojtyla returned to "insist stubbornly on what was beginning to be called the spirit of Assisi," affirming that in the city of St. Francis "it was disclosed in an extraordinary way, the unique value that prayer has for peace; and indeed we cannot have peace without prayer, and the prayer of all, each according to his own identity and in the search for truth."[344] Already in the closing ceremony, moreover, the pope had hoped that that day would be the beginning of a journey and not remain an end in itself. "We continue to spread the message of peace. We continue to spread the spirit of Assisi," he said.

Riccardi continued, recalling the thirty years of Assisi:

> For this reason, since 1987, I matured the choice with my friends of the Community of Sant'Egidio, that the intuition of John Paul II should be continued, gathering religious leaders . . . . I was struck by the desire of so many religious leaders to get out of their particular point of view and to place themselves on a broader horizon: what—a few years later—we would call the global world. Often a closed world imprisons believers with ancient conflicting logics, with new fanaticism and nationalisms. In the meeting there is a liberation of all this.

Not a few thought, even in the Roman Curia, that the day in Assisi should remain a unique event. But the Community of Sant'Egidio, strongly encouraged by John Paul II, decided to repeat that event by starting to organize, year after year, in a different city and country, international meetings in the "spirit of Assisi." The first two events were in Rome in 1987 and 1988. On September 1, 1989, the Prayer for Peace, entitled "War Never Again," was held in Warsaw, exactly fifty years after the outbreak of the Second World War, in a crowded Castle square. Sixty-eight days later, the Berlin Wall would be pulled down. A whole day was dedicated to the pilgrimage to Birkenau and to the memory of the Shoah, with the full involvement of all religious leaders, including Muslims, when many countries with an Islamic majority still did not recognize the Holocaust, ignored it, or, worse, denied it. Peace also passes through the recognition of the suffering of others, of the history of persecution that has hit the other. The value of peace cannot be fully appreciated if one has no experience, or one loses memory of the horror of war. The patient work over thirty-five years has brought together and united different religious worlds, respecting diversity, repudiating violence, and removing the foundation under the feet of those tempted by radical hatred, going through many difficult historical phases since the belief that there is no alternative to dialogue. It is releasing the energy of peace, involving political leaders, intellectuals, nonbelievers, and many ordinary citizens in an agenda of dialogue and cooperation for the good of the human family. Over the years, participation from Israel has been important, starting with that of Chief Rabbi Israel Meir Lau and many others.

Marco Impagliazzo, president of the Community of Sant'Egidio, recently wrote:

> The coexistence between women and men of different faiths and cultures in the globalized and urbanized world is an irrepressible

and unchangeable reality through walls and borders. Religions entering into history, emerging from the temptation of self-referentiality, finding more and more spaces and themes for dialogue—not least that relating to the defense of the environment—represent the possibility of establishing a peaceful and integrated coexistence, an alternative to an illusory homogenization of communities on a national and other basis, which in history has already manifested all its danger.[345]

The last of these meetings, which had the title "No One Is Saved Alone: Peace and Fraternity" took place, as mentioned before, in Rome on October 20, 2020. On that occasion, Pope Francis, speaking at the event about the journey of the spirit of Assisi and thanking the Community of Sant'Egidio that carries it out annually, said:

> The Assisi meeting and its vision of peace contained a prophetic seed that by God's grace has gradually matured through unprecedented encounters, acts of peacemaking and fresh initiatives of fraternity. Although the intervening years have witnessed painful events, including conflicts, terrorism and radicalism, at times in the name of religion, we must also acknowledge the fruitful steps undertaken in the dialogue between the religions. This is a sign of hope that encourages us to continue cooperating as brothers and sisters.[346]

Andrea Riccardi, born in Rome in 1950, is an authoritative and well-known voice on the international scene. Full professor of contemporary history since 1981, he has taught in numerous Italian universities. Various universities around the world have awarded him with an honorary degree or doctorate. Expert in contemporary humanistic thought, academic of the Catholic Church in the modern and contemporary age, but also of the religious phenomenon as a whole and of religious cohabitation in the Mediterranean, he is the author of numerous publications translated into different languages. Riccardi has been awarded numerous prizes and awards, including the 2004 Balzan Prize for humanity, peace, and brotherhood among peoples and the 2009 Charlemagne Prize awarded to people and institutions that have particularly distinguished themselves in promoting a united Europe and the spread of a culture of peace and dialogue. Riccardi was the Italian Minister for International Cooperation and Integration in Mario Monti's government from 2011 to 2013. Since 2015, he has been president of the Dante Alighieri Society.

Riccardi is also known for having been the founder, in 1968, of the Community of Sant'Egidio, when he was only eighteen.[347] The Community of Sant'Egidio, born as a Roman presence, has become an international presence in seventy countries. Women and men of all ages and from different cultural and social backgrounds are committed to helping the poorest, the children, the elderly, the alone, the sick, the disabled, the homeless, immigrants, refugees, and many others, fighting against all forms of racism and discrimination, as well as promoting numerous development projects in the South of the world. Sant'Egidio is also known for its work in favor of peace and dialogue around the world. In particular, Riccardi played a mediating role in various conflicts and contributed to the achievement of peace in countries that include Mozambique, Guatemala, Ivory Coast, and Guinea. More recently, he has initiated reconciliation processes in South Sudan and the Central African Republic. The magazine *Time* in 2003 included him in its list of thirty-six modern heroes of Europe who have distinguished themselves for their professional courage and humanitarian commitment.

Riccardi was awarded the Moshe Rosen prize in 2019 by the Conference of European Rabbis to honor—as stated in the award—the many-yeared commitment of the Community of Sant'Egidio against anti-Semitism, hatred, and intolerance, and for religious freedom and dialogue between religions. On that occasion, Riccardi said: "Only memory that has become a people's concern and is passed on to the younger generations is a powerful barrier against anti-Semitism and hatreds which, despite past horrors, promptly reemerge and roam around our Europe and the world like a nightmare. This worries us today, due to the rekindling of those hatreds that resurgent nationalism brings with it. Anti-Semitism is the first chapter of the book of horrors and hatreds, which we hoped forever confined to the library. Too many irresponsibly open the pages of this book!"

David Rosen, who has known the Community of Sant'Egidio closely for many years, said in the laudatio he gave on that occasion:[348]

> Sant'Egidio is not just an organization that helps the poor all over the world, it is a community, a community of bonds between people, and it is a community of spirituality, it is a community of prayer. It is the community that values and emphasizes—in a world saturated with intense materialism—the transcendent power of the divine spirit in the life of human society. Andrea Riccardi coined this expression of the "weak strength of prayer" .... This is the insight that there are huge and impressive things we need to do in life, but what is lasting is the perseverance of true dedication and devotion, especially the perseverance of the spirit. And this is manifested in the world with prayer.

"The Holy Scriptures begin with human figures who do not recognize their responsibility and who fall in front of the question 'Where is your brother?'" Chief Rabbi Pinchas Goldschmidt, president of the Conference of European Rabbis, said at the start of the Moshe Rosen award ceremony. "The Community has made this question its own to respond to conflicts and people in need, without distinction of belonging."[349]

David Rosen, peer and personal friend of Riccardi, fine and intelligent companion on the journey of the spirit of Assisi, protagonist of many dialogue meetings, has contributed decisively to the strengthening of relations between the Catholic and Jewish world, as well as to the strengthening of the interreligious dialogue at the international level. Rosen was a gateway and a bridge in Sant'Egidio's friendship with the Jewish world.[350] His bond with Riccardi is both spiritual and human, a sign of that special alliance between the Jewish communities and the Community of Sant'Egidio around the world to put a stop to the dehumanizing force of intolerance. Rosen defined the particularity of the interreligious work of the Community of Sant'Egidio as follows:

> The guide of the "spirit of Assisi" was taken by the Community of Sant'Egidio, which deserves the credit not only for having promoted it but also for having it refined. What was being refined? The recognition—and this is part of the charisma of the Community of Sant'Egidio—that true universalism cannot be achieved by reducing everyone to a minimum common denominator. True universalism is when we can cultivate our particularities in the respect and celebration of each other's identities. It is when our different religious traditions are respected for what they are. When there is no attempt to proselytize or to undermine the integrity of the other. In fact, we can become truly universal when we respect the particularities of the other. And this was the method that the Community of Sant'Egidio began in 1987 in the meeting following the one in Assisi with a prayer in separate places, each according to its own tradition. Such meetings of dialogue and prayer have taken place year after year in cities all over the world, like different streams that have flowed into this powerful river of unity in diversity. This is the great vision that Andrea Riccardi has cultivated in his Community and which has in fact had its impact throughout the Catholic Church and beyond and is a testimony for all of us. We can truly say that the Community of Sant'Egidio has brought forward not only the spirit of Assisi, but the true spirit of *Nostra aetate*, the true spirit of the Second Vatican Ecumenical Council. Above all, the incredible process of reconciliation between

Christians and Jews. And this was evident since 1982 with the terrible terrorist attack on the Great Synagogue of Rome, when the Community showed solidarity, and the members of the Community joined the Jews in that moment of prayer simply to show solidarity. There have been marches and vigils and every year the Community remembers the deportation of the Jews, remembers the tragedy of the Shoah in Rome and in various cities around the world, trying to educate the younger generations on the universal importance of the message that comes from the Shoah,[351] as well as Sant'Egidio's commitment to bring young people, but also religious leaders to Auschwitz to learn those lessons. In doing so, it is recognized that, just as it is important to preserve the particular heritage of each community, there is something universal in the particular suffering of the Jewish people. Anti-Semitism is actually a problem for all of humanity. Andrea Riccardi has talked about it several times. As Tolstoy says, since the Exodus, freedom has spoken with a Hebrew accent. This means that when Jews are denied freedom, society is rotten. And therefore the need to remember the lesson of the Shoah, and to always warn against the challenge and danger of anti-Semitism, is a human obligation and above all a historical Christian obligation, in particular a Catholic obligation: this is what the Community teaches. In this sense it is the continuity of the message of the "spirit of Assisi," the spirit of *Nostra aetate*, the spirit of the Second Vatican Ecumenical Council, the spirit of the popes who have loved the Community of Sant'Egidio, in particular John Paul II and now Pope Francis .... Andrea Riccardi continues to be a blessing for the Jewish community ..., with the Community of Sant'Egidio he testifies the extraordinary divine presence in the world.

Hans Küng[352]

Dr. Ahmed Abbadi

An Interreligious Hero: Hans Küng

On April 6, 2021, Hans Küng, ninety-three years old, died peacefully in his sleep. It could be said that Hans Küng made good use of his seven decades of adult life. He wrote well over fifty books and too many articles to count. He meaningfully contributed to global events across all fields of life: spiritual, political, social, environmental, economic, artistic, and more. Perhaps most significantly, he influenced how people around the world see themselves and others, holding up a giant mirror so that we all might see ourselves, individually and collectively, more clearly.

As someone who physically and metaphorically traversed such broad expanses for so long a time and whose footprints remain large and deep, he collected a library of opinions, sentiments, and descriptions by those who, in some way, crossed his wide-ranging path. In positive terms, he was called "one of the most influential theologians of the twentieth century"[353] and a "renowned scholar and prolific writer."[354] Some were a little less positive, referring to him to as divisive, with some claiming him to be radical and controversial, and others going further to call him a heretic.[355]

Yet there is another word to describe Hans Küng that also begins with an *h*. While this other depiction hasn't followed him as persistently as that of heretic, it certainly is worthy of the life of dedication and distinction that he lived, and one that I hope will soon be fastened to his name: *hero*.

The original meaning of hero—its Greek root—is that of protector or defender, which accords with Küng's lifelong actions to defend and protect his Catholic faith, to which he was unflinchingly committed. But he was also an uncompromising defender and protector of the whole of humanity, and he knew that this work required extraordinary interreligious effort. Indeed, he famously hung the promise of peace between nations on the peace between religions. Thus, the well-being and survival of humanity could not be detached from a culture of respect and mutual recognition between religious communities.

But the transcendent promise of interreligious harmony and global peace demands sacrifice. If, in the words of the scholar Joseph Campbell, who dedicated his life to the study of heroes and their journeys, "a hero is someone who has given his or her life to something bigger than oneself,"[356] then we can say that Küng is a hero who gave his life to the pursuit of interreligious understanding and the welfare of members of his extended, global family. In doing this, he opened our eyes to what an interreligious hero looks like.

I would like to suggest ten notable elements that epitomize Küng's heroic journey and that deserve consideration and mention here.

Courage

A hero—Küng's stature could not carry the privilege and burden of this designation without embodying and thus demonstrating courage. As the poet David Whyte tells us, courage is a word that "tempts us to think outwardly, to run bravely against opposing fire . . . rewarded with medals, but a look at its linguistic origins is to look in a more interior direction and toward its original template."[357] Both its Latin root *cor* and its later French derivation *coeur* mean heart. In tying together the wise notions of both Campbell and Whyte, I would say that the courage of a hero stems from a connection to something bigger than oneself, which emanates from and is motivated by love.

If a defining aspect of the courage of a hero is knowing who, what, and how one loves and dedicating a life toward acting on and deepening that love, then Hans Küng's heroism shone through his love for his beloved brothers and sisters in humanity. In Küng's case, this love was dependent on and animated by faith in the Divine, for, as he famously said, "In the last resort, a love of God without love of humanity is no love at all." It is this courage rooted in love and faith that threads its way through all of the other features of Küng's interreligious heroism, enlivening and strengthening each one. Above all, it took a special kind of courage for Küng to build a global interreligious movement around common basic values that would connect people from different cultures, religions, and nations in a constructive way so that they could live well together.

Honesty

It is through Küng's heart and the love that guided and compelled him that another ingredient of his heroism illuminated his life. As the Jewish psychiatrist Viktor Frankl famously said, "What is to give light must endure burning." Küng's honesty, his insistence on speaking truth to power and on holding truth above institutional dogma, might have burned his own fingers as well as those toward whom his honesty was directed. It may not have been easy for some to hear Küng say that the West made mistakes and carried some responsibility for the violence over caricatures of the Prophet Mohammed.[358] But, because he linked honesty with insight about ourselves and others, he joined his statement with a call for reflection in both the Western and Islamic worlds.

His honesty was anchored in belief and fortitude; his were honest calls to friends and colleagues of any and no religion to make changes, so that they could be more honest with themselves and with others. It was something that he could ask for only because he practiced such honesty himself. For he knew that without honesty, trust could never be built between different religious communities. And, without trust, there could be no real mutual engagement, which he believed was undoubtedly the only thing that could save humanity from itself.

Humility

Küng's uncompromising honesty was unyielding and essential for his perseverance in the face of recriminations. His was a heroic honesty that was linked to a complicated humility—complicated, because many might have found that adjective surprising when associated with someone of such charisma and larger than life *élan*.

Perhaps his humility was the source of his confidence, a confidence that allowed him to invite and respond to internal and external critique. As the human rights scholar and activist Richard Falk said, "Küng respects those with responsibilities in the domain of power and seems genuinely aware of the fallibility of his own ethical intuitions, thereby insisting on subjecting his own ideas to continuous reflection and self-criticism."[359]

To walk along this knife's edge of humility and confidence, he did not elevate his own ideas above all others; instead, his humility drove his deep sense of respect for others and their ideas, including those from different religions and belief systems. He was not one to discount, dismiss, or deride spiritual beliefs and practices to which he did not adhere and which may have been very much outside of his own theological frame of reference.

Had he assumed an air of superiority regarding his beliefs, it is unlikely that six thousand people from diverse religions would have discussed the document that he prepared for the second Parliament of the World's Religions with his global ethic presented in it. It's unlikely that more than two hundred chosen religious representatives would have signed and adopted the *Declaration toward a Global Ethic*. It is unlikely that leaders from all world religions would have agreed, for the first time in history, upon core elements of a common ethic: namely, humane treatment of all human beings and the Golden Rule, nonviolence, peace and justice, truthfulness, equal rights, and partnership.

Vision

When writing about courage, the Greek historian Thucydides contended, "The bravest are surely those who have the clearest vision of what is before them, glory and danger alike, and yet, notwithstanding, go out to meet it."

Throughout his life, Küng spoke about vision, both the necessity of having one and the perils of not. For Küng, the necessity of vision could never be ignored nor postponed nor in any way compromised. His insistence on vision was absolute and was central to his interreligious work. He was insistent in his writings about a new paradigm for humanity and its religions and was equally insistent about defining the vision and way toward the new paradigm, an effort that would never end, because the search for truth is itself an ongoing process.

Thus, Hans Küng believed that the world was moving towards a completely new way of thinking about and looking at issues that affect humanity. In discussing a change of consciousness, he began with a concern that what is missing from influential political thought and cultural space is a realistic vision of the future. He spent his entire life galvanizing and uniting as many people as he could around this new and shared vision of a better and more just future for everyone on the earth. It was a vision rooted in the *Global Ethic*, which he insisted was essential if the vision were to be fulfilled. "A better world order," Küng proclaimed, "will ultimately be brought in only on the basis of:

- common visions, ideals, values, aims and criteria;

- heightened global responsibility on the part of peoples and their leaders;

- a new binding and uniting ethic for all humankind, including states and those in power, which embraces cultures and religions. There can be no new world order without a new world ethic, a global ethic."

He boldly proclaimed that this consensus of values would be "a decisive contribution to overcome the crisis of orientation which has become a real world problem."[360]

Scorching Clarity

Those with vision, whose sights are fixed on a distant horizon, sometimes suffer from abstruseness and struggle to clearly delineate the vision and how to move towards its realization. In contrast to this handicap, the scholar of interreligious studies and author of the "Dialogue Decalogue" Leonard Swidler,[361] spoke about Küng's "scorching clarity," which he wielded in different ways.

Küng was sensitive to the problematics that vex each and every one of us in our modern experience, and he sought to address them head-on. To do so, however, he knew that to be heard—which is also to be helpful—he needed to be clear. Thus, he wrote in an unencumbered, comprehensible manner, so that anyone, from any religious or nonreligious persuasion, could read his writings with ease, so much so that scientific theologians criticized him for being a popularizer.

But there was another purpose behind his popular and prolific output. He was interested in deconstructing complexity but, even more importantly, in helping others learn how to do this themselves. He remarked that one's goal should be "to show that we can help a human being, young or old, to find a good way in this rather complicated situation."[362] The task of bringing together world religions, for the first time, to agree on a unified vision and global ethic, was a task of immense complexity, requiring immense clarity for it to work. But Küng knew that he could not be the only one with such clarity and that a task such as this one would require a global, interreligious army of clear-eyed combatants.

Functional Action

Küng's ability to deconstruct complexity and to offer clarity was necessary for another of his objectives. He would not allow his visions for humanity at large to be hollow aspirations with no hope of realization; they had to be functional and practical. Further, whenever he offered critique and criticism, he was quick to accompany them with suggestions and plans for their implementation.

His commitment to functionality found expression in his effort to identify a minimum ethical consensus among all religions that he saw as both a possible and necessary project due to the emergence of global developments. The minimum ethical consensus was the mechanism that allowed him to take a metaphorical vision, "a community of destiny on our spaceship earth," link it to a digitally shared awareness of various struggles for truth and justice and make a global norm project—the *Global Ethic*—a functional action.

Thus, Küng presented a clear vision made functional when he coined the acclaimed aphorism: "No peace among nations without peace among religions. No peace among religions without dialogue between the religions. No dialogue between the religions without fundamental research into the religions."[363]

Intellectual Effort

The third and final line of his celebrated saying above points to Küng's deep and formidable commitment to his pursuit of knowledge, which cannot be elided in any serious and heroic endeavor to change global consciousness and forge interreligious unity for the sake of human survival.

As a Catholic theologian and professor, he dived deeply into and contributed significantly to scholarship in his own Catholic faith and Christianity more broadly. Such diving made it possible for him to engage with the highest echelons of power and knowledge within the Church regarding his reform proposals. While the waters of his own religion were deep—and he continued to explore their depths—he sought to dive into the oceans of other religious traditions, too, knowing that any credible and meaningful interreligious effort with the potential for functional traction would necessitate an intellectual intimacy with all of them as well. In his late fifties, he began to publish works on Hinduism, Islam, Buddhism, Judaism, and Chinese religions.

Later, as his interreligious work became more interdisciplinary, integrating discourses on politics, international human rights, and economics, he ensured that he was ready and prepared to responsibly and seriously embark in these new domains:

> I was therefore responsible for the first draft of this *Declaration of Human Responsibilities* and for incorporating the numerous corrections suggested by the statesmen and the many experts

from different continents, religions and disciplines. Therefore I identify completely with this declaration. However, had I not been occupied for years with the problems, and had I not finally written "Global Ethic for Global Politics and Global Economics," published in 1997, which provides a broad treatment of all the problems which arise here, I would not have dared to formulate a first draft at all in close conjunction with the 1948 *Declaration of Human Rights* and the 1993 *Declaration toward a Global Ethic* which required a secular political continuation. Such declarations are therefore not products of naiveté but fruits of an intellectual effort.[364]

Invitation

One might be intimidated by Küng's formidable scholarly rigor and daunting intellectual authority, and yet a hallmark of his personal character and professional approach was his inclusive and inviting manner. He invited everyone, including those with whom he disagreed, those who were of no faith, and even those who had hurt him and whom he had offended, to join him on the journey toward creating a religiously harmonious, global community.

As Küng said, the *Declaration toward a Global Ethic*, which is his most recognizable interreligious endeavor and which has, since 1993, been a pivotal axis around which global interreligious movements for international peace have revolved, invites all, believers and also nonbelievers, to commit to its tenets and live in accordance with it.[365] And, while his invitations to friend and foe alike were laced with good cheer and friendliness, he was always clear that the invitation he was issuing was for the heroic cause that was larger than himself and everyone else, namely, peace among religions for the survival of humanity.

Optimism

During his lifetime, Küng met with resistance and challenges that brought hardship and anguish. Yet he remained optimistic. He indefatigably confronted, as Richard Falk extols, "the central challenge of mobilizing the positive potentialities of religion, politics, and economics as a normative counterweight to the destructive tendencies that are otherwise likely to engender a bloody era of 'culture wars' and 'religious wars.'"[366]

Küng brandished his optimism like a weapon against the waves of criticism and disparagement of those who didn't believe that religions could agree on much of anything. He held high the torch of optimism in the bleakest hours of interreligious strife, including after the tragedies of 9/11 and the cartoons of the Prophet Mohammed, so that there could be a lighted path toward forgiveness and healing and a renewed vigor to continue developing research projects and publications about world religions and global ethics issues, promoting the *Declaration toward a Global Ethic* and the many projects and activities of Küng's Global Ethic Foundation.[367]

Küng's heroic and divinely inspired courage to say yes, even in the most challenging of moments, recalls the great second secretary-general of the United Nations, Dag Hammarskjöld, who reminded us, "For all that has been, Thank you. For all that is to come, Yes!"[368] Over a decade after he retired from his active professorship and became emeritus, but well before he slowed in his writing, lecturing, and other pursuits, Küng published a personal testimony, *What I Believe*. In it, he spends a lot of time questioning, contemplating, and then affirming his approach of saying yes to life. He entitles a section "No Fear of Deep Waters," in which he writes: "The act of saying Yes, venturing fundamental trust, risking trust in life: in that way and only in that way I can go on living my life, that is, adopt a positive fundamental attitude . . . ." Küng describes that feeling of trust, which is inseparable from saying yes, as the joy that he "experienced as a child while swimming, when for the first time I had the experience that the water really supported bodies, even mine, that I entrusted myself to the water, that all alone—without support or any aids—I could trust myself to the water."[369]

Perseverance

Plato, both in *The Republic* and in *Laches*, describes courage as a sort of perseverance, a perspective later echoed by Thomas Aquinas in his rumination on the cardinal virtues, where courage takes the form of fortitude. At his death at age ninety-three, with seventy years of a life spent bringing members of the extended global family together on common ground, Küng's interreligious heroism assumed a near-unrivaled bearing.

He walked his long and enduring path with stirring and almost superhuman perseverance. It is a perseverance that he believed in and which he happily and with unfaltering faith and trust bequeathed to the next generation.

In a speech entitled "Towards a Universal Civilization," which he delivered at a conference in Malaysia in 2010, he spoke with optimism and clear vision of that which was on the horizon:

> The change of consciousness needed here is a task for the new century, the "world century." Some of the older generation, to which we belong, might be sceptical. But it is for the younger generation to realize decisively the sketch for the future presented here. As the famous French writer Victor Hugo says, the future has many names: "For the weak it is the unattainable. For the fearful it is the unknown. For the bold it is the opportunity."[370]

The Next Interreligious Hero: Rabbi David Rosen

Perhaps the most fitting way to express appreciation for the interreligious work to which Küng committed his life would be to accept his invitation to courageously persevere in uniting all of humanity in a bond of trust-oriented by the global ethic vision[371] and to be inspired by these ten elements of the heroism that he fashioned while he was with us. We all carry the responsibility to do what we can to realize this vision.

If we look at the life of Rabbi David Rosen, we see the ten elements of interreligious heroism shining along the path of peace and reconciliation that he has forged. Rabbi Rosen has given his life to building partnerships among religious communities whose centuries-long histories are an account of wariness and suspicion. To do this, he has had to be both honest and humble, with those in his own Jewish community as well as the other religious communities with whom he has spent decades walking side by side. He has held out his hand, just as he grasped the hand held out to him, offering and accepting invitations to step across what may seem like chasms between communities.

I have known Rabbi Rosen for many years. We have spent considerable quality time together, whether through participating in the formalities of international meetings or sitting comfortably at home surrounded by family. Across all of these rich and varied moments, I have had the pleasure of knowing an elegant spirit who always honors his word, who cares very deeply, and whose wisdom has been cultivated through his unwavering desire to evolve. He has not allowed any of his life's experiences to pass by him, unobserved and insufficiently reflected upon. Quite the contrary. Thus, he has learned precious and needed skills that few really possess: how to manage his feelings, when to speak and when not, and how to sculpt hopes and tailor them to the readiness of the audience before him. He has mastered the subtle art of invisibility, knowing when it is more effective to increase or decrease his visibility. As a result, he is well regarded and well respected by those of all faiths and none.

In the darkest of moments, Rabbi Rosen has held fast to a clear vision of interreligious unity and global well-being undergirded by a shimmering optimism that promises "indeed, the best is yet to come." It is this courage, driven and sustained by love, that humanity desperately needs in order to continue Küng's call, and it is this courage, love, and wisdom that Rabbi Rosen truly embodies.

Dharma Master Hsin Tao

Dr. Maria Reis Habito

I HAVE CHOSEN TO write about my teacher, Dharma Master Hsin Tao, abbot of the Wu Sheng Monastery on Ling Jiou Mountain, and Founder of the Museum of World Religions, both located in Taiwan, as an interfaith hero. A hero is a person who faces and overcomes challenges with courage, creativity, and grace. There are many challenges on the spiritual path, and it would not be possible to find an interfaith hero who is not at the same a hero in his or her own faith tradition.

My teacher, whom we call Shihfu-Master, gave concrete expression to his vows to save all beings by creating a Buddhist monastery, where not only more than a hundred nuns and monks dedicate their lives to spiritual practice and altruistic service on a daily basis, but where also countless lay disciples in different parts of Asia, the US, and Europe find a spiritual home and direction. In addition to that, Shihfu has created another sacred space, a platform to foster understanding, respect, and love among religions, and to launch worldwide interfaith initiatives—namely, the Museum of World Religions.

Shihfu was born in 1948 to Chinese parents in the eastern part of the country, which was then called Burma, today's Myanmar. Orphaned at age four, he became a child solder at age eight, witnessing the suffering and destruction brought on by war from a very young age. At age twelve, he was transferred by the army back to Taiwan, where he continued his training in a military school. He became a monk at age twenty-five, finding that devoting his entire life to the spiritual search would be the only way to answer the question of why there is so much suffering in the world and what can be done about it. Not being satisfied by the traditional training provided by the monastery, he spent ten years meditating in graveyards and two years fasting in a cave on Ling Jiou Mountain on the east coast of Taiwan, where the present monastery is located.

I first met Shihfu in 1980, when I was a twenty-year-old student of Chinese language and culture at Shihfan University in Taipei. At the time, Shihfu lived in a small hermitage on a lake, and the unlikely fact that I would meet him in such a hidden place was explained to me as the result of a deep Karmic affinity.

Already during that first visit, I could feel the magic that at first scared but also attracted me to this young Buddhist master, namely the clarity and peace that he radiated, his charisma. To my surprise, I would find that whenever I spent a weekend in the hermitage during subsequents visits, away from the hustle and bustle of my Taipei student life, I would return with a sense of inner peace and joy that had eluded me before. I ascribed this sense of peace and joy to the simple fact of having been in Shihfu's presence, even though he would mostly spend his time in meditation while I was at the hermitage. But there were times, of course, when we had conversations—interfaith conversations—and my inability to answer Shihfu's questions about God and the spiritual life in a way that was satisfactory, even for myself, propelled me on a deeper spiritual search. Thus after I returned to Germany, I decided to enroll in Chinese/Japanese studies and philosophy at the University in Munich, to delve more deeply into both the Eastern and Western spiritual traditions.

This decision came with encouragement but also an admonition from Shihfu, who told me that with regards to Buddhism, more than book learning, I needed to really start practicing meditation to understand what I would be writing about.

In Chan/Zen Buddhism, all forms of language and notions are at best understood like a finger pointing to the moon and at worst as a hindrance that keeps us stuck in concepts and ideas that prevent us from realizing the ineffable reality behind those words. That reality itself can only be accessed through meditation, through the opening of heart and mind to what is transcendent, luminous, eternal, and, at the same time, immediate and intimate.

Here is one example of how Shihfu taught me the reality behind notions and images, which was transformative for me. Arriving at the hermitage with fruits and flowers in one of the early days, Shihfu took them from me and offered them up on the altar before a seated white figure, which reminded me of a Madonna. Having read that Buddhism does not worship idols, I asked him, "Shihfu, I thought that in Chan Buddhism, you do not worship idols? Who is that figure?" In response, he looked at me with a wide smile and said: "This is not an idol. This is you!"

You can imagine my confusion. This is me? How so? What does he mean? Shihfu then explained that the figure is the Bodhisattva of Great Compassion, who has realized emptiness—our true, infinite nature beyond the confines of the small ego self, this self-nature that is no other than boundless compassion. Boundless compassion is our true nature and the true nature of the universe. What has stayed with me as a spiritual opening and challenge was not the explanation but his direct reference: "This is you!" This is one example of a transformative Chan teaching that Shihfu has mastered with great skill. In Chan, the teacher points directly "to the heart and mind"[372] of the student, eliciting immediate responsiveness, often in the form of doubt or bewilderment, which becomes the engine to open up new horizons of realization.

All of Shihfu's teaching is aimed at helping people to realize their enlightened nature, which is also called "our true face, before our parents brought us into the world." This true face is beyond any form or content, thus empty: clear, luminous, and eternal, unaffected by time and space. While in Buddhist terminology, this original nature or quality that all living beings share is called Buddha-nature, Shihfu explains it as God's eternal Spirit for his Western students. Far from trying to convert his Western students to Buddhism, Shihfu is always encouraging them to rediscover their spiritual roots in the Abrahamic tradition and to deeply realize the eternal quality of God's Spirit—which is the eternal quality of their own spirit—in their own lives and then live it out in love and compassion.

Shihfu's own practice to discover his original face cannot but be described as heroic. Ten years of meditation in graveyards (with up to sixteen hours of meditation per day) were followed by two years of fasting in the cave on Ling-Jiou Mountain, taking only water and nine pills of a Chinese herbal medicine daily to help him physically survive. As he was reduced to skin and bones from the fast, he was in constant pain, because all bodily tissues that cushion the nerves from direct touch had shrunk away.

But the experience of that kind of pain became a vehicle for his enlightenment. As he describes it: "As I was struggling with this physical pain, I kept asking myself: 'Is there anything at all in this that is not in pain?' It is strange, but that which knew that the body is in pain, that itself seemed to be just fine. That which knows the pain, knows of no pain! This is how it gradually dawned on me that there is something deep within ourselves that does not suffer, even if we are half-dead from pain. This taught me not to focus my attention on the pain or mind it at all, but to instead pay attention to that inside which knows of no pain and can never be destroyed, no matter what. And so I discovered that in our heart-nature, which does not undergo the pain of life and death, but is free from the suffering of *samsara*."[373]

The realization of the heart/mind nature is the core energy of all of Shihfu's activities and teachings. Leaving the cave in 1985, he set out to establish the Wu Sheng Monastery and, soon after, surprised his followers by announcing his mission of building a Museum of World Religions as a contribution to world peace. The vision of the museum is based on the teaching of the Flower Garland (Avatamsaka) Sutra, which tells the story of the pilgrim Sudhana to fifty-three different teachers in his search for enlightenment. Finally arriving at the tower of Buddha Maitreya, he has a vision of the interconnectedness of all aspects of reality, described in the image of Indra's net, which covers the entire universe. Each eye of the net contains a shining jewel that reflects the entirety of all of the other jewels. For Shihfu, the various religions represent the teachers on the way to spiritual realization; they are deeply linked and reflect each other like shining jewels. During his long retreat and fast, Shihfu came to clearly realize that all tensions, conflicts and wars, all the suffering he experienced as a child soldier, stem from what he calls a religious blindness, namely our basic ignorance about the deep interconnectedness of all forms of life on earth. He thus vowed to find a way of addressing this ignorance.

The museum and its central task to impart this vision of interconnectedness and harmony in new and creative ways was born out of Shihfu's religious vows:

> I have been vowing to attain enlightenment since I was 16 or 17 years old. Even today, I am still working hard in this very important direction . . . . All human beings, regardless of their creed, color, religion, and cultural background—are our brothers and sisters; all conditions good and bad are stepping stones towards perfect awakening. If you have *Prajna* (nondual) wisdom as your meditative tool, you know that all people and conditions can co-exist harmoniously and beautifully, and we must depend on each other to thrive in this world.
>
> Living in an interdependent world like this, we should do our best to eliminate all conflicts and misunderstandings, and to use our wisdom and compassion as our new interpersonal skills in dealing with each other. If you have wisdom and compassion, you can flourish whereever you go. You can co-create a sacred space for yourself and others right here right now. So my vows of helping and benefiting others come from my *Prajna* wisdom, which has to be actualized in day-to day living. When I decided to make a great vow for myself and others, a creative concept came into my mind—I wanted to build a Museum—a unique museum dedicated to all major religions in the world.[374]

So, from 1991 on, Dharma Master Hsin Tao and a group of nuns and followers started traveling throughout Asia, Western Europe, Russia, the USA, Canada, North Africa, and the Middle East to visit sacred sites, establish contact with religious leaders and communities, and learn about museums. These trips included attendance at the World Parliament of Religions conference in Capetown, South Africa, in 1999 and participation in the Summit of World Religious Leaders held at the UN in 2000. The information about these trips, the meetings with religious leaders, visits of communities, discussions with museum specialists, etc. were fully shared with followers in Taipei and other towns, who could either read about them in the museum newsletter or watch films about them in the monastery. The motivation and involvement of the community became central in the task of building the museum, since the US$66 million for its establishment was raised from donations. If the museum, which opened in 2001, is itself a unique contribution to interfaith education, the fact that a Buddhist community raised all the money to build the museum as its gift to the world is certainly unique as well. None of this would have been possible without Shihfu's genius in touching the hearts of his followers and conveying his vision to them in a way that would lead to its realization.

Based on Shihfu's vision and guidance, the museum content was developed by a team of scholars from the Center for the Study of World Religions under the guidance of Prof. Lawrence Sullivan, and the design was furbished by the renowned New York-based Ralph Appelbaum company. There is no space to go into the details about the innovative content here, descriptions of which can be found elsewhere. Suffice it to say that the flow of the museum exhibits is designed to bring about a transformative experience about the spiritual dimension of life, as the visitor starts a pilgrimage through time and space, starting from the Creations Theater, leading through the Five Stages of Life, which are recognized and celebrated in all religions, culminating in a vision of the world of interconnectedness in the Avatamsaka Golden Globe, leading into the Great Hall of World Religions with its interactive exhibits.[375]

About two thousand students per year go through the special Life-Education classes offered at the museum, which are designed to help the students discover the value of their own lives and that of others in the light of religious teachings and to lay the foundations of understanding, respect, and love for people of all religious traditions and cultures. This respect and love is also fostered by special religiously themed exhibits, activities, and celebrations, which attract about fifty thousand visitors throughout the year.[376]

Through the process of building the museum, Shihfu and the Ling Jiou Mountain community established close ties of friendship and cooperation with religious leaders and communities in different places of the world and in Taiwan itself, where Shihfu helped establish a ten-faith coalition of religious leaders and communities who regularly come together at the museum for spring prayer and collaborate in charity work and disaster relief.

To carry out the educational and interfaith work of the museum internationally, its outreach organ, the Global Family for Love and Peace, a UN-affiliated NGO, was founded in 2002. As a response to the events of September 11, 2001, the GFLP started organizing a series of international Buddhist-Muslim dialogues to foster greater understanding, friendship, and cooperation between Buddhist and Muslim populations in fifteen different countries of Asia, Europe, North Africa, and the US, including at the UNESCO in Paris and the UN headquarters in New York. Defining the topics and co-organizing these dialogues with our local partners has been part of my work as international program director.[377] But we have also been participating in and hosting meetings of different international interfaith organizations at the monastery and museum—such as the 2005 meeting of the Elijah Interfaith Institute, of which Shihfu is a board member; the Goldin Institute; and the Pontifical Council for Interreligious Dialogue, to name just a few—always incorporating public events for the wider population of Taipei and Taiwan to make them part of the interfaith life. Rabbi David Rosen, also a board member of the Elijah Institute, is one of our dear friends who attended the 2005 meeting at the monastery, and we much enjoy meeting in different venues, as our work, especially around ecological issues, intersects.

The ecological activities arose from Shihfu's concern that, in spite of the rich interfaith work carried out by the museum and the GFLP in the last twenty years, the mission of the museum—"Love for All Forms of Life"—has not yet been adequately expressed, especially in view of the ecological crisis that is facing the earth community. Thus was born the project of the University of Life and Peace in Myanmar, which is envisioned as an interdisciplinary institution of learning that will implant the seeds of love for the earth in its students and train them to help resolve the environmental crisis both from a spiritual and scientific approach. The process of establishing the university is another example of a method of interfaith cooperation that brings together leaders of different faith traditions in Myanmar who support the project.

The lesson that I carry with me from having known Shihfu for more than forty years is that it takes great courage to explore the depths of our own being and that it takes just as much courage to work towards the realization of the daunting tasks that call upon us to be part of this exploration process. In Buddhism, this process is called "aving oneself by saving others, an expression that describes the way of the Bodhisattva, whose path is based on the vow to never rest until all beings have been liberated from suffering, since the suffering of others is understood as one's own suffering. It is the genius of a religious leader not only to visualize the concrete task at hand on this path but to touch and inspire the wider community to walk this path together.

Sheikh Abdullah Nimer Darwish

Rabbi Michael Melchior

Introduction

BESIDES PERHAPS MY OWN father, I can think of no leader who has inspired and influenced me to pursue peace more than Sheikh Abdullah Nimer Darwish, blessed be his memory. Sheikh Abdullah for me embodied how it is possible to simultaneously be a devout Islamic leader deeply connected and committed to the Muslim world and the Palestinian cause and at the same time a passionate champion of religious peace, working side by side for years with his Israeli rabbinic partner, myself, who am committed to Judaism, Israel, and Zionism. There was not a leader on either side of the Israeli Palestinian conflict with whom the sheikh was not in close contact in order to promote these goals. He was in nearly daily contact with Palestinian President Yasser Arafat and later Abu Mazen and still remained close and respected by the leaders of Hamas. He was also respected and in contact with the prime ministers and presidents of Israel, the leaders of most of Israel's political parties, and Israel's Jewish religious leaders. All respected him immensely, sought his advice and often used his services as what may be called an insider mediator.

Sheikh Abdullah's Story

Sheikh Abdullah was born in Kafr Qasim, an Arab town not far from Tel Aviv, in 1948 and passed away in 2017. In 1956, the Kafr Qasim Massacre occurred, leaving family members of his killed by Israeli soldiers. This tragic event had a profound impact on him and led him initially to have great animosity towards the state of Israel and its military. After the 1967 war, he traveled to Nablus in the West Bank to study Islam and was exposed and connected to the Muslim Brotherhood. Upon his return to Kafr Qasim in 1972, he established the Islamic Movement as a social and

317

educational enterprise and became one of the greatest proselytizers of Islam in Israel and the Palestinian territories.

Once, he told me a story of how he, as an unmarried man, introduced the Islamic practice of religious women covering their hair with a hijab to women in Israel and Palestine. At the time, no one had that tradition nor knew how a hijab should look. The sheikh turned to a tailor in Hebron and gave him instructions of how to design one, according to Islamic law books. When he returned to Kafr Qasim, for the first time ever, a married woman donned the hijab he had designed. From there, the tradition spread. The sheikh explained to me, laughing, that many of his students believed that the hijab had to be in the exact form and color as the first one. I recall telling him how this reminded me of great Hassidic masters, where traditions sometimes developed according to how the followers believed was the right practice of their master without that ever having been the master's intention.

Towards the end of the 1970s, he was one of the founders of Usrat Al-Jihad (family of Jihad), the origin of the Islamic Jihad, committed to liberating Palestine with violence and establishing an Islamic state in place of the State of Israel. Although it never used violence against people, the organization collected weapons and destroyed property. As a result, Sheikh Abdullah was imprisoned in an Israeli jail in 1981 and released three and a half years later. Even during his time in prison, he was their ultimate leader. When rules were broken, he would always take the blame upon himself, although everyone knew he could not have physically committed the transgressions (the sheikh was physically impaired from birth and could not move one of his arms). In prison, he devoted much of his time to studying and thinking about the fundamental sources of Islam, and as a result he went through an incredible transformation. Years later, he retold the story of what he said to his many followers who came to greet him upon his release in 1984:

> Gentlemen, I, your sheikh, am from now on the first soldier for peace between Palestinians and Israelis. I am not saying that I am the first soldier to make peace, because I am cowardly, no. I do so because I am strong! Strong in my faith, strong in the deep faith that on this land, both people should live![378]

For many, his transition to being a soldier of peace came as a total surprise or even as a shock. Some saw him as a traitor to the cause he had founded, but he did not care. He felt with all his heart that he was following the true Islam. This is what Allah expected from him, and he was willing to pay the price for his transition.

Sheikh Abdullah believed in the Palestinians' right to self-determination, to freedom, and to securing a future for their children based upon a two-state solution. Inside Israel, he did everything he could to help integrate the Muslim community to life in the state—including full economic, educational, and political integration. He declared that once, he had believed that a majority of Jews would convert to Islam, and therefore all of Palestine could become Islamic. Now he understood that this would never happen. Therefore, the Muslims in Israel should live according to the laws of the state as a native minority, working hard to obtain full and equal rights but never using violence as a means of obtaining these rights. He understood that for this to happen, the Islamic Movement needed to function as a democratic movement that would participate in municipal elections, which inherently meant recognition of the State of Israel. His decision to recognize the State of Israel stemmed from his religious belief and not simply on a pragmatic, temporary political solution.

The success of the Islamic Movement in the municipal elections led to Sheikh Abdullah's historic decision in 1996 to participate in the national Knesset election, splitting the Islamic Movement into two factions. Sheikh Ra'ed Salah broke off from Sheikh Abdullah, who had been his leader and mentor, and formed the Northern Branch of the Islamic Movement, while Sheikh Abdullah continued to be seen as the leader of the Southern Branch of the Islamic Movement. Sheikh Ra'ed Salah and the Northern Branch were supported by the leading Muslim Brotherhood decision-maker, Sheikh Yussef Al Karadawi, who forbade participation in Israeli national elections. Yet this did not deter Sheikh Abdullah's position that this decision was the right one for his community of religious Muslims holding Israeli citizenship.

Our Relationship

My personal relationship with Sheikh Abdullah began with sporadic meetings in the late 1990s and was formalized after a Middle East interfaith summit in Alexandria in 2002. I had initiated the summit together with my friend and Palestinian colleague, the late Sheikh Talal Sider, and others. Sheikh Sider had been among the founders of Hamas but later strongly believed in a solution of peace and had become an independent minister in the Arafat cabinet. Sheikh Abdullah knew Sheikh Talal very well and through him heard about the Alexandria summit. Sheikh Abdullah invited me to his home and spoke of his admiration and the courage it took to create the Alexandria summit at the peak of the second Intifada (Israeli-Palestinian violence, 2000–2005). Before anything else, he received me with such personal warmth that we forged a friendship that grew much stronger than I can describe. Our relationship intrigued many of those who met us, who had difficulty in understanding how a staunch Zionist believer, a former Israeli cabinet minister like myself, could have such a close relationship with such a leading Islamist figure. At our first meeting, we envisioned what a future peace would look like. We hardly needed a discussion. In thirty minutes, we had solved all the issues over which the negotiators on both sides had racked their brains for a decade, including borders, settlements, refugees, Jerusalem and Temple Mount/Haram al-Sharif. Then we agreed on why the Oslo process that we both had supported had gone sour. We both, for years, had spoken to our own communities about the missing link of religion, about opening the tent of peace to include religious leaders and their communities. We had discussed that when a car drives so many times into a dead end, it sometimes needs to reroute to ultimately get to its destination. It is not that the destination of peace was wrong—there is no existence, no life and no future without peace—but there is a need to reroute the road towards peace to include religious leaders in it.

Establishing the Religious Peace Initiative

After President Bush presented his Roadmap for Peace in the Middle East, we began to formalize our cooperation. Eventually, in 2007, we established the Middle East Religious Peace Initiative (RPI), which Sheikh Abdullah also called the Religious Roadmap for Peace. Under the leadership of Sheikh Abdullah, our Muslim colleagues established Adam Centers in Gaza, Ramallah, and Kafr Qasim, which worked in close cooperation with Mosaica in Jerusalem, where I continue to serve as the president. We wished to remove step by step all the obstacles which had been in the way of the political peacemakers, even when the politicians were sincere and had good intentions. Our main purpose was to restore in the hearts of the traditional and religious populations on both sides the idea that it is possible to make peace between Judaism and Islam, the idea which then can be a basis for political peace. We wanted to show that there are excellent partners for this process, and that the vast majority of both peoples wholeheartedly wish for this to happen.

We were in total agreement that the purpose of our work was not to create another dialogue group but to form a different reality for our children. Our method was to work with the so called extremists on both sides to solve problems that everybody thought were unsolvable. Through this, we could forge true friendships and create trust, which is the necessary key to taking on the greater challenges of saving thousands of lives and paving the path to solving the core issues of the conflict.

I had many talks with Sheikh Abdullah about religious law and interpretations. I could always raise with him the most difficult questions, such as the verse in the Qur'an (7:166) which tells of the Jews turning into apes. Sheikh Abdullah looked at me and said, "Muslim men can marry Jewish women, they need not convert even. Do you really think that we would permit our men to marry apes?! Read the context in the Qur'an. As well as other negative sources about Jews. The context is of Jews who do not observe their own tradition and do not follow the laws of the Sabbath. The Torah says much harsher words about those who do not observe the Sabbath!" This taught me that misconceptions can often be the basis of animosity. At the same time, the sheikh stressed that we live today in a democratic and pluralistic society; just as we are loyal to our own belief and traditions, we must also be tolerant of others.

Speaking Out against Hatred and Violence

Sheikh Abdullah taught me many lessons on life. Once, I gave an interview on Israeli television about anti-Semitism. Afterwards, he called me and said that the interview was fine. I answered that when you say fine, it means that it wasn't anything special. He said: "Listen. When you speak about anti-Semitism, you have the experience, you know the material, but you will always speak from the perspective of someone battling for his own interests, even totally legitimate interests. When you speak on Islamophobia, you speak with grandeur and with passion. It is surprising to the listener and therefore much more convincing." He suggested, "Let us make a deal. You, the rabbi, will speak about Islamophobia, and I, Sheikh Abdullah, founder and leader of the Islamic Movement, will speak out on anti-Semitism." He kept his word until his last breath. In hundreds of interviews all over the Arab world and in front of great audiences both in Israel and in the Palestinian territories, he would explain the perils of anti-Semitism and Holocaust denial, how these phenomena were against the essence of human and Muslim behavior.

Once, in 2007, I brought him to speak in front of the Global Forum for Combating Antisemitism, arranged by the Israeli Ministry of Foreign Affairs. I explained to him that he would meet great skepticism and opposition in the crowd of several hundred Jewish leaders from all over the world, including a few who believed with all their heart that nothing good could come from any political Islam. He said that he was convinced that if I were at his side translating, nothing could go wrong, that we had passed much greater hurdles than this. In a lengthy exposé, he spoke from his heart on all the difficult issues. He explained from where he came and where he was today, saying that precisely because he was not a Muslim Zionist but rather a true Islamist, he recognizes the State of Israel and the perils of anti-Semitism. He added that he was the right partner for peace and security not only for all citizens of the State of Israel, but also for a future Palestinian state. He spoke with such passion and answered all the most difficult questions in such a convincing way that it left practically all the skeptics in the audience in awe.

The sheikh could sometimes surprise even me with his forward thinking. I was once offered the position to chair the World Zionist Organization. It was important for me to hear how Sheikh Abdullah would react to this suggestion, having in mind the image of Zionism in the Muslim world. He immediately answered that if I decided this was right for me, the work for religious peace would not be an obstacle. To be sure, our Muslim partners would not become Zionists, but it would be important for them to see a fine, humane face of Zionism devoted to promoting religious peace.

Towards the end of the 90s, Sheikh Abdullah wrote a religious ruling that forbade suicide bombings against Israelis, in opposition to the ruling of Sheikh Karadawi, who permitted and encouraged it at the time (though later he retracted this ruling). Whenever he spoke to Palestinian leaders and big crowds in Palestinian cities, he would always remind them that their goal could be reached only without violence. He unfailingly condemned any attack, and his heart went out to the victims, although he often could be furious at the behavior of Israel's army.

Hearing of the terrorist attack on a synagogue in Har-Nof in 2014 during the morning prayers, he immediately called me to express his disgust and sympathy with the victims. He was willing to go on any media channel and say that this was a double crime in the eyes of Islam: a crime against humanity, when innocent human beings are murdered, and a crime against a holy place, when this savage murder takes place in a synagogue.

Expanding Our Network and Gaining Legitimacy

Sheikh Abdullah opened the door for me to become acquainted and forge relationships with key leaders throughout the Arab and Muslim world, leaders who influenced thousands of younger leaders and also provided them the opportunity to become acquainted with me and the Religious Peace Initiative (RPI). This was essential, particularly because we attempt to keep most of RPI's work under the radar and out of the public eye. He gave me the most precious gift of all: his leading protégé, Sheikh Raed

Bader. Sheikh Raed, under the guidance of Sheikh Abdullah, had studied Islam with the greatest legal minds in Palestine and Jordan and became a great legal authority, who then did not leave the side of Sheikh Abdullah. While early in our collaboration, I would go with Sheikh Abdullah to meetings, audiences, and panels, it became clear that, due to his health limitations, I needed to develop the same relationship with his star pupil. We would, after thorough consultations with the sheikh, go to one meeting after another throughout the Muslim world, as well as with leading rabbis—often rabbis far from my views—including religious Zionist rabbis who lived in the West Bank. The sheikh would sit in the Adam Center and wait for our reports upon returning, extremely pleased with the progress, which was much faster than he had anticipated.

More and more, we understood that the secular peace process had been a threat to religious leaders. The threat was not because of the territorial issues, which are largely solvable, but because those who promoted the secular peace often wished to promote a package deal that would uproot religion from society. The more traditional religious public feared a post-religious reality following a secular peace. While secularism plays a legitimate part in our existence, the combination of a difficult peace solution and aggressive secular proselytizing, motivated by the desire to wipe away the core of traditional existence, was more than any peace process could bear.

We offered a religious peace map from inside our religions, not in order to exclude the secular but in order to change the whole approach to peace. This immediately challenged and opened the hearts and minds of many of those who had been skeptical or outright opposed to the secularized peace process. It was both a change of language and of substance. Sheikh Abdullah took immense pleasure in seeing that so many leaders, including many of those who in 1985 had rejected his transition, now admitted that he had been right all along, just many years ahead of his time.

In 2015, Sheikh Abdullah delivered a momentous speech at the Ha'aretz Peace Conference, in which he spoke about the Religious Peace Initiative:

> The devil's assertion "either we OR you" should be eradicated. No! The truth is: "we AND you." We shall live together, each in our independent state, and I, the soldier of peace will continue making peace with my Jewish religious friends . . . .

> With my brother and friend Rabbi Melchior, we established together the coalition of Jews and Arabs for peace, and we founded the Religious Peace Initiative. It is not very different from other initiatives, other than the fact that we included

religion. This is to say to others "gone are the days when clerics are the obstacle to peace." We removed the obstacles and for those who do not want to participate with us in making peace, either Muslims or Jews, sit on the sidelines and let us pave the way! Shalom Aleichem![379]

The process of acceptance of Sheikh Abdullah's views culminated under sad circumstances. First, he fell ill and was in a coma for a period. Prayers were said for him all over the Muslim world from believers of all factions of Islam. Many who had not even heard about the sheikh now became acquainted with his whole philosophy for the future of Islam. Sheikh Abdullah, with G-d's help, pulled through and had a couple of years in which he enjoyed the new consensus around himself and religious peace. However, the greatest culmination was at his funeral and in the tent of mourning. Hundreds of thousands showed love and devotion. It was as if his death united us all around this great leader. He was eulogized in person and over the phone on loudspeakers by the leaders of the Palestinian authority and Hamas, as well as by leaders from all over the Muslim world. Chief Rabbi David Lau sent his eulogy, and Rabbi Avi Gisser, one of the leading settler rabbis, spoke warmly of his friendship with the sheikh. The head of the northern faction, Sheikh Raed Salah, kissed his forehead and eulogized him, in this way symbolizing that he was the true leader.

This was the first time I had attended a Muslim funeral. I stood at the very end of the crowd, among Jewish friends, and suddenly I was called to eulogize. I was totally unprepared for being permitted to do this and was overwhelmed by the grief of the moment. There was a total silence in the crowd. My throat was choked. At first, I could hardly utter a word, the tears running freely down my cheeks. The essence of my words was speaking to the sheikh:

> You promised me, when we began our journey, that you would never leave my side. Now, Allah has taken you away from my side, and I am orphaned. We are all orphaned, without our leader, without our Tzaddik. But at this solemn moment we promise that we shall continue the roadmap of the sheikh. We shall continue our commitment to create peace, security, and happiness for the generations of both peoples to come.

Dr. Mansour Abbas, the political leader of the Islamic party Ra'am, is another protégé of Sheikh Abdullah. He has been part of the Religious Peace Initiative for years. He is now implementing the philosophy of the sheikh in his efforts to change relations of Jews and Arabs in Israel and radically improve the lives of the Arab minority.

Celebrating Rabbi David Rosen

Over the years, Sheikh Abdullah crossed paths with Rabbi David Rosen on several occasions. This is not surprising, since there is hardly anyone in the religious world promoting peace with whom Rabbi Rosen did not meet, speak, create a relationship. As with Sheikh Abdullah, everyone holds great respect for Rabbi Rosen's passion and total commitment to promoting dialogue, connections, and ultimately peace. I have known Rabbi Rosen for well over forty years. We have worked on parallel paths, as well as together, with very similar visions of how we would like to see the world. Among our many collaborations were years of dialogue with Christian and Muslim leaders in East Jerusalem in the second half of the 90's and Rabbi Rosen's active participation in the Alexandria summit in 2002, as well as his always active participation and involvement on the board of Mosaica—The Religious Peace Initiative.

Rabbi Rosen has followed and contributed immensely to the changes in the Christian, particularly the Catholic, world. I know of no greater expert with whom to consult on matters of relationships with the Christian world than Rabbi Rosen. This gave him the insight that, just as change could happen between Jews and Christians, so it could also happen between Jews and Muslims. Actually, as he expresses it, it is much easier with the Muslim world, because our religions and history in many ways are so much closer. He is one of the few who first recognized the great evolution taking place in the Muslim world. He is the most eloquent presenter of the Jewish prophetic ideals for peace so desperately needed to bring good forces together instead of the polarization in every forum all over the world. Rabbi Rosen expresses the demand from other religions—not least from our own religion—to interpret and reinterpret our sources and the fundamentals of our religions. Religion is the main force influencing the world, and we, as believers, can do so much good utilizing the precious tool that G-d has given us.

We are now celebrating Rabbi David's seventieth birthday—the number of years taken from Adam (he reached 930, not 1000) and given to the original David, King David, who reached seventy, in order for there to be messianic hope in the world that stems from the house of King David. I wish for Rabbi David Rosen that he will continue to go from strength to strength in preaching and enabling a world which the Messiah would like to join.

Azza Karam

KATHERINE MARSHALL

Azza Karam as a Remarkable and Pioneering Interfaith Heroine

IN AUGUST 2019, IN Lindau, on an island hard by the point where Germany, Austria, and Switzerland meet, the World Assembly of Religions for Peace (RfP) elected a new secretary general, Dr. Azza Karam. The election marked a first both for Religions for Peace, an ambitious alliance of religious communities, and for world interreligious organizations. They selected a woman and a Muslim, someone with a wide range of experience in diverse fields that extended well beyond religious matters, thus breaking molds of patriarchal religious traditions. The Religions for Peace assembly erupted in applause as William Vendley, RfP's long-time secretary general, handed the symbolic reins of office and leadership to a determined woman.

What makes Azza Karam an interfaith heroine? In the short period that she has exercised formal interreligious leadership, she has exemplified a deep commitment to an inclusive approach that draws on the finest teachings and practice of diverse religious traditions, as well as modern secular ideals. She has arrived at her interreligious leadership via paths that differ from any other recent leader, which have taken her through different institutions, enriching her experience of life and institutional challenges. She has, over her life and career, faced demands that have tested her interpersonal skills in countless ways. In short, she fits no traditional molds but has through her life experience acquired gifts of knowledge, relationships, and insights.

Distinctive qualities that mark Karam as a leader include a well-integrated combination of deep respect for the human rights foundations for religious engagement in world affairs and, flowing from that, convictions that give intellectual and pragmatic meaning to understandings of equity. She is steeped in the spirit behind the global consensus on the United Nations

Sustainable Development Goals[380] and their foundations. These reflect an interconnected web that links human development (people), prosperity (a flourishing life), peace (well beyond the absence of conflict), environmental focus and justice (honoring and protecting the planet), and partnership that works to being out the best of each and every human being.

Courage in Pioneering New Leadership Models

"I am not afraid." That comment, expressed during an interview exchange between us some years ago,[381] epitomizes a central quality that marks Karam as an exemplary interreligious leader. She needs that courage, as she navigates the intricacies of multiple religious traditions, institutions, and global agendas that demand the constructive engagement of multiple religious actors. She has long shown the qualities and caliber of a pioneer leader, setting new courses in a traditionally masculine landscape. She does not shy from the complexities of the interreligious landscape and the issues she confronts on an hourly basis, taking each with care, subtlety, and vision. These issues require fine intellectual qualities that include a capacity to draw from different intellectual and theological disciplines, as well as knowledge and understanding of varying positions. Negotiation skills in their finest sense are a fundamental asset of interreligious leadership. They must be built on a willingness to listen, probing deeply into different perceptions and interests. Karam stands out as a model of courageous, feisty personal engagement and leadership in an especially demanding field.

It would be a mistake either to underestimate the challenges that have confronted Azza Karam as an interreligious leader or to frame those obstacles as insurmountable. The challenges for any interreligious leader are daunting, but never more so than in this critical time in history. Responding to the urgent, fast-paced imperatives of the twenty-first century is no mean task. She has needed to define and gain acceptance for new directions in a highly diverse community. She must also face the reality that appreciation for religious roles in world affairs in many global institutions is fragile and imperfect, and new demands arise, it seems, on a daily basis. But with unquestionable intelligence and knowledge that spans different disciplines and perspectives, alongside gifts of personal leadership, Karam has demonstrated that she is eminently suited to the challenge. Her longstanding engagement with the complexities of interreligious relationships and the challenges of working for sustainable peace in different world regions and global institutions represent a rare mix. In short, the task and challenges are large and mounting, but Karam shows that her qualities and determination suit her remarkably well for the leadership role she plays at this moment in history.

Paths to Leadership

Born and raised in Egypt, Karam studied at the American University in Cairo, and began her career and personal activism working in Egypt, then in the wider Arab region, with involvement in Lebanon, Syria, and Jordan. She became increasingly interested in democracy, human rights, and gender through working with practical issues on the ground. She was obliged in this context to approach the roles of religion in nuanced ways, taking into account both secular and religious perspectives and stripping away facile stereotypes, something that marks her to this day.

An important step came when Karam took on the challenge of working for the United Nations Development Programme (UNDP) on the Arab Human Development Reports.[382] This series of reports stands out for its thoughtful and path-setting analysis and engagement with many of the toughest issues facing the region. In this context, she interacted with wide-ranging ideas and institutions, engaging with governments, civil society, and religious communities. She worked with organizations that were prepared to go against the general taboos that have been justified through religion; some of these are still articulated by religious leaders. She shone a spotlight on the many organizations inspired by their religious beliefs that work to provide needed services to their religious communities, with an understanding and an appreciation that this is about human rights and—as many would put it in their own idiom—human dignity, first and foremost.

Karam is also a noted scholar, well respected for her analytic work, writing, and public presentations. She holds a professorship of religion and development at the Vrije Universiteit in Amsterdam, in The Netherlands. Her PhD in 1996, from the University of Amsterdam, focused on political Islam and became her first book, published in Arabic (her mother tongue) and in English. She has studied diverse topics but always adds new insights on the links between belief and action. Karam has focused in many forms on the roles that women play within religious communities, exploring both the challenges they face and the gifts they bring. She has published widely over the years—in several languages—on international political dynamics, including democratization, human rights, peace and security, gender, religious engagement, and sustainable development. As a scholar, her knowledge of her own Muslim religious tradition is deep and constantly exploratory. She is gifted with a boundless intellectual curiosity.

Karam's advocacy, academic work, and inspiration have carried through to years of operational work and activism, first with Religions for Peace's international hub in New York (where she developed the Global Women of Faith Network), then with the United Nations Population Fund (UNFPA). There she worked closely with Thoraya Obaid, the executive director, dealing with highly sensitive issues around women's rights and the challenges to them.

Thus Karam's paths to interfaith leadership have formed her as an inspirational figure who can draw on diverse experience across sectors, world regions, and religious traditions. Azza brings intellectual gifts and rigorous discipline, keen awareness of Muslim religious traditions, and robust operational experience that ranges from the community level to global institutions that are part of the United Nations. Her experience thus spans local community work and high policy realms, public and private, secular and religious, intellectual and pragmatic.

In each chapter in her career, Azza Karam has traced new paths of leadership and developed new, innovative programs that promise wide and lasting impact. Her tangible achievements include the much admired innovations reflected in the Arab Human Development Reports and the formation and building of a worldwide network of women, working from the vantage point of their religious traditions and institutions. Working for long years in the often contested United Nations family planning division (UNFPA), she kept constantly at the center of her vision the ideals and core principles that link religious traditions, asserting repeatedly that anti-women, harmful traditions shall not be undertaken "in our name."

In short, Karam has developed and lived, in widely diverse settings, a leadership model and experience that are marked by vision, courage, grit, and compassion.

Interactions with Azza Karam

I came to know Azza Karam best through working together to meet five shared challenges that confronted us both as we worked in different institutions and with separate perspectives in the first two decades of the 2000s.

The first challenge was to contend with the sharp polarization of religious views around gender roles, including notably family planning. At UNFPA, where Azza was in a leadership position, assaults came from different directions: feminists who were critical and suspicious of efforts to engage with religious views and different religious institutions that were sharply critical of UNFPA's very mandate and work, to the point of physical threats to those involved in meeting women's most urgent needs. Azza Karam played central roles in establishing core principles and building a common ground that demonstrated the most positive sides of religious traditions and beliefs. This took grace and courage but also in-depth analytic work to appreciate concerns and opportunities for fresh thinking. Working with UNFPA's Executive Director Thoraya Obaid, UNFPA reached out to religious communities and formed important alliances that made progress possible in various world regions. Karam and I worked together on a UNFPA report[383] that exemplifies the deep analytic work that she inspired and led and the sustained effort to establish common ground and build a robust alliance.

Second, the fragmentation of efforts both by United Nations agencies seeking to engage constructively with faith-inspired development work and by those religious bodies themselves emerged as an increasingly serious impediment to understanding and progress. It inspired an ambitious interagency task force[384] that drew on experience and leadership within many United Nations agencies that Karam built and led. The task force has highlighted the depth of experience of several agencies, defined and documented issues and tensions that often arose from misunderstandings or gaps in knowledge, and helped in linking their work to the broad efforts that underpinned the seventeen Sustainable Development Goals (SDGs) that were approved by the United Nations General Assembly in September 2015.

A third challenge was against the backdrop of both perceived and actual patriarchal attitudes towards women, notably in religious leadership echelons. Engaging the women who all too often are essentially invisible both to religious and secular actors demands a constant and sensitive attention. It also meant knowing and hearing women leaders and integrating them in policy settings and identifying the priority issues that concerned them. Karam has consistently contributed to this effort. She was part of a consortium of scholars and practitioners who contributed to a project by Georgetown University's Berkley Center for Religion, Peace and World Affairs that focused on shining light on the peacebuilding work of women inspired by religious beliefs and networks.[385] Religions for Peace's network of women of faith is an enduring legacy of her persistent focus on women's roles within religious communities.

A fourth challenge has been to address what we term religious illiteracy, an all too common phenomenon among many diplomats and humanitarian and development specialists. The resulting blindness goes alongside negative and often simplistic preconceptions about multilateral and government bodies among religious communities and gaps in knowledge that loom large. Karam played a central role in efforts to develop strategic learning exchanges[386] that opened dialogues, which played material roles in turning glazed eyes or hostility into practical and far better informed engagement.

And fifth, a central challenge in engaging and linking faith-inspired work on development and humanitarian work is skepticism about the evidence that documents the work and assesses its quality. Karam and I were involved in a consortium of scholars and activists that shaped a special issue of the respected *Lancet* publication exploring religious engagement in health. We jointly wrote the introductory framing of that effort in 2015, and Karam co-authored other papers.[387] More recently, in the fall of 2020, Karam was part of a Georgetown University symposium that explored different facets of the response to the COVID-19 emergency, with an interview that was the foundation of a segment on religious responses.[388]

Contemporary Challenges

Azza Karam now leads the complex, sprawling, carefully crafted and balanced, fifty-one-year-old interreligious body Religions for Peace, which is dedicated to interfaith harmony and to broadly understood work to advance world peace. In her inaugural address, Karam laid down some clear markers for her leadership, which notably included an unambiguous commitment to human rights. She also stressed the priority of building strong operational links between ordained clerics and religious institutions and other formal and less formal religious leaders, notably for diverse programs focused on fighting poverty, which take their inspiration from religious faith. She committed herself to supporting central roles for women and young people as integral facets of the interreligious movement and action.

Stepping into the role of leader of Religions for Peace at this historic moment demands fresh strategic thinking that builds on the organization's long history and complex organizational structure but is also open to new departures and approaches. The interreligious leadership position does not carry with it expectations and frameworks set in concrete; the role requires great creativity and flexibility, coming at an unprecedented period. The world and thus Religions for Peace have faced the COVID-19 emergency that began at the moment Karam took on the leadership office. It has blocked many forms of engagement, as lockdowns stymied relationships and interactions. Each and every religious institution has been forced to adapt sharply and instantaneously to new restrictions and demands. In this demanding period, Azza Karam first shone the spotlight on RfP's ninety-two interreligious councils in every world region, raising funding that is making possible a wide range of locally driven, innovative projects that have been marked by interreligious cooperation. She has been tireless, demanding, and creative in engaging leaders and institutions on wide-ranging issues, which have included approaches to peace and to more specialized topics like the debt of poorer countries.

The leadership challenges of this period would have tested any leader, but Karam's persistence, determination, and creativity stand out as exceptional.

In this pioneering work, Karam works closely with Rabbi David Rosen in his central role as a leader within the Religions for Peace family and alliance. David Rosen's respect for Karam's gifts and contributions played significant roles in the bold decision to break molds and appoint her to the position of secretary general. He has served as a a stalwart supporter for Karam's strategic initiatives. Theirs is a synergy of intellect and principles that enrich both Religions for Peace and the interreligious movement.

Blu Greenberg

Dr. Deborah Weissman

It is sometimes observed that women have an easier time in dialogue with each other than do men. Some people have suggested that there is less ego involvement and more empathy. I tend to think the reason is that women have been marginalized in all of their communities, particularly in institutionalized religion, and thus have an immediate basis for identification with the other.

Blu Greenberg, a founder of JOFA (the Jewish Orthodox Feminist Alliance) and perhaps the most important voice of Orthodox Feminism in the twentieth century, recognized but did not accept that marginalization. She has not only fought for greater participation of women in all aspects of religious life but has been a strong advocate of interfaith dialogue among women and between men and women.

Bluma (I understand that at some point, she legally changed her name to Blu) Genauer was born in Seattle on January 21, 1936, the daughter of Rabbi Sam and Sylvia. Blu's family were observant Jews, and she had a yeshiva education on the East Coast. Blu received a BA in political science from Brooklyn College, an MA in clinical psychology from the City University of New York, and an MS in Jewish history from Yeshiva University. Along the way, she met her future husband, Irving (Yitz) Greenberg, and they married in 1957. Growing up as a rabbi's daughter may well have prepared her for the role she assumed later as a rabbi's wife.

Blu has referred to herself as a "transition woman."[389] She and I were both privileged to have had, at different times, Professor Nehama Leibowitz as one of our teachers of Bible. Nehama was a unique trailblazer in her own way but disavowed any connection with feminism. Blu and I have lived in our lifetimes through huge transitions in the status and role of Jewish women. We are about half a generation apart in terms of age, and that slight difference, plus our very different backgrounds in terms of Jewish observance, might account for the difference with which we perceive and experience the rate of change regarding women in Judaism.

Yitz dedicated his book *The Jewish Way: Living the Holidays* "to Blu, who taught me the meaning of covenantal Love."[390] Together, they raised five children. They have at least twenty-three grandchildren. It is one of the characteristics of Blu that, among Orthodox Jews, she is an outspoken feminist; among feminists, she is an outspoken champion of the family. This makes her position challenging, but she always comports herself with grace and humor, as well as with no small measure of courage.

I first met Yitz when I was in college in the late 1960s. I often was a guest in their home, including for Shabbat dinner. Although Blu and Yitz had their own five children and other guests as well, they often hosted guests from other religious traditions. The presence of such a diverse group can enhance and enrich the Shabbat experience of all who are at the table and was a formative element in my own journey into interfaith.

It was through Yitz that Blu initially encountered the world of inter-religious dialogue. As she says, "I am indebted to my husband for bringing me into the world of dialogue, and even more for what he taught me about conducting it with integrity . . . . I have come to appreciate interfaith dialogue as one of the central spiritual forces in my life, along with family, feminism, Israel, singing in shul on Shabbat . . . forces that generate a powerful, autonomous surge of emotion, accompanied by feelings of deep gratitude that I was elected to be a Jew."[391]

Yitz and Blu were pioneers in post-Shoah Jewish-Christian dialogue. Yitz says in his book *For the Sake of Heaven and Earth*,[392] of his decision to get involved in Jewish-Christian exchange in 1962: "I joined the dialogue, very frankly, not to come to love and understand Christians, but really kind of to say 'stop teaching hatred about me.'" They were motivated by the challenge: "How do you get Christians to reformulate their thinking about Judaism?" As Yitz recounts, the Christians they met were so wonderful, open, sympathetic to the Jews, and ashamed of what Christianity had done in the Holocaust that, as time went on, the Greenbergs became more and more appreciative and respectful of Christianity in general.

Some of Blu's role models in dialogue have been Catholic nuns, especially Sister Rose Thering. As Blu said to me in conversation, "Just to have known people of such moral vision as Sister Rose would alone make the whole interfaith journey worthwhile to me."

Beginning in 1978 and lasting in various forms for a dozen years, a group called Women of Faith in the Eighties served as a home for Blu. By 1982, her reputation as a key figure in Jewish-Christian dialogue was recognized when she was invited by the World Council of Churhes to join seven women of other faiths to prepare papers for the Decade for Women meeting scheduled for Nairobi in 1985. The role she played in this group ended up having a life-transforming effect upon me. In June of 1988, through the World Council of Churches, I underwent a life-transforming experience for which I have Blu to thank.[393] WCC invited about sixty women from all over the world, representing nine different religions, to a week-long conference in Toronto, on religion, politics, and feminism. Blu Greenberg nominated me to attend. Blu had known me primarily from Jewish feminist activities; I hadn't yet done much interfaith work.

The nine religions represented at the Toronto conference were Judaism, Christianity, Islam, Buddhism, Hinduism, the Sikh and Baha'i faiths, Native American Indian spiritual traditions, and the Wiccan religion. I was on a panel on the Israeli-Palestinian conflict with a Quaker from Palestine and a Catholic nun from Lebanon. I suggested, let's not dwell on the past, let's look to the future; we want a better future for our children and grandchildren. What can we do to bring that about? After the talk, Blu reminded me, "Don't forget history." This was part of her great wisdom. I don't think I was forgetting history, but in retrospect, I realize that the achievement of peace will involve perhaps not acceptance but at least an acknowledgement of our different narratives.

Each religious group was given a time slot—morning or evening—in which to share with the rest of us some prayers or ritual that typify their community. The Jews were given Friday evening, with Blu as the unofficial leader of the Jewish delegation. It should be noted that, for many years, the Jews who engaged in interreligious dialogue were largely non-Orthodox and, in many cases, nonobservant Jews. Blu Greenberg was one of the pioneers of Orthodox religious Jews participating wholeheartedly in inter-religious activities. Sometimes Orthodox Jews feel more comfortable in dialogue with Christians or members of other faiths than with Reform and Conservative Jews. Blu can dialogue and cooperate with all of them.

Putting together a *Kabbalat Shabbat* service and then the Shabbat table ritual with eight Jewish women from different denominations was in itself no small feat. Despite our own intrareligious differences, we did succeed in organizing a candle-lighting ceremony and an abbreviated *Kabbalat Shabbat* service. Friday morning, we went around to the other groups with a question and a request. The question we asked, mainly of the Muslims and Hindus, was, if we also provide grape juice, would it be offensive to you if we had wine on the table? The answer they gave was, "No, but thanks very much for asking." The request was preceded by an explanation that it is our custom to sing at the Shabbat table, so that if the groups had any songs from their traditions that they wanted to share with the rest of us, we would be happy to photocopy the words in advance.

During the evaluation session of the conference, a great many participants—mostly non-Jewish women—reported that the highlight of the conference for them had been the Shabbat. Since that conference, I have become deeply involved in interreligious dialogue. The conference in Toronto was really my first international exposure to this field, and I will be ever grateful to Blu for that wonderful introduction.

Blu is a great supporter of Israel but also a critic of some government decisions. Her concern for peace led her, in 1989, to help establish the Dialogue Project to promote communication between Jewish and Palestinian women. She participated in the conference on the Responsibility of Jews, Christians and Muslims for Peace in Jerusalem, hosted by the Reference Group on Inter-Religious Relations of the World Council of Churches, in Thessaloniki, Greece, in 1996.

The dialogue with Palestinians has sometimes been a source of pain and frustration. Blu accompanied the Palestinian women on a visit to Gaza, and the group also came to Israel. The group disbanded after Oslo but Blu's support of peace movements remains. In 2002, she participated in the Global Peace Initiative developed from the first World Summit of Women Religious and Spiritual Leaders in Geneva.

In 2016, we both were invited, together with about three hundred male rabbis from different streams within Judaism and a handful of women (mostly "the wives of ") to a conference sponsored by an evangelical Catholic group, the Neocathecumenal Way. The group is philo-Semitic and very supportive of Israel. They also have enormous material resources and a stunningly beautiful conference center in the Galilee. Jews were invited from throughout the world to spend several days with leaders of this movement in an atmosphere of fellowship and spirituality. Many of my Catholic friends warned me and even tried to dissuade me from attending, as this group is known for its reactionary tendencies.

There were no women on the program. Some of us protested, and permission was finally given to Blu to speak. A few other women took advantage of the opportunity and at least posed questions. But additionally, I found very problematic a film that we saw, extolling the virtues of a family—American members of the movement—with nineteen children! This seemed a standard that was hard to reconcile with feminist notions of women's self-actualization. If a woman is pregnant or breastfeeding throughout all of her fertile years, it is not only physically and physiologically taxing, but it does interfere with doing almost anything else.

The film featured a scene in which the entire family of twenty-one was gathered around a long table to carry out family Scripture study, led by the father. The text he chose was Genesis 22, the binding of Isaac. After reading it dramatically, his first question to the family was: "Would you have the love of and commitment to God and be prepared to make the kind of sacrifice that Abraham was prepared to make?"

I have taught that text myself but in very different contexts. I had great difficulty with the father's pedagogic choice of text and opening question and his apparent discouragement of independent thinking. I concluded that the movement were Catholic fundamentalists.

I was wondering what Blu thought of all this. At dinner that evening, I asked her for her view, and she said, "Israel needs all the friends we can get." I was disappointed in Blu's response but tried to understand it from her perspective. She is so deeply committed to garnering support for Israel that she seems willing to overlook other things which, to me, seem as important.

We share a delicate balancing act of feminism, modernity, Halakha (Jewish religious laws), support for Israel, and interfaith openness, but I suppose these can be balanced differently by different people.

Most of all, Blu is what we call in Yiddish a fine Mentsch (human being). One of her memorable statements, which may at first glance appear trivial but, regrettably, is far from that: "The essential Orthodox Jew . . . must be honest, ethical, respectful of other human beings, responsible in relationships, reliable in their word."[394] This also translates into her attitude when dealing with disagreements. One of the important things one can learn from Blu—and this is a vital lesson for interfaith engagement—is how to disagree in a cordial, elegant, and friendly way.

A great tragedy befell the family in 2002, when Blu's son J. J., not yet thirty-seven, was killed when his bike was crashed into by a truck driver in Israel. The family donated five of his organs to other patients. There were over a thousand people present at the funeral. It was a blazing hot day. Typical of Blu's concern for others, the family made sure we were all supplied with bottles of water.

In 2015, Blu received an honorary doctorate for her lifetime achievement at Bar-Ilan University, a university under Orthodox auspices in Israel. A mutual friend of ours told me on that occasion that Blu was being similarly honored by the Jewish Theological Seminary in New York, the flagship of the Conservative movement within Judaism. To be thus honored by both Orthodox and Conservative Jews represents Blu's great capacity for both intrareligious and interreligious dialogue.

In conclusion, I would like to bring some words of Yitz's from his preface to *The Jewish Way*:

My wife, Blu, has been intellectual companion and best friend, inspiration and early warning system, source of constant appreciation and most honest critic. I have learned to depend on her judgment and to ignore her wisdom only at my peril. Her humanness and love, her religious model, her ability to juggle the contradictions of life without self-pity or resentment have been the anchor of my life for more than thirty years. The dedication of this book to her is but a grain of sand on the shores of a boundless sea.[395]

Blu is not alone in serving as a model for balancing sensitivity to feminist concerns and to modernity, along with commitment to Halakha and interfaith openness. Rabbi David Rosen, a friend and collaborator since the mid-1980s, is himself a model for balancing these concerns. Not only is he a giant of interreligious dialogue, he is also a staunch supporter, over many years, of women's Torah education and the enhancement of women's roles in the synagogue and community. The many threads of life and ideals by means of which our lives are interwoven are part of the greater whole to which Blu, as much as Yitz, Greenberg also belongs.

The Anonymous Hero[396]

Dr. William Vendley

Meeting

WE MET AT THE airport baggage claim in Lome, Togo. It was May 1999. My bag came from New York; his didn't arrive. A small man with a battered heavy Sony video recorder slung over a thin shoulder, his eyes flickered faintly as they politely swept past. He looked lost. Venturing, I asked: "Where are you going, friend?" He said: "To the peace talks." He added: "I don't know if I can go. I don't have the money for the visa fee."

We were headed to the same place. I paid the five dollars for the visa and welcomed him into my taxi. Before sharing more about him, I'll offer background.

On March 9, Agence France Press (AFP) ran a story on their wire service dealing with a singular event in the agonizing drama unfolding in then one of the poorest countries on earth, Sierra Leone. Previous stories told of the people of Sierra Leone's decade-long struggle for political freedom, of their courage in successfully holding democratic elections, of their crushing disappointment at the military coup in 1998, of the headlong descent into violent chaos; and of rebel boy soldiers—made high on drugs—hacking off the hands and feet of village farmers—mothers, children, and fathers—whom they suspected of supporting the government.

The AFP story on March 9 marked a possible turning point. It chronicled rebel leader Foday Sankoh ordering his soldiers to observe a cease-fire and release some hostages. The press report added somewhat cryptically: "Sankoh was flanked by religious leaders from the Inter-Religious Council." Other press reports on other press services filled out these cryptic remarks. We could learn that Sierra Leone's Inter-Religious Council had already held consultations with President Kabba, engaging in him a willingness to begin peace negotiations. Digging deeper, we learned that the Inter-Religious Council had also been in extended contact with

343

the rebels in the bush and that the rebels had released fifty-two children to its Women of Faith group. That enabled the women to bring the children to President Kabba to help build the political conditions essential for dialogue in the war-exhausted country. The rebels agreed to the peace talks on the condition that the Inter-Religious Council be invited as an informal participant and as guarantor of the talks' procedural propriety. President Kabba had requested their presence as well.

A section of a cable that I was privileged to view from Ambassador Okelo, the UN secretary-general's representative, addressed to UN Secretary-General Kofi Annan, provided an assessment of these facts. It stated plainly that the peace process would not have been possible in Sierra Leone without the Inter-Religious Council and its partnership with Religions for Peace.

I had firsthand experience of the nightmare in Sierra Leone, as the religious communities in the country had invited Religions for Peace to accompany them in forming their Inter-Religious Council, affiliating it with Religions for Peace and advancing its peacemaking during the civil war. As the then secretary general of Religions for Peace, I engaged in a kind of relay with my trusted colleague Stein Villumstad, each of us staying in Sierra Leone for several weeks at a time, then passing the baton to the other to carry on the work. Through our partnership with our religious friends in Sierra Leone, we had frequent meetings with President Kabba and extended encounters with the rebel commander Foday Sankoh, his war lords, and his army of boys swept into the rebel movement.

Back in Lome, the taxi set off for the site of the peace talks. My airport acquaintance showed me press credentials and shared that he was there to film the talks for Sierra Leone's government. As we rode along, I had an idea: would my airport friend do us a favor? If we purchased extra tape cassettes, would he film the religious leaders in their roles in the peace talks? He gladly agreed.

I felt a thrill as we proceeded to our destination. I began imagining the video of the religious leaders playing their indispensable roles in the peace talks. I pictured myself showing it to the governments, foundations, and philanthropists who, in funding Religions for Peace, were taking a chance on the efficacy and efficiency of the religious communities as problem solvers. The film, I felt sure, would provide convincing evidence that their bet on Religions for Peace was yielding results—and perhaps convince them to invest further in our efforts. We arrived at the venue. My encounter in the airport was turning out to be an unexpected blessing.

Peace talks are slow, often tedious. In Lome, the talks had three senior mediators with three distinct mandates: from the UN, the Organization of

African Unity (the predecessor of the African Union), and the Economic Community of West African States (ECOWAS). These highly experienced negotiators soon arrived at a pragmatic formula: let the religious leaders informally visit the rebel and governmental representatives at night to discern incremental areas of agreement that could assist the formal proceedings the next day. This process had the trust of the conflicting parties, and it significantly reduced the hurdles of pride and protocol that could derail the formal proceedings. It offered insider knowledge and nimble flexibility and protected both sides from heading down blind alleys.

Throughout the talks, the formal mediators repeatedly attributed their progress to the behind-the-scenes work being done by our partners: "Due to the role of Sierra Leone's religious leaders, we made progress last night" and "Once again, it is thanks to Sierra Leone's religious leaders that we have made a substantive advance" and so on. Each time these luminous pearls fell from the lips of these hard-boiled political mediators, I would instantly look at the videographer, only to find that he was invariably focused on something else, anything else really, other than the political mediators attesting to the importance of the religious leaders. Then, when religious leaders would be formally called upon to speak, followed by praise from all the parties, my videographer friend would again invariably fail to point the camera at what I so desperately wanted him to capture.

Concerned, I spoke to my new friend politely, asking him to please try to capture on film these remarkable attestations to the value of the religious contributions. His face clouded as I spoke. He seemed hurt that I should try to tell him how to do his job. My effort failed. During the long and tedious peace talks, there were chords of praise for the religious leaders from all sides, but none of it was captured on film.

I needed a new approach. During a break, I decided to engage my new friend in conversation. Maybe, I thought, if I actually got to know him a little better on a personal level, I could also get my request through. "What," I began, "do you think of the Inter-Religious Council?" After a thoughtful pause, "They are us," he said. "Our mixed families and neighborhoods of Muslims and Christians, and our hopes to be together." An elegant answer. I asked him to tell me his story.

He began by sharing quietly that his young wife had died of a treatable illness because the war had exhausted all the medicine in the country. Then, he shared that his daughter, too, had perished needlessly, again due to a war-related absence of medical service. He told me that his now three-year-old son had sickle cell anemia and that he was struggling to take care of him by himself. He spoke quietly in a matter-of-fact fashion while sharing his experience on January 6, 1999 when the rebels invaded Freetown, his home city.

He had gotten up early as his young son slept to dash off to the market to get him an egg. As he hurried home, the rebels broke through, and he had to seek shelter in a house packed with thirty or so terrified people. Rebels breached the door and summarily shot eight or nine in the head. He told me how he had tried to lean back against the wall to appear less visible, all the while gripped by fear for his son sleeping alone back home. He remained trapped in that house for thirty-six hours. Periodic executions punctuated the reign of terror. As his anguish for his little boy grew, all he could do was offer his Muslim prayers.

He told me his story, his mild eyes direct, his quiet voice never changed. He told me how he eventually escaped and reunited with his son, who had survived because a Christian neighbor had taken him in. He finished in the same quiet voice: "But, thank God, peace has come at last to Sierra Leone."

Before the thunder of his gentle spirit, I felt small and fell quiet. I had gotten him to tell his story in the hopes that I could persuade him to capture what I wanted on film. Despite his harrowing story, he was unspeakably dignified. The man who had suffered so profoundly seemed simply to know that peace is God's gift, and that this gift is offered even where its presence cannot be fathomed.

A Plenitude of Teachers

In my life, I have had my share of good teachers and a plenitude of co-teachers. Let me single out my decades of searching partnership with the radiant Rabbi David Rosen, to whom I joyously dedicate this reflection. Whenever possible, our decades-long searching was nurtured within the warmth of his family home, as David, his wife Sharon, and their children welcomed me into the restoring rest of their loving celebration of Shabbat. From uniquely gifted and effective ambassadors of multifaith goodwill like Rabbi Rosen, to unsung laborers working in their neighborhoods, each person in Religions for Peace co-taught and co-learned. Together, we opened our hearts in sharing, discerning, and acting. Side by side and full of principled respect, we also prayed or meditated in each other's presence. We built bonds of solidarity that embraced our differences. "Different Faiths, Common Action" was more than our motto; it was a description of our sweet labor.

An enduringly necessary first step was to teach ourselves to unite in taking concrete action in response to mutually discerned threats to peace, those forces that degrade human dignity, erode the common good, and threaten our home, the earth.

Gradually, however, we also began to teach each other that our respective religions—each in its own way—anticipates a fullness of peace in its radiant positivity. We learned from each other that for religious traditions, peace includes a positive state of personal and social flourishing. Words like *Shalom, Salaam,* and *Shanti* are ciphers for these holistic religious visions of peace.

Importantly, we also began to recognize that it is each religious tradition's respective positive vision of peace that brings into bold relief for its believers the bitter contradictions and failures, both personal and collective, and the corrosive social exclusion that deeply wounds our human experience. We only really see the threats to peace in the light of our more foundational positive visions of peace. Ironically, the deeper the threats to peace, the more we are pressed to plumb the radical positivity of peace. This far-reaching insight is a bridge to explaining the importance of my Lome friend, an unexpected teacher.

Seeing the Teacher

The fact of evil poses a profoundly disturbing question. It pushes beyond the reach of intelligence into the core of our hearts. It is a question for me—as a Catholic Christian—about love, about our desperate need for it and our possibility of abiding in it. Love, for me, is also the interreligious question, although I welcome that it can be framed and pursued in widely different religious terms.

In the odd light cast by the fact of evil, I beheld my Lome friend as a teacher of love.

The love that can abide in the midst of evil, I have learned, is not cheap and can never be mastered, only lived into. Teachers of this love arise wherever but often when our encounter with evil becomes unavoidable.

Evil, in my tradition, is an absence, a contraction of the flooding fullness of existence. When evil breaks into the open, it almost forces us—if we hold our gaze—to acknowledge that we, persons and societies, contradict and fail to cultivate our deepest potential for goodness. We conspire to inflict damage—sometimes lethal damage—upon one another, often perversely calling it good. Typically, we hold off the hideousness of these moments, using self-screening rationalizations to avoid seeing that we have inverted the scales of value, prizing personal or group gain over the well-being of all.

In the inverse epiphanies of evil unmasked, we can see more clearly as relational beings that, in hurting the other, we hurt ourselves. We can know that we are, in varying degrees, both victims and victimizers. We can see clearly that we and our society have become infected and that the infection does not spare our religious institutions.

Somehow, by bearing great evil, my Lome airport friend embodied with force the question of what God is doing about evil. Does God care? Does God abandon us in our vulnerability to evil? Or, does God offer to enter into our hearts as Love, so that—humbled, healed, and newly empowered—we, victims and victimizers, might engage in collaboration with Love to help transform personal and social evil?

Over time, and with the help of persons like my Lome teacher, I have come to realize that the religions' most ruthlessly honest admittance of human vulnerability to evil disclose profound possibilities for concrete multireligious collaboration to overcome it.

Love, my religious tradition's answer to the ubiquity of evil, is inevitably my innermost lens. It has helped me to see that each religious tradition counsels its own practices to heal the ravages of evil. These practices underlie the multireligious commitments to address evil, based upon unflinching honesty, repentance, restitution, and reconciliation; common calls for the transformation of social structures that hurt us into ones that help us; sober summons to self-sacrifice for others and our common good; calls for the voluntary bearing of innocent suffering, for returning good for evil, for forgiveness, unrestricted compassion, and love.

At bottom, each tradition appeals to a mysterious good more radical and ultimately more powerful than evil, a mystery experienced as both gift and task. It follows for me that, even if a unity of faiths is not possible, a unity in the mystery of love is.

In the blaze of sunshine that gladdens the heart, the religions increasingly unite in the labor for the rights that protect and the virtues that build up the human heart. In the night of evil, each speaks in its own tongue of a love anchored beyond human vicissitudes. It is a love that my Lome friend expressed in his bearing perhaps even more than with his quiet words: "But, thank God, peace has come at last to Sierra Leone."

Fathers and Children

Muhammad Abdul Rauf

Imam Feisal Abdul Rauf

THERE HAVE BEEN MANY individuals whose examples and writings on interfaith understanding and relationships have had a profound influence upon me, so many that I have forgotten more than those whose names I can remember. But if I were forced to name one, it would have to be my late father, Muhammad Abdul Rauf. He was a graduate and life-long employee of al-Azhar University in Egypt. Al-Azhar sent him as part of a delegation to Kuwait in 1947 to establish a religious institute there, where I was born the following year.

He was sent in 1950 to study at Cambridge University in England and in 1955 to the then British colony The Federation of Malaya to start a Muslim College. Malaya won its independence in 1957 and joined in 1963 with other regional states that were British colonies to create the nation known since as Malaysia.

My interfaith experiences with him began from my earliest days, where, as a child growing up in Malaya in the 1950s, I witnessed his deep personal friendship and mutual love for the late Swami Satyananda, who was then the leading Hindu leader in Malaya, who came from Sri Lanka (then known as Ceylon). I was too young then to fathom any religious discussions they had. Unfortunately, Swami Satyananda passed away when I was around ten years old.

My father was sent by al-Azhar University in 1965 to be director of the Islamic Center of New York, then the only mosque in all of New York City, except for the mosques of Elijah Muhammad, whose followers were known as the Black Muslims.

It was in New York that I had the good fortune to accompany him and meet several of the great Jewish rabbis and scholars of that time, such as Rabbi Louis Finkelstein at the Jewish Theological Seminary and Rabbi Marc Tanenbaum, with whom he had regularly weekly interfaith meetings, then called ecumenical meetings, for a stretch of time.

As I reflect on my father's approach to interfaith relations, I recognize the centrality of friendship to his practice of relations across religions. What my father did, probably above and beyond all other contributions to interfaith relations, was to engage in personal relationships, to make friends. Friends of other faiths would be invited to our home for lunches and dinners, during which ideas and areas of common work serendipitously developed on which he then cooperated with his counterparts. Personal relationships provide the foundation for healthy interfaith relations. As our dining room table could testify, there is a kind of organic growth that leads to maturation of projects.

The emphasis on individuals and personal relationships also led to what might be considered ultimately his greatest achievement: being with people at times of crisis. His energies were stretched far too thin, but the prime example of this was in the aftermath of the Six-Day War, during which time it was emotionally difficult to be a Muslim and an Egyptian in NYC. My father accepted every invitation he possibly could to speak at Jewish synagogues. At that emotionally very difficult time for us as Egyptians and Muslims, I was surprised by how willing my father was to accept these invitations—and even more surprised by how much his Jewish hosts appreciated his presence My father often quoted the Qur'anic verse 2:62: "Indeed those who believe, the Jews, the Christians, the Sabeans, whoever believes in God and the Last Day and does good, will have their reward with their Lord. They will have no fear, nor will they grieve" to demonstrate the Qur'an's attitude to peoples of all faiths. He also accepted the Qur'anic command to its believers to "believe in God, His Angels, His Scriptures, His Messengers, saying 'We make no distinction between any of His Messengers'" (2:285) All the Prophets whom God sent to all of humanity are our Prophets. This perhaps is the most interfaith imperative to Muslims.

While I consider the personal angle primary, there is also an important scholarly or intellectual angle to my father's interfaith work. Two of his important published works were the result of his interfaith relationships and were prompted by his non-Muslim partners: one by professor of sociology Morroe Berger of Princeton University, the other by William Baroody, then president of the American Enterprise Institute.

Professor Berger urged my father to translate a book written by Professor Labib al-Said of al-Azhar University, the man responsible for the first recording of the whole Qur'an in the 1960s on phonograph records by one of the leading Qur'anic reciters in Egypt of his day, Sheikh Mahmud Khalil al-Hussary. This book made available to English readers a play-by-play of the efforts to record the whole Qur'an with its correct recitation on phonograph. In the foreword, my father expresses how "throughout the project, we have been encouraged by the courtesy, perseverance and understanding of Dr. Morroe Berger, who originated the idea of this adaptation and coordinated the work (with a grant to the American Research Center in Egypt from the United States Office of Education)." He also expresses his gratitude to Dr. Bernard Weiss, who worked together with Professor Berger and my father in editing my father's translation. Dr Weiss shaped the book, creatively revised the text, expanded certain points (in consultation with my father and Professor Labib), and restructured chapters and contents, thus recasting the original Arabic work into a well-integrated and readable book.[397]

In this book, Professor Said describes his difficulties in getting the authorities at al-Azhar to agree to the project and how his difficulties paralleled the difficulties of the Prophet's companions when urged by Umar al-Khattab, who later went on to become the second caliph after the Prophet Muhammad, to press his predecessor Caliph Abu Bakr to put the whole Qur'an into writing before the demise of those who had memorized it. The reader may think it noteworthy that this work, on something as fundamental to Islam, a book on the Qur'an, was the product of a collaboration with Jewish friends. But in our house it was natural. In my growing up days, I noticed how much my father admired the literary and academic works of non-Muslim scholars on Islam, some whom he knew, like Arthur Arberry, who translated the Qur'an and many other works, providing English speaking readers with an understanding of Islam. I remember him discussing with admiration with a colleague of his from al-Azhar, Dr. Muhammad Zaki Badawi (who later became head of the Muslim College in England) some of the insights of Ignaz Goldziher in his writings about Islam. Openness to interfaith engagement went hand in hand with academic rigor, discipline, and the quest for receiving truth or relevant understanding wherever it could be found, regardless of religious affiliation.

The second project took place in 1984, when William Baroody invited my father to write a sequel to what Baroody calls a seminal essay, written by my father. The essay was titled "The Islamic Doctrine of Economics and Contemporary Thought," and it was contributed by my father to the first volume of essays from the American Enterprise Institute's summer institutes on Religion and Economics, *Capitalism and Socialism: A Theological Inquiry.*

In a sequel book, titled *A Muslim's Reflections on Democratic Capitalism*, my father used the ideals of democratic capitalism, as they developed in Jewish-Christian writings, to describe the alternative vision of Islam, proceeding throughout by comparison and contrast. By searching and quoting relevant verses of the Qur'an and sayings of the Prophet Muhammad, the Hadith, my father found that most features of a democratic capitalist economy were in accord with Islamic revelation.[398]

As rabbis, priests, and imams, our primary work is to minister to the members of our respective faith communities, and that certainly took the lion's share of my father's time and energy. Most of his interfaith work was in speeches he gave and in participation in ecumenical meetings, leaving little time for published works.

An important friendship and venue for my father's interfaith contribution was the Dallas-based Thanks-Giving Square. My father visited an annual convening there since its inception in the 1960s, at the invitation of its president and founder Peter Stewart. My father and Peter Stewart deeply loved and respected each other, and Peter would always visit us and join the family for lunch or dinner whenever he visited New York. They believed that leaders from the various faith communities, standing together, making joint appearances and statements on their theological common grounds, played an important role in urging the members of their respective faith communities to befriend members of other faith communities and seek common ground.

Though a regular attendee, my father could not attend the Thanks-Giving meeting in 1990, as he was in Malaysia completing the end of his tenure as the first rector of the International Islamic University in Kuala Lumpur. He asked me to attend on his behalf. It is there that I first met Rabbi David Rosen.

Rabbi Rosen then impressed me as the most persuasively articulate, the most good-looking, the most artistically and musically talented rabbi I had ever known. With his artistic left hand, he sketched numerous amazing drawings of human and still life around us, and regaled us with his competent command of the piano on the premises. Little did I know then that our life paths would intertwine over the succeeding years in many ways that I could not have then imagined!

One particularly noteworthy occasion took place in 2001, when Rabbi Rosen invited me to join him and speak at the quarterly Board of Governors meeting of the American Jewish Committee on December 10, exactly ninety days after the fateful day of 9/11. This was another time when being an Arab and a Muslim in New York was about as unpopular as it could possibly be. It was a great surprise for me to see how graciously the board members welcomed my presence that day and expressed their sincere desire to have better and improved personal and institutional relations with Muslims and Muslim organizations in the United States.

These life experiences taught me how important it was, during times of tensions and crisis between faith communities, that faith leaders make an even more concerted effort to channel the divine commandment and mandate to love one another as we love ourselves, to calm down the passionate emotions of the day that arouse and stir our human sentiments against each other.

Rabbi Rosen's personal attributes are what make him an exceptional rabbi. One has to have a sensitive ear to respond appropriately to the divine call to "Hear, O Israel . . . !" in its multiple biblical occurrences, a call that reverberates as powerfully to Muslims, who derive great pleasure from hearing God when the Qur'an is recited by an artistic reciter with a beautiful voice. It takes an artistic appreciation of beauty to sketch and verbally articulate God's beauty and power to admiring congregations, like his namesake the Prophet David did in singing God's praises accompanied by his harp, the ancestor of the modern piano.

Throughout the past three decades, Rabbi Rosen and I developed a personal and professional friendship that manifested itself in joint appearances at multiple venues, from interfaith events at academic institutions to the annual meetings at the World Economic Forum, where after 9/11 a special initiative was launched to improve West-Muslim world relations. We also worked together in attempting to normalize relations between Israel and a couple of Muslim majority nations, in cooperation with the late Shimon Peres, an effort that faced enormous political headwinds.

Although we did not succeed in the attempt as we would have liked, I have always believed that the attainment of such objectives is analogous to chopping down a tree with an axe. It takes many continuing swings until that last particular swing that fells the tree. Until then, the effort must continue, often with other players who will continue our efforts, much as we ourselves continue the efforts of our predecessors.

I have been deeply shaped by my father and his approach to relations with members of other faiths. My father's friendly relationships with non-Muslims impacted me personally, in that they urged me to befriend people of all faiths and all races. When I was appointed imam of Masjid al-Farah, I too welcomed the opportunity to interact with leaders of other faith communities, especially the Christian and Jewish communities who were the majority in New York City.

Moreover, I have followed in his footsteps by becoming a scholar-imam who not only writes about religion in a way that meets the rigors of academia but speaks at the same time in the public interest, meeting the spiritual imperatives of our time. My father taught me the saying of the Prophet Muhammad's cousin that we have to bring up our children for a time different from our own—which meant that I had to deal with circumstances different from my father's, yet maintaining the perennial teachings and values of our faith.

Personal friendships have been the foundation of my work across religions. I consider myself blessed to have had meaningful friendships with Jews, Christians, Hindus, Buddhists, and others. For all the importance of our mutual collaboration and following in the footsteps of my father, the most foundational aspect of my relationship with David Rosen is ultimately the fact that we are friends. We have broken bread together. From that foundation of friendship, we share the quest of being relevant to the needs of our communities and to the specifics of our time. Jointly, we strive to build a future in which our faith communities will thrive together in peace.

Rabbi Wolfe Kelman[399]

Rabbi Naamah Kelman and

Rabbi Levi Weiman-Kelman

WHAT AN HONOR TO write about our interfaith hero, our father. Rabbi Wolfe Kelman z"l[400] was in the first generation of rabbis involved in interfaith dialogue. As Abraham Joshua Heschel's confidante and advocate, he sat right behind the front seat of history. He crossed the Petrie Bridge in Alabama in 1965, marching behind Heschel and Martin Luther King Jr. and was behind the scenes of the historic breakthroughs with the Vatican. In our home, Pope John XXIII and the Rev. Dr. Martin Luther King Jr. were heroes. But Wolfe Kelman did not only walk in Heschel's shadow; he cast his own.

Wolfe was active in dialogues as Vice President of the Rabbinical Assembly of the Conservative Movement, through the efforts of the American Jewish Committee. His local Upper West Side involvement with co-religionists such as Rev. Dean Jim Morton of the Cathedral of St. John the Divine made him a respected leader. He spoke fondly of his various connection with cardinals in New York and Rome, particularly Cardinal Bea.

At our Shabbat table, on a regular basis, you might find a Catholic priest or a Protestant minister. As a scion of a Chasidic dynasty and many generations of rabbis, our father saw the divine spark in every single human being; when and where he could, he would light that spark to teach, guide, support, hold. His security in his identity as a Jew allowed him to open his heart and his home—our home—to the other, often to the widow, the orphan, and the stranger.

Wolfe lost his father at age thirteen, and his revered mother remained a widow her entire life. So he had a special bond, an obligation to widows, orphans, and strangers his entire life. Born in Eastern Europe, he emigrated to Canada as a boy, served in the Royal Canadian Air Force during World War II, and moved to the US after the war. He arrived at the Jewish Theological Seminary in 1945 and never left until his death in 1990. Those post-war years were full of optimism and change. The interfaith movement was born with the civil rights movement. Our father's commitment to equality and justice was fueled by his deep Jewish belief and practices. Unlike Orthodoxy at that time, he embraced dialogue. He even forgave those co-religionists of other faiths who turned out to have been born Jewish.

We have a fond memory of our father coming home and sharing the fact that in his recent dialogue encounter, the priest was a former Jew, the minister a former Jew, and the Buddhist a former Jew. While the Jewish establishment shunned these connections, our father found it amusing and inevitable. "Where is the interfaith dialogue in this encounter?" he laughed—and yet he showed up. Of course, many encounters involved Christians from birth. Here, too, he brought the wonderful combination of his Chasidic legacy, Canadian civility, and American know-how.

He loved to attend Christmas Mass, usually at the Cathedral of St. John the Divine, where his friend Dean Jim Morton presided. "I celebrate the birth of a Jew," he said, "but Easter is a different story." Levi remembers that every December 24th, my father brought me along as he and Rabbi Heschel attended midnight Mass at St. John the Divine. It was late, and I quickly fell asleep on my father's lap. Only as an adult did I realize how challenging it was for these two Galitzianer Hassidim to make this gesture of respect and even love to Jim Morton, dean of the cathedral. When it came time for communion, we quietly slipped out.

We grew up singing the hymn "Amazing Grace" at our Friday night table, not just when Christian guests were present. Wolfe learned this hymn through his involvement in the civil rights movement. He believed that this hymn was deeply religious and universal and did not mention Jesus. Every Seder after he marched in Selma, we sang "We Shall Overcome" in a Hebrew version. Those songs were our *zemirot*, ritual songs sung at the festive Shabbat table, following our family's custom.

Our father's private and public practice was to be inclusive, emphasizing what we share. He often said: "Unity and not uniformity." This was especially relevant when talking about Jews. He used this approach when attending political meetings in Israel with Orthodox and Ultra-Orthodox rabbis. He was passionate about finding the common ground, but when he could not, he would hold his own ground.

Breaking out of his sheltered childhood in Toronto, life in the big city of New York and particularly on the Upper West Side was like an endless, joyous parade of intellectuals, clergy, activists, seekers, writers, and singers, so many of them finding shelter, food for thought, and food to eat in our home. The festival of ideas, opinions, and insights was breathtaking but always accompanied by humility and humor. Our father or usually our mother could smell a phony from miles away. Wolfe took other humans seriously but warned us never to take ourselves too seriously.

He detested ultimate black-and-white truths. He often said, "Simple truths are either/or; profound truths are either *and* or." We were taught to hold multiple ideas in our head but remain faithful to our deepest values.

There is the well-worn story of the rabbi trying to mediate a squabble, where he told each side: You are right. The rabbi's wife intervened: How can they both be right? The rabbi responded: You, too, are also right.

That was not our father. Even though he had the capacity to hold multiple perspectives in balance, he still had the ability to take sides and in particular to see the angle of the oppressed and the downtrodden. The story that fits him better is the Chasidic tale, where a rabbi comforts the "one who was not right." In interfaith dialogue, this is essential. Wolfe could listen with great compassion to those with whom he did not agree, never wavering in his own beliefs. He had a remarkable ability to hold perspectives in balance, seeking truth, an appreciative view of the other, and especially practical care for the other in terms of social activism. In the framework of interfaith dialogue, this amounted to an application of the rabbinic call (Avot 1,2) to practice Torah (representing truth) with *avodah* (service) and *gemilut chassadim* (charitable actions, representing commitment to social justice).

In his capacity as Executive Vice President of the Rabbinical Assembly, Wolfe Kelman was an active member of IJCIC (International Jewish Committee for Interreligious Consultations).[401] He often went to Europe for interfaith meetings. While Heschel became very involved in the anti-war movement that involved clergy, our father avoided such engagement. In his professional role, he determined that he could not take certain political stands publicly. Unlike his beloved mentor and teacher, as a representative of a rabbinical organization, he could not take public stands on political matters like the Vietnam war. He never stopped his children from going to anti-war rallies. The two authors of this piece, his children, have taken different stands on this issue, as we shall presently describe.

In the 1970's, through his connection with Heschel, our father met Jacob Teshima. Jacob was born to Abraham Teshima, who had founded the Makuya Movement in Japan sometime after World War II. With the defeat of Japan and the aftermath of the atomic bombs on Hiroshima-Nagasaki, a number of new religious movements were born. Abraham founded a Christian sect that combined aspects of Shintoism, Buddhism, and some Judeo-Christian ideas, creating a substantial following with deep connections to Israel. Abraham sent his oldest son and heir apparent to Israel to learn Hebrew and the Bible in the late 60s. In Israel, Jacob discovered Jewish thought and the study of Jewish mysticism. Hence, he decided to move to NYC to pursue a doctorate with Heschel. Jacob became a *ben-bayit*, a member of the family, in our home. He was joined by his wife and his growing family. In 1974, our father was invited to visit Jacob in Japan and meet with the leadership and followers of Makuyah. One highlight of this trip was his spontaneous decision to join an ecstatic prayer service and walk on burning coals. Reciting the mantra "Yah Ribon" (God is our Sovereign) as he quickly made his way across, he shared that he didn't feel anything until he noticed that it wasn't that bad. Then it hurt. This act of respect and affirmation was typical. He did not participate in any service that contradicted his faith, but if he felt that he could support another without comprising his own, then why not? As if burning coals were not enough, he also found himself under a freezing waterfall. This was Wolfe Kelman, celebrating others celebrating God.

Wolfe sought to light the divine spark in every human being. This came directly from his Chasidic background, which he expanded to other religions. He loved humanity with all its weaknesses and foibles. On the one hand, he was the descendant of Chasidic Rhyschizer nobility; on the other hand, he was also a refugee. He came to Canada as a child, his family escaping poverty and persecution. He never forgot the support and openness of Canada and, later, the opportunities that America afforded him. "For you were a soujourner in the land of Egypt" (Deut. 10:19). He was forever indebted and wanted to offer everyone, regardless of race, religion, and eventually gender, the opportunities of equality.

In 1990, a month before our father died, Levi was privileged to accompany our father (who was in ill health) to Rome as he participated in a meeting of IJCIC. The sheer joy that he took in these meetings and the respect he showed for the Jews and Christians who pioneered interfaith dialogue continues to inspire us.

Each one of us carried on our father's interfaith vision and engagement in a different manner. Here it is best that each one of us speak for himself or herself.

Levi: I took my father's commitment to interfaith a bit further. While in rabbinical school, I spent significant periods of time in Christian monasteries (especial the unique Taizé, an ecumenical community in France), Hindu ashrams (led by Swami Satchidananda), Sufi communities (with Pir Vilayat Inayat Khan), and Buddhist centers (Chögyam Trungpa Rinpoche). I have maintained a close relationship with the brothers at Taizé. Being a congregational rabbi has allowed me to express my commitment to interfaith work in a variety of ways. At my congregation in Jerusalem, Kol HaNeshama, we end every service with a Jewish prayer for *shalom* (peace), but we add a line from a Muslim prayer for *salaam*. Whenever visiting clergy are present, I ask them to lead us in a prayer for peace from their own traditions. Christians studying for the ministry or the priesthood often find their way to my congregation, and I have been blessed to develop close ties to a community of Augustinian monks from Würzburg, Germany. I also had the honor of being a founding member of an international group of religious leaders committed to peace work.

Naamah: In 1992, I attended my first interfaith conference in Japan. There I met Rev. Hans Ucko of the World Council of Churches, who became instrumental in my involvement in dialogue for the following twenty years or so. Through him, I ended up participating in interfaith activities all over the world: Switzerland, India, South Africa, and more, for meetings with representative of many faiths. I was often the first woman clergy/rabbi that attendees met. I was involved in bringing this dialogue to Palestinian Christians in Israel, through the work of Rabbi Ron Kronish. As I moved up the leadership ladder at Hebrew Union College, where I now serve as dean, I became less available to travel. I also wanted to encourage younger women clergy to take invitations sent to me. Of particular importance is the incorporation of interfaith work into the programs and curricula at Hebrew Union College. Regarding our program with Christian and Muslim teachers, the Teachers' Room, now in its sixth year, has impacted over 240 teachers. We are presently working with seventy-five additional teachers to change the nature of dialogue and understanding of the other in Jerusalem. In 2000, we began work in the emerging field of spiritual care. We have been training Jews and Christians in pastoral care. Based on our experience, we have developed tools that we consider could serve the Israeli-Palestinian conflict by sharing narrative. With the Rossing Center and the Holy Land Trust, we created a program called Healing Hatred.

I am deeply proud of the initiative of my staff, which created a prayer room for all faiths on our campus. I believe we are the only institution in Jerusalem that has such a space to serve the growing numbers of staff and students who are Muslim and Christian.

We are proud to be second-generation interfaith partners and even prouder that some of our children are third-generation. Rabbi David Rosen, scion of a distinguished rabbinic family, like our father, embodies the same ease and self-confidence in his identity, making dialogue and conversation a place of mutual respect, often seasoned with humor and warmth. David, like our father, speaks with great intelligence, based on deep Torah knowledge. Both are memorable public speakers filled with wit and clarity. David is a calming presence but can be clear and firm when necessary. Whereas David might look for a piano to play when tensions rise in dialogue, our father would have hummed a *niggun* or told a story. Like our father, David has nurtured his next generation to uphold a beacon of light and hope in this broken world.

Rabbi Mickey (Michael) Rosen

Rabbi Shlomo Dov Rosen

It is a great privilege for me to write about my father, the late Rabbi Dr. Mickey (Michael) Rosen, and his interreligious engagement, in a book that honors his brother, Rabbi David Rosen. In what follows, I shall attempt to spell out an orientation towards interfaith engagement that I associate with my father and that may seem striking and unconventional. I believe this orientation speaks of him and that its roots can be traced to my grandfather, the father of both my father and his brother David Rosen, the celebrated English rabbi Yaakov Kopul Rosen. It is an orientation with which I also find affinity in my own work.

Rabbi Mickey Rosen: A Spiritual Orientation

In that spirit, I would like to begin with a citation in which my father references my grandfather:

> "My father used to say that, throughout the Bible, the image of the righteous person is that of the tree. The meaning of this is that that even though the roots are circumscribed to one particular place, the branches and the shade the tree affords extend to a great distance. This is a metaphor for education. A person who is deeply rooted and who has strong positive identity has the ability to forge relations with the other and to impact his surroundings . . ."

> However, today, it is not easy for me to simply repeat his idea. I would, in the first instance, draw a distinction between a positive identity that is accompanied by humility and one that is accompanied by a sense of triumph. We witness people who are deeply rooted, who are well educated, yet they are totally self-absorbed in their narcissistic self-justification.

We should not act self-confidently, simply relying on the
force of Torah. Rather, we must engage in interior reflection,
without which we will readily be drawn into temptation.[402]

This passage sums up key features of who my father was. He continues the teachings of his own father, profiling what is most urgent and vital to
him—a vision of social justice that emanates from a spiritual interiority.

This interiority, a spiritual grounding deep within oneself and
in relationship to God, is key to forming an attitude to the other. This
perspective runs as a leitmotif in my father's work, in its various expressions—spiritual, pedagogic, institutional, and reflective. Several passages
from his book *The Quest for Authenticity* spell out this orientation.[403]
Even though they were articulated with reference to the hero of this work,
Rabbi Simcha Bunim of Przysucha, they speak as much of the author of
these lines as they do of the hero he describes.

For a person to embark on a path of truthfulness requires not only the
analytical demand for self-criticism but the spiritual acumen to recognize
that there is a spark of the Divine within each person.[404]

The ability to combine passion with self-analysis is rare. On the whole,
passion by its very nature operates as an emotional totality, usually commit-
ting the person to one uncompromising particular point of view, whereas
the ability to be self-analytic comes with a certain hesitancy, an ability to see
different aspects of the situation.[405]

For Przysucha, equanimity meant that a human being could be so
attuned, focused, and centered on God's presence that whatever happens
to the person does not fundamentally disturb that focus. It is the stage a
person reaches in which the reality of God puts everything else into perspective. Equanimity is thus the hallmark of someone who is there, who
has reached the point of authenticity. This has consequent implications
for the way he relates to society. With equanimity, one can easily come
to a lack of concern for what other people think of you. Or, to put it another way, someone who has touched his inner core can develop a sense of
self-confidence outside the theater of public ego massage, in which other
people's approval is of no major consequence.[406]

Taking our cue from these citations, we may appreciate how my father
applied this vision to his engagement with other faiths. I would characterize my father's attitude to other religions as a kind of religious colorblindness. By that, I mean that many distinctions that are crucial for others did
not meaningfully exist for him or did not matter and that my father had
the capacity to see beyond the conventions of public opinion and the differences it profiled. The colorblindness to which I refer is the source of a

new vision. Disengagement from non-intrinsic hurdles and background noise frees one to see spiritual value in others. It is a condition in which a deeply religious person ignores distractions and, as a consequence, is able to identify and connect with the spiritual in other religious people. Both of these features come from the same source of internal depth, whence one might draw spiritual insight.

My father's singular perspective and interfaith contribution was perhaps in this very sense of equanimity of which he speaks in the citations above. Making a non-issue out of an issue, a mere mirage out of a surging sea gushing with ancient sea monsters, involves more than courage and activism. It requires a certain kind of disengagement from deep-seated distractions. This was the product of a fundamentally religious mode of existence, a deep interior grounding in the spiritual universe that he inhabited. It is such disengagement that I refer to as a kind of religious colorblindness, in which one does not even see that which others find compellingly forbidding.

His involvement with Archbishop Desmond Tutu is a case in point. In 1986, he invited Tutu to speak at Yakar in England (he later came to speak in Jerusalem, in 1999). The sight of a bishop talking in an Orthodox synagogue is far from common and should not be taken for granted. On the communal side, it involved a period of preparation, and on the archbishop's side, the symbolic and considerate gesture of tucking his pectoral cross into his cassock. Primarily, it required a rabbi who engaged reality from a somewhat purist spiritual and ethical perspective, rather than thinking in terms of typical communal norms and the political and theological distractions that forge those norms. Here is how my father communicated the importance of the moment:

> Why is Yakar going to such lengths in its involvement with the campaigns against apartheid and racism? Simply because the Jew has no monopoly on suffering or persecution. He may have suffered more than any other people. He has definitely been persecuted more consistently than any other people. But the question remains: what does *he* do with that experience? Is he to turn inwards, to become so insular as to be unconcerned with any racist experience other than his own? . . . There is an alternative reaction, and that is to *use* our experience, to follow the injunction in the Torah that appears more often than any other: "You shall love the stranger because *you* were strangers in the land of Egypt."

My father's vision was at one and the same time deeply spiritual and deeply engaged in terms of its social consequences. This found expression in the institution he founded and in the activities he carried out. To these I now turn.

Yakar as an Instrument of Interfaith Work

My father founded the Yakar Institute in memory of his own father (YaKaR is the acronym of Yaakov Kopul Rosen), first in London (1978), then in Jerusalem (1991), and finally in Tel Aviv (2007—run today by my brother, Rabbi Chananel). Yakar has always been, from the very outset, an educational institution, synagogue, and cultural center, all wrapped into one. A central aim of my father was to engage social and cultural issues from a religious perspective. Sometimes the issues were political. Whether concerning the PLO, Northern Ireland, or apartheid in South Africa, current affairs were debated within a synagogue by religious Jews, as religious Jews.

In 1997, several years after founding the Yakar Institute in Jerusalem, my father invited Benjamin Pogrund to run within it a Center for Social Concern. The center became a hub for engaging other religions and cultures. Yakar did groundbreaking work with Muslim and Jewish educators. Meetings with Muslims eventually matured into a Beit Midrash-Madrasa program at Yakar, bringing together educators from both religions. In addition, public events were held on comparative perspectives of Islam and Judaism. The range of topics discussed reflects the deep-seated conviction that religion, spirituality, and ethics are all one. Topics included conflict resolution, the other, repentance, fundamentalism, women in law, art in religion, the end of days, the love of God, peace, holy sites, freedom, pluralism and chosenness, teaching non-violence, Judaism and Islam, Hinduism and Judaism (the roots of dialogue), art in Islam and Judaism, mysticism and its significance, and more. The educators' Beit Midrash also included a Christian component. And Christianity naturally featured in the public meetings, particularly concerning the perspective of each religion on the other. The public events provided platforms for various exceptional leaders, Muslim and Jewish, who were involved in groundbreaking work. It was also a way for the public to hear analyses from innovative leaders doing interfaith. Unsurprisingly, David Rosen was a speaker on several occasions at these events.

I do not think that, for my father, interfaith engagement was an aim in itself. Rather, he was invested in spiritual and ethical endeavors, and it was only natural to engage that spirituality in others and to work with members of other faiths over ethical issues, including towards mutual understanding. What I call religious colorblindness describes that spiritual place where irrelevant distinctions do not feature, which enables one to engage with members of other faiths and religions naturally, to further the spiritual and ethical aims that one has in common. It is, furthermore, an internal place, in which the very distinctions between spirituality, ethics, and the arts, also do not feature. This seamlessness is evident from the above list of topics that featured in events at Yakar as part of my father's interfaith work.

The Legacy of Rabbi Kopul Rosen

In contemplating my father's personality and spiritual grounding and answering what enabled him to be so different to many others in these ways, we must trace a line back to my grandfather. My father's guiding light in most things was his own father, who was, by all accounts, somewhat larger than life. It would seem that my grandfather had little care for mediocracy or for how the things one should do would be received by the general public. Although he passed away in the early 60s, and I grew up on his knees only figuratively, my grandfather's exceptional personality always seems vivid. Remarkable charisma, creativity, and intelligence seem to have allowed him to get away with creating colossal institutional innovations, making a real mark on the world, even if Providence recalled his star before its jubilee on earth.

Rabbi Dr. Kopul Rosen was born in 1913, in Notting Hill, London, not long after his parents arrived in England from Poland. He found himself speaking publicly and teaching from a young age, and after being sent to pre-war Eastern Europe to study, he returned to England to take up a series of rabbinical posts. (My father was born in Glasgow in 1945, when his father was rabbi there.) Communal rabbinics, however, seems to have proved too narrow and constricting for my grandfather. After a few wider national offices (principle rabbi of the Federation of Synagogues, head of the Mizrachi in England), he threw himself into the creation of Carmel College, which he founded and ran until his untimely passing, at age forty-eight, from leukemia (when my father was seventeen years old and David eleven).

Carmel College was a boarding high school, modeled on both the English tradition of refined and elite education and Jewish values of study and religious life. It was also a microcosm for my grandfather to create a mode of Jewish living that could truly contribute to the world. For that reason, the openness to interreligious interaction and natural meetings between Jews and gentiles on campus must have had an amplified effect on all and presumably left a pivotal impression on his children. The oldest of the siblings, my uncle Rabbi Jeremy Rosen, recalls this period:

> Soon after, my father severed his ties with community institutions and the family moved out into the English countryside, where our Jewish life revolved entirely around the school. It was clear to us all that he was delighted to be independent and able to create just the sort of dynamic intellectually open and vibrantly orthodox atmosphere outside of the community, without having to be accountable to anyone. He made us all aware of his distaste for communal institutions and hierarchies.
>
> The campus welcomed both Jewish and non-Jewish thinkers, scholars, artists, and musicians. Regular visitors were clerics such as Reverend Witton-Davies, the archdeacon of Oxford, and Reverend James Parkes, who devoted his life to Jewish-Christian reconciliation. Academics such as Alan Bullock and Isaiah Berlin rubbed shoulders with Israeli scholars and cultural icons. Discussion was open and often critical of all aspects of Western society. My father's library included the works of Rabindranath Tagore and Swami Vivekananda, alongside Chaim Moshe Luzzatto, the Tanya, Rav Kook, and Rav Dessler. This ecumenical, independent, and critical atmosphere was how we were brought up: to be open to the world and to difference. It was in this idyllic atmosphere on the banks of the River Thames in Oxfordshire that we were brought up. It came naturally to us therefore to feel unfettered by conventional attitudes, both to religion and prejudices.

While my grandfather's involvement in interreligious dialogue may not have taken on institutional dimensions, it was presumably an important feature of his person and was based on cultivating meaningful personal relationships. It is therefore no surprise that all three of his rabbinical sons have done serious work in the arena of interfaith. As in other arenas, each of the men seems to have appropriated, carried forth, and developed elements of his father's nature in his own particular creative manner. Their common context allows us to better comprehend the exceptional work of all three.

The Foundations of Religious Conviction

With my father, as presumably with his own also, when common perceptions were deemed unreflective, one could distinguish a sliver of zest in his allowing his convictions to guide him against the current. I once made the fatal mistake of asserting to my father that something he was doing was totally unaccepted in most religious circles. He took no time to make it perfectly plain to me that I would do better with any other argument. Again and again my father would recite in his sermons the couplet from Yeats's "The Second Coming":

> The best lack all conviction, while the worst
> Are full of passionate intensity.

Yet to what did this ideology lead? A religious colorblindness. An anti-climax of normalizing the impossible, as if it were taken for granted. How? My argument is that the secret ingredient often lacking in charismatic ideologues is the internal anchoring and directedness that comes from religious spiritual-ity. This would seem to be something he learned from his father.

As with his father, an almost obsessive preoccupation with global issues of moral import combined in my father with intense investment in spiritual internalization, prayer, and soulful singing. If, for some of his congregants, his fiery sermons on social justice clashed with and even marred the soulful prayer service he led, for him, it was all one. Spiritual interiority guides one to trust in God and gives space for a certain qui-etude in the throes of moral excitement. This interiority is precisely what enabled his ideology to bring him to this religious colorblindness, where distinctions that entrap others simply do not feature.

For this reason, my father's mode of religious work must necessarily be the outcome of maturity, both spiritual and intellectual. Internal and authentic religious anchoring and an appreciation of complexit require maturity and development. This was true not only of my father's work with members of other religions but of his educational endeavors. He would open groundbreaking projects, team up with unexpected people, and often go out on a limb. It was often not easy, growing up, to identify with what my father was doing. That was part of the nature of his own spiritual place and the way he educated. Once, presumably when I was in my early twenties, my father remarked to me:

> I would not have agreed with what I now do at your age. I would
> be very suspect of anyone your age who would agree with what
> I do.

I no longer remember to what my father was referring at the time, but it makes little difference. Many of the projects he began and which he struggled to move forward were copied by others, or otherwise became the norm some time later. It is not simply that he was ahead of his time.

More fundamentally, such is the fate of those with an internal compass, creativity, and audacity.

This theme of requiring time to grow into a mode of behavior was an integral part of our education, and it is coupled with the idea that this growth should eventually unite one with creative actors of old. These are hallmarks of authenticity within a lived tradition. Of course, there is deep spiritual comfort in finding that one's own mature and personally authentic journey coalesces with that of one's predecessors. I think this was very important for my father and part of what enabled him to be both so traditional and so creatively audacious. My father loved to tell a Chassidic story, the punchline of which is an old man recounting to a young Chassidic master a message from a previous master. The old man recounts that, as a child, he had witnessed a master of a previous generation doing the exact same thing as the younger master later did, and that the old man, when a child, had been told by the earlier master that one day a future master would come and do just as he had done. The old man recalled that he was told those many years earlier: "Tell him, 'I was here before you.'"

Rabbi David Rosen:
The Making of an Interfaith Hero

SHARON ROSEN

MY HUSBAND AND LIFE partner, David Rosen, always claims that his passion for interfaith was born out of his religious commitment to social justice. I can vouch for that. Both immigrants to Israel from Britain, we met in Jerusalem during the winter of 1972 when David was twenty-one and a rabbi serving as an army chaplain down at the Suez Canal, which, at that time, was Israel's border with Egypt. His trademark eloquence already evident, a gift inherited from his illustrious father Rabbi Kopul Rosen, David dazzled me with his belief in God as a divine, positive force in the world and with Judaism's essential beauty—so much so that we were engaged to be married a few weeks later. But I have no recollection of us talking about other religions or the world of interfaith until we found ourselves in Cape Town in 1975.

South Africa: The Birth of a Passion

As fate would have it, David was appointed in January 1975 as rabbi to the Green and Sea Point Hebrew Congregation, the largest Orthodox Jewish congregation in South Africa and possibly the world. At that time, in the halcyon days of Cape Town's Jewish community, the congregation was approximately two thousand families strong, located in a city famed for its beauty on the one hand and steeped in the ugliness of apartheid on the other. The race laws and their accompanying discrimination against people who were not lily white were at their height, and I remember us contemplating how we could possibly remain in a country whose laws were so clearly inimical to religious teachings and to our values in general. The biblical message that all human beings are created in the divine image and the call to love one's neighbor as oneself was totally contrary to what we were experiencing there, where love, care, and compassion seemed limited to one's own parochial community.

David thought long and hard about how he could use the highly influential position in which he found himself to make a difference, not only within his own congregation but in society as a whole. While the Cape Jewish community was racially homogenous, other religions did cross racial and ethnic divides. He decided that if one could build interfaith bridges across Christianity, Islam, and Judaism in the Cape, this could provide an opportunity to meet people of different races on an even footing. By getting to know one another, barriers would be broken down, ignorance and misperceptions dispelled, bigotry combatted, and trust built. David, then and now, believes in the power of relationship building as the key to reducing prejudice.

Using his enthusiasm and powers of persuasion, David met with priests, pastors, imams, and other rabbis in Cape Town and presented the following message: despite our differences, the things that bring us together—profound values like our belief in God, holiness, and compassion—are so much more important than the things that keep us apart. It is our responsibility to work together for the benefit of our communities so that we can become more than our separate parts. Generally, the message worked, and David thus became a pioneer of interfaith relations, founding and chairing the Cape Inter-Faith Forum: Council of Jews, Christians and Muslims (now the Cape Town Interfaith Intitiative) in 1976, at a time when interreligious gatherings of religious leadership were few and far between in the world at large, let alone in the Cape, South Africa. In time, the members of the forum became both professional colleagues and dear friends whom we often hosted in our home.

David loves to tell the story of his first encounter with a dominee (minister) from the Dutch Reformed Church of South Africa, familiarly known as "the Nationalist Party at prayer" by those who condemned the Church's justification of apartheid and support for the ruling National Party. David had made an appointment to meet with the dominee in the hope that he too could be persuaded to join the Cape Inter-Faith Forum. David had heard that the dominee was meeting with Catholics, which, at that time in ecumenically divided South Africa, was considered almost as dangerous as fraternizing with people across the color bar; so he thought he might be a likely candidate for the forum. David acknowledges that interfaith relationship building cannot be limited only to the people with whom one feels comfortable. Changing attitudes leading to transformation often takes place among the most unlikely of people and in the most unlikely of circumstances.

The dominee listened to David's spiel about how the things that bring us together are so much more important than the things that keep us apart, after which he retorted in a strong Afrikaans accent, "But that is not true, the most important thing in my life keeps us apart—the fact that you do not believe in our Savior, the Lord Jesus, and for that you will go to hell! I must save you from that fate!" With surprising presence of mind, David told the dominee that if he wanted to save him, then the forum was a perfect place to acquaint himself with Jewish beliefs in order to better understand the devil for the purpose of conversion. The dominee did join the forum, listened, learned, engaged in dialogue, and became more open to different beliefs and attitudes. He proved that the process works.

David also learned how ignorant he was of other religions and what an enriching experience multifaith encounters were for him. He says, "I was stunned to discover how ignorant other religious leaders were about me and my heritage, yet I reflected that I was part of the problem too, as I didn't know them and had all kinds of misconceptions. To be represented correctly, I would need to represent them correctly myself, and I knew, with shared values, we all had an obligation to work together to celebrate the greater sum of our different parts." He found this process deeply enriching.

Interfaith meetings also deepened his understanding and love of his own religion. It made him consider, to put it anthropomorphically, why God had created such a variety of religions on earth. What is the significance and meaning of this for the world? David came to the conclusion that if the omnipresent All-Knowing creates and guides us in all our diversity, and that we are all created in the divine image, then that richness of diversity is part of what constitutes godliness. Moreover, how can God be encapsulated into one religious form and system, when that Omnipresence is beyond time and human matter? The conclusion for David was that the divine presence wants humankind to serve him in diverse ways, so long as by doing so we hold to a common moral standard. When people of faith meet with others in their fullness and belief in the one moral God, then in fact that meeting is a reflection of the divine presence itself.

Almost invariably, in the extraordinary number of speeches and presentations David has given over the years on what is a successful prescription for interfaith dialogue, he has invoked the three cardinal principles advocated by Lutheran Bishop Krister Stendahl, who died in 2008. Bishop Stendahl, whom David personally met several times after his election as bishop of Stockholm in 1984, said the following, according to David's recollection:

- Seek to understand the other the way she or he understands herself or himself (and not as you would interpret the other);

- Always view the other community by the best in them and not the worst;

- Leave room for holy envy. By this, Bishop Stendahl meant that you must not assume that aspects of another religious faith you admire must necessarily also be found in your own tradition.

All three principles reinforce the values and actions that David has sought to bring to interfaith dialogue: listen, learn, connect, discuss, understand, respect, admire, share. In this way, the process becomes a source of inspiration, blessing, and collaboration for the purpose of what Jews call *Kiddush Hashem*—praising God's name in the world.

Interfaith dialogue did enable David to cross the color bar in South Africa, but it was viewed with suspicion by the powers that be. I remember a march taking place in Cape Town in the aftermath of the 1976 Soweto Uprising, which had resulted in hundreds of men, women, and children being killed by the South African police. Courageous religious leaders involved in the Inter-Faith Forum, like the Anglican dean of Cape Town, Edward (Ted) King, led their mixed-race communities through the streets of the city in protest against police brutality. David was there, too, but knew that his white congregation, who were generally rather nervous, if not fearful, of his outspokenness gave him some protection from the more deadly actions of white nationalists.

Nevertheless, we realized it was time to leave Cape Town in July 1979 after we discovered that our home phone was being tapped, we had received anonymous death threats targeting our children, and our temporary work visas were not renewed. Looking back on those years today and seeing the flourishing of interfaith activities in Cape Town, a city that now strives for egalitarianism, David can be proud that he had some hand in getting the ball rolling.

Ireland: A Jewish-Christian Romance

By November 1979 we were ensconced in Dublin, Ireland, where David had accepted the position as chief rabbi. The Jewish community was small but vibrant, with several synagogues, over sixty organizations, and a Jewish school covering the gamut of ages from kindergarten to university. One of the more exciting aspects of David's role was that it had national stature, as the position was enshrined in the Irish Constitution as fifth in state after the president of Ireland and the various Catholic and Anglican primates. David often quotes a predecessor in the role, Lord Immanuel Jakobovits, the second chief rabbi of Ireland, that 95% of the Irish population were Catholics, 5% were Protestants, and he was chief rabbi of the rest! However, despite the size of the Jewish community, David enjoyed a high profile among the wider population, with official broadcasts twice a year on state television for the Jewish holidays, as well as regular appearances on numerous popular talk shows. He received hundreds of letters, mostly from Christians, thanking him for his TV messages and asking him for texts. He also had official roles to play in national ceremonies, such as the induction of the newly elected president of Ireland, which took place during our tenure, and in the annual St. Patrick's Day parade in Dublin.

Ireland was a highly religious country when we lived there. It had joined the European Economic Community (EEC) in the early 1970s, from which it was benefitting economically, but it had a conservative and very traditional feel to it, and the Church was still powerful. Six weeks before our arrival, Pope John Paul II had visited Ireland, the first trip of any pope to the country. More than one third of the Irish population poured into Phoenix Park, Dublin, for the public Mass that took place there. I remember one of the activities we played with our young children on our thirty-minute walk to and from synagogue on wintry Sabbath mornings in December was to count the number of Christmas trees in the front windows of houses. There was rarely a house without one—and we knew the ones that did not were Jewish. Catholic society was more likely to admire and trust a Jew who practiced the laws of her or his faith than one who had eschewed them. Thus, we received a warm welcome on our arrival and a society ripe for interfaith activities.

Soon after our arrival, we were invited to the state National Theatre to see a Seán O'Casey production of *Juno and the Paycock*. We hardly understood a word due to the actors' broad Dublin accents, but we were astonished and delighted to receive a warm welcome in perfect Hebrew from the Catholic archbishop of Dublin and primate of all Ireland, Rev. Dermot Ryan, whom we met for the first time during the play's intermission. Thus began a warm and collaborative relationship, which subsequently led to the establishment in 1981 of the Irish Council of Christians and Jews as a national member organization of the International Council of Christians and Jews (ICCJ) headquartered in the Martin Buber House, Heppenheim, Germany. At that time, Sir Sigmund Sternberg, a family friend, was president of the ICCJ and encouraged David's interest and involvement in interfaith in what became a lifelong mentorship until the former's death in 2016. David was also to become president of the ICCJ in later years.

David's interest in interfaith had by now developed into a passion, and he put his Cape Town experience to good use. He had observed firsthand the power of interfaith to build relationships, based on knowledge and trust, and personally experienced the enrichment of his own faith through the process. He knew that Jews and Christians in Ireland could benefit from this relationship; moreover, it could set a precedent for building stronger intrafaith as well as interfaith connections between religions in Ireland as a whole. While we were living in the south of the island in a relatively peaceful Republic of Ireland, we were constantly aware of the Troubles—the term given to the decades-long conflict between Protestants and Catholics over the border in Northern Ireland—that was taking the lives of thousands of people and which was at its worst during our sojourn there in the early 1980s.

In contrast to the Catholic and Anglican leadership whose responsibilities covered the populations both north and south of the border, officially the Chief Rabbinate of Ireland only had responsibilities for the Jewish community south of the border. There is an old joke told of a Belfast Jew who was held up at gunpoint by a man snarling, "Are you Catholic or Protestant!" The Jew tremblingly answers, "I'm Jewish," to which the man responds, "Well, are you a Catholic Jew or a Protestant Jew?" There is some truth to the joke, as Jews were divided by the border, with the Jews in Northern Ireland generally identifying with the Protestant majority and Jews south of the border identifying with the Catholic majority there. Nevertheless, for practical reasons, the Irish Chief Rabbinate did care for the needs of their northern Jewish neighbors, which resulted in frequent cross-border visits; so, to all intents and purposes, there was an opportunity once again for interfaith processes to be engaged in reducing conflict.

One Saturday afternoon during the height of the Troubles in 1981, when Margaret Thatcher was the UK prime minister and Catholic prisoners from the Irish Republican Army (IRA) in Belfast's infamous Maze Prison were on hunger strike in protest at the treatment they were receiving, the front doorbell of our home rang. Knowing it was not a member of the Jewish community, as they would not use the chief rabbi's electric doorbell on the Sabbath, David opened the door to find three burly Irishmen waiting on the porch. They recognized David. Seemingly surprised to directly connect with him at the front door without an intermediary, they introduced themselves as members of Sinn Féin (the so-called political arm of the IRA) and asked to speak with him. David invited them into our home and listened to their request.

They said that Bobby Sands was on the verge of death in Maze Prison and that they wanted to prevent this at all costs. They continued that if Catholic prisoners start dying, "all hell will break loose," and they asked David if he could use his position to prevent the catastrophe. They wanted him to get a message to Margaret Thatcher to pull back before they all fell over the precipice. When David asked why they had turned to him, one of the men answered in a strong Irish brogue, "Our Catholic leaders are no good, she won't listen to them; we're sure not going to the Protestants, so you're all that's left! We've also heard you and know you can bridge divides. Maybe you can do something here." David did try and reached out to the British Prime Minister through Immanuel Jakobovits, who was now the chief rabbi of the UK and the Commonwealth; but the "lady [was] not for turning," and, subsequently, ten of the hunger strikers died, which exacerbated the bitter conflict. Religious engagement can bridge divides, but one clear lesson is that it needs time and a process of trust building before there is any chance of success.

It took approximately a year for the developing bonds among Catholic, Protestant, and Jewish leaders to cement before David founded the Irish Council of Christians and Jews, the first interfaith organization ever to be established in Ireland. The inauguration was hosted by Archbishop Ryan in the archbishop's palace and included the Anglican archbishop, Primate of Ireland Henry McAdoo, senior members of the Jewish Representative Council of Ireland, and other Christian leaders. The first working meeting took place in Church of Ireland premises in September 1981, chaired by David. The goal of the council was to promote understanding and friendship between Christians and Jews. This was accomplished through various activities, including interfaith conferences and guest lectures to which the general public was also invited.

The council enjoyed a close collaboration with the Irish School of Ecumenics, originally founded by the Jesuit Fathers in Milltown, Dublin, but subsequently part of Trinity College Dublin. David became a member of its faculty. Together with Sr. Carmel Niland from the Sisters of our Lady of Sion, a deeply compassionate and caring woman in an extraordinary Catholic holy order working to heal Catholic-Jewish relations pursuant to the Second Vatican Council, they established and taught a post-graduate course on Jewish-Christian relations. David found himself marking doctoral theses on the subject of interfaith relations although, ironically, he himself had never gone to university. He had attended the English boarding school founded by his late father but had left before the end of his secondary schooling to study at a religious seminary in Jerusalem. After four years of religious study and then army service, we married and left immediately for South Africa, so David had not found time to study at university, with the result being that he is mostly an autodidact.

Through interfaith meetings locally and internationally, David met with senior Catholic leaders around the world and was invited to address interreligious gatherings, such as conferences held by the International

Jewish Committee for Interreligious Consultations (IJCIC), which was established as the official Jewish dialogue partner of the Pontifical Commission for Religious Relations with the Jews. Many years later, David was to become chairman of this committee.

Moreover, because there was no Israeli ambassador in situ at the time in Ireland, the chief rabbi not only represented the Jewish community but also served as a de facto representative of the State of Israel. As a result, David met with major international Jewish figures who sometimes visited Ireland on diplomatic issues. One such leader was Abraham Foxman, the national director of the powerful American Jewish organization the Anti-Defamation League (ADL). We struck up an instantly warm relationship with Abe and his wife Golda when we hosted them for a Shabbat meal in our Dublin home, which was to have future significance for David's career in general and in interfaith in particular. Abe invited David to be in contact when he left his position as chief rabbi.

Christian-Jewish Relations

Our five years in Dublin were interesting and fruitful, but we had promised ourselves when we left Israel that we would return to Jerusalem from the Jewish diaspora by the time our oldest child was ten years old. We kept to our word. We wanted our children to grow up as Israelis and experience the joy of Jewish life in their own homeland. We found ourselves in the first few days of 1985 in an absorption center in Jerusalem, unsure of what we were going to do or where we were going to live; but, within two months, David had been offered the position of dean of the Sapir Institute, an educational center in Jerusalem's Old City whose purpose was to introduce primarily Jewish secular youth to the Jewish library. At the same time, he contacted Abe Foxman, who serendipitously was looking for someone to work on interfaith relations based out of the ADL's Jerusalem office. The ADL has always placed great importance on interfaith relations as a route to reducing discrimination and had promoted Rabbi León Klenicki, an influential advocate on the topic, in 1984 as its director of interfaith relations in the US. David and León became the ADL's co-liaison to the Vatican and remained close colleagues until David left the ADL in 2001, after being offered a position as international director of interreligious affairs at the American Jewish Committee (AJC), a dream job, as he called it, which enabled him to focus exclusively on interfaith activities.

The position with the ADL afforded David the opportunity to continue his passion for interfaith professionally and to hone his expertise in

Catholic-Jewish relations. He maintained regular contact with the Pontifical Commission for Religious Relations with the Jews as a result of the ADL's prominent position in IJCIC and visited Rome at least once a year. With the help of his colleague and dear friend Lisa Palmieri-Billig, ADL's representative in Italy to the Holy See, David was introduced to Andrea Riccardi, who in 1968 founded, in the wake of the second Vatican Council, the heartwarming Catholic Sant'Egidio movement, which devotes itself to caring for the poor and working for peace. It is committed to pursuing the vision of Pope John Paul II's groundbreaking international, interfaith Prayer for Peace meeting in Assisi in 1986 and consequently focuses on international, interfaith peacemaking. Annually, Sant'Egidio holds an international, interfaith conference in a different country, which culminates in a highly moving candlelighting ceremony, where hundreds of leaders from different religions and countries congregate together to embrace and sign a declaration of peace. Over the years, these meetings have provided an opportunity for faith leaders to build profound bonds of trust leading to joint cooperation. David assisted Sant'Egidio in recruiting Jewish Israeli and other religious leaders for their events and became one of their principle Jewish representatives. Sant'Egidio leaders have visited Israel regularly over the decades and have joined us for many Shabbat meals in friendship, discussion, and song. Eating, singing, and practicing religious rituals together is a marvelous recipe for building long-lasting trust.

Lisa also introduced us to another exceptional, spiritual, Catholic movement that is dedicated to uniting the world in love. Founded during World War II by Chiara Lubich, whom we were privileged to know and also host for Shabbat in our home, the Focolare Movement now has over two million followers in 182 nations around the world, including Israel, all dedicated to a life of profound Catholic faith, while working to build diverse relationships based on dialogue and love. A woman is always elected head of the Focolare, signifying an important message from a religion known for its highly patriarchal leadership, and we are proud to count among our friends the recently elected head, Margaret Karam, its first Arab leader, who hails from Haifa, Israel's third largest city. The Focolare, too, hold international interfaith events. I remember well David and me singing Sabbath table hymns as a program item at one meeting in the Focolare retreat at Castel Gandolfo, outside Rome.

The first time (of many to follow) that David had a personal conversation with Pope John Paul II was at another Prayer for Peace vigil that the pontiff held in Assisi in January 1993, this time focusing on special prayers for a solution to the conflict in the Balkans. David was the main Jewish representative at the event and remembers the pope recounting to him his wartime experiences during World War II and his friendships with Jews in Poland. David had an experience there that he would never forget. The timing of the meeting meant that David needed to spend Shabbat in Assisi, so that he would not have to travel on the Sabbath itself. He was invited to partake of a meal on the Friday night in the beautiful Saint Francis of Assisi Monastery (kosher vegetarian food was provided). He joined the hundreds of monks in the impressive refectory and was startled to hear the abbot calling them to attention to stand and listen in prayerful silence to David's sanctification over the wine—a ritual that introduces all festive Jewish meals and which refers to the chosenness of the Jewish people. This would not be the last time that David would wonder what his ancestors would have made of such an astonishing spectacle after two thousand years of Jewish suffering at the hands of Christians.

No doubt the highlight for David during the early 1990s was when the then Israeli Deputy Foreign Minister Yossi Beilin invited David to join the five-person Israeli delegation that negotiated full diplomatic relations with the Vatican. Despite burgeoning Catholic-Jewish interfaith activities after the Second Vatican Council, the Vatican still did not recognize Israel as a sovereign state. While not overtly stated, this policy seemed to stem from concern that recognition might harm the safety of Christian communities in Arab countries that were at war with Israel. However, the Madrid Conference in 1991, which attempted to revive the Israeli-Palestinian peace process through negotiations involving Israelis, Palestinians, and other Arab countries, gave the Vatican an excuse to start its own negotiations with Israel.

By now, the Israeli Foreign Ministry was well acquainted with David's Catholic-Jewish expertise. Moreover, it was in dire need of a person who had David's command of English and would be a worthy religious counterpart to the Catholic leaders in the Vatican delegation. David's special role was to resolve tensions around differing interpretations of the relationship by concocting constructive language in the formal document that would gloss over these differences and enable acceptance by both sides. The Fundamental Agreement between the Holy See and Israel establishing full relations was finalized inside a beautiful room in the Vatican on December 29, 1993. Once again, David had the uncanny feeling that his ancestors were looking down at him from above, shaking their heads in amazement at his involvement in such a historical event of interfaith diplomacy—and with no less an institution than the Holy See itself!

This event also included some emotional turmoil and a modicum of disappointment for David. Yossi Beilin had informed him that he wanted David to be the first Israeli ambassador to the Vatican. After all, David knew the setup intimately, was trusted by the Catholic hierarchy, and had the sensitivity to know how to handle relationships on both sides, particularly as in Israel there was still a great deal of suspicion, if not anger, regarding Christian sentiment and Catholic past behavior towards Jews. David was quite excited about this new direction in his life, but the Vatican discovered Beilin's intention from a leaked Israeli media report. At the kosher-catered dinner that night, hosted by Archbishop Tauran, who was then secretary for Relations with States (in effect the Vatican foreign minister), the archbishop asked Beilin not to appoint a rabbi as the first Israeli ambassador, claiming that a seasoned diplomat was needed to conclude the unresolved financial and legal issues. This was a highly unusual intervention, particularly as all Vatican ambassadors, or papal nuncios, as they are called, are themselves clerics. The delegation returned to Israel to the Foreign Ministry the following day and, walking past a small demonstration of Jews holding placards with the message "We have not forgotten the Crusades," the bilateral Fundamental Agreement was finally signed.

Rumors of David's rejection by the Vatican had reached the ears of Professor Zvi Werblowsky, a doyen of interfaith and head of the Department for Comparative Religions at Hebrew University. When David confirmed that the rumors were indeed true, Werblowsky was incredulous and immediately contacted his friend Cardinal Joseph Ratzinger (later elected Pope Benedict XVI), who also expressed surprise and said he would inquire with Secretary of State Sodano. According to Werblowsky, Cardinal Ratzinger rang back abashedly to inform him that Sodano had confirmed that this was the advice he had received from his predecessor Cardinal Casaroli, who still wielded enormous influence. The real reason, which I divulge here for the first time, is that the Vatican still feared Muslim negative reactions to the bilateral agreement and that the appointment of a rabbi as Israeli ambassador would rub salt into the wounds by highlighting a unique, Christian-Jewish relationship with Israel. The irony of this story is that twenty-five years and eight Israeli ambassadors later, the financial and legal issues for which the Vatican gave as an excuse the need for a seasoned ambassador have still not been resolved. Nevertheless, in retrospect, the position of ambassador would likely have limited David's breadth of interfaith operations, which grew exponentially in the 1990s.

Not all of David's interfaith activities were taking place overseas. He became involved with the Israel Interfaith Association and the Jerusalem Rainbow Club, where intellectual discussions across the Abrahamic religions were held. He also co-founded the Inter-Religious Coordinating Council in Israel (ICCI) in 1991, whose purpose was to act as an umbrella body for networking among some seventy-five Christian, Palestinian/Muslim, and

Jewish institutions to harness the teachings and values of the three Abrahamic faiths and to promote Jewish-Arab coexistence.

In the early 1990s, David also became the first professor of Jewish studies at the newly built and exquisitely designed Brigham Young University Jerusalem Center for Near Eastern Studies on the Mount of Olives in East Jerusalem. The center afforded the opportunity for approximately 170 Mormon students studying at Brigham Young University in Utah to spend a semester in Jerusalem experiencing firsthand the land in which Jesus was born and to learn about the three Abrahamic religions. This was David's first contact with Latter-Day Saints, which developed into deep and lasting relationships with its leadership at the highest level and its students.

Another highlight during this period, which reflected David's international stature in Jewish-Christian relations, was the holding of the first ever international Jewish-Christian conference in 1994, entitled Religion in Secular Society. While two years in the making, serendipitously the meeting took place a month after the signing of the Fundamental Agreement with the Vatican, which opened the floodgates for Christian leaders who were yearning to visit the Holy Land. Christian leaders above the level of bishop were invited from ninety countries, and they came in droves. Cardinal Maria Martini, the highly popular archbishop of Milan, agreed to open the conference; Cardinal Joseph Ratzinger closed it; and Palestinian Michel Sabbah, archbishop and Latin patriarch of Jerusalem, spoke in the intermediate session. Christian luminaries from other denominations included the Anglican archbishop of Canterbury, George Carey; president of the World Council of Churches Reverend Lois Wilson; and the evangelical scholar Marvin Wilson.

On the Jewish side, South Africa's Chief Rabbi Cyril Harris and France's Chief Rabbi René Sirat, Rabbi Leon Ashenazi (Manitou), and US Rabbi Irving (Yitz) Greenberg were leading speakers from overseas. Nearly one thousand religious leaders packed into the largest conference center in Jerusalem for the two-day event chaired by David. The conference was electric as enthusiasm abounded, and the relationships developed through this meeting have lasted decades. The Israeli Foreign Affairs and Tourism Ministries were ecstatic by the amazing success of the conference, which resulted in extensive positive media coverage for Israel. Both ministries made films extolling interfaith relations as the way to herald a new era in Israeli-international cooperation.

Three Pontiffs

Pope John Paul II's dream to visit the Holy Land for the centenary came to fruition in the year 2000, and David was on hand to ensure that the visit was successful. He had been dubbed "the pope's rabbi" in a CNN interview, and the nickname stuck. He helped with the planning in the Vatican and in Israel and participated in many events during the pilgrimage. He was on hand when the pope paid a visit to the Chief Rabbinate and listened with anticipation when the pontiff requested the setting up of an annual bilateral commission between the Chief Rabbinate and the Vatican for dialogue on issues of common interest. David quips that the Chief Rabbinate did not have meetings with other Jewish denominations, let alone with Christians, but one cannot refuse when the request emanates from a pope! As the Chief Rabbinate needed someone with expertise in Christianity for these dialogues, David became its honorary advisor on matters of interfaith. For the past twenty years, he has represented the rabbinate in many interfaith meetings, at home and abroad, and for a variety of religions. The Chief Rabbinate has clearly come a long way in opening up to other faiths since that groundbreaking Christian-Jewish conference in 1994.

With the death of Pope John Paul II, Benedict XVI was elected to succeed him in 2005. David's relationship with him as Cardinal Ratzinger blossomed into a friendship which lasted beyond the latter's resignation in 2013. On a trip to the Vatican in 2016 to participate in Pope Francis's visit to Rome's Great Synagogue, we enjoyed a wonderful meeting with the pope emeritus in his home in the Vatican Gardens behind Saint Peter's Basilica. While physically frail, his mind was as sharp as ever, and we spent an hour reminiscing about past events and discussing Jewish-Catholic relations. Benedict had firmly followed John Paul II's path, cementing the "inseparable bond" between Judaism and the Catholic Church. During his pilgrimage to Israel in 2009, David took part in various events. We have, for posterity, a photo of the pope with a broad smile, holding hands with David, their arms in the air, almost in triumph, at the end of the trip. David always felt that Pope Benedict had received an unfair rap from the media, which did not see his emotional depth but portrayed him as a dour figure, sandwiched between the media-savvy and charismatic John Paul II and the friendly, down-to-earth Pope Francis.

Pope Francis has followed the path laid out by his predecessors regarding Jewish-Catholic relations, with the result that David has met him, as with the other popes, more than a dozen times. Following his pilgrimage to the Holy Land, in which David also participated, Pope Francis convened a special service entitled Prayers for Peace in the Holy Land in the

Vatican Gardens in the presence of Shimon Peres and Mahmoud Abbas, president of the Palestinian Authority. David was honored to represent the Jewish delegation in leading the prayers and was complimented by the pope on his singing abilities.

David's preeminent role as the key global Jewish spokesperson to the Vatican and its preferred representative was highlighted by two unique events. In 2010, in the first ever invitation issued by the Vatican to a Jew, David addressed the Special Synod on the Middle East, providing a Jewish perspective on Christians in the Middle East. In 2015, the Pontifical Commission for Religious Relations with the Jews released a document on the occasion of the fiftieth anniversary of *Nostra aetate,* surveying the theological and educational changes of the Church in relation to Jews and Judaism over the course of the past fifty years. Among other things, the document affirmed that the Church has no active mission to convert the Jews and that the religious responsibility of Jews is to be loyal to their Torah. In another first, David was invited to address the press conference releasing this Vatican document, where he highlighted the significance of the document as well as some of its lacunae. The Vatican clearly trusted both David's profound knowledge of the issues and his fair and sensitive approach.

Among the many awards David has received over his career, three stand out. In 2005, David was awarded a papal knighthood—Commander of the Order of St. Gregory the Great—by Pope Benedict XVI for his efforts at promoting Catholic-Jewish reconciliation. In 2010, he was made a Commander of the British Empire (CBE) by HM Queen Elizabeth II for his significant contribution to interfaith relations; and in 2016, he was awarded the archbishop of Canterbury's Hubert Walter Award for Reconciliation and Interfaith Cooperation by Archbishop Justin Welby.

Jewish–Muslim Relations

The Cape Inter-Faith Forum enabled David's first forays into understanding Islam through connection with Muslims themselves, but it wasn't until we returned to Israel in 1985 that these opportunities expanded, first with his involvement in the Israel Interfaith Association and the ICCI, and then when he co-founded Rabbis for Human Rights in 1998 in response to violations against Palestinians in the West Bank. Once again, David's vision of Judaism as a religion in pursuit of social justice, with a belief that all human beings are created in the divine image, informed his actions.

In 1993, the World Economic Forum (WEF) invited David to speak on a panel on Religion and International Relations in the context of the conflict in the Balkans. From then on, David was invited back annually to the WE. We attended for nearly two decades, meeting Muslim leaders from many countries, including those with which Israel did not have diplomatic relations. David became a stalwart of the C-100 (approximately one hundred cultural, political, and religious leaders) set up by the WEF to promote understanding between Islam and the West after the devastating 9/11 attacks in the US. Generally, the opportunity to build profound connections with a variety of senior religious leaders of different faiths was one of the great gifts we received from participating in the WEF meetings in Davos, Switzerland, but also at regional meetings in Muslim countries like Jordan, Morocco, and Turkey, during those formative years of bridge building.

In 2001, when the Al-Aqsa Intifada (the second Palestinian uprising against Israel) was causing the deaths of thousands of Israelis and Palestinians, Father Andrew White, an emissary of the Anglican Archbishop of Canterbury George Carey, visited Rabbi Michael Melchior, then Israel's Deputy Foreign Minister, and David, to discuss an idea that had originated with Shimon Peres—how interfaith dialogue could be used to calm the waters. Canterbury had developed a close relationship with Al-Azhar, the most prestigious university for Islamic learning in Cairo. The result of these deliberations, which included British, Egyptian, Israeli, and Palestinian religious leaders, politicians, and diplomats, was an overnight interfaith meeting in January 2002 in Alexandria, hosted by Sheikh Muhammad Tantawi, Grand Imam of Al-Azhar and facilitated by Carey, where the *Alexandria Declaration* was signed by more than a dozen senior Christian, Jewish, and Muslim leaders from the Holy Land, of which David was one. The declaration was a joint pledge by the religious leaders to work together for a just and lasting peace and called on Israeli and Palestinian political leaders "to work for a just, secure and durable solution" to the conflict. Sadly, the efforts did not have the desired results, and the Intifada raged for a further deadly three years. But it did begin a process that brought Israeli and Palestinian, Christian, Muslim, and Jewish religious leaders together within different frameworks to promote peace in the region.

The Council of Religious Institutions of the Holy Land (CRIHL), convened by the Norwegian Reverend Trond Bakkevig, was one such framework in which David was heavily invested. It included the senior religious leaders from the Chief Rabbinate, the Palestinian Authority, and the Christian denominations of the Holy Land, and worked to maintain open channels of communication among the different religious institutions and to promote mutual respect in pursuit of an enduring peace. However, despite regular educational and other activities over a period of more than ten years, ultimately CRIHL was doomed to fail, given that political developments were veering in the opposite direction.

It became only too clear that while engagement with religious actors is essential in conflicts where there is a religious dimension, miracles cannot be wrought when there is no political willingness. This was also true regarding the time and effort David invested in supporting Alain Michel's Hommes de Parole organization, which hosted three international meetings that included hundreds of Israeli and Palestinian imams and rabbis to promote peace in the region.

Jewish–Muslim Relations:
Beyond Enemy Borders

Not long after the Oslo Accords were signed in 1993, the first ever delegation of Indonesian Muslim leaders visited Israel, and, at the request of the Israeli Foreign Affairs Ministry, we hosted them for a Shabbat dinner. This was the beginning of a firm friendship with Abdul Rahman Wahid, known as Gus Dur, head of the Nadhlatul Ulama, the largest Muslim organization in Indonesia, with more than fifty million members. Not long after, Gus Dur was elected president of Indonesia and hosted a group of Jewish leaders at an Abrahamic conference in Jakarta that David attended, entering on his Israeli passport with the prior permission of the Indonesian authorities, despite there being no diplomatic relations between the two countries. Ever since, David's relations with Indonesian Muslim leaders have blossomed. Even during the pandemic this past year, David has been lecturing in webinars to Indonesian universities and other organizations that have enjoyed attendance in the thousands.

In 2008, David was invited to an unprecedented interfaith meeting hosted by King Abdullah of Saudi Arabia in Madrid. In the wake of the 9/11 attacks on the US, the king had begun a slow process of opening up Saudi Arabia to other religions, and the Madrid meeting was the first time that Jews were invited to attend such an event. David was invited as the international interreligious director of the AJC, so there was some consternation in Saudi Arabia when they discovered, through a sensational media report, that not only did he have Israeli citizenship, but he also lived in the country. He subsequently heard that there was an emergency meeting in the Saudi Foreign Ministry to decide whether they should rescind the invitation. In the end, they concluded that it was to Saudi advantage to include him in the meeting. To criticism that he was Israeli, they could point to the fact that he had been invited as a prominent interfaith leader from an important US organization. However, at the same time, they were protected from criticism that they were ignoring the world center of Judaism by not inviting someone from Israel.

David returned excited from this meeting. He spoke of how suspicion and fear turned to incredulity, then to curiosity and interest, when he spoke with Muslim leaders who had never before met a Jew. David was introduced to Saudi King Abdullah in Madrid (he was later to be hosted by the king in his Moroccan country palace in 2015), and the meeting itself would have ramifications for David's future path in life.

In its wake, Saudi Arabia established an intergovernmental, interfaith dialogue center in Vienna, bringing Austria and Spain on board, as well as the Vatican which had observer status. The King Abdullah bin Abdulaziz International Centre for Interreligious and Intercultural Dialogue (KAICIID) set up a founding, governing board of seven people from diverse faiths, including Muslims from Saudi Arabia, Lebanon, and Iran. David became the Jewish representative on the board and has devoted an extraordinary amount of time over the past twelve years in service to the organization and its efforts to seed and grow interreligious dialogue around the world. The organization has developed into one of the leading players in the field of interfaith and has provided David with even greater opportunities to reach out to the Muslim world.

Just before COVID-19 abruptly ended most international travel, David made his first trip to Saudi Arabia in February 2020 as a KAICIID board member and in a first in Saudi history, King Salman hosted a rabbi, who was also an Israeli, in his royal palace in Riyadh. No less exciting for David was a meeting with a group of about eighty Saudi young people one evening during the visit, who engaged him in conversation. In echoes of our first meeting with the primate of all Ireland related above, a young woman in a full burka came over to David and welcomed him to Saudi Arabia—in Hebrew!

In 2017, through KAICIID, David met Dr. Muhammad bin Abdul Karim Al-Issa, the former Saudi minister of justice and the newly appointed secretary general of the Muslim World League who has taken this organization in a very different and constructive direction from where it had been previously. In his efforts to present a more enlightened approach, Dr Al-Issa has visited synagogues and strongly condemned anti-Semitism and Holocaust denial. He and David have established a good working relationship, which has born promising dividends. Dr. Al-Issa reached out to Bawa Jain, the secretary general of the World Council of Religious Leaders, to hold a UN interfaith conference on Responsible Leadership in Modern Society. At the same time, David and Bawa arranged for Dr. Al-Issa to address the executive council of the AJC, which resulted in a memorandum of understanding with

David Harris, AJC's CEO, whereby Dr. Al-Issa agreed to participate in a joint pilgrimage to Auschwitz on the occasion of the seventy-fifth anniversary of its liberation in January 2020.

David joined Al-Issa at this profoundly moving event that left lingering images in the world's media of a delegation of senior Muslim leaders from different countries, including those with no diplomatic relations with Israel, prostrating themselves in prayer at the Auschwitz memorial to the victims. The following day, the delegation held joint prayers at the Polish Nozyk synagogue, where both David and Al-Issa spoke to those present. That evening, AJC hosted a Shabbat dinner in the Warsaw Castle that was also attended by Polish political, religious, and civic dignitaries. David led the Shabbat service, whose liturgy had been translated into various languages, including Arabic, enabling the participation of all guests. David returned to Israel after this trip with such optimism for Jewish-Muslim mutual respect that one could almost imagine the Messiah had arrived!

David has had long associations with various multifaith organizations, including the World Parliament of Religions and United Religions Initiative (URI) but none as profound as his relationship of more than thirty years with Religions for Peace (RfP), a global interfaith movement and network that spans ninety national and six regional interreligious councils. It began when he met Dr. John Taylor, its secretary general, in the mid-1980s, but it was only when Dr. William (Bill) Vendley took over the position in 1994, resulting in extremely close bonds of friendship to this day, that David's involvement became intense. He has been a president of RfP and a member of its executive committee for decades, providing constant advice and counsel often on highly sensitive issues, a role he continues to play in support of the present secretary general, Professor Azza Karam, who was elected in 2020.

One of the many friendships David has developed through RfP is with Sheikh Abdallah bin Bayyah, who is currently the moderator of its executive committee. Sheikh Bin Bayyah established the Forum for Promoting Peace in Muslim Societies and invited David to participate in the forum's conferences, held primarily in Abu Dhabi. These meetings reflected the changes that were already taking place in the Gulf states well before the recent signing of the Abraham Accords that established diplomatic relations with Israel. Sheikh Bin Bayyah also convened the groundbreaking gathering in Morocco under the auspices of King Mohammed VI in January 2016 that issued the *Marrakesh Declaration*, based on the historic Charter of Medina that was promulgated by the Prophet Mohammed and which affirmed full civil rights of non-Muslims in Muslim majority societies. David and I were the only Jewish Israelis present at that unprecedented meeting, again reflecting the high regard in which the Muslim organizers hold him.

Jewish Relations with Religions of the East

RfP also provided tremendous opportunities for David to build sustained connections with the Dharmic religions that heretofore had been quite sporadic. He developed a trusting relationship with the leadership of Rissho Kosei Kai, a global Buddhist movement, headquartered in Tokyo, whose mission is to promote peace in the world through religion. Its founder, Rev. Nikkyo Niwano, helped to establish RfP, and the organization still plays a crucial role in supporting RfP financially and strategically. Subsequent visits to Japan also built lasting connections with leaders from the Oomoto, a new religion originating from Shintoism, as well as the Makuya Christian movement, who are strong supporters of Israel. Visiting Hiroshima in 1996, on the fifty-first anniversary of the deadly atom bomb detonation, we were hosted at the Makuya Center and spent a wonderful evening chatting and singing in Hebrew.

When writing about Buddhist friendships, I must make mention of David's relationship with the Dalai Lama. They met originally when the Dalai Lama visited Israel for the first time in 1999 at the invitation of the Friends of Tibet in Israel for an event sponsored by the Israeli government. However, due to pressure from the Chinese government on Israel not to officially receive this world religious figure, the visit was publicized as an interfaith event, which the Foreign Affairs Ministry asked David to host. Thus, the Dalai Lama participated in the Jubillenium Interfaith Summit, which David convened on the shores of the Sea of Galilee. Another religious leader participating in the summit was the late W. D. Muhammed, the leader of the Black American Muslim community, who, like David, was a president of RfP. It was exciting to see these world religious leaders in Israel and to provide them with firsthand experience of the significance of the state for the Jewish people. The Dalai Lama showed particular interest in how the Jews had managed to revive the Hebrew language and turn it into the living language of their country. He voiced a wistful desire for a similar resurgence of the Tibetan language for his exiled people.

In addition to further meetings with the Dalai Lama on his later visits to Israel, David also participated with him on major international, interreligious panels in Seattle, Washington (together with Bishop Desmond Tutu); at Emory University in Atlanta, Georgia; and at Melk Abbey, Austria, where they both received lifetime achievement awards, together with Dr. Ahmed el-Tayeb, the current grand imam of Al-Azhar.

On the Hindu side, several notable relationships were forged, and these have been associated with some important events. Swami Dayananda, one of India's foremost teachers of the philosophical system of Vedanta, sought to establish relations with Jewish leadership and more specifically with the Chief Rabbinate of Israel. David was instrumental in realizing the meetings between the Chief Rabbinate and a gallery of noted Hindu leaders. The Israeli Ministry of Foreign Affairs, in particular the ambassador in New Delhi, was very interested in sponsoring this dialogue out of a recognition that this could deepen and sustain the bilateral diplomatic relationship. AJC, too, served as a co-sponsor.

The first summit took place in New Delhi in 2007 with the attendance of one of Israel's chief rabbis, and the second in Jerusalem in 2008, in which several members of the Chief Rabbinate Council participated, including both chief rabbis. During the first summit there was also a meeting with leaders from all the religious communities in India. This led to David's friendship with the late Sheikh Muhammad Ilyasi, who headed the All India Organization of Imams of Mosques that embraces over half a million imams, as well as his son Umeir. David brought them together with a delegation of other Muslim leaders to Israel despite strong Muslim protests in India.

At both these bilateral summits, theological concerns were prominent. Hindu leadership was at pains to point out why Hindu image worship did not mean that Hindus were idolaters. Rather, they believed in one universal power behind and within the cosmos. In the words of Swami Dayananda, (to which I can personally attest), "You [Jews] say there is only one God, and we say there is nothing but God."

David has developed personal friendships with other Hindu gurus, notably with Pujya Swami Chidanand Saraswati, president and spiritual head of the Parmarth Niketan Ashram in Rishikesh, India, and his deputy, Sadhvi Bhagawati Saraswati. In November 2016, Swami Chidanand hosted an eighteen-person AJC delegation who attended the annual Hindu celebration of Dev Diwali on the Ganges in the holy city of Varanasi, a pilgrimage attended by one million Hindus. David was the keynote speaker at the gathering and spoke of the growth of Hindu-Jewish relations globally and the empowering of interreligious dialogue based on common love of the Divine.

David has also developed a special friendship over decades with a prominent Sikh leader, Bhai Sahib Mohinder Singh, president of the Guru Nanak Nishkam Sewak Jatha community in Birmingham, UK. We have had the pleasure of hosting Bhai Sahib, one of the most spiritual and caring leaders I have had the privilege of meeting, at our Shabbat table as well. I see this as a miniscule return for the incredible vegetarian hospitality he and his co-religionists have offered us and thousands of others at various interfaith forums we've attended.

One important arena in which David has been interacting with Hindu and other prominent religious leaders is the Elijah Board of World Religious

Leaders, of which he has been a member since its foundation in 2003. The forum is characterized, as the Dalai Lama has stated, by profound and intimate engagement among top-tier religious leaders, on matters of spiritual concern and on the practice of leadership across religions. As with so many other organizations, David was instrumental in helping to conceive the forum to birth. He continues to support Rabbi Dr. Alon Goshen-Gottstein as he launches various intellectual and media projects that address the concerns of religious leaders, scholars, and the broader public. One memorable moment referred to above was when Pope Benedict and David held hands at the center of a host of local religious leaders, singing and praying for peace in Nazareth, during the pope's pilgrimage. The moment was planned and orchestrated by Alon as a way of enhancing the positive message of Pope Benedict's visit, and he relied on David for its realization. This is but one example of how Alon's creative mind and David's availability as a friend, advisor, and partner over a period of twenty-five years have combined to lend Elijah's initiatives greater impact and outreach globally. We have enjoyed a family friendship with Alon and his wife Therese for many years and have shared Shabbat meals together in Jerusalem. It is Alon's innovative mind and generosity of spirit that sparked the idea for this book of essays honoring David for his seventieth birthday and brought it to fruition.

Finally, speaking of sacred meals, I would be remiss not to mention how David's love for interfaith has intersected with another great passion of his, a commitment to the *mitzva* (religious commandment) to steward sentient beings and care for the environment. We have been a vegetarian family for over forty years, but, six years ago, we took the next step and became vegans. This has enabled David, without dissonance between belief and action, to become a prominent and much sought-after Jewish spokesperson on interfaith platforms throughout the world, invoking the moral call found in Judaism to care for all God's creation.

As David turns seventy years of age, his passion and commitment to interfaith is as strong as ever, and his energy to forge trusting relationships across religions and cultures is undiminished. My own life's trajectory has been greatly impacted by David's activities through the beauty I have experienced in accompanying him on his interfaith journey and through the friendships we have developed on the way. My own profession in the field of religious engagement is a direct corollary of this. I am fortunate that my life partner is also my most trusted advisor. For this, I am deeply grateful.

Conclusion:
Appreciating Interreligious Heroes

Dr. Alon Goshen-Gottstein

I WOULD LIKE TO begin this summary view of our project by considering first different types of dialogue or engagement, moving from that to an identification of traits, characteristics, and spiritual orientations that contribute to the making of an interreligious hero.

As outlined in the volume's introduction and as made evident in its structure, interreligious or interfaith relations or dialogue are not one thing. They are a large family of activities, approaches, and practices, all of which combine to create the broad field of interreligious relations. Some would refer to this field as the interfaith movement, though often that designation relates more to on-the-ground relations than to the full scope of engagement—including the more theoretical, reflective, and spiritual dimensions—that have received particular attention in this volume. Significantly, none of the figures surveyed in the book were the man and woman in the community who simply cultivated good relations with his or her neighbor. Bill Vendley's contribution comes closest to profiling this aspect, as he speaks of his teacher, the anonymous interreligious hero. Yet this hero, too, and Bill's particular perspective are focused on the role of religion in peacemaking. Given the nature of the project and the profile of contributors, almost all interreligious heroes described are scholars and religious leaders. This allows us then to explore what might be termed the high end of the interfaith arena. If, indeed, the heroes represent this high end, one wonders to what extent this amounts to an invitation to the broader field, the movement, to follow suit or to incorporate more fully the dimensions that are often missing from interfaith engagement and that are characteristic of the work of these heroes.

In the framework of a book that honors a rabbi who is active in interfaith relations, I allow myself the following application of a famous rabbinic maxim, in order to capture what seems to me the most basic typology of interfaith activities that emerges from the present volume. The beginning of the mishna tractate Avot, where key moral and philosophical lessons of the early rabbis are captured, states:

> Shimon the Righteous was one of the last of the men of the great assembly. He used to say: the world stands upon three things: the Torah, service [of God], and acts of human kindness.[407]

Key values are appreciated in terms of how they sustain the world. For the rabbis, this is a statement referring to the cosmic effects of religious behavior. The world is mystically or secretly, invisibly, sustained by proper religious behavior, and such behavior can be classified in line with one of three primary virtues. Torah study is the most salient, the hallmark of rabbinic culture. Reference to service would relate to temple service and its sacrifices. However, prayer is also understood as service, thereby pointing to the eventual rise in the value of prayer as a prominent feature of Jewish religious life. Acts of human kindness include charity, good deeds to the other, and the range of actions that express love, compassion, and care for the other.

Let us now consider the relevance of this foundational teaching to interreligious engagement. Here, too, the goal is to sustain the world. Yet such sustaining is understood in much more concrete and measurable terms. Whether it be sustaining the world in face of violence, war, or ecological disaster, there is a very concrete sense to sustaining the world. Protecting, sustaining, supporting, or establishing would be relevant nuances that capture varying dimensions of the meaning of religious activity from the Jewish perspective and of interfaith activity from the broader perspective.

Yet, in this extension of the rabbinic teaching, it is not only deeds of human kindness that provide the foundation for sustaining the interconnected world of humanity and the webs of relationships of which it consists. Torah and prayer are also part of what sustain it. In the context of interfaith activities, the fuller sustaining that humanity requires is not only physical but spiritual. This spiritual sustaining involves the sharing of knowledge, wisdom. It involves a quest of the mind, and it points to a fundamental activity that is relevant to relations across religions—study. Reviewing the contents of this volume, one realizes how central study is to much of what is being presented. The classical archetypes are teachers, whether by letter or by example. Scholars increase understanding of other religions and offer the means of redefining the view of other religions. Through scholarship, religions redefine themselves and make room for the other.

Prayer points to another dimension of interfaith engagement. Understanding requires deepening, and such deepening engages the heart, not only the mind. Prayer, service of the heart, the approach to God and to the spiritual life, is at the core of the spiritual life. Accordingly, some of the most important voices of interreligious engagement, whether we consider these in relation to spiritual exemplars or later practitioners, are concerned not simply with the ideas of the other religion but with its spiritual reality. A discovery of the fullness of the spiritual reality of God is understood by some as involving a fuller appreciation of the spiritual, mystical, or prayer life of another religion. Ramakrishna's spiritual gluttony is an extreme expression of this, as are the spiritual pursuits of Rabbi Zalman Schacter. But throughout this volume—and not only in those listed under the specific heading of those who seek a deeper appreciation of the spiritual reality of another religion—we encounter interreligious pursuits as part of the quest for God, beyond the quest for a sustained and whole world.

And, of course, blessed are the peacemakers, that third type of interfaith hero, who manifest the ideal of deeds of human kindness as a metaphor for all the life-keeping processes that drive so much of contemporary interfaith activity. One of the important recognitions that emerges from the presentation of many, though not all, of the individuals surveyed under the rubric of "Engaged and Peace Activists" is just how deeply their engagement in projects that are life-sustaining and world-sustaining are more than just instance of interreligious dialogue in the service of contemporary needs. For more than half the personalities surveyed (and this does not exclude the same being true for others, regarding whom we have not been informed by our authors), their peace or social activism flows deeply from the fundamentals of their worldview and spiritual experience. It is because they are so deeply touched by a profound spiritual recognition that they are moved to act and to serve. We may say, because their service of the Divine or the Ultimate is so deep, they are driven to serve humanity and the world.

Thus the ensemble of the testimony of interreligious heroes is an invitation to the depth that is captured in the threefold rabbinic maxim, as it is applied more broadly to religion in general and to interreligious relations.

Which leads me to David Rosen. One way of describing how he is positioned within the broader interfaith arena could be with reference to the rabbinic maxim. It would be lovely to depict anyone as the ideal and harmonious balance of all three dimensions and activities. In some way, this is also true, both as far as Jewish ideals are concerned and as far as interreligious heroes go. Yet, already in the mishna, we note a tension.[408] Naturally, people tend to be one thing or another. Heroes manifest some traits more fully than others. So, while acknowledging that all dimensions have some expression in all religious personalities, I would venture the following description of what seems to me an appropriate means of describing his particular interreligious presence. David, I submit, is an individual who holds in exquisite balance the two poles of Torah study and deeds of human kindness. Lest anyone consider this a triviality, I hasten to add that already in the mishna and throughout Jewish history, these ideals are held in tension. A creative tension often privileges one over the other. Holding them in balance is therefore far from obvious. Yet this is what David's interfaith ministry is about.[409] Let me explain.

As we learn from Sharon's presentation of David's growth into the domain of interreligious relations, the impetus was that of good deeds. Fighting apartheid, increasing understanding among different factions in Ireland, supporting the cause of peace, enhancing understanding between religions that have been in conflict for centuries, as well as caring for the environment and a host of other life-keeping causes—these are all expressions of good deeds carried out in relation to the world. Yet, when one observes what David does—and I have observed him in numerous contexts over a quarter of a century—what he does most of all, and probably best of all, is to teach. He brings the wisdom of Judaism to the particular context, to the specific conversation, even as he draws out the wisdom of the other and makes both of these part of the larger storehouse of wisdom that is put at the service of humanity or the community. David does not go on the picket line, nor does he engage in politics. His cause is served by teaching, by Torah, in the broadest sense, as it complements and serves the needs of global human kindness.

Even this vision of two major avenues of service held in balance does not do justice to the particularity of David's mission and his unique gifts and positioning. It is not simply that David teaches. Rather, the teaching in which he engages is expressive of a very unique service, a way of living the interreligious vocation unlike any other. As I review the various types described in this book, I cannot identify a single person who could serve as the paradigm or precedent for David. He does not teach at a university, he does not write books, he does not revision Jewish theology, nor does he forge new frontiers in interreligious experience. What then is the key to the universally recognized success of this individual? I submit that David's uniqueness in the interfaith arena is precisely that he does not fit into any of the molds created by predecessors, neither by earlier generations nor by present-day colleagues. His greatness is that he has been able to forge a new modality for interfaith contribution. I would term this representative interfaith engagement or perhaps diplomatic interfaith engagement. Sharon tells of how David was nearly appointed to the post of Israel's first ambassador to the Vatican. Whether or not appointed to the post, an ambassador is precisely what David is. David is Judaism's foremost—and possibly only—ambassador to the world of interfaith. There is no other personality that has that representative function, devoted exclusively to representing

Judaism in a variety of interreligious forums. All other actors do various other things and are invited to speak for Judaism on the sidelines, in accordance with the relevant subject and context. David, by contrast, has made a name for himself as Judaism's representative *par excellence*, which is precisely why his name is nearly synonymous with interfaith and Judaism. David's ambassadorial career has been far greater and far more fulfilling than a nominal appointment to a diplomatic post might have provided. He has, over the course of several decades, become Judaism's unique ambassador to world religions or to the interfaith reality, as this is expressed in a multitude of interfaith organizations and circumstances. It is thus only after we have studied the various historical and typological expressions of interreligious heroes that we can appreciate how David Rosen draws on these precedents, how he brings together distinct approaches, and how he combines all of these into what is truly a unique interfaith ministry—a representative and ambassadorial Jewish presence to religious leaders and institutions of the world and of world religions.

It takes a very particular skill set and personality to attain such status. It requires clear thinking, brilliance, articulateness in speech, ability to distill a message and to always be relevant. It also builds on a set of human and social skills, not to mention the good looks and excellent sense of dress, of which Feisal Abdul Rauf reminds us. But all these are put in the service of a higher vision that is then translated into this unique ministry. That vision, I submit, is furnished by the balance of Torah as teaching and message with acts of kindness. as a code for all the life-upholding activities, peacemaking and more, that are served by the interfaith enterprise. The service of God in teaching and caring and the service of others in friendship and relationship come together in a compelling way in the person of Judaism's first and only interfaith ambassador.

Recognizing David's unique position and mission leads us to an examination of key dimensions of what makes an interfaith hero, as these have emerged from our essays. As noted in the introduction, the significance of this question is not simply theoretical. It is a question that has educational and even spiritual consequences. It therefore deserves more specific attention.

Some themes have struck me as they have appeared time and again across multiple essays. To these I now turn.

The first of these is friendship. It is striking how centrally friendship and personal relations feature across the project. Transformations occur as a consequence of personal relations. Friendship provides the fuel for advancing interfaith growth and understanding, in all its expressions. The notables of the history of interreligious engagement are all described as having had formative and transformative friendships. That some essays do not feature this dimension does not mean it was lacking in the hero's life. It may speak to the limitations of space or the specific focus an author chose to give. We know enough of many of those individuals to know that is not the case. Friendship, I submit, is a major dimension in the formation of an interreligious hero. It may seem trivial, but nevertheless worth stating, that an important key to David Rosen's own success in this field is his capacity to develop friendships over decades and across religions. This is one of the major points that emerges from Sharon's description of David's path in the interfaith world.

A second point of note has to do with the attributes of an interfaith hero, or of interfaith heroes, inasmuch as not all heroes will feature all attributes. Across all sub-categories of the book, authors describe not only ideas, achievements, and historical processes. These are supported and have their counterpart in the description of the characteristics, personality traits, and even spiritual attributes of the interreligious heroes. I would not want to put forward the suggestion that the more attributes there are, the higher an individual scores on a purported interreligious hero ladder. More simply, it is enough to suggest that character traits are essential to the making of a hero. This seems a sensible proposition in relation to any hero, whatever the domain. The characteristics that are relevant to the making of an interreligious hero may have specificity of their own, in view of the task at hand. It is therefore worth considering the kinds of traits that authors have put forth. What follows is suggestive and does not seek to be exhaustive of all fine personality traits and characteristics that have been surveyed in this book. It is enough that we recognize that heroic virtues are part of the making of an interfaith hero.

I begin with simple *Menschlichkeit*, the Yiddish term for being a thoughtful, considerate, and caring human being. Debbie Weissman profiles this as one of the qualities of Blu Greenberg. I think it is broader in scope. While heroes can be eccentric and at times even defy commonly practiced ideal virtues, there is an even stronger case to be made for forming human relationships as a virtue constitutive of interreligious heroes. After all, constructing bridges across religions involves creating relationships. The human and relational element is thus key.

Several essays feature clearly the heroic attributes. Cardinal Parolin devotes a section in his essay to the character qualities of Cardinal Bea. As he notes, "Cardinal Bea exemplified several attitudes essential to interreligious dialogue." The attitudes he describes are broken down into pairs, holding within each pair a constructive tension. These include stability and flexibility, humility and determination, patient tenacity and courageous process. I note that they are also very applicable to David Rosen. In fact, his involvement in the drafting of multiple interfaith statements and his long-term investment in bringing about change in a variety of multilateral relationships and advancing global causes from an interfaith perspective is in some ways similar in type to the tasks that lay before Cardinal Bea. One therefore notices the parallels in character traits that are required for successful realization of such tasks.

Another interfaith hero who has been engaged in long-term processes, the drafting of key texts, and the quest to advance a broad-based multireligious effort for the common good is Hans Küng. Ahmed Abbadi constructs his presentation of Küng in terms of ten heroic virtues. A review of these traits, extracted from Abbadi's essay, is a fascinating exercise in imagining heroic behavior, especially as it applies to the interfaith arena. The qualities listed by Abbadi are courage, honesty, humility, vision, scorching clarity, functional action, intellectual effort, invitation (to others), optimism, perseverance. I am struck by how much overlap there is between this description and that offered by Cardinal Parolin. I imagine the dimensions described by Abbadi could have equally been applied to Cardinal Bea and likely to many other workers in the field of interfaith. They are then the stuff from which interreligious heroes are made.

Cardinal Koch refers to the distinction alluded to in the introduction between imitable and inimitable characteristics of great individuals. With reference to Pope John Paul II, he recognizes his charisma as an inimitable quality. Nevertheless, the working assumption is that others can learn from his chosen hero. He therefore proceeds to suggest qualities in this interreligious hero that can inform the person and work of others. Here are his suggestions, and these take us into slightly different ground than the characteristics we have already encountered. These include openness and esteem towards others, interest in the other (one might say curiosity), empathy, fearlessness, courage, trust in God, and trust in the other. I find this a beautiful and inspiring list of qualities. It hits me personally in what seems to me precisely the way that the person and work of interreligious heroes should inspire others.

Speaking of popes, it is not without interest to note some original attributes suggested by Therese Martine Andrevon Gottstein in her description of Pope John XXIII. Here we come across a fundamental love of humanity (possibly akin to the *Menschlichkeit* cited above), intellectual greed (in other words, an avaricious desire for knowledge), interior freedom, indifference to opinions (mockery) of others, obsession with peace, and, finally, simplicity and patience. As we look at these qualities they all make sense. They are somehow appropriate for individuals who seek to bring about change and peace and to advance understanding between religions. The point is not to establish a definitive list. Rather, it is to point to a domain that provides the foundation for interreligious heroism, the person and his or her attributes. In fact, it is these attributes that account for why being an interreligious hero is a spiritual reality or achievement. It is not only because the individual is working in the domain of religion. It is because, in order to realize the vision and mission of an interreligious hero, in all the variety that we recognize belongs to the category, one must manifest traits that depend on one's spiritual quality and are expressive of it. The spiritual life is therefore the foundation of the work of the interreligious hero. I would add that work in the interreligious domain in turn enhances and deepens the spiritual life of the practitioner. Spiritual growth and interreligious action and engagement dialectically reinforce each other.

As we touch on the more explicitly spiritual domain, I would like to mention points made with reference to two individuals described in our collection. Archbishop Pizzaballa studies Abraham Joshua Heschel, an important instance of an interreligious hero chosen from another tradition. I was struck by his description of Heschel as someone who possessed a "profound unity that he demonstrates in himself and that he tries to achieve for others: a complete man, in the biblical sense of undivided." Pizzaballa goes on to tell us that identity is grounded in faith, understood as a profound relationship with God, prior to any religious affiliation. This is a powerful statement relating to the religious moorings that make interfaith engagement truly a matter of faith. Among the several hundred occurrences of the term *faith* in our collection, most use the term as synonymous with religion. Only a handful relate to faith as a foundational dimension of the religious life. I believe this quote is the only one to bring to light the depth of the recognition that the ideal or heroic practice of interfaith must be grounded in deep faith, understood in the way Pizzaballa proposes.

In similar vein, Rabbi Shlomo Dov Rosen describes his father Mickey, David's brother. Rosen seeks to affirm a core quality that defines his father's spiritual life and that also finds expression in relation to other religions. He puts forth an ideal of interiority, spiritual grounding deep within oneself and in relation to God and the expression of deep personal authenticity. Here again we have a way of identifying the spiritual ground and character traits that find expression throughout an individual's spiritual life, including in the domain of interreligious work.

Perhaps we can draw these statements together through the following proposition. Interfaith work is not divorced from the totality of the person and her or his spiritual life. It is, rather, a further expression of the depth of the spiritual life and one more arena for its realization. In this reading, an interreligious hero is not simply a person of great achievements in the domain of interfaith relations. Rather, it is a person whose greatness, personal attributes, and overall spiritual orientation find expression in all fields of life. Working to advance any aspect of interfaith relations draws on the broader quest for perfection and realizes the person's internal heroism as it finds particular articulation in the field of interfaith relations. Looking back at the ensemble of essays, I would say that the greater part of the essays describe not only individuals who were heroic in the field of interreligious relations and their various sub-domains and expressions; rather, they describe individuals who possessed personal greatness, spiritually informed, and who applied themselves to relations across religions as an outcome, expression, and fruit of the totality of their spiritual lives.

In conclusion, I would like to return to David Rosen and to the family context, just described by his nephew Shlomo Dov. As noted in the introduction, one of the lessons of this project is how interreligious work is extended across generations. Shlomo Dov provides us with significant insight regarding his father Mickey, as well as David's father, Kopul Rosen. Reading this essay and thinking of David in a cross-generational perspective, I was led to the following reflections. It is precisely when one considers not only actions and achievements but also personality qualities and traits that the following recognition emerges. In order to appreciate him, one must recognize in David a Rosen scion. David is a true Rosen, drawing on the gifts and particularities of the father he lost at a young age.

Like his brother Mickey burning passion for a social vision of Judaism is coupled with a core commitment to Judaism, study, and an interior spirituality. David does not apply these in the same way as did his brother. There are differences in their education and modes of service. Consider, however, David's beginnings in South Africa and how his interfaith career was launched in the fight against apartheid. The same naturalness of approach found expression in Mickey's invitation of Desmond Tutu to Yakar. Consider David's voice on a range of global issues, bringing to public forums Judaism's social vision. It is the same voice that both Kopul Rosen and Mickey Rosen, David's father and brother, brought to the world through their respective institutions. Consider how naturally David engages other religions, often casting aside boundaries and conventions that others in the Orthodox camp would never consider crossing. Where does this ease of spirit come from? I have just offered an accounting for it that is more than likely.

Returning to the core of spirituality that informs the interreligious quest, and returning to Shlomo Dov's description of his father in terms of authenticity, I wonder out loud if this very authenticity, even if it finds varying expressions, is not itself a Rosen trait. Divergence and nuance among the brothers (including David's other brother Jeremy, who also has an important track record in this domain) and across the generations is natural. The common thread that runs across generations, now extending into a third generation, through the work of both David's and Mickey's children, is that of religious authenticity. Appreciating this trait is not only a tribute to the individual members of the Rosen family; it is a testimony and an invitation to authentic religious practice and to its expression in all interfaith relations.

Endnotes

Introduction (pgs 1–10)

1. Sanhedrin 82a.

2. My own contribution is something of an exception here. I did not intend to write for this volume, considering that initiating the project and editing the volume was sufficient. However, Geshe Tashi Tsering, who had undertaken to write about the Dalai Lama, was in a hospital in India, during COVID days, and let me know he could not deliver on his promise. Considering the importance of the Dalai Lama to the interfaith arena over the past several decades, I felt he should not be missing from our collection. I therefore reworked an essay that was published previously internally among Elijah scholars and used it to describe His Holiness as an interreligious hero. I had previously dedicated a book titled *Luther the Antisemite* to the memory of Krister Stendahl, describing him as one of my heroes. This does accord with the view that scholars communicate readily as interfaith heroes across religions.

3. There was also no attempt throughout this book to define interfaith or interreligious. The terms serve interchangeably. While I have a preference for the latter, the area of relations and reflection described in this book can be described using either term.

4. See Alon Goshen-Gottstein, *Religious Genius: Appreciating Inspiring Individuals across Traditions* (New York: Palgrave, 2017). A follow-up volume titled *Religious Geniuses: Case Studies* is scheduled to appear in the *Interreligious Reflections* series, in which the present volume also appears.

5. It is theoretically possible that certain types of interfaith work will feature specific dimensions of what is an interreligious hero. I have not attempted such a correlation, in part due to the circumstances that inform the present project.

6. See discussions in *Religious Genius*. The question of imitability is the conceptual thread that runs across the essays assembled in Richard Kieckhefer and George Bond, eds., *Sainthood: Its Manifestations in World Religions* (Berkeley: University of California Press, 1988).

7. Author's original title: "Pope Francis, Missionary of Inter-Faith Dialogue in the Footsteps of Saint Francis of Assisi."

St. Francis and Pope Francis (pgs 13–19)

8. In ch. 12 of the *Regola definitiva* (*the Rules of Life or the Order*), made up of only four verses, the first two verses talk about the sending of the Brothers among the Saracens and the infidels (Segretario Generale Giustizia, ed., *Sussidi Cefid: Il Dialogo*

Ecumenico e Interreligioso [Assisi: Centro Francescano Internazionale per il Dialogo Assisi, 2011], 156).

9. Pope Francis, address to representatives of the communications media, given at Paul VI Audience Hall, Rome, Mar. 16, 2013.

10. Cf. Robert F. Kennedy Jr. and Dennis Nolan, *Saint Francis: A Life of Joy* (New York: Hyperion, 2005), 2, 25.

11. *General Constitution of the Franciscan Missionary Brothers of the Sacred Heart of Jesus* (https://www.franciscancaring.org/road_to_brotherh.html).

12. Francis, *Fratelli tutti* (https://www.vatican.va/content/francesco/en/encyclicals/documents/papa-francesco_20201003_enciclica-fratelli-tutti.html), §3.

13. Francis, *Fratelli tutti*, §3, quoting the *Regula non bullata* of Francis of Assisi.

14. Cf. *Nostra aetate* (www.vatican.va/archive/hist_councils/ii_vatican_council/documents/vat-ii_decl_19651028_nostra-aetate_en.html), §4.

15. Francis, address at the Synagogue of Rome, given on Jan. 17, 2016. Cf. also Francis, address on the occasion of the courtesy visit to the two chief rabbis of Israel, May 26, 2014.

16. Francis, *Laudato sì*, §16 (https://www.vatican.va/content/francesco/en/encyclicals/documents/papa-francesco_20150524_enciclica-laudato-si.html).

17. Francis, *Laudato sì*, §70.

18. *Catechism of the Catholic Church*, 340, as cited in Francis, *Laudato sì*, §86.

19. Francis, *Laudato sì*, §220.

20. Francis, *Evangelii Gaudium* (www.vatican.va/content/francesco/en/apost_exhortations/documents/papa-francesco_esortazione-ap_20131124_evangelii-gaudium.html); *Acta Apostolicae Sedis* 105 (https://www.vatican.va/archive/aas/documents/2013/AAS-indice2013.pdf), 1190; cited in Francis, *Laudato sì*, §89.

21. Francis, *Laudato sì*, §92.

22. Francis, *Laudato sì*, §42.

23. Francis, *Laudato sì*, §92.

24. Francis, *Laudato sì*, §91.

25. Francis, *Laudato sì*, §93.

26. Pope John Paul II, *Centesimus annus* (www.vatican.va/content/john-paul-ii/en/encyclicals/documents/hf_jp-ii_enc_01051991_centesimus-annus.html); *AAS* 83 (https://www.vatican.va/archive/aas/documents/AAS-83-1991-ocr.pdf), 831. Francis, *Laudato sì*, §93.

27. New Zealand Catholic Bishops Conference, *Statement on Environmental Issues* (Sept. 1, 2006), cited in Francis, *Laudato sì*, §95.

28. Francis, *Fratelli tutti*, 271.

29. Author's original title: "Chaitanya Mahaprabhu: A Dialogical Dance."

30. Chaitanya's family name was Nimai or Visvambhara Misra. At the time of initiation in the ascetic order, his given name was Krsna Caitanya. He is popularly known as Chaitaya Dev or Chaitanya Mahaprabhu.

31. Cited in Edward C. Dimock Jr. and Tony Stewart, eds. and trans., *Caitanaya Caritamrta of Krsnadasa Kaviraja, Antyalila* (Cambridge: Harvard University Press, 1999), 992–95.

Chaitanya Mahaprabhu (pgs 21–27)

32. Cited in Swami Saradeshanand, *Sri Chaitanya Mahaprabhu* (Kolkata: Advaita Ashram, 2005), 368.

33. For life and works of Chaitanya, see Walther Eidlitz, *Krsna Caitanya: The Hidden Treasure of India, His Life and Teachings,* translated by Mario Windisch et al. (Stockholm: Almquest & Wiksell, 2014).

34. Kiyokazu Okita, "Singing in Protest: Early Hindu Muslim Encounters in Bengali Hagiographies of Chaitanya," in *Bhakti and Power: Debating India's Religion of the Heart,* edited by John Startton Hawley et al. (Seattle: University of Washington Press, 2019), 159–70.

35. Margaret Case, ed., *Govindadeva: A Dialogue in Stone* (New Delhi: IGNCA, 1996).

36. Cf. F. S. Growse, *Mathura: A District Memoir* (Reprint, Delhi: Pilgrims, 1998), 184–271.

37. See Shrivatsa Goswami, "Bhakti and Power from the Inside: A Devotee's Reading of What Chaitanya Achieved," in Hawley et al., eds., *Bhakti and Power,* 179.

38. Gopal Narayan Bahura, "Govind Gatha," in Case, ed., *Govindadeva,* 201.

39. Harold Coward, ed., *Studies in Indian Thought: The Collected Papers of Prof. T. R. V. Murti* (Delhi: Motilal Banarasidass, 1983), 23, 27.

40. The system of thought in this school is understood as expansion of the seed statement from *Bhagavata Purana* (1.2.11): "Vadanti tat tattvavidas tattvam yaj jnanam advayam" (Those who know the reality declare it to be the non-dual knowedge). Chaitanya preferes the term *advaya* (non-dual) over *advaita.* T. R. V. Murti explains the difference: "*Advaya* is knowledge free from the duality of the extremes (*antas* or *drsti*s) of 'is' and 'is-not', being and becoming, etc. It is knowledge free from conceptual distinctions. *Advaita* is knowledge of a difference-less entity—*Brahman* (Pure Being). *Advaya* is purely *epistemological* approach; *advaita* is *ontological*" (*Studies in Indian Thought: Collected Papers of Professor T. R. V. Murti,* edited by Harold G. Coward [Delhi: Motilal Banarsidass, 1996], 182).

41. *Bhagavata Purana* 3.28; 11.19–29.

42. *Bhagavata Purana, Rasapancadhyayi,* bk. 10, chs. 29–33.

43. It is the highest spiritual realization in Chaitanya's way where the non-dual absolute, manifesting in human form as Krishna, sports in Vrindavan with the infinite number of Gopis, the cowherd women symbolizing the spiritual seekers of the divine love. See Graham M. Schweig, *Dance of Divine Love: The Rasa Lila of Krishna from the Bhagavata Purana, India's Classic Sacred Love Story* (Princeton: Princeton University Press, 2005).

44. "Sraddham bhagavate sastre, anindam anyatra eva hi" (*Bhagavata Purana* 11.3.26).

45. "Atmendriya priti iccha tara nama kama, krishnendriya priti iccha dhare prema nama" (A. C. Bhaktivedanta Swami Prabhupada, *Caitanya Caritamrta of Krsnadasa Kaviraja: Adilila* 4.141 [Alachua, FL: Bhaktivedanta Book Trust International, 1984], 202).

46. "Atmasukhdekhe gopir nahika vichar, krsna sukher hetu kare saba byabahara" (Prabhupada, *Adilila* 4.149, 202).

47. "Apani karimu bhaktabhava angikare, apani acari bhakti shikamu sabare, apane na kaile dharma shikhana na jaya" (Prabhupada, *Adilila* 3.18–19, 178).

48 "Apani acari bhakti karila pracara" (Prabhupada, *Adilila* 4.37, 190).

49. A. C. Bhaktivedanta Swami Prabhupada, *Caitanya Caritamrta of Krsnadasa Kaviraja: Antyalila* 20, sl. (verse) 5–6 (Alachua, FL: Bhaktivedanta Book Trust International, 1984), 994.

50. He was part of the larger Visnava tradition. His movement is called Gaudiya Vaisnavism. The global Hare Krishna movement or ISCKON follows Chaitanya. See Edwin F. Bryant et al., eds., *The Hare Krishna Movement: The Postcharismatic Fate of a Religious Transplant* (New York: Columbia University Press, 2004).

51. See Margaret H. Case, *Seeing Krishna: The Religious World of a Brahman Family in Vrindaban* (New York: Oxford University Press, 2000); John Stratton Hawley, *Krishna's Playground: Vrindavan in the Twenty-First Century* (New Delhi: Oxford University Press, 2020), ch. 6 "Being Shrivatsa," 218–65.

52. Right after World War One, a famous entrance was that of an Englishman, Ronald Nixon, who later became known as Yogi Krishna Prem, a mystic follower of Chaitanya.

53. In the company of Prof. Harvey Cox, a great champion of a dialogical culture.

Guru Nanak Dev Ji (pgs 29–37)

54. Thomas Carlyle, *On Heroes, Hero Worship, and the Heroic in History* (Reprint, London: Electric Book Co., 2001), 3.

55. Carlyle, *On Heroes*, 91.

56. Carlyle, *On Heroes*, 17.

57. *Guru Granth Sahib* (Reprint, Amritsar: Shiromani Gurdwara Parbandhak Committee, 1983), 471.

58. *Guru Granth Sahib*, 468.

59. Bhai Gurdas Ji (https://www.searchgurbani.com/bhai-gurdas-vaaran/index/vaar).

60. *Guru Granth Sahib*, 141.

61. Harbans Lal, "Guru Nanak Pioneered Interfaith Dialogues, Associations, and Global Scriptures," in Hardev Singh Virk, ed., *Interfaith Dialogues: Sikh Perspectives* (New Delhi: Guru Nanak Foundation, 2020), 120.

62. Bhai Gurdas Ji (https://www.searchgurbani.com/bhai-gurdas-vaaran/index/vaar).

63. See Devinder Singh Chahal, "Nanak the Guru and His Philosophy," *Understanding Sikhism: The Research Journal* 12, nos. 1–2 (Jan.–Dec. 2010), 8–22.

64. *Guru Granth Sahib*, 96.

65. Guru Gobind Singh, *Akal Ustat in Dasam Granth* (Reprint, Amritsar: Bhai Chattar Singh-Jiwan Singh, 2011), v. 86.

66. As cited in Jaswant Singh Neki, *Guru Granth Sahib and Its Context* (New Delhi: Bahai Vir Singh Sahitya Sadan, 2007), 11.

67. *Guru Granth Sahib*, 966.

68. Neki, *Guru Granth Sahib*, 23.

69. *Guru Granth Sahib*, 661.

70. One of my first forays into the interfaith movement was to visit Pope John Paul II in 2000, at the beginning of the new millennium. Subsequently, my engagement has substantially grown through such key events, as at the CPWR event in Barcelona, where we served nearly 7000 people daily with langar—the provision of food in an egalitarian manner to all. Serving langar is such a fundamental part of the Sikh ethos that we have continued that tradition, serving all, irrespective of their faith. For example, we continued the tradition of serving langar at the Ram Katha event in Birmingham, at the CPWR event in Salt Lake City, and, most recently, during the pandemic, through our youth organization Nishkam Swat. Other key projects have included hosting major conferences such as the Elijah Board in Amritsar and the Globalisation for Common Good in Kericho, Kenya. I have also been involved with colleagues to launch a Charter for Forgiveness and Reconciliation and have been working to establish a Museum of World Religions in conjunction with the University of Birmingham.

71. As cited in a translation by Bhai Sahib; publication information unavailable.

72. Guru Gobind Singh, *Akal Ustat,* 270.

73. *Guru Granth Sahib*, 864.

Śrī Rāmakṛṣṇa (pgs 39–47)

74. Author's original title: "Śrī Rāmakṛṣṇa (1836–1886): The Mystic Saint of Modern India."

75. Mahendra Nath Gupta, *Sri Ramakrishna Kathamrita,* 2 vols. (Kolkata: Udbodhan Karyalaya, 1986–1987). Swami Nikhilananda, trans., *The Gospel of Sri Ramakrishna* (Chennai, Ind: Sri Ramakrishna Math, 1996), 511.

76. Romain Rolland, *La vie de Ramakrishna*, (Paris: Delamain et Boutelleau, 1929); E. F. Malcolm-Smith, trans., *The Life of Ramakrishna: A Study of Mysticism and Action in Living India* (Almora, Ind.: Advaita Ashrama, 1931).

77. Swami Vivekananda, *Complete Works of Swami Vivekananda*, 9 vols., 12th ed. (Kolkata: Advaita Ashrama, 2013).

78. Christopher Isherwood, *Ramakrishna and His Disciples,* 2nd ed. (Hollywood: Vedanta Press & Catalog, 1980).

79. Sri Aurobindo, "The Synthesis of Yoga Introduction V," *Arya: A Philosophical Review* 5 (1914) 303–12. A compilation appears in Sri Aurobindo Ashram Trust, *The Synthesis of Yoga* (Pondicherry: Shri Aurobindo Ashram Publication Dept., 1999).

80. Swami Saradananda, vol. 1 of *Sri Ramakrishna Leela Prasanga,* 5 vols., 12th ed. (Kolkata: Udbodhan Karyalaya, 1960); vol. 2 of *Sri Ramakrishna Leela Prasanga,* 5 vols., 11th ed. (Kolkata: Udbodhan Karyalaya, 1963). Swami Chetanananda, trans., *Sri Ramakrishna and his Divine Play* (St. Louis: Vedanta Society of St. Louis, 2003).

81. Swami Tapasyananda, *Sri Ramakrishna Life and Teachings,* 3rd ed. (Chennai: Sri Ramakrishna Math Chennai, 2018), 74.

82. Nikhilananda, *Gospel of Sri Ramakrishna*, 111.

83. Nikhilananda, *Gospel of Sri Ramakrishna*, 511.

84. Swami Vivekananda, *Complete Works*.

85. Swami Gambhirananda, *History of the Ramakrishna Math and Mission*, 3rd ed. (Kolkata: Advaita Ashrama, 1983), 36–37.

86. For the most recent articulation of Śrī Rāmakṛṣṇa's contribution to this field, see Ayon Maharaj, *Infinite Paths to Infinite Reality: Sri Ramakrishna and Cross-Cultural Philosophy of Religion* (Oxford: Oxford University Press, 2018).

'Abd Al-Qâdir Al-Jazâ'irî (pgs 49–59)

87. John W. Kiser, *Commander of the Faithful* (New York: Monkfish, 2008), 15.

88. Kiser, *Commander of the Faithful*, 19.

89. Kiser, *Commander of the Faithful*, 26.

90. Kiser, *Commander of the Faithful*, 27.

91. Kiser, *Commander of the Faithful*, 104.

92. Qur'an, IV: 125.

93. Kiser, *Commander of the Faithful*, 244.

94. Kiser, *Commander of the Faithful*, 286.

95. Kiser, *Commander of the Faithful*, 273.

96. Kiser, *Commander of the Faithful*, 288.

97. Kiser, *Commander of the Faithful*, 297–99.

98. Cited in Kiser, *Commander of the Faithful*, 301–2.

99. Kiser, *Commander of the Faithful*, 302.

100. Letter to Bishop Louis-Antoine Pavy, cited in Kiser, *Commander of the Faithful*, 302.

101. Kiser, *Commander of the Faithful*, 303.

Claude Montefiore (pgs 63–69)

102. Benjamin Jowett, cited in Lucy Cohen, *Some Recollections of Claude Goldsmid Montefiore* (London: Faber and Faber, 1940), 47.

103. In a letter to Schechter, dated Sept. 8, 1903, Montefiore writes, "I have often defended the Rabbis etc. & have shown myself a disciple of yours" (cited in J. B. Stein, *Lieber Freund: The Letters of Claude Goldsmid Montefiore to Solomon Schechter* [Lanham, MD: University Press of America, 1988], 45). See also the preface to Montefiore, *The Hibbert Lectures 1892: Lectures on the Origin and Growth of Religion, as Illustrated by the Religion of the Ancient Hebrews 1892* (Reprint, Whitefish, MT: Kessinger, 2007).

104. Some of his writings were simply word-by-word commentaries of both the Hebrew Bible and New Testament; others were sermons written for ordinary Jewish

congregations; still others were written for a general Jewish audience; finally, the largest number of works were written with a Christian (and often a scholarly Christian) audience in mind.

105. Victor de Waal, "The Centenary of the London Society for the Study of Religion: Friedrich von Hügel, Claude Montefiore and Their Friends," *Theology* 110 (2007) 251–59.

106. Montefiore, *Outlines of Liberal Judaism: For the Use of Parents and Teachers* (London: Macmillan, 1912), 212.

107. *Dabru Emet: A Jewish Statement on Christians and Christianity* (https://icjs.org/wp-content/uploads/2020/06/Dabru-Emet.pdf); *To Do the Will of Our Father in Heaven: Toward a Partnership between Jews and Christians* (https://www.cjcuc.org/2015/12/03/orthodox-rabbinic-statement-on-christianity/).

108. Montefiore, *The Synoptic Gospels* (London: Macmillan, 1909), 1:cxxxv.

109. Montefiore, "The Significance of Jesus for His Own Age," *Hibbert Journal* 10 (1911–1912), 773.

110. Montefiore, *Synoptic Gospels* (London: Macmillan, 1909), 2:326–27.

111. "On the one hand was the artificiality of a hair-splitting and barren erudition, and on the other the fresh directness of the layman and the son of the people; here was the product of long generations of misrepresentation and distortion, there was simplicity, plainness and freedom" (Wilhelm Bousset and Hugo Gressman, *Die Religion des Judentums im späthellenistischen Zeitalter* [Tübingen: Mohr, 1926], 67).

112. Montefiore, *The Old Testament and After* (London: Macmillan, 1923), 576.

113. Nahum Glatzer, ed., *Franz Rosenzweig: His Life and Thought* (New York: Schocken, 1961), 19.

114. Louis Jacobs, *Montefiore and Loewe on the Rabbis* (London: Liberal Jewish Synagogue, 1962), 4.

115. Montefiore, *Rabbinic Literature and Gospel Teachings* (London: Macmillan, 1930), 239.

116. Montefiore and Herbert Loewe, eds., *A Rabbinic Anthology* (London: Macmillan, 1938), xxiv.

117. Cohen, *Some Recollections*, 189.

Martin Buber (pgs 71–76)

118. Author's original title: "Martin Buber and the Jewish-Christian Dialogue."

119. On this subject, see the contributions written by Jewish scholars in *Lexikon für Theologie und Kirche* 2 (1994) 737ff; and in *Religion in Geschichte und Gegenwart* 1 (1998) 1087–89.

120. Extensive literature (until 1981) in the field of art. See Buber in *Theologische Realenzyklopädie* 7 (1981) 253–58. From the Catholic side, see especially Hans Urs von Balthasar, *Einsame Zwiesprache: Martin Buber und das Christentum*, 2nd ed. (Cologne: Johannes, 1993); Bernhard Casper, *Das dialogische Denken: Franz Rosenzweig, Ferdinand Ebner und Martin Buber* (Munich: Alber Philosophie, 2002); Karl-Josef Kuschel, *Martin Buber: Seine Herausforderung an das Christentum* (Gütersloh: Gütersloher, 2015).

121. Buber, *Schriften zum Chassidismus*, Werke 3 (Munich: Kösel, 1963). English version: *Tales of the Hasidim*, translated by Olga Marx, 2 vols. (New York: Schocken, 1947, 1991).

122. Buber, *Schriften zur Bibel*, Werke 2 (Munich: Kösel, 1964). English version: *On the Bible: Eighteen Studies*, edited by Nahum N. Glatzer (Syracuse, NY: Syracuse University Press, 2002).

123. For Buber's reflections on this, see Buber and Franz Rosenzweig, *Die Schrift und ihre Verdeutschung*, Werke 2 (Munich: Kösel, 1964). English version: *Scripture and Translation*, translated by Lawrence Rosenwald with Everett Fox (Bloomington: Indiana University Press, 1994).

124. Buber, *Schriften zur Philosophie*, Werke 1 (Munich: Kösel, 1962). English version: *The Knowledge of Man: Selected Essays*, edited by Maurice S. Friedman (Reprint, n.p.: Humanities, 1988).

125. On this and the following, see Buber, *Zwei Glaubensweisen*, Werke 1, 657; cf. 178. English version: *Two Types of Faith*, translated by Norman P. Goldhawk (Syracuse, NY: Syracuse University Press, 2003).

126. Cf. W. Kasper, *Juden und Christen: Das eine Volk Gottes* (Freiburg: n.p., 2020), 19–29.

127. Jan-Heiner Tück, ed., *Die Beschneidung Jesu: Was sie Juden und Christen heute bedeutet* (Freiburg: n.p., 2020).

128. Pontifical Biblical Commission, *The Jewish People and Their Sacred Scriptures in the Christian Bible* (https://www.vatican.va/roman_curia/congregations/cfaith/pcb_documents/rc_con_cfaith_doc_20020212_popolo-ebraico_en.html).

129. Schalom Ben-Chorin, *Brother Jesus: The Nazarene Through Jewish Eyes*, translated by Jared S. Klein and Max Reinhart (Athens: University of Georgia Press, 2018). The exegetically difficult and much discussed question as to whether and to what extent we can contrast Jesus's faith in God and the faith in Jesus as the Christ in this way or whether the foundations of the later Christology are not rather already laid in Jesus himself, at least implicitly, cannot be dealt with in this context. Cf. von Balthasar, *Theodramatik* 2/2 (Einsiedeln: n.p., 1978), 116ff.

130. Buber, *Gottesfinsternis: Betrachtungen zur Beziehung zwischen Religion und Philosophie*, Werke 1. English version: *Eclipse of God: Studies in the Relation between Religion and Philosophy* (Princeton: Princeton University Press, 2013). Buber understands this eclipse of God as a consequence of faith understood as *pistis*, cf. *Zwei Glaubensweisen*, 776ff. He thus connects to some worldly forms of Christian mysticism, but with hardly the same understanding as in the Pastoral Constitution of Vatican II, *Gaudium et spes* (1965).

131. Buber, *Begegnung: Autobiographische Fragmente* (Stuttgart: Kohlhammer, 1961), 43ff. English version: *Meetings: Autobiographical Fragments*, edited by Maurice Friedman (London: Routledge, 2013).

132. Cf. Rosenzweig, *Der Stern der Erlösung*, Ges. Schriften 2 (The Hague: Nijhoff, 1976), 386ff. English version: *The Star of Redemption*, translated by Barbara E. Galli (Madison: University of Wisconsin Press, 2008).

133. Buber, *Zur Geschichte des Dialogischen Prinzips*, in *Das dialogische Prinzip: Ich und Du. Zwiesprache. Die Frage an den Einzelnen. Elemente des Zwischenmenschlichen.*

Zur Geschichte des dialogischen Prinzips, Werke 1 (Gütersloh: Gütersloher, 1999). English version: "On the History of the Dialogical Principle," in *Between Man and Man,* translated by Ronald Gregor Smith (London: Routedge & Kegan Paul, 1947).

134. Buber, *Prophetie, Apokalyptik und die geschichtliche Stunde,* Werke 2. English version: *The Prophetic Faith* (Princeton: Princeton University Press, 2019).

135. Cf. Kasper, *Juden und Christen,* 43ff.

Abraham Joshua Heschel (pgs 87–91)

136. Author's original title: "Abraham Joshua Heschel: The Firebrand Snatched from the Fire of Nazism, Who Ignited Our Relationships with the Divine Pathos."

137. They include Rabbi Dov Maer of Mezeritch (the Great Maggid), Rabbi Abraham Joshua Heschel (the Rav of Apt), and Rabbi Pinhas of Koretz.

138. As A. J. Heschel himself stated, "No Religion Is an Island," *Union Seminary Quarterly Review* 21, no. 2 (1966) 117.

139. Cf. Heschel, *Il messaggio dei Profeti,* translated by A. Del Bianco (Rome: Borla, 1981), 6.

140. Cf. Heschel, *Il messaggio dei Profeti,* 14.

141. Heschel, *Il messaggio dei Profeti,* 54.

142. Heschel, *The Earth Is the Lord's: The Inner World of the Jew in Eastern Europe* (New York: Schuman, 1950), 64.

143. Cf. Heschel, *God in Search of Man: A Philosophy of Judaism* (New York: Farrar, Straus & Cudahy, 1955), 311.

144. Alon Goshen-Gottstein, "No Religion Is an Island: Following the Trail Blazer," *Shofar* 26.1 (2007) 73.

145. Cf. Adolfo Lippi, *Elezione e passione: Saggio di teologia in ascolto dell'Ebraismo* (Torino, It.: Elledici, 1996), 81.

146. Cf. Heschel, *God in Search of Man,* 3–22.

147. Heschel, *God in Search of Man,* 23.

148. Cf. Paul Ricoeur, "Note introductive," in Richard Kearney and Joseph Stephen O'Leary, eds., *Heidegger et la question de Dieu* (Paris: Grasset, 1980), 19.

149. Cf. Edward K. Kaplan, *Spiritual Radical: Abraham Joshua Heschel in America, 1940-1972* (New Haven, CT: Yale University Press, 2007), 235–76; Alexander Even-Chen and Ephraim Meir, *Between Heschel and Buber: A Comparative Study,* Emunot: Jewish Philosophy and Kabbalah (Boston: Academic Studies Press, 2012), 273–78.

150. Ephraim Meir, "Da *Nostra Aetate* a Papa Francesco: Una retrospettiva ebraica," in Gabriella Caponigro, ed., *Figli di Abramo: Il dialogo fra religioni cinqunt'anni dopo* Nostra Aetate (http://www.edizioniets.com/priv_file_libro/3348.pdf), ch. 3.

151. Heschel, "No Religion," 124.

152. See Goshen-Gottstein, "Heschel and Interreligious Dialogue: Formulating the

Question," in Stanislaw Krajewski and Adam Lipszyc, eds., *Abraham Joshua Heschel: Philosophy, Theology and Interreligious Dialogue* (Wiesbaden: Harrassowitz, 2009), 161. Throughout the article (161–67), Goshen-Gottstein precisely starts from the thought of the rabbi to formulate questions of great importance, which intend to trace the future of interreligious relations.

153. Heschel, "No Religion," 119.

154. Heschel, "No Religion," 123.

155. Pope Francis, "Discorso del Santo Padre Francesco a una delegazione dell'American Jewish Committee"' (http://www.vatican.va/content/francesco/it/speeches/2019/.march/documents/papa-francesco_20190308_american-jewish-committee.html).

156. The Center for Jewish-Christian Understanding and Cooperation, *To Do the Will of Our Father in Heaven: Toward a Partnership between Jews and Christians* (https://www.cjcuc.org/2015/12/03/orthodox-rabbinic-statement-on-christianity).

157. David Rosen, *Faithfulness to Tradition and Peacemaking in the Middle East* (https://www.rabbidavidrosen.net/wp-content/uploads/2016/02/Faithfulness_to_tradition_and_Peacemaking_in_the_Middle_East.pdf).

Pope John XXIII (pgs 95–101)

158. Pope Pius X, "*Pascendi Dominici gregis*: Encyclical of Pope Pius X on the Doctrines of the Modernists" (https://www.vatican.va/content/pius-x/en/encyclicals/documents/hf_p-x_enc_19070908_pascendi-dominici-gregis.html).

159. Pope John XXIII, *Journal de l'âme* (Paris: Cerf, 1964), 142. Gottstein's translation here and for following citations.

160. Iliana Raïtchéva, "Monseigneur Roncalli et sa mission apostolique en Bulgarie" (https://bnr.bg/fr/post/100382712/monseigneur-roncalli-et-sa-mission-apostolique-en-bulgarie).

161. Martino Diez, *Jean XXIII ami des Turcs* (https://www.oasiscenter.eu/fr/jean-xxiii-ami-des-turcs).

162. According to the International Raoul Wallenberg Foundation, he saved between 24,000 and 80,000 "cousins and compatriots of Jesus," as he called them. See https://www.raoulwallenberg.net for more information.

163. André Kaspi, *Jules Isaac ou la passion de la vérité* (Paris: Plon, 2002), 229–35.

164Pope John XIII, *Journal de l'âme*, 394.

165. As cited in *L'Orient-Le Jour*, "Jean XXIII, le pape du concile, diplomate et Don Camillo" (https://www.lorientlejour.com/article/863060/jean-xxiii-le-pape-du-concile-diplomate-et-don-camillo.html).

Cardinal Augustin Bea (pgs 103–108)

166. Author's original title: "Cardinal Augustin Bea: Father of the Conciliar Declaration *Nostra aetate*."

167. Stjepan Schmidt, *Augustin Bea: The Cardinal of Unity*, translated by Leslie Wearne (New Rochelle, NY: New City, 1992), 500.

Pope John Paul II (pgs 111–116)

168. Author's original title: "Pope John Paul II as an Ice-Breaker in the Jewish-Catholic Dialogue."

169. Pope John Paul II, "Homily of His Holiness John Paul II" (https://www.vatican.va/content/john-paul-ii/en/homilies/1979/documents/hf_jp-ii_hom_19790607_polonia-brzezinka.html).

170. Pontifical Commission for Religious Relations with the Jews, "We Remember: A Reflection on the *Shoah*" (https://www.bc.edu/content/dam/files/research_sites/cjl/texts/cjrelations/resources/documents/catholic/We_Remember.htm).

171. John Paul II, "Prayer of the Holy Father at the Western Wall" (https://www.vatican.va/content/john-paul-ii/en/travels/2000/documents/hf_jp-ii_spe_20000326_jerusalem-prayer.html).

172. "Die Begegnung zwischen dem Gottesvolk des von Gott nie gekündigten Alten Bundes und dem des Neuen Bundes ist zugleich ein Dialog innerhalb unserer Kirche, gleichsam zwischen dem ersten und zweiten Teil ihrer Bibel" (John Paul II, "Begenung von Papst Johannes Paul II. mit Vertretern der jüdischen Gemeinde" [https://www.vatican.va/content/john-paul-ii/de/speeches/1980/november/documents/hf_jp_ii_spe_19801117_ebrei-magonza.html]).

173. Commission for Religious Relations with the Jews, "'The Gifts and the Calling of God Are Irrevocable' (Rom 11:29): A Reflection on Theological Questions Pertaining to Catholic-Jewish Relations on the Occasion of the Fiftieth Anniversary of 'Nostra aetate' (No. 4)" (http://www.christianunity.va/content/unitacristiani/en/commissione-per-i-rapporti-religiosi-con-l-ebraismo/commissione-per-i-rapporti-religiosi-con-l-ebraismo-crre/documenti-della-commissione/en.html).

174. "Die jüdische Religion ist für uns nicht etwas 'Äußerliches,' sondern gehört in gewisser Weise zum 'Inneren' unserer Religion. Zu ihr haben wir somit Beziehungen wie zu keiner anderen Religion. Ihr seid unsere bevorzugten Brüder und, so könnte man gewissermaßen sagen, unsere älteren Brüder" (John Paul II, 'Ansprache von Johannes Paul II' [https://www.vatican.va/content/john-paul-ii/de/speeches/1986/april/documents/hf_jp-ii_spe_19860413_sinagoga-roma.html]).

Cardinal Joseph Bernardin (pgs 127–131)

175. Author's original title: "A Blessing to Each Other: The Interreligious Vision of Cardinal Joseph Bernardin."

176. Joseph Bernardin, *A Blessing to Each Other: Cardinal Joseph Bernardin and Jewish-Catholic Dialogue* (Chicago: Liturgy Training Publications, 1996).

Rabbi Irving Yitz Greenberg (pgs 135–141)

177. Author's original title: "Rav Yitz: An Interfaith Hero."

178. Irving Greenberg, "Theology after the Shoah: The Transformation of the Core Paradigm," *Modern Judaism* 26.3 (Oct. 2006) 213–39; 227–28.

179. Greenberg, "Personal Service: A Central Jewish Norm for Our Time," *Contact* 4.1 (2001) 3–4.

180. Greenberg, *For the Sake of Heaven and Earth: The New Encounter between Judaism and Christianity* (Philadelphia: Jewish Publication Society, 2004), 196.

181. Greenberg, *For the Sake*, 201–3.

182. Rodger Kamenetz, *The Jew in the Lotus: A Poet's Rediscovery of Jewish Identity in Buddhist India* (Northvale, NJ: Aronson, 1998), 49.

183. Greenberg, *For the Sake*, 31–32.

184. Greenberg, *For the Sake*, 37.

185. Greenberg, *For the Sake*, 38.

186. Greenberg, *For the Sake*, 39.

187. Greenberg, *For the Sake*, 69.

188. Greenberg, "Voluntary Covenant" (https://rabbiirvinggreenberg.com/wp-content/uploads/2013/02/2Perspectives-Voluntary-Covenant-1987-CLAL-2-of-3.pdf), 38.

189. Greenberg, *For the Sake*, 26.

190. Greenberg, *For the Sake*, 49.

191. Greenberg, *For the Sake*, 105.

192. Greenberg, *For the Sake*, 69.

Abdurrahman Wahid (pgs 143–150)

193. Bret Stephens, "The Last King of Java," *Wall Street Journal*, Apr. 7, 2007 (https://www.wsj.com/articles/SB117591182092262904).

194. Ron Kampeas, "Ex-Premier Fights for Moderate Islam," Jewish Telegraphic Agency, May 16, 2008 (https://www.jta.org/2008/05/16/culture/ex-premier-fights-for-moderate-islam).

195. Abdurrahman Wahid and Israel Lau, "The Evils of Holocaust Denial," *Wall Street Journal*, June 12, 2007 (https://www.libforall.org/lfa/media/2007/WSJ_The-Evils-of-Holocaust-Denial_06-12-07.pdf).

196. Seth Mydans, "Abdurrahman Wahid, Sixty-Nine, Is Dead; Led Indonesia for Two Years of Tumult," *New York Times*, Dec. 30, 2009 (https://www.nytimes.com/2009/12/31/world/asia/31wahid.html).

197. This statement was facilitated by the Elijah Interfaith Institute and has since been reissued by its Board of World Religious Leaders. See https://elijah-interfaith.org/addressing-the-world/elijah-board-of-world-religious-leaders-endorses-anti-terrorism-statement.

198. Jeff Jacoby, "Defeating Islamic Extremism" (https://www.libforall.org/lfa/media/2006/Boston-Globe_Defeating-Islamist-Extremism_01-22-06.pdf).

199. Wahid, ed., *The Illusion of an Islamic State: How an Alliance of Moderates Launched a Successful Jihad against Radicalization and Terrorism in the World's Largest Muslim-Majority Country*, translated by C. Holland Taylor (Jakarta: Wahid Institute, 2011), 36.

200. With the permission of the author, this paragraph and the subsequent three paragraphs are drawn (with some modifications) from Timothy Samuel Shah et al., *Indonesia Religious Freedom Landscape Report 2020* (Washington, DC: Religious

Freedom Institute, 2020); available at https://www.religiousfreedominstitute.
org/publication/indonesia-religious-freedom-landscape-report. The report's primary author, Dr. Shah, has joined the Center for Shared Civilizational Values as a
founding board member and its director of strategic initiatives.

201. James M. Dorsey, "The Battle for the Soul of Islam," *Current Trends in Islamist
Theology* 27 (Oct. 2020), 106–27; 123, 107.

Fethullah Gülen (pgs 153–160)

202. Author's original title: "Fethullah Gülen: Tradition Embracing the Age."

203. Ali Ünal and Alphonse Williams, *Advocate of Dialogue: Fethullah Gülen* (Fairfax,
VA: Fountain, 2008), 316–17.

204. Ibrahim Özdemir, "Mandela and Gülen" (http://fgulen.com/en/press/columns-
en/ibrahim-ozdemir-todays-zaman-mandela-and-gulen).

205. Zeki Saritoprak and Ali Ünal, "An Interview with Fethullah Gülen," *Muslim World*
95.3 (2005) 456 (https://doi.org/10.1111/j.1478-1913.2005.00104.x).

206. Fethullah Gülen, *Key Concepts in the Practice of Sufism* (Clifton, NJ: Tughra,
2007), xxii.

207. Translated by author from Gülen, *Insanin Ozundeki Sevgi* (Istanbul: Ufuk Kita-
plari, 2003), 146–47.

208. Heon Kim, "Gülen's Dialogic Sufism: A Constructional and Constructive Factor
of Dialogue" (http://citeseerx.ist.psu.edu/viewdoc/download?doi=10.1.1.517.643
0&rep=rep1&type=pdf).

209. Jon Pahl, *Fethullah Gülen: A Life of Hizmet* (Clifton, NJ: Blue Dome, 2019), 239.

210. Translated from Gülen, "Diyalogda Israr" (https://www.herkul.org/kirik-testi/
diyalogda-israr/).

211. Translated from Gülen, "Sozde Degil Ozde Muslumanlik" (https://www.herkul.
org/tag/yasatmak-icin-yasama/).

Sheikh Abdullah Bin Bayyah (pgs 163–168)

212. Author's original title: "Sheikh Al-Allamah Abdullah Bin Maḥfūz Bin Bayyah."

213. See https://www.acommonword.com for more information.

214. See https://www.rfp.org/resources/marrakesh-declaration-on-the-rights-of-relig
ious-minorities-in-predominantly-muslim-majority-communities/ for more information.

Mahatma Gandhi (pgs 171–178)

215. Cited in Margaret Chatterjee, *Gandhi's Religious Thought* (Notre Dame: University of Notre Dame Press, 1983), 17.

216. Mahatma Gandhi, *All Men Are Brothers*, compiled and edited by Krishna Kri-
palani (New York: Continuum, 2001), 57.

217. Gandhi, *All Men Are Brothers*, 72.

218. Gandhi, cited in https://www.mkgandhi.org/god/ramanama/11myrama.html.

219. Gandhi, *The Voice of Truth*, edited by Shriman Narayan (Ahmedabad, Ind.: Na-vajivan, 1969), 265.

220. Gandhi, *Voice of Truth*, 268.

221. Gandhi, *All Men Are Brothers*, 54.

222. Gandhi, *Voice of Truth*, 268.

223. Gandhi, *Voice of Truth*, 265.

224. Gandhi, *Voice of Truth*, 267.

225. Gandhi, cited in https://www.mkgandhi.org/god/ramanama/11myrama.html.

226. Gandhi, *All Men Are Brothers*, 58.

Thomas Merton (pgs 181–187)

227. Thomas Merton, *The Seven Storey Mountain* (New York: Harcourt Brace Jovanov-ich, 1978), 178.

228. Matthew Kelty, *Flute Solo* (Garden City, NY: Image, 1980), 101–3.

229. Merton, *The Asian Journal of Thomas Merton: Edited from His Original Notebooks*, edited by Patrick Hart et al. (New York: New Directions, 1971), 124–25.

230 Dalai Lama, as cited in Paul Wilkins, ed., *Merton by Those Who Knew Him Best* (San Francisco: Harper and Row, 1984), 145.

231. Merton, *Contemplative Prayer* (New York: Image, 1971), 67.

232. Augustine, as cited in Merton, *Contemplative Prayer*, 33.

233. Merton, *Conjectures of a Guilty Bystander* (New York: Image, 1968), 156.

234. Benedict, prologue from *The Rule of St. Benedict*, v. 49. See https://christdesert.org/prayer/rule-of-st-benedict/prologue-verse-45-50/.

235. Merton, *New Seeds of Contemplation* (New York: New Directions, 1972), 60.

236. Merton, *New Seeds of Contemplation* (New York: New Directions, 1972), 72.

237. Merton, *New Seeds of Contemplation*, 291.

238. Merton, *Asian Journal*, 308.

Rabbi Zalman Schachter-Shalomi (pgs 189–195)

239. Author's original title: "Lessons from a Pioneer: Rabbi Zalman Schachter-Shalo-mi." This essay is based on the author's article "Reb Zalman, Neo-Hasidism, and Inter-Religious Engagement: Lessons from My Teacher," *Tikkun* 32.4 (Nov. 2017) 40–47.

240. Zalman Schachter-Shalomi with Edward Hoffman, *My Life in Jewish Renewal: A Memoir* (Lanham, MD: Rowman & Littlefield, 2012), 65.

241. Schachter-Shalomi with Hoffman, *My Life in Jewish Renewal*, 66.

242. Schachter-Shalomi with Hoffman, *My Life in Jewish Renewal*. From its inception in 1775, the HaBaD school (Lubavitch is the Russian town in which the dominant line of leaders resided from 1813 to 1915) envisioned itself as an intellectually rigorous

form of Hasidism, with a sophisticated set of teachings on theology, worship, and spiritual development. See Naftali Lowenthal, *Communicating the Infinite: The Emergence of the HaBaD School* (Chicago: University of Chicago Press, 1990). This is an often-overlooked aspect of the dynasty today, because it has become such a successful mass outreach organization in the post-Holocaust era.

243. See for example, "Toward a New and Kerygmatic Credo," published on the Shalom Center website (https://theshalomcenter.org/node/1395).

244. Schachter-Shalomi with Hoffman, *My Life in Jewish Renewal*, 156.

245. See, for example, Schachter-Shalomi, introduction to *Fragments of a Future Scroll: Hassidism for the Aquarian Age* (Germantown, PA: Leaves of Grass, 1975), 6. In this same brief text, he goes on to say that in order to meet the needs of this rising generation, Jewish teachers must become more open to and adept at sharing Jewish mystical resources with countercultural seekers, in addition to making thoughtful use of insights and techniques from other traditions.

246. This volume is an edited translation of the work of Rabbi Dov Baer of Lubavitch, the second leader of the HaBaD-Lubavitch dynasty, by the British rabbi and scholar Louis Jacobs.

247. Schachter-Shalomi, "November 24, 1963, Schachter to Merton," in *Merton and Judaism: Holiness in Words; Recognition, Repentance, and Renewal*, edited by Beatrice Bruteau (Louisville: Fons Vitae, 2003), 201.

248. Schachter-Shalomi with Hoffman, *My Life in Jewish Renewal*, 90.

249. Schachter-Shalomi with Hoffman, *My Life in Jewish Renewal*, 90.

250. Schachter-Shalomi with Hoffman, *My Life in Jewish Renewal*, 91.

251. For more on this meeting, see my article "Howard Thurman's Mentorship of Zalman Schachter-Shalomi," in *Interreligious Studies: Dispatches from an Emerging Field*, edited by Hans Gustafson (Waco, TX: Baylor University Press, 2020), 228–35. Part of what Reb Zalman (a self-described mystic) enjoyed so much about studying with Thurman was that the dean consciously blended academic study with embodied practice and personal reflection. This included labs in which Thurman made use of music, movement, and meditation. Reb Zalman patterned his teaching after Thurman early in his career. See Schachter-Shalomi, "What I Found in the Chapel," in *My Neighbor's Faith: Stories of Interreligious Encounter, Growth, and Transformation*, edited by Jennifer Howe Peace et al. (Maryknoll, NY: Orbis, 2012), 208–11.

252. Sara Davidson, *The December Project: An Extraordinary Rabbi and a Skeptical Seeker Confront Life's Greatest Mystery* (New York: HarperOne, 2014), 78.

253. Schachter-Shalomi, "February 6, 1964, Schachter to Merton," in *Merton and Judaism*, 198–99.

254. Schachter-Shalomi with Hoffman, *My Life in Jewish Renewal*, 160–61.

255. Reb Zalman's engagement with Merton and other Catholic monastics actually played a concrete role in the development of both the Jewish Renewal and Havurah movements. See my forthcoming article, "Envisioning a *Jewish* Monastic Community: Zalman Schachter-Shalomi, Catholicism, and the B'nai Or Fellowship" *Studies in Christian-Jewish Relations* (2022).

256. See Schachter-Shalomi, "Toward a New and Kerygmatic Credo" (https://thesha-lomcenter.org/node/1395).

257. See Susan Goldstein, "Rabbi Zalman Schachter-Shalomi Extended Interview," *Religion and Ethics Newsweekly*, Sept. 30, 2005 (http://www.pbs.org/wnet/religion andethics/2005/09/30/september-30-2005-rabbi-zalman-schachter-shalomi-extended-interview/9753).

Raimon Panikkar (pgs 197–204)

258. Author's original title: "Raimon Panikkar, My Teacher and 'Hero': Raimon Panik-kar (1918–2010); On a Personal Note."

259. First published in 1957, the book has had several English editions up until 1982. Above quote from Raimon Panikkar, preface, *The Unknown Christ of Hinduism* (Bangalore: Asian Trading Corporation, 1982). Panikkar continued and deep-ened this Hindu-Christian dialogue—bringing it to a genuine dialogue between religions—by publishing *The Vedic Experience Mantramanjari: An Anthology of the Vedas for Modern Man and Contemporary Celebration* (Berkeley: University of California Press, Berkeley, 1977). Panikkar has also enriched Christology by his yet one more book, *Christophany:The Fullness of Man* (Maryknoll, NY: Orbis, 2004), originally published in Italian in 1999.

260. Panikkar, *The Intra-Religious Dialogue* (New York: Paulist, 1978).

261. It should be mentioned that Panikkar did commit himself to dialogue with athe-ists. His book *The Silence of God: An Answer of the Buddha* (Maryknoll, NY: Orbis, 1989) bears witness to this (the original, *El Silencio del Dios*, was published in Spanish in 1970).

262. The previous section is a summary of Panikkar's article, "Towards a Dialogical Dialogue," *InterCulture* 20.4 (Oct.-Dec. 1987) 14–39 (http://iimarchives.org/wp-content/blogs.dir/25/files/2017/06/inter97a-transforming-christian-mission-into-dialogue.pdf).

263. Panikkar, *Myth, Faith, and Hermeneutics: Cross-Cultural Studies* (New York: Pau-list, 1979).

264. Panikkar, *Myth, Faith, and Hermeneutics*, 2.

265. Panikkar, *Myth, Faith, and Hermeneutics*, 4–9.

266. The terms kairological and chronological derive from the Greek roots *kairos* and *khronos*. We could roughly say that *kairos* is the moment, and *khronos* is an event. Whereas *khronos* moves logically, sequentially, or consecutively, *kairos* happens at a significant time.

267. Also published in India, three editions—1977, 1989 and 1994—by Motilal Banar-asidass in Delhi.

268. Panikkar, *Mysticism, Fullness of Life,* edited by Milena Carrara Pavan, *Mysticism and Spirituality: Opera Omnia* 1 (Maryknoll, NY: Orbis, 2014), v.

269. Preface to Felix Machado, *Jnaneshvari: Path to Liberation* (Mumbai: Somaiya, 1998).

270. Panikkar, *Mysticism, Fullness of Life,* xiii–xxv.

Thich Nhat Hanh (pgs 207–213)

271. Thich Nhat Hanh, *Living Buddha, Living Christ* (New York: Riverhead, 1995); Thich Nhat Hanh, *Going Home: Jesus and Buddha as Brothers* (New York: Riverhead, 1999); Thich Nhat Hanh and Daniel Berrigan, *The Raft Is Not the Shore: Conversations Toward a Buddhist-Christian Awareness* (Maryknoll, NY: Orbis, 1975).

272. Thich Nhat Hanh, *Going Home*, 195.

273. Martin Luther King Jr., "Letter from Dr. Martin Luther King Jr. Nominating Thich Nhat Hanh for the Nobel Peace Prize in 1967" (https://plumvillage.org/letter-from-dr-martin-luther-king-jr-nominating-thich-nhat-hanh-for-the-nobel-peace-prize-in-1967/).

274. Thich Nhat Hanh, *Living Buddha, Living Christ*, 5–6.

275. Thomas Merton, "Nhat Hanh Is My Brother" (https://plumvillage.org/thomas-mertons-words-on-thich-nhat-hanh/).

276. Daniel J. Adams, "Thich Nhat Hanh Then and Now." Unfortunately, the author does not give his source. Archived on the website of the Merton Center at Bellarmine University (http://merton.org/ITMS/Seasonal/20/20-3Adams.pdf).

277. One of their dialogues is filmed and available on YouTube: "Uncommon Conversations: Thich Nhat Hanh and Br. David Steindl-Rast and Gratefulness" (https://www.youtube.com/watch?v=AZKsOfYURtI).

278. David Steindl-Rast, foreword to Thich Nhat Hanh, *Living Buddha, Living Christ*, xv–xvi.

279. Thich Nhat Hanh, *Living Buddha, Living Christ*, 151.

280. Thich Nhat Hanh, *Being Peace*, edited by Arnold Kotler (Berkeley: Parallax, 1987), 89.

281. Thich Nhat Hanh, *Going Home*, 160–61.

282. Eihei Dogen, *Genjokoan*, translated by Shohaku Okumura (https://brightwayzen.org/wp-content/uploads/2014/11/For-BWZ-Chant-Book-Genjokoan.pdf).

283. Thich Nhat Hanh, "The Art of Prayer" (https://plumvillage.org/about/thich-nhat-hanh/interviews-with-thich-nhat-hanh/thich-nhat-hanh-answers-weekly-magazine/).

284. Thich Nhat Hanh, "Art of Prayer."

285. Thich Nhat Hanh, *Going Home*, 180–81.

286. Thich Nhat Hanh, *Going Home*, 182–83.

287. Thich Nhat Hanh, "Art of Prayer."

288. Thich Nhat Hanh, *Going Home*, 202.

Chiara Lubich (pgs 215–221)

289. Chiara Lubich, *Christian Living Today: Meditations* (Hyde Park, NY: New City, 1997; first published in Italian as *Meditazioni* [Rome: Città Nuova, 1959]), 51–52, based on a text originally written in Oct.1947.

290. Lubich, "Acceptance Address" (https://www.templetonprize.org/laureate-sub/address-by-chiara-lubich/).

291. From article 1 of the General Statutes of the Work of Mary (Focolare Movement), with modifications approved by the Pontifical Council for the Laity on Mar. 15, 2007. Printed as a booklet for Focolare use; unavailable URL.

292. "Address of Chiara Lubich to Members of *B'nai B'rith* and Other Members of the Jewish Communities of Argentina and Uruguay," in *Walking Together: Jews and Christians in Dialogue in Rome, Jerusalem, and Buenos Aires*, edited by Joseph Sievers and Miriam Girardi (Rome: n.p., 2013), 20.

293. Lubich, *The Art of Loving* (New York: New City, 2005), 29.

294. Lubich, "The Interreligious Dialogue of the Focolare Movement," unpublished presentation in Aachen Cathedral (Germany), 13 November 1998.

295. Lisa Palmieri-Billig, in *Chiara Lubich and the World Religions: Together Towards the Unity of the Human Family*, Conference Proceedings Castel Gandolfo, Rome, Mar. 17–20, 2014, edited by the Center for Interreligious Dialogue of the Focolare Movement (Bengaluru, Ind.: ATC, 2017), 35.

296. Palmieri-Billig, in *Chiara Lubich and World Religions*, 34–35.

297. Cited in Roberto Catalano, "Christian-Muslim Dialogue: The Experience of Chiara Lubich and the Focolare Movement," *Encounter* 385 (2013), 2.

298. Imam Ronald Shaheed, in *Chiara Lubich and World Religions*, 236.

299. Lubich, video message, Dec. 25, 1973, with English translation at https://www.focolare.org/en/news/2011/12/24/siate-una-famiglia-2/.

The Dalai Lama (pgs 225–231)

300. Dalai Lama, *Toward a True Kinship of Faiths: How the World's Religions Can Come Together* (New York: Doubleday, 2010).

Swami Dayananda Saraswati (pgs 233–238)

301. This is not a modern nineteenth- or twentieth-century notion. It is basic to normative Hinduism and Sikhism. Take, for example, the *Jnanesvari* of the early thirteenth century, which tells us: "As a matter of fact, God so fills every nook and cranny of the world that every object must succumb before His infinite omnipotence" (R. D. Ranade, *Mysticism in India: The Poet-Saints of Maharashtra* [Albany: SUNY Press, 1983], 64). See also Ranade, *Mysticism in India*, 63–64, on the ultimate uselessness of images and anthropomorphism.

302. *Declaration of Mutual Understanding and Cooperation* (http://frfnet.org/1st-Hindu-Jewish%20Summit%20Report-Final.pdf), 46.

Eva Fleischner (pgs 241–247)

303. Author's original title: "A Luminous Presence: Eva Fleischner."

Bishop Kenneth Cragg (pgs 249–254)

304. Kenneth Cragg, *Call of the Minaret* (New York: Oxford University Press, 1956).

305. Martin Forward, "'Is Thine Heart Right, as My Heart Is with Thy Heart?': A Christian Spiritual Theology for Dialogue with Muslims,'" in David Thomas with Clare Amos, eds., *A Faithful Presence: Essays for Kenneth Cragg* (London: Melisende,

2003), 371–83; 371.

306. Cragg, *Call of the Minaret*, 173.

307. It is unlikely that Cragg directly named the series, but the very concept of the series was influenced by Cragg's *Call of the Minaret*, which had recently been published. The very language re. taking off shoes is profoundly Craggian.

308. Max Warren, introduction, in Kenneth Cragg, *Sandals at the Mosque* (London: SCM, 1959), 9–10.

309. Wesley Ariarajah, "Dialogue, Interfaith," in *Dictionary of the Ecumenical Movement*, edited by Nicholas Lossky et al. (Geneva: WCC, 2002).

310. Cragg, "The Credibility of Christianity: Reflections on the Christian 'Temper' in the World" (Jan. 14, 1967), incorporated in "Kenneth Cragg: An Appreciation (1913–2012)," *Current Dialogue* 54 (July 2013) 83–90 (https://www.oikoumene.org/sites/default/files/File/Dialogue_54.pdf).

311. Cragg, *Call of the Minaret*, 356.

312. Sharon is of course a person who deserves to be recognized for her own contribution to interreligious dialogue and peace-building.

313. Author's original title: "Dr. Mary C. Boys, SNJM: A Model of Dedication to Christian-Jewish Rapprochement."

Mary Boys (pgs 257–261)

314. Mary C. Boys, "Questions 'Which Touch on the Heart of Our Faith,'" *Religious Education* 76.6 (Nov.–Dec. 1981) 636–56. The title comes from a statement of the French Bishops' Committee for Relations with Jews, Apr. 16, 1973 (https://ccjr.us/dialogika-resources/documents-and-statements/roman-catholic/other-conferences-of-catholic-bishops/cefr1973).

315. Boys, *Biblical Interpretation in Religious Education: A Study of the Kerygmatic Era* (Birmingham, AL: Religious Education Press, 1980), 2.

316. Boys, ed., *Seeing Judaism Anew: Christianity's Sacred Obligation* (Lanham, MD: Rowan & Littlefield, 2005).

317. See Boys and Sara S. Lee, *Christians and Jews in Dialogue: Learning in the Presence of the Other* (Woodstock, VT: Skylight Paths, 2006); and Boys, *Jewish-Christian Dialogue: One Woman's Experience* (Mahwah, NJ: Paulist, 1997), 40–50. See also the special issue of the journal *Religious Education: Religious Traditions in Conversation* 91.4 (Fall 1996), edited by Boys and Lee.

318. Daniel Lehmann, quoted at 07:18–8:32, in "Metaphors for a Unique Relationship," *Walking God's Paths: Jews and Christians in Candid Conversation* (video series), produced by Philip A. Cunningham et al. (Boston: Center for Christian-Jewish Learning at Boston College, 2004), episode 5 (https://ccjr.us/dialogika-resources/educational-and-liturgical-materials/curricula/wgp-1).

319. Actually, this sculpture was in a sense doubly inspired by Mary. For her book *Has God Only One Blessing?: Judaism as a Source of Christian Self-Understanding* (New York: Paulist, 2000), she asked a member of her religious community, artist Paula Mary Turnbull, SNJM, to create a post-*Nostra aetate* reimagining of the medieval motif of Synagoga and Ecclesia. The two statuettes she crafted present Synagogue and Church as women of equal dignity proudly displaying respective symbols of their traditions. Joshua Koffman's sculpture built upon this depiction

by portraying the two women as interacting together as *chavruta* partners.

320. In addition to numerous articles and book chapters, see her books *Has God Only One Blessing?* and *Redeeming Our Sacred Story: The Death of Jesus and Relations between Jews and Christians* (New York: Paulist, 2013).

321. Commission of the Holy See for Religious Relations with the Jews, "Notes on the Correct Way to Present Jews and Judaism in Preaching and Catechesis in the Roman Catholic Church" (1985), I:2.

322. Commission of the Holy See, "Notes on the Correct Way," I:8.

Ecumenical Patriarch Bartholomew (pgs 271–278)

323. "Inter-Religious Dialogues Organized by the Ecumenical Patriarchate" (https://www.apostolicpilgrimage.org/inter-religious-dialogue/-/asset_publisher/Vm7b-Vj09xVVt/content/inter-religious-dialogues-organized-by-the-ecumenical-patri archate/32008?inheritRedirect=false).

324. An important collection of the patriarch's addresses on this subject is *In the World, Yet Not of the World: Social and Global Initiatives of Ecumenical Patriarch Bartholomew* (New York, Fordham University Press, 2010).

325. "Religions and Peace: Address of His-All Holiness Ecumenical Patriarch Bartholomew at the Al-Azhar and Muslim Council of Elders' Global Peace Conference," Apr. 28, 2017 (https://www.oikoumene.org/resources/documents/religions-and-peace-address-of-his-all-holiness-ecumenical-patriarch-bartholomew).

326. These principles are studied in detail in John Chryssavgis, "Ecumenical Patriarch Bartholomew and Interfaith Dialogue: Mystical Principles, Practical Initiatives," in *Muslim and Christian Understanding: Theory and Application of "A Common Word*," edited by W. El-Ansary and D. Linnan (New York: Palgrave Macmillan, 2010), 81–90.

327. https://www.oikoumene.org/resources/documents/religions-and-peace-address-of-his-all-holiness-ecumenical-patriarch-bartholomew.

328. *Encyclical of the Holy and Great Council of the Orthodox Church* (https://www.holycouncil.org/-/encyclical-holy-council), para. 17.

329. Bartholomew I, *Encountering the Mystery: Understanding Orthodox Christianity Today* (New York: Doubleday, 2008).

330. *Patriarchal and Synodal Encyclical of 1902* (https://www.ecupatria.org/documents/patriarchal-and-synodal-encyclical-of-1902/).

331. "1920 (1): A Beautiful Letter from the Church of Constantinople" (https://www.oikoumene.org/news/1920-1-a-beautiful-letter-from-the-church-of-constanti-nople).

332. *For the Life of the World: Toward a Social Ethos of the Orthodox Church* (https://www.goarch.org/social-ethos), para. 57.

333. *For the Life of the World,* para. 57.

334. Bartholomew I, "Statement by Ecumenical Patriarch Bartholomew at Yad Vashem Holocaust Memorial" (https://mfa.gov.il/MFA/AboutIsrael/History/PapalVisit/PopeFrancis/Pages/Statement-by-Ecumenical-Patriarch-Bartholomew-at-Yad-Vashem-Holocaust-Memorial-27-May-2014.aspx).

335. See Michael Plekon, "The Sacrament of the Brother/Sister in the Lives and Thought of Mother Maria Skobtsova and Paul Evdokimov," *St. Vladimir's Theological Quarterly* 49, no. 3 (2005) 313–34.

336. "La vie et la mort de Mère Marie sont aussi prophétiques pour nous, orthodoxes en Occident, pour tant de jeunes qui souhaitent l'amour et le risque, mais ne savent plus où trouver Dieu. Dieu est au centre, Il est au cœur des êtres et des choses, dans la densité même de la matière, dans la souffrance et la création partagées, nous dit Mère Marie. . . . L'Église n'est rien d'autre que le monde en voie de déification; dans l'Église, le monde n'est plus un tombeau, mais une matrice" (Olivier Clément, preface to "Mère Marie Skobtsov, Le Sacrement du Frère" [https://www.pagesorthodoxes.net/saints/mere-marie/mmarie-intro.htm#preface]).

Rev. Nikkyo Niwano (pgs 281–286)

337. Author's original title: "My Grandfather, My Hero: The Great Challenge of Openness."

338. Nikkyo Niwano, *Heiwa e no michi*, 111–13.

339. Niwano, *Heiwa e no michi*, 321–22.

340. Niwano, *Kono michi*, 127.

341. "The Kyoto Declaration of the First World Assembly, 1970" (http://www.wcrp.or.jp/en/wcrp1_1970.html).

342. Author's original title: "Andrea Riccardi, the Community of Sant'Egidio, and the 'Spirit of Assisi.'"

Andrea Riccardi (pgs 289–294)

343. 1986 was also the year in which a pope entered a synagogue for the first time in history. It was the historic visit of John Paul II to the synagogue in Rome, welcomed by Chief Rabbi Elio Toaff and by the entire community.

344. John Paul II, "To the Roman Curia at the Exchange of Christmas Wishes," Dec. 22, 1986 (https://www.vatican.va/content/john-paul-ii/it/speeches/1986/december/documents/hf_jp-ii_spe_19861222_curia-romana.html). In Italian.

345. Marco Impagliazzo, "The 'Spirit of Assisi' to the Test of History," in *In the Open Sea of History: Studies in Honor of Andrea Riccardi*, edited by Jean Dominique Durand et al. (Rome: Bari, 2021), 45–68; 68.

346. Pope Francis, "Address of His Holiness Pope Francis" (https://www.vatican.va/content/francesco/en/homilies/2020/documents/papa-francesco_20201020_omelia-pace.html).

347. On Sant'Egidio, see www.santegidio.org.

348. The English version of the text shown here and in other citations is by various translators.

349. "Premio 'Moshe Rosen' ad Andrea Riccardi" (https://www.santegidio.org/pageID/30284/langID/it/itemID/33096/Premio-Moshe-Rosen-ad-Andrea-Riccardi.html).

350. A sign of this special bond is the greetings received on the occasion of the fiftieth anniversary of the Community of Sant'Egidio from Yad Vascem, on Feb. 7, 2018.

Hans Küng (pgs 297–306)

351. In July 2007, the Community of Sant'Egidio received the Gold Menorah, awarded by Bené Berith in the presence of the chief rabbi of Israel, Yona Metzger.

352. Author's original title: "Interreligious Heroism: The Legacy of Hans Küng and the Opportunity of Rabbi David Rosen."

353. "Radical and Controversial Thinker 1985" (https://www.rte.ie/archives/2020/0506/1136800-hans-kung-theologian/).

354. Patricia Lefevere, "Hans Küng, Celebrated and Controversial Swiss Theologian, Has Died," *National Catholic Reporter,* Apr. 6, 2021 (https://www.ncronline.org/news/people/hans-k-ng-celebrated-and-controversial-swiss-theologian-has-died).

355. These descriptions are drawn from the articles written about Hans Küng and cited above, as well as an interview in the *Spiegel* (Marcus Grill, "I Don't Cling to This Life," Dec. 12, 2013 [https://www.spiegel.de/international/zeitgeist/controversial-theologian-hans-kueng-on-death-and-church-reform-a-938501.html]; an obituary in the *Irish Times* (Derek Scally, "Germany Salutes Divisive Theologian and Ratzinger Adversary," Apr. 7, 2021 [https://www.irishtimes.com/news/world/europe/germany-salutes-divisive-theologian-and-ratzinger-adversary-1.4531403]); two articles in the *National Catholic Reporter* (John Wilkins, "Ripples Spread Out from Hans Küng's World," May 2, 2014 [https://www.ncronline.org/news/people/ripples-spread-out-hans-k-ngs-work]; and Leonard Swidler, "Hans Küng Knows Church's Problems—and That Change Is Inevitable," May 1, 2014 [https://www.ncronline.org/news/people/hans-k-ng-knows-churchs-problems-and-change-inevitable?_ga=2.203265298.203439946.1630166290-1204899081.1630166290]; and an article in the *New York Times* (Kenneth A. Briggs, "Küng's Views Meet Positive Response in U.S.," Dec. 13, 1981 [https://www.nytimes.com/1981/12/13/us/kung-s-views-meet-positive-response-in-us.html]).

356. Joseph Campbell with Bill Moyers, *The Power of Myth* (New York: Anchor, 1991), 91.

357. David Whyte, *Consolations: The Solace, Nourishment, and Underlying Meaning of Everyday Words* (Vancouver, BC: Many Rivers, 2015), 39.

358. Hans Küng: "First, I want to say that I condemn this outbreak of violence and that I find the offensive remarks of Iranian President Ahmadinejad completely unacceptable. But it is also crucial that the West reflect on the situation and accept that it has made many mistakes," in "The West Has Made Many Mistakes" (https://www.dw.com/en/the-west-has-made-many-mistakes/a-1894970).

359. Richard Falk, "Hans Kung's Crusade: Framing a Global Ethic," in *International Journal of Politics, Culture, and Society* 13, no. 1 (Fall 1999) 63–81.

360. Küng, "Towards a Universal Civilization," *Islam and Christian-Muslim Relations* 11, no. 2 (2000) 229–34.

361. Swidler, "Hans Küng Knows Church's Problems."

362. "Radical and Controversial Thinker 1985."

363. Küng, as cited in "The Global Ethic Project" (https://www.global-ethic.org/the-global-ethic-project/).

364. Küng, "Global Ethic and Human Responsibilities," paper submitted to the High-Level

Expert Group Meeting on "Human Rights and Human Responsibilities in the Age of Terrorism," Apr. 1–2, 2005, Santa Clara University, CA (http://www.oneworlduv.com/wp-content/uploads/2011/06/hkung_santaclara_univ_global_ethic_human_resp_2005.pdf).

365. "Declaration toward a Global Ethic" (https://www.global-ethic.org/declaration-toward-a-global-ethic/).

366. Küng, "Global Ethic and Human Responsibilities."

367. Global Ethic Foundation (https://www.global-ethic.org).

368. Küng offers a different quote from Dag Hammarskjöld, a quote that frames his deliberations about venturing a yes: "I don't know Who—or what—put the question, I don't know when it was put. I don't even remember answering. But at some moment I did answer Yes to Someone—or Something—and from that hour I was certain that existence is meaningful and that, therefore, my life, in self-surrender, had a goal" (Küng, *What I Believe* [London: Bloomsbury, 2010], 100).

369. Küng, *What I Believe*, 10–11.

370. Küng, "Towards a Universal Civilization."

371. Global Ethic Foundation (https://www.global-ethic.org/global-ethic/).

Dharma Master Hsin Tao (pgs 309–315)

372. Different from Western languages, there is only one word in Chinese for both heart and mind: 心 *xin*.

373. Maria Reis Habito, ed. and trans., *The Way of the Heart: Teachings of Dharma Master Hsin Tao* (n.p.: Create Space, 2016), 45–46.

374. Hsin Tao, *The Power of Zen Meditation* (Bloomington, IN: Balboa, 2018), 54, 56.

375. Reis Habito, "Master Hsin Tao's Vision: The Museum of World Religions," in vol. 3 of *The World's Religions after September 11*, edited by Arvind Sharma (Westport, CT: Praeger Perspectives, 2009), 3–12. For the Museum of World Religions, see https://www.mwr.org.tw/mwr_en.

376. Reis Habito, "Museum of World Religions in Taipei: Educating towards Respect, Tolerance and Love," in *Houses of Religions: Visions, Formats and Experiences*, edited by Martin Roetting, Religious Studies in Interfaith Contexts 1 (Münster: LIT, 2021), 119–33.

377. See Bhikkhuni Liao-Yi and Reis Habito, eds., *Listening: Buddhist-Muslim Dialogues 2002–2004* (Taipei: Museum of World Religions Development Foundation, 2005); Liao-Yi and Reis Habito, eds., *Heart to Heart: Buddhist-Muslim Encounters in Ladakh* (Tapei: Museum of World Religions Development Foundation, 2012).

Sheikh Abdallah Nimer Darwish (pgs 317–325)

378. Sheikh Abdullah Nimer Darwish speaking at the Ha'aretz Israel Conference on Peace, Nov. 12, 2015 (https://www.youtube.com/watch?v=41i75A_y3ww).

379. See n1.

Azza Karam (pgs 327–333)

380. United Nations Department of Economic and Social Affairs: Sustainable Development (https://sdgs.un.org/).

381. "A Discussion with Azza Karam, Senior Advisor on Culture, UNFPA" (https://berkleycenter.georgetown.edu/interviews/a-discussion-with-azza-karam-senior-advisor-on-culture-unfpa).

382. United Nations Development Programme: Human Development Reports (http://hdr.undp.org/en/arab-states).

383. *Religion, Women's Health and Rights: Points of Contention and Paths of Opportunities* (https://www.unfpa.org/publications/religion-womens-health-and-rights).

384. See, for example, https://www.partner-religion-development.org/fileadmin/Dateien/Resources/Knowledge_Center/UNIATF-ToR-and-2014-Overview.pdf.

385. Susan Hayward and Katherine Marshall, eds., *Women, Religion and Peacebuilding: Illuminating the Unseen* (Washington, DC: United States Institute of Peace, 2015).

386. "Partnering with Faith Organisations in Development, Health and Humanitarian Work, Rome, 22–24 October 2013" (https://newunkampus.unssc.org/course/info.php?id=29).

387. Azza Karam et al., "The View from Above: Faith and Health" (https://www.thelancet.com/journals/lancet/article/PIIS0140-6736(15)61036-4/references).

388. "Global Challenges: Pandemic and World Order; Religion" (https://www.youtube.com/watch?v=zHiqZXoV7q8&list=PLEZIphLsXAiwKCzPUpYsqx2jNuQV0oxCf&index=11).

Blu Greenberg (pgs 335–340)

389. Blu Greenberg, *On Women and Judaism: A View from Tradition* (Philadelphia: Jewish Publication Society of America, 1981), 178.

390. Irving Greenberg, *The Jewish Way: Living the Holidays* (New York: Simon & Schuster, 1988), 5.

391. B. Greenberg, "My Interfaith Friendships: Blessings and Challenges," in Sue Levi Elwell and Nancy Fuchs Kreimer, *Chapters of the Heart: Jewish Women Sharing the Torah of Our Lives* (Eugene, OR: Cascade Books, 2013), 118–29; 119.

392. I. Greenberg, *For the Sake of Heaven and Earth: The New Encounter between Judaism and Christianity* (Philadelphia: Jewish Publication Society, 2004).

393. The full story is available in my *Memoirs of a Hopeful Pessimist: A Life of Activism through Dialogue* (Jerusalem: Urim/K'tav, 2017).

394. B. Greenberg, *On Women and Judaism*, 19.

395. I. Greenberg, *The Jewish Way*, 10.

The Anonymous Hero (pgs 343–348)

396. Author's original title: "A Teacher."

Muhammad Abdul Rauf (pgs 351–356)

397. Titled *The Recited Koran: A History of the First Recorded Version,* by Labib as-Said, translated and adapted by Bernard Weiss et al., the book was published by Darwin Press (Princeton, NJ) in 1975.

398. The book is available to be downloaded in pdf format on the American Enterprise Institute's website at https://www.aei.org/research-products/book/a-muslims -reflections-on-democratic-capitalism/.

Rabbi Wolfe Kelman (pgs 359–363)

399. Authors' original title: "Truths Our Father Told Us."

400. Z"l means "may his memory be a blessing."

401. IJCIC member organizations include the American Jewish Committee (AJC), Anti-Defamation League (ADL), B'nai B'rith International (BBI), Central Conference of American Rabbis (CCAR), Israel Jewish Council for Interreligious Relations (IJCIR), Rabbinical Assembly (RA), Rabbinical Council of America (RCA), Union for Reform Judaism (URJ), Union of Orthodox Jewish Congregations of America (OU), United Synagogue of Conservative Judaism (USCJ), and World Jewish Congress (WJC).

Rabbi Mickey (Michael) Rosen (pgs 365–372)

402. *Voices of Yakar* (an internal weekly handout), Aug. 2000.

403. Michael Rosen, *The Quest for Authenticity: The Thought of Reb Simhah Bunim* (Jerusalem: Urim, 2008).

404. Rosen, *Quest for Authenticity,* 137.

405. Rosen, *Quest for Authenticity,* 149.

406. Rosen, *Quest for Authenticity,* 204–5.

Conclusion: Appreciating Interreligious Heroes (pgs 397–406)

407. Avot 1,2.

408. In my reading of the first chapter of Avot, the chapter offers an upacking of this mishna by featuring distinct voices that favor either the one activity or the other.

409. A necessary clarification: I speak here of David's interfaith ministry, not of his life as a rabbi nor as a member of the Jewish community. Some of the authors who have written about David have had a hard time distinguishing the two, for obvious reasons, not knowing the internal workings of Jewish life and community. Significant as these may be, they are beyond the frame of the present discussion.

About the Contributors

Abbadi, Dr. Ahmad

Dr Abbadi is the Secretary General of the Rabita Mohammadia des Oulé-mas (Muhammadan League of Religious Scholars) in Morocco. From 1992 to 1994, Dr. Abbadi was a visiting scholar in residence at DePaul University and the University of Chicago. In 2014, Dr. Abbadi was appointed by His Majesty the King as a member of the Higher Council for Education, Training and Research in Morocco.

Adamakis, Metropolitan Emmanuel

During his service to the Church, His Eminence Metropolitan Emmanuel has become an advocate for peace and dialogue. He has served as Metropolitan of France, Exarch of the Ecumenical Patriarchate (election 2003), and Co-President of the World Conference of Religions for Peace (WCRP) In charge of Interreligious Dialogue with Judaism and Islam on behalf of the Ecumenical Patriarchate. In 2021, he was appointed elder hierarch of the Patriarchate of Constantinople.

Amos, Dr. Clare

Until her retirement in 2018, Dr. Clare Amos was head of the interreligious office at the World Council of Churches, focusing on relations between the Abrahamic faiths. Prior to moving to Geneva in 2011, she had worked in a similar capacity for the Anglican Communion in London. Dr. Amos has had a long involvement with the Middle East and interreligious concerns (for which her interreligious hero was partially responsible), having lived for a number of years in both Jerusalem and Beirut.

Andrevon Gottstein, Dr. Thérèse Martine

Thérèse M. Andrevon Gottstein has been involved in the study of Judeo-Catholic relations for some thirty years. A specialist in Catholic theology of Judaism since the Second Vatican Council, she teachers at the Catholic University of Paris and at Domuni University. She is also a member of an ecumenical research group of Christian theologies relating to Judaism, as well as a member of the Elijah Interfaith Institute. She has authored and edited several publications in the field of Christian theology of Judaism.

Anli, Ibrahim A.

Ibrahim Anli is a civic entrepreneur and researcher with a career record that bridges nonprofit and academic experience. Ibrahim was a visiting researcher at the Hebrew University of Jerusalem in 2007–2008. He holds a BA in Economics from Istanbul University, an MA in Conflict Analysis and Resolution from Sabanci University, and a certificate in Strategic Management for Leaders of NGOs from Harvard University. He presently directs the Rumi Forum.

Atmapriyananda, Swamiji

Swami Atmapriyananda has been Vice Chancellor of Ramakrishna Mission Vivekananda University since 2005. A physicist by training, he joined the Ramakrishna Order in 1978. A much sought-out lecturer, he is one of the important contemporary expositors of the philosophy of Sri Ramakrishna and Swami Vivekananda. He has been active with the Elijah Interfaith Institute's Board of World Religious Leaders for the past fifteen years.

Boys, Prof. Mary

Mary Boys is an American scholar specializing in religious studies and a prominent voice in Christian-Jewish relations. She is Dean of Academic Affairs and McAlpin Professor of Practical Theology at Union Theological Seminary in the City of New York. She was formerly Professor of Religious Education at Boston College. Mary is a member of the Sisters of the Holy Names.

Ceric, Imam Dr. Mustafa

Grand Mufti Dr. Mustafa Ceric is the Reis-ul-Ulema emeritus—President of the Council of Ulema—in Bosnia-Herzegovina. He graduated from Al-Azhar University in Cairo and afterwards accepted the position of Imam at the Islamic Cultural Center in the United States. During his tenure at the Center, he earned a PhD in Islamic Theology at the University of Chicago.

Cunningham, Dr. Philip A.

Dr. Philip A. Cunningham is Professor of Theology (specializing in Christian-Jewish relations) and Director of the Institute for Jewish-Catholic Relations of Saint Joseph's University in Philadelphia. He has served as president of the International Council of Christians and Jews and on the Advisory Committee on Catholic-Jewish Relations for the United States Conference of Catholic Bishops.

Goshen-Gottstein, Dr. Alon

Rabbi Dr. Alon Goshen-Gottstein is acknowledged as one of the world's leading figures in interreligious dialogue. He has been Director of the Elijah Interfaith Institute, which he founded, since 1997. His work bridges the theological and academic dimensions with a variety of practical initiatives, especially involving world religious leadership. A noted scholar of Jewish studies, he has held academic posts at Tel Aviv University and has served as Director of the Center for the Study of Rabbinic Thought, Beit Morasha College, Jerusalem. A multi-volume series of interfaith studies edited by him is published by Wipf and Stock. He has published around twenty monographs and edited collections in Jewish studies, interfaith studies, and Jewish theology of religions.

Goswami, Acharya Shrivatsa

Acharya Shri Shrivatsa Goswami comes from a family of eminent scholars and spiritual leaders at Sri Radharamana Mandir of Vrindavan. He is a leading figure in the Vaishnava tradition, representing the leadership of the Bhakti (devotional) movement, in a school dating back to the sixteenth-century figure of Chaitanya. He has lectured at major universities worldwide and toured extensively to participate in conferences on philosophy and religion. One of the focuses of his present work is the alliance of religion and conservation. He is a member of the Elijah Interfaith Institute's Board of World Religious Leaders.

Griswold, Bishop Frank

Frank T. Griswold is a former Presiding Bishop and Primate of the Epis-copal Church and is a member of the Elijah Interfaith Institute's Board of World Religious Leaders. He is the author of several books and has taught and lectured in the United States and in many other parts of the world. For him, interfaith encounter and the various ways the Mystery at the heart of our existence is named, celebrated, and draws us into an ever widening communion of fellow seekers is a source of healing for a fractured world, in which religion too often divides rather than unites.

Habito, Dr. Maria Reis

Dr. Maria Reis Habito is the International Program Director of the Museum of World Religions and the Director of the Elijah Interfaith Institute USA. She was a research fellow at Kyoto University and completed her PhD at Ludwig-Maximilians-Universität. Dr. Reis Habito frequently represents Dharma Master Hsin Tao in international meetings and forums.

Kasper, Cardinal Walter

Cardinal Walter Kasper is President emeritus of the Pontifical Council for Promoting Christian Unity. He is a noted theologian who has published extensively. From 2001 to 2010 he was the Vatican's top official in charge of relations with the Jewish people.

Kelman-Ezrachi, Rabbi Naamah

Rabbi Naamah Kelman was appointed Dean of the Taube Family Campus of HUC-JIR in Jerusalem on July 1, 2009. Rabbi Kelman is very involved in Jewish and Zionist Pluralism and Renewal in Israel as a founder of Panim: Jewish Renewal in Israel and has served on its Board. Rabbi Kelman was the first woman ordained by the Hebrew Union College in Jerusalem in 1992.

Kessler, Dr. Edward

Dr. Edward Kessler MBE is the Founder and Director of the Woolf Institute and a leading thinker in interfaith relations, primarily Jewish-Christian-Muslim relations. He is a Fellow of St Edmund's College, Cambridge, as well as a Principal of the Cambridge Theological Federation. Kessler, with Martin Forward, founded the Centre for the Study of Jewish-Christian Relations (CJCR) in 1998.

King, Prof. Sallie B.

Sallie B. King is Professor emerita of Philosophy and Religion at James Madison University and Affiliate Faculty, Department of Theology and Religious Studies, Georgetown University. Her work is in the areas of Buddhism, interreligious dialogue, and the cross-cultural philosophy of religion. She is a previous President of the Society for Buddhist-Christian Studies and member of the Christian and Interfaith Relations Committee of the Friends General Conference (national Quaker organization). She is a Buddhist and a Quaker.

Koch, Cardinal Kurt

Cardinal Kurt Koch is a Swiss prelate of the Catholic Church. He has been a cardinal and President of the Pontifical Council for Promoting Christian Unity since 2010. He was the bishop of Basel from 1996 until 2010. In 2010, Koch was appointed a member of the Congregation for the Oriental Churches and the Pontifical Council for Interreligious Dialogue.

Koskinen, Bishop Lennart

Bishop Koskinen is a clergyman in the Church of Sweden. He was Bishop of Visby between 2003 and 2011. Koskinen obtained his doctorate in theology at Uppsala University in 1980. Koskinen is also a member of the Elijah Interfaith Institute's Board of World Religious Leaders.

Machado, Archbishop Felix

Archbishop Machado worked as Undersecretary in the Pontifical Council for Interreligious Dialogue, Vatican, from 1999 to 2008. Presently, he serves as Chairperson for the Office for Interreligious Dialogue of the Federation of Asian (Catholic) Bishops' Conferences (FABC) and as Chairperson for the Office for Interreligious Dialogue of the Catholic Bishops' Conference of India (CBCI). He is not presently Archbishop of Vasai, India.

Marshall, Katherine

Katherine Marshall is a Senior Fellow at the Berkley Center for Religion, Peace, and World Affairs, where she leads the center's work on religion and global development, and a Professor of the Practice of Development, Conflict, and Religion in the Walsh School of Foreign Service. She helped to create and now serves as the Executive Director of the World Faiths Development Dialogue. She is also vice president of the G20 Interfaith Association.

Melchior, Rabbi Michael

Melchior is the rabbi of an active congregation in Jerusalem, Chief Rabbi of Norway, and Former MK and Minister in the government of Israel. He is also President and Founder of Mosaica—The Middle East Religious Peace Initiative and a variety of social, environmental, and educational initiatives.

Mohinder Singh, Bhai Sahib Ahluwalia

Bhai Sahib is third in line of Spiritual Leaders of Guru Nanak Nishkam Sewak Jatha (Birmingham) UK since 1995. In the interfaith context, Bhai Sahib is a member of the Elijah Interfaith Institute's Board of World Religious Leaders and the European Council of Religious Leaders; Trustee of Religions for Peace International and President of Religions for Peace UK; supporter of the Council for a Parliament of the World's Religions; Trustee and Chair of the Museum of World's Religions (UK) working group; and patron of United Religions Initiative (UK) and Divine Onkar Mission. In 2012, he received a Papal Knighthood of St Gregory the Great from Pope Benedict XVI.

Niwano, Rev. Kosho

Rev. Kosho Niwano, President-Designate of Rissho Kosei-kai, devotes herself to sharing the teachings of the Lotus Sutra with Rissho Kosei-kai members both in Japan and overseas. She actively engages in international interreligious dialogue and cooperation, serving as Co-Moderator of Religions for Peace International and as a member of the Board of Directors of the King Abdullah Bin Abdulaziz International Centre for Interreligious and Intercultural Dialogue.

Pallavacini, Imam Yahya

Imam Yahya Pallavicini is Chairman of the COREIS Islamic Religious Community in Italy; Vice-President of the MJLC (Muslim-Jewish Leaders Council Europe) in Vienna; Ambassador for ICESCO (Dialogue among Civilizations) in Rabat; and Executive Member of the WMCC (World Muslim Communities Council) in Abu Dhabi.

Parolin, Cardinal Pietro

Cardinal Parolin is an Italian prelate of the Catholic Church. A cardinal since February 2014, he has served as Secretary of State for the Vatican since October 2013 and a member of the Council of Cardinal Advisers since July 2014. Before that, he worked in the diplomatic service of the Holy See for thirty years.

Pawlikowski, Prof. John

Professor Pawlikowski is Professor emeritus of Social Ethics at Catholic Theological Union, Chicago. He is founding Director of the Catholic-Jewish Studies Program at Catholic Theological Union, was President of the International Conference of Christians and Jews for six years, and now holds the title of Honorary Life President at ICCJ.

Pizzaballa, Archbishop Pierbattista

Patriarch Pierbattista Pizzaballa OFM is an Italian prelate of the Catholic Church who has been the Latin Patriarch of Jerusalem since November 6, 2020. He had been Apostolic Administrator of the Latin Patriarchate since 2016. A Franciscan friar, he served as Custos of the Holy Land from 2004 to 2016. Much of his pastoral work has been with Hebrew-speaking congregations, and he has close ties to Jewish leaders, while also having been a vocal supporter of the Palestinians.

Onaiyekan, Cardinal John Olorunfemi

Cardinal John Olorunfemi Onaiyekan is a Nigerian prelate of the Roman Catholic Church. He was Archbishop of Abuja from 1994 to 2019 and was made a cardinal in 2012. He has served as President of the Christian Association of Nigeria, President of the Catholic Bishops' Conference of Nigeria, and Bishop of Ilorin.

Rambachan, Prof. Anantanand

Anantanand Rambachan is Professor of Religion at St. Olaf College. From 2013 to 2017, Professor Rambachan was Forum Humanum Visiting Professor at the Academy for World Religions at Hamburg University, Germany. He is a member of the Theological Education Steering Committee of the American Academy of Religion; a member of the Advisory Council of the Centre for the Study of Religion and Society, University of Victoria; an advisor to Harvard University's Pluralism Project; and a member of the Elijah Interfaith Academy.

Rauf, Imam Feisal Abdul

Imam Abdul Rauf is an American Imam of note. He is Sufi by orientation, a thinker, author, peace activist, and longtime practitioner of interfaith dialogue. From 1983 to 2009, he served as Imam of Masjid al-Farah, a mosque in New York City. He is the author of several books on Islam, including *Defining Islamic Statehood: Measuring and Indexing Contemporary Muslim States* (2015) and *Moving the Mountain: A New Vision of Islam in America* (2012).

Rose, Rabbi Or N.

Rabbi Or N. Rose is the founding director of the Miller Center for Inter-religious Learning and Leadership of Hebrew College. Among his publications are *Rabbi Zalman Schachter-Shalomi: Essential Teachings* and *Words to Live By: Sacred Sources for Interreligious Engagement* (both co-edited volumes published by Orbis).

Rosen, Sharon

Sharon Rosen is Global Director of Religious Engagement at Search for Common Ground, the world's leading non-governmental organization dedicated to peacebuilding. Sharon provides strategic oversight and technical expertise to Search field offices and is the Lead Curriculum Developer of a three-part toolkit on the Common Ground Approach to Religious Engagement.

Rosen, Rabbi Shlomo Dov

Rabbi Shlomo Dov Rosen is presently the Communal Rabbi and Director of Yakar - Jerusalem, a fellow at the Truman Institute, and Ram (lecturer) in Yeshivat Machanaim. He was previously the Communal Rabbi of the Beit Yosef synagogue and Ram at Yeshivat Eretz HaTzvi. He has published on pluralism, distributive justice, and angelology. He is involved in interfaith work (with an emphasis on theology) both in and outside of Yakar.

Sievers, Prof. Joseph

Prof. Joseph Sievers has taught Jewish history and literature of the Hellenistic period at the Pontifical Biblical Institute since 1991. In addition, he served as Director of the Cardinal Bea Centre for Judaic Studies at the Pontifical Gregorian University from 2003 to 2009. He has published several books and many articles, primarily in the areas of Second Temple history (especially Flavius Josephus) and Christian-Jewish relations.

Sperber, Rabbi Daniel

Rabbi Daniel Sperber is Professor of Talmud at Bar-Ilan University in Israel and an expert in classical philology, history of Jewish customs, Jewish art history, Jewish education, and Talmudic studies. He also serves as Rabbi of Menachem Zion Synagogue in the Old City of Jerusalem. In 2010, Rabbi Sperber accepted an appointment as honorary Chancellor of the non-denominational Canadian Yeshiva and Rabbinical School in Toronto.

Spreafico, Bishop Ambrogio

Bishop Spreafico was ordained as a priest in 1975. Since July 2008, he has been Bishop of Frosinone-Veroli-Ferentino. As a scholar of sacred Scripture and biblical spirituality, he has taught at the Pontifical Biblical Institute in Rome and at the Theological Faculty of the Pontifical Urban University, where he has been Rector for a long time. Since May 2010, he is the Chairman of the Commission for the Evangelization of Peoples and the Cooperation between Churches of the Italian Episcopal Conference. In May 2011, he was appointed by Benedict XVI as a member of the Congregation for the Causes of Saints.

Staquf, Imam Yahya Cholil

Imam Yahya Cholil Staquf is the Secretary General of the world's largest Muslim organization, the Nahdlatul Ulama (NU) Supreme Council, Indonesia. He is a distinguished Muslim scholar and co-founder of a global movement (Humanitarian Islam) that seeks to reform obsolete tenets of Islamic orthodoxy that enjoin religious hatred, supremacy, and violence.

Turkson, Cardinal Peter

Cardinal Turkson is a Ghanaian cardinal of the Catholic Church. He was President of the Pontifical Council for Justice and Peace from October 24, 2009 to January 1, 2017. Pope Francis named him the first Prefect of the Dicastery for the Promotion of Integral Human Development, which began operations on January 1, 2017, a post he continues to hold. He previously served as Archbishop of Cape Coast.

Vendley, Dr. William Fray

Dr. William Fray Vendley was the Secretary General of the World Conference of Religions for Peace (WCRP). He is a member of its World Council and coordinates the activities and projects of WCRP's Inter-Religious Councils in seventy countries and in five regions, including Africa, Asia Europe, Latin America, and the Middle East. He is a member of the Council on Foreign Relations.

Yanklowitz, Rabbi Shmuly

Shmuly Yanklowitz is a rabbi, activist, and author. In March 2012 and March 2013, *Newsweek* and the *Daily Beast* listed Yanklowitz as one of the fifty most influential rabbis in America. Yanklowitz has served as a delegate to the World Economic Forum.

Weiman-Kelman, Rabbi Levi

Rabbi Levi Weiman-Kelman is the President of Rabbis for Human Rights. He was ordained by the Jewish Theological Seminary. He has been on the forefront of the struggle for religious pluralism and justice in Israel's highly polarized society.

Weissman, Dr. Deborah

Dr. Deborah Weissman is a specialist in Jewish education. She has had extensive experience in teacher training, religious feminism, and interfaith teaching and dialogue, having served for two terms as President of the International Council of Christians and Jews, the first Jewish woman (and only the second woman at all) to have served in that position in over fifty years.

Williams, Archbishop Rowan Douglas

Dr. Rowan Douglas Williams is a Welsh Anglican bishop, theologian, and poet. He was the 104th Archbishop of Canterbury, a position he held from December 2002 to December 2012. Previously the Bishop of Monmouth and Archbishop of Wales, Williams was the first Archbishop of Canterbury in modern times not to be appointed from within the Church of England.